1 9 8 8

Diminishing Fictions

Essays on the

Modern American Novel

and Its Critics

BRUCE BAWER

Diminishing Fictions

Essays on the Modern

American Novel and Its Critics

GRAYWOLF PRESS/SAINT PAUL

Grateful acknowledgment is made to the editors and publishers of the
following newspapers and periodicals in which many of the essays in this
collection were first published: *The American Spectator, Arrival, Commentary,
London Review of Books, The New Criterion, Notes on Modern American
Literature, The Wall Street Journal,* and *The Washington Times.*

Publication of this volume is made possible in part by grants from the National
Endowment for the Arts and the Bush Foundation, and by contributions to
Graywolf Press from many generous individuals, foundations and
corporations. Graywolf Press is a member organization of United Arts.

ISBN I-55597-109-I
Library of Congress Catalog Card Number 87-83084
CIP Data on back page

FIRST PRINTING, 1988
3   5   7   9   8   6   4   2

Published by GRAYWOLF PRESS
Post Office Box 75006
Saint Paul, Minnesota 55175
All Rights Reserved

Acknowledgments

There are two people without whom this book would not exist: Hilton Kramer and Dana Gioia. My debts to both of them are extraordinary.

Many of the essays in this book would be much the poorer if not for the perceptive comments and suggestions of Erich Eichman at *The New Criterion*. I extend my grateful thanks to him and to the other editors who oversaw the original publication of these essays: at *The New Criterion*, Donna Rifkind and the late Eva Szent-Miklosy; at *The Washington Times*, Colin Walters and Lauren Weiner; at *The Wall Street Journal*, David Brooks and Claudia Rosett; at *Commentary*, Neal Kozodoy; at *The Nation*, Elizabeth Pochoda; at *Arrival*, Bill Katovsky, Emily Zukerberg, and Tim Carroll; at *NMAL*, Lee Richmond; at *The London Review of Books*, Mary-Kay Wilmers and Madeleine Nicklin; and at *The American Spectator*, Wladyslaw Pleszczynski and Andrew Ferguson. I also thank my editors at Graywolf, Scott Walker and Sheila Murphy, and my agent, Beth Vesel. The essay on Glenway Wescott was written during a term of residency at the Djerassi Foundation in Woodside, California, for which I am forever grateful to the Foundation and its director, Sally Stillman.

Finally, this book represents a good portion of the work of several years, during which time I have been buoyed by the encouragement and support of a number of people. Aside from the dedicatees, I must mention Carol Bawer, Randall Babtkis and Carolyn Cooke, Tom DePietro and Dorothy Heyl, Peter Fedorowich, Michael Frank, Sari Friedman, Gloria Glickstein, Lenny Hort and Laaren Brown, Michael Kwart, Phillis Levin, Glenn Levine, Dorothea Matthaus, Sanford Operowsky, Chip Teply, Sarah Wenk, Judy White, and Harriet Zinnes. Their love and friendship have sustained me beyond measure.

BRUCE BAWER

Contents

For my parents
NELL *and* TED BAWER
and for
CHRIS DAVENPORT

I

Diminishing Fictions:
Four Decades of the Novel

S UMMER 1985

The question . . .

is what to make of a diminished thing.

—R OBERT F ROST, "The Oven Bird"

O ne day a few years back, when I was in graduate school, a professor and I were chatting idly about Hemingway, Fitzgerald, Faulkner, Dos Passos—writers that I had been reading lately, and that, as he told me, he had lionized as a teenager in the 1930s. "Who is it you kids look up to now?" he asked. "Who are your idols? Who do you think is writing the Great American Novel these days?" I considered the question. To be sure, there were contemporary American novelists that I respected, that I read with pleasure; but none of them meant to me what Hemingway and company had meant to my professor. The fact was, I didn't wait breathlessly for *anybody's* next novel; there was no magnificent vision, no grand style out there that had changed my life. "Nobody," I said, and was myself surprised—and more than a little dismayed—that this should be my answer. He nodded grimly, as if he'd expected nothing else—indeed, as if he'd asked the question precisely in order to confront me with my own reply.

It was not—and is not—a pleasant verdict to render. But there it is, like it or not: the American novel *has* lost a good deal of its prewar glory; it *doesn't* matter quite so much anymore; it is no longer the flagship of the American arts, the most conspicuous of the mirrors we hold up to ourselves. Whether the golden age of the American novel was the 1850s (*The Scarlet Letter, Moby-Dick*), the 1880s (*The Adventures of*

Huckleberry Finn, The Portrait of a Lady, The Rise of Silas Lapham), or the 1920s (*The Age of Innocence, The Enormous Room, An American Tragedy, The Great Gatsby, The Sun Also Rises, The Sound and the Fury*) is open to question, but it would be difficult indeed to support the contention that any American novel published during the four decades since World War II has been quite worthy of comparison with the masterpieces of these earlier periods.

Why is this so? The explanation offered up by the professors and critics usually runs more or less as follows: Freud, Darwin, and World War I shook the assumptions about the meaning and continuity of human life on which the novel (especially at its nineteenth-century zenith) was once based; World War II, the Holocaust, and the Bomb destroyed them. There is indubitably a great deal of truth in this, even if the doubt, disillusion, and despair that have characterized the work of many a postwar American novelist seem more than a bit contrived. Many of the major American novels written before World War II, after all, were thick with doubt, disillusion, and despair; but there's despair and there's *despair*. What saved these prewar novels from being mere testaments of doom was the fact that their protagonists, as a rule, were men and women of substance. Doomed or not, they were genuine heroes, who actively sought to construct for themselves a life built upon useful work or positive beliefs or order or happiness or love. Titles like *The Titan* and *The Great Gatsby* are only partly ironic. Gatsby *is* great, not for his wealth but for the tenacity with which he clings to a dream of innocence; even Jake Barnes, the hopeless, emasculated wretch in *The Sun Also Rises* who has left innocence far behind, is a man of stature by virtue of the stoic faith with which he accepts his personal fate; and so on. Even the most tormented of these pre-World War II protagonists had a grandeur about him, a true tragic dimension, and if, at the end of the book, he was destroyed by a universe that was indifferent to his fate, the feeling was that something *important* had been done in. Someone of value, someone whose existence in the universe made an ethical and emotional difference, had waged the good fight against the forces of futility. There *were* such things as courage, character, moral strength, beauty, truth, devotion. Whether they had triumphed or not, they meant something. They were good. And by recognizing this, in spite of their nearly overwhelming *Angst,* the great prewar American novelists demonstrated memorably that one thing, at least, which gives a novel significance and dimension is its creator's zealous devotion to that part

of every human soul that fights in the interests of these virtuous attributes. These writers' accomplishments affirmed, in short, that there
is an aesthetic value that proceeds from a deeply rooted belief in the
nobility of human feeling.

So it was, alas, in the prewar American novel. In the most celebrated
postwar novels, by contrast, there has generally been more compulsive
doom and gloom than there has been forceful opposition to it; the poor
wretches whose lives and thoughts and souls are at the centers of these
novels have typically been less tragic than pathetic, less heroes than
ciphers. This is not to suggest that one should condemn a novel simply
because it takes a gloomy view of the world. It is only to observe that in
one book after another, the major novelists of our day have, intention-
ally or not, allowed their relentless negativism to work against the best
interests of the form itself; wittingly or unwittingly, they have
renounced the vitality, the abundance, and the breadth of artistry that
for more than two centuries have consistently distinguished the great
novels of the world. Many postwar novelists, of course, feel that they
have no choice. They are convinced that we live in an age of chaos and
fragmentation; that the novel, whose roots lie in the eighteenth century's love of order, is a relic; and that a contemporary novelist, consequently, is incapable of rendering as full and faithful a picture of his
society as did his predecessors in ages past. I am speaking here, naturally, not of the major American novelists of the prewar era who continued to publish fiction after the war (the most notable of whom,
Hemingway and Faulkner, won their Nobel Prizes for books published
during this period), but of the younger generations of writers who have
established the dominant literary tone of the post-1945 era, and in
whose books a narrow and artistically unprofitable passivity has been
the rarely broken rule. It is, after all, not only Saul Bellow, among our
postwar novelists, who has concerned himself with victims, not only
John Updike who has chronicled the timid movements of contemporary American rabbits on the run; one postwar novelist after another
has directed his attention to such inert folk. There have, to be sure, been
prominent novels (mostly Beat or Beat-influenced) whose protagonists
have managed to escape this epidemic of psychic stagnancy. But, as if to
suggest the impossibility, in the postwar world, of meaningful (let
alone heroic) action, these protagonists have tended to assert themselves in, to say the least, refractory ways: by engaging in aimless
movement (Jack Kerouac's 1957 *On the Road*), by practicing obsessive

debauchery (William Burroughs's 1966 *Naked Lunch*), by committing outrageous atrocities (Norman Mailer's 1965 *An American Dream*), or by participating in one type or another of nihilistically conceived, if often entertaining, nuttiness (Joseph Heller's 1961 *Catch-22*, Ken Kesey's 1962 *One Flew Over the Cuckoo's Nest*, Kurt Vonnegut's 1963 *Cat's Cradle*, Tom Robbins's 1976 *Even Cowgirls Get the Blues*, John Irving's 1978 *The World According to Garp*).

The American novel, then, has travelled a bumpy road these past forty years. Among its more distasteful manifestations during this period have been the metafictional novel and what we may call the "workshop novel," both of which I propose to discuss presently. Perhaps the most striking novelistic phenomenon of all, however, has been the annexation of fact—whether straight or twisted, autobiographical or historical—onto the crumbling house of fiction. Though the reasons for this turn of events are no doubt as diverse and as complicated as the writers involved, two or three generalizations seem fair. First, since World War II the interest of the American public in serious fiction has declined precipitously; whereas in the prewar years novels sold twice as well as books of nonfiction, the postwar years have seen those figures reversed, and it is likely that some novelists have noticed this and acted upon it. Second, some novelists have patently decided that novels consisting entirely of invented stories and characters can do little or nothing to illuminate the important truths of our age, and that the incorporation of significant public figures or events into a novel is bound to lend it greater validity. To some of these novelists, of course, the "important truths" are not metaphysical or psychological but social and political in nature, and the real public figures and events which they inject into their novels tend to be drawn from the sociopolitical realm. Third, more and more postwar novelists—like their poetry-writing contemporaries—have become fascinated with the Self (which is often a nice way of saying that they have become fascinated with themselves). Some of these writers may well feel, with Philip Roth, that in a civilization too complex to be captured in a novel—an America whose boisterous day-to-day history is, as Roth has written, "a kind of embarrassment to one's own meager imagination"—a turning inward is the novelist's only resort. At any rate, what it all comes down to is one single dismaying fact: that in the past forty years, many of our most highly regarded novelists have lost respect for the fictional way of truth.

The most famous contemporary American novelist to find himself walking the non-fiction trail is, of course, Norman Mailer. Though he is probably the most well-known novelist of our time, his fictional corpus is an awfully dreary one. *The Naked and the Dead* (1948), his competent but rather tiresome imitation of Dos Passos, has been succeeded by one ill-aimed Existential stab after another into the dark belly of existence: *Barbary Shore, The Deer Park, An American Dream, Why Are We in Vietnam?, Ancient Evenings, Tough Guys Don't Dance.* While most of these novels read as if they were, for Mailer, dismal chores — books motivated primarily by a vague feeling that to be America's greatest writer one must produce novels (a conviction that would seem be the sole legacy of the Age of Hemingway)—such books of nonfiction as *Advertisements for Myself, The Prisoner of Sex,* and *Miami and the Siege of Chicago* have been marked by a liveliness, a naturalness, an exuberance that Mailer's fiction rarely possesses. As anyone who has read one or two of these nonfictional books knows, their chief topics are invariably (a) events and personalities of national prominence (be they in politics, boxing, crime, or literature) and (b) Norman Mailer. This fearsome duality owes a lot, it should be said, to the ethos of the "New Journalism," with its unqualified regard for the notion that, in any work of reportage, the reporter is as important a part of the story as anything else.

Despite *Marilyn* and its ilk, however, the overall emphasis of Mailer's nonfiction has been decidedly political. The mere fact that he entitled one of his novels—one of his *fictional* novels, no less—*Why Are We in Vietnam?* would seem to suggest that he is inclined, at times anyway, to mistake the political issues of the moment for the metaphysical questions of the ages. As we know, Mailer has run for elective office (and lost); he has even dreamed of being president. Indeed, in a 1956 *Village Voice* piece, he proposed at least half seriously that the Democrats nominate Ernest Hemingway to run against Eisenhower—but even that colossal egomaniac failed to share Mailer's notions about the proper role of the novelist in the national life. Mailer's greatest critical triumphs, as it happens, have been two books that were extremely political, the remarkable *Armies of the Night* (1968) and *The Executioner's Song* (1979)—both volumes of nonfiction that Mailer, in the wake of Truman Capote's "nonfiction novel" *In Cold Blood* (1965), presented to the world as novels.

Though American writers have not taken up the "nonfiction novel" in droves, many of the most celebrated of them have, like Mailer, continued to plug tediously away at the novel-as-fiction, while proving far more engaging as purveyors of nonfiction. Among these writers are Gore Vidal, whose acerbic essays are a good deal more captivating than his bloated, oddly inert novels (some of the more recent of which—*Burr, 1876, Lincoln,* etc.—are, at any rate, not so much works of fiction as they are slightly reshaped hunks of history); Joan Didion, whose sensitive, clever pieces in *Slouching Towards Bethlehem* (1968) outshine such dark, dry little fictions as *Play It as It Lays* (1970); Mary McCarthy, whose literary essays and lovely memoir, *Memories of a Catholic Girlhood* (1957), are unquestionably more valuable than facile novels like *The Groves of Academe* (1952) and *The Group* (1963); James Baldwin, whose racial and sexual rage are more eloquently expressed in his essays, *Notes of a Native Son* (1955), than in such variously flawed novels as *Go Tell It on the Mountain* (1953) and *Giovanni's Room* (1956); and Joyce Carol Oates, whose relentless prolificity seems less damaging to her essays, somehow, than to her increasing pointless and prolix works of fiction.

Other contemporary novelists, meanwhile, especially since the mid-Sixties, have spiced their fiction liberally—and, at times, radically —with historical figures and events, often for obvious political reasons. William Styron, for instance, at a time when black militancy was at its height, published the controversial *Confessions of Nat Turner* (1967), which took the form of a memoir of the famous insurrectionist, and which seemed to count among its purposes the justification of violence in the service of emancipation. E. L. Doctorow wrote *The Book of Daniel* (1971), an uneasy, politically obsessed hodgepodge of fact and fancy based on the case of Julius and Ethel Rosenberg, and containing passages that appeared to belong not in a novel but in a political tract:

> The final existential condition is citizenship. Every man is the enemy of his own country. E V E R Y M A N I S T H E E N E M Y O F H I S O W N C O U N T R Y. Every country is the enemy of its own citizens. . . . in war the soldier's destruction is accomplished by his own Commanders. It is his government which places a rifle in his hands, puts him up on the front, and tells him his mission is to survive. All societies are armed societies. All citizens are soldiers. All Governments stand ready to commit their citizens to death in the interest of their government.

Doctorow also gave us *Ragtime* (1975), which was lauded on publication for the "charming" way it incorporated real-live, turn-of-the-century folks like J. P. Morgan and Booker T. Washington into an invented story, but which (as some readers have come to recognize) was essentially an indictment of the American system. In a similar vein, Robert Coover wrote *The Public Burning* (1977), a fantastic vision of the Cold War in which the central figures are the lovable Rosenbergs and the invidious Richard M. Nixon. Coover is not the only novelist to have made Nixon a character; Philip Roth and Joseph Heller, for example, have both published rather silly novels—*Our Gang* (1971) and *Good as Gold* (1979), respectively—set in the Nixon White House. (Even Herman Wouk has recently gotten into the act with a potboiler called *Inside, Outside* about a Nixon administration appointee.) Yet another manifestation of the cult of fact is Styron's powerful but troubling *Sophie's Choice* (1979), which mixes real-life Nazi figures with fictional characters, and in which Styron introduced his protagonist, a young Virginia writer named Stingo, in such a way as to make the reader feel that this *must* be the young Bill Styron. Similarly—though in connection with less devastating matters—Oates began her most admired novel, *them* (1969), by saying that "This is a work of history in fictional form," and proceeded to inject herself, as the heroine's teacher, "Miss Oates," into the narrative. Clearly, both Styron and Oates were acting upon the peculiarly post-World War II notion that "a work of history in fictional form" is, for one reason or another, to be preferred to a plain old work of fiction.

These are—is it necessary to say this?—rather disturbing developments. Though all too many of our postwar writers seem to believe otherwise, to insert real public figures, living or dead, into a book of fiction, or to "prove" a point about historical events by distorting them and their consequences, is not necessarily the way to greater truth; such practices can, on the contrary, in the hands of ignorant or ill-meaning authors, serve to propagate misconceptions about important chapters of American history. This is not to suggest that history has no place at all in the novel, or that our contemporary novelists are the first to render their own versions of historical fact. The *Iliad* and *Odyssey, Henry V* and *Julius Caesar, War and Peace* —it would be difficult to list all the classic works of literature which have been inspired by famous people or historical incidents. In our own country and century, *An American Tragedy* was based on a heavily publicized court case. Indeed, it is not the incorporation of fact into postwar American fiction, per se, that distresses one so much as it is the meager artistic merits of the literary works that have been the products of the widespread adoption of this approach. If Homer, Shakespeare, Tolstoy saw history as a means of illuminating timeless human truths—and if Dreiser, feeling the same way, took a murder case out of the headlines of the day and broadened it into a universal story of the human condition—our contemporary novelists tend to do the opposite: to narrow the human condition down to the spirit of the age (a smaller theme), and to narrow that, in turn, down to the events and issues of the hour. If no postwar American novel stands out above the rest—if none has, in other words, succeeded in transmuting contemporary life into deathless art—we can, I believe, place a good deal of blame on the inclination of our novelists to perceive the human condition in our time and country as little more than a gloss on our political and social history.

This is true not only of the nonfiction-happy writers that I have mentioned, but even, to some extent, of such inveterate writers of fiction as Saul Bellow and John Updike. Bellow, for example, has published a number of ambitious, thoughtful, and ponderous novels—*Dangling Man, The Victim, The Adventures of Augie March, Seize the Day, Henderson the Rain King, Herzog, Mr. Sammler's Planet, Humboldt's Gift,* and *The Dean's December*—in which he has, as a rule, been more concerned with expressing his ideas and opinions than with rendering a convincing fictional universe. To him a novel represents, in the main, an opportunity to air his views on American life; and a protagonist (whether he be Augie March, self-consciously "American, Chicago-born," or Henderson, whose cry of "I want, I want, I want" is apparently the pathetic postwar American equivalent of Kurtz's tragic "The horror! The horror!") is not so much a representative man as an out-and-out symbol of an uneasy age. One would not, to be sure, think for a moment of denying the manifold virtues of Bellow's novels—most notably the sense they almost always convey, à la Dostoevsky, that one is in the presence of a rich and vibrant intelligence, a mind that is painfully aware of the precise emotional contours of passion and suffering. Yet at the same time it would not be unfair, I believe, to call Bellow's books "novels-as-essays," and to suggest that his *To Jerusalem and Back: A Personal Account* (1976), a work of nonfiction, is perhaps more representative of his true strengths.

Which brings us to Updike, who for better or worse is probably the closest thing we have to a laureate of postwar middle-class American life. In several of his novels he has, by his own admission, attempted to represent the spirit of American life under various presidential administrations (*The Centaur,* Truman; *Rabbit, Run,* Eisenhower; *Couples,* Kennedy; *Rabbit Redux,* Johnson; *A Month of Sundays,* Nixon; *Rabbit is Rich,* Carter)—the underlying assumption manifestly being that a change of administration makes that much of a difference in the life of the spirit. Accordingly, *A Month of Sundays* (1975) begins: "Forgive me my denomination and my town; I am a Christian minister, and an American. [Shades of *Augie*!] I write these pages at some point in the time of Richard Nixon's unraveling." Page two of *Rabbit is Rich* (1981) finds our excuse for a hero, Harry Angstrom, remembering his father-in-law who had "[l]oved to talk Republican . . . and when Nixon left him nothing to say he had kind of burst. Actually, he had lasted a year into Ford. . . ." Most political of all, perhaps, is *The Coup* (1978), whose narrator is an African dictator given to outbursts of hatred toward "the simultaneously most expansionist and most avowedly idealistic of power aggregations"—that is, the United States; the book, utterly unconvincing as a character portrait, is a true novel-as-essay on the subject of American foreign policy. While straining desperately to "say" something about life in the American century, then, Updike doesn't really manage, in these uniformly accomplished but oddly uncompelling novels, to say very much at all about *life.* His protagonists, like Bellow's, are invariably intended to symbolize The Contemporary Condition; like Bellow, he seems more interested in taking his protagonists through a series of tellingly archetypal present-day adventures than in structuring novels that provide balanced and believable pictures of contemporary American lives. Like Bellow, he has therefore been inclined to make many of his novels rather desultory in form—or, to put it otherwise, "picaresque."

This polemically motivated taste for the picaresque is a common one among major American novelists of the postwar era. The most important postwar novel by a black writer, Ralph Ellison's *Invisible Man* (1952), might in fact be described as a contemporary black odyssey, a self-conscious parable of the twentieth-century "black experience." Though Ellison's novel succeeds artistically in spite of this contrivance, the slighter novels of Philip Roth, which make use of this same device to describe the American Jewish experience, often do not. To be sure, the adventures through which Roth has led his protagonists in such novels as *Letting Go* (1962) and *The Professor of Desire* (1977) have had very little to do with politics and a good deal to do with the authorial self-fascination that I have spoken of. *Portnoy's Complaint* (1969) and *The Breast* (1972), on the other hand, while they are obviously the products of an egocentric sensibility, might well be best understood as egregiously "with it" acts of social hyperawareness—that is to say, as Roth's contribution to the sexual revolution. Like Updike, Roth has, in latter days, appeared to be the victim of a falling-off of imaginative energy, manifested by, among other things, the production of several novels concerned with the adventures of a single protagonist who, in several key particulars, resembles Roth himself. Updike, of course, has the *Rabbit* novels, and Roth has what he has now dubbed the *Zuckerman Bound* series: *The Ghost Writer, Zuckerman Unbound,* and *The Anatomy Lesson.* The latter volume—representing as it does an elaborate act of vengeance on Irving Howe (who appears in the novel as Milton Appel) for his criticisms of *Portnoy* —is probably the apotheosis of Rothean self-absorption. Indeed, it may well represent the epitome of the blinkered, solipsistic tendencies that have afflicted the American novel in the post-war era. For a writer of Roth's importance to base an entire novel upon his irritation over a single review of one of his previous novels seems almost to be an offense against the form itself. For in so doing he trivializes the novel, places a petty act of personal revenge on the same level as the comprehensive depiction of human society that is the novel's traditional province. Interestingly, both he and Updike—by ironically coupling, in the titles of *Rabbit Redux* and *Zuckerman Unbound,* the silly-sounding names of their protagonists with adjectives that are redolent of antediluvian literary majesty—appear to be acknowledging this relative narrowness of scope, to be saying, in effect, "Please don't expect too much of me."

Many of the writers I have mentioned have produced valuable novels. But too often these novels have been valuable more for their comprehensive documentation of the social mores of our era than for their literary artistry. The more ambitious, in fact, our best novelists have become—the more strenuously, that is, they have attempted to define the nature of the beast or the spirit of the age—the less successful they have been. Joseph Epstein, in reviewing Bernard Malamud's novel *God's Grace* (1982), put it memorably: "Poor Malamud, the larger he strains to become, the smaller his talent begins to appear." Especially in the light (or, rather, the gloom) of Mailer's excrementally infatuated epic *Ancient Evenings* (1983), and the latest, rather disappointing works of Bellow and Updike, this observation might well serve as an apt verdict upon the achievement of all our major postwar American novelists.

In a sense, the most satisfying postwar American novels have been the work of writers who have decided *not* to try to outdo *Ulysses* or Hemingway or Faulkner or to write something definitive about the American century, but who have chosen rather to investigate various corners of the human heart. Among the books—plain and ornate, realistic and fantastic—that belong in this category are William Maxwell's wonderfully sensitive story of Midwestern adolescent life, *The Folded Leaf* (1945); J. D. Salinger's colloquially written tale of a perturbed prep-school Huck Finn, *The Catcher in the Rye* (1951); May Sarton's luminous portrait of an aging woman's lonely struggle for "peace, order, and poetry," *Mrs. Stevens Hears the Mermaids Singing* (1965); Edmund White's arresting Kafkaesque sketch of life in a summer beach colony, *Forgetting Elena* (1975); and Toni Morrison's enchanting, fantastic story of small-town black life, *Song of Solomon* (1977). One might also mention the oeuvres of such disparate figures as Eudora Welty and Louis Auchincloss, and a number of less familiar individual novels, including *Finistère* (1951) by Fritz Peters, *Mrs. Bridge* (1959) by Evan S. Connell, and *Totempole* (1965) by Sanford Friedman. Such works have little in common except that they have been artistically more successful, overall, than the productions of our so called literary "heavyweights." If most of these books fail to explore the heart as broadly or deeply as *Ulysses*, they do evince a pleasing consistency of vision, of style, of tone; if the perceptions that they convey are not always of a Dostoevskian profundity, they are at least expressed with undeniable elegance. Many of the most admirable postwar novels have been the work of Southerners—writers who are manifestly the heirs of Faulkner, though they have operated on a somewhat smaller scale. The more evocative and compelling of these works—aside from the novels of Welty—have included Truman Capote's *Other Voices, Other Rooms* (1948) and *Breakfast at Tiffany's* (1958), Styron's *Lie Down in Darkness* (1951), Harper Lee's *To Kill a Mockingbird* (1960), and Walker Percy's *The Moviegoer* (1961). Compared to the would-be epic poems of Mailer, Bellow, Updike, and such, these writers' novels are exquisite lyrics. It might be argued, indeed, that if the postwar era has not been notable for Great American Novels, it has produced its share of "small classics."

Opposed, in style and scope and everything else, to these pleasant novelistic oases is that sprawling Kalahari Desert of literature known as "metafiction." The writers who have won the greatest celebrity for practicing this strange, surrealistic adaptation of literary modernism — among them, John Barth (*Giles Goat-Boy, Letters*), William Gaddis (*JR, The Recognitions*), Don DeLillo (*Running Dog, The Names, Ratner's Star*), John Hawkes (*Second Skin, The Lime Twig*), and Thomas Pynchon (*Gravity's Rainbow, V.*)—give the impression that they consider themselves the only writers of the postwar era who have been ready, willing, and able to capture the *Zeitgeist,* to write the *Ulysses* of postwar America. The chief problem with the metafictionists, unfortunately, is that they have been even more distracted from the human condition than "mainstream" writers like Mailer and Bellow; like those writers, they have been eager to define the spirit of the age, but they don't seem to think that the spirit of the age has very much to do with the *human* spirit. Their novels, consequently, tend to be marked not by a desire to make sense of human society (which is, after all, the novel's traditional concern) but by an effort to proclaim, usually in language as inelegant, inaccessible, and pseudoscientific as possible, the tyranny and ineluctability of inanimate systems—whether governmental, military, or corporate. Not only does metafiction hold these systems culpable for the depersonalization and fragmentation of post-World War II civilization —and, therefore, for the supposed obsolescence of the conventional novel—but it equates them with the indomitable mysteries of existence.

What's more, since many metafictionists are products of the English Department, they seem never to get used to the idea that the writing of fiction is an act of creation involving the manipulation of language, and consider it clever to remind us constantly of this amazing circumstance. They are, in short, more interested in writing about writing than in writing about anything else. This scrap of John Barth's *Letters* (1979) is typical:

> ... when we say N O V E L , for example, we refer at once to at least 5 things: (a) (what we take to be) a document in the guise of an extended fiction of a revolutionary character; (b) a 5-year plan for the composition of that document; (c) a five-year plan for effecting, in part by means of that document, certain novel and revolutionary changes in the world; (d) the title of a (also known as RN) and the code name of b and c; and (e)

the code name for this Novel Revolution itself and the 5 several years of its implementation. . . .

Need I add that, like the Mailers and Updikes, the Barths and Pynchons rarely lose sight, for long, of the newspaper headlines? From the closing pages of *Letters,* this sample passage:

> . . . the Author outlines this last on Tuesday, July 4, 1978. The U.S. Bicentennial was celebrated, in the main, quietly, two years since, by a citizenry subdued by the Watergate scandals, the presidential impeachment hearings, the resignation of President Nixon, and his full and complete pardon by President Ford, himself defeated four months later by President Carter, with whom this week's polls show only 23% of the electorate to be satisfied. The post office has raised the first-class postal rate to 15 ¢ per ounce. Vice-President Mondale has returned from private talks with Egyptian President Sadat and Israeli Prime Minister Begin meant to renew the stalled Middle East peace negotiations. New fighting in Lebanon. *RN,* ex-president Nixon's memoirs, is #3 on the New York *Times* list of nonfiction best-sellers. . . .

Though educated, nonacademic Americans have shown little interest in exploring this fogbound literary territory, the canon-compilers on campus—who have kept metafiction alive—tend to regard it as *the* significant fictional mode of our time. And academia is, frankly, where these books belong. Though some of them do have redeeming aesthetic qualities (Pynchon's short 1966 novel *The Crying of Lot 49,* for instance, has a certain offbeat charm), they are, as a rule, designed to appeal to the sort of sensibility that is more suited by nature to textual research than to literary criticism, that confuses pretentiousness with profundity, and that mistakes ponderousness for stylistic innovation. Metafiction is based, moreover, on the notion that literature has less to do with making sense of the world—how, the metafictionists ask, can one make sense of something that is senseless?—than with glossological game-playing.

Within limits, of course, there is nothing wrong with playing with words; the main problem is that writers like Hawkes and Gaddis have made such a dull game of it. And an unimaginative one, too: for despite all the academic hoopla over the "innovativeness" of these books, the game doesn't vary all that much from one to the other. The most notable exception to this rule is Vladimir Nabokov. Though he has written books that are notoriously unnavigable (for example, the gigantic 1969 *Ada*), and though all of his published works (especially the 1962 *Pale Fire,* which takes the form of a series of scholarly annotations) are ideal dissertation fodder, Nabokov stands head and shoulders above the rest of the metafictional crowd. He is one postwar American novelist (or, more precisely, Russian-turned-American) whose postmodernistic game-play is successful, especially in the brilliant *Lolita* (1958), where the linguistic sport is witty and apt, exquisitely underlining that wonderful novel's central concern with the faithful representation of human feeling.

Alas, Nabokov has had no successors. The prospects for the American novel are, at present, as bleak as they have ever been. For metafiction has not been the only inauspicious consequence of the postwar academic institutionalization of literature. While the English departments of America have been busy inflating the reputations of the Barths and Pynchons, the creative writing programs have been busy too, distributing advanced degrees to armies of students who have learned how to make "workshop fiction"—spare, elliptical exercises in tone, metaphor, and (above all) obsessive surface detail that, although often well written, seem in most instances to have been deliberately shorn of passion, force, animation, and originality.

The writers who have made this brand of fiction the literary wave of the Eighties tend, like their master of masters Raymond Carver, to favor the short-story form, and the novels they do write—for instance, Ann Beattie's *Chilly Scenes of Winter* (1976) and *Falling in Place* (1980), Jayne Anne Phillips's *Machine Dreams* (1984), Elizabeth Tallent's *Museum Pieces* (1985), and Elizabeth Benedict's *Slow Dancing* (1985)—are inclined to be so narrow in scope and modest in their ambitions that many of them read like extended short stories. Indeed, some of these novels *are* short-story collections in disguise (Susan Kenney's *In Another Country,* Andrea Lee's *Susan Phillips,* Louise Erdrich's *Love Medicine,* all published within the past year). Whatever the genre, these authors are inclined to write frequently in the present tense; to favor the short declarative sentence (*very* short and *very* declarative); to be preoccupied with domestic details (cooking, dishwashing, laundry), with the most banal of contemporary phenomena (TV commercials, trailer parks), and with brand names; to transmit clues to the nature of a protagonist's personal torments as dryly and emotionlessly as if those torments were just so many trite domestic details; and to think that surface details, if piled up high enough, can help us to see through to the heart.

Many of them cheerfully refer to themselves as children of television, and acknowledge the influence of the soap opera and music video upon their work; while they may also be described, in a sense, as the descendants of John Updike, John Cheever, and J. D. Salinger, their prose, alongside that of Updike and Salinger and Cheever, looks all the more vapid and mechanical. If the metafictionists are fruitlessly "experimental," these writers, who seem to aim not for some literary ideal but for the pages of *The New Yorker* (or a Knopf contract), are dismayingly unexperimental—and just plain unimaginative. One novel or story after another consists of passages that sound exactly like this:

> Holly, swinging her legs from the kitchen stool, lectures her mother on natural foods. Holly is ten.
>
> . . . Holly wants to eat peanuts, soyburgers, and yogurt. Waldeen is sure this new fixation has something to do with Holly's father, Joe Murdock, although Holly rarely mentions him. After Waldeen and Joe were divorced last September, Joe moved to Arizona and got a construction job. Joe sends Holly letters occasionally, but Holly won't let Waldeen see them. At Christmas he sent Holly a copper Indian bracelet with unusual marks on it. It is Indian language, Holly tells her. Waldeen sees Holly polishing the bracelet while she is watching TV.
>
> Joe McClain is punctual, considerate. Tonight he brings fudge ripple ice cream and a half-gallon of Coke in a plastic jug. He kisses Waldeen and hugs Holly.
> Waldeen says, "We're having liver and onions, but Holly's mad 'cause I won't make Soybean Supreme."
> "Soybean *Delight*," says Holly.
> (Bobbie Ann Mason, *Shiloh and Other Stories*)

Or this:

> As soon as Mrs. Harrington got home, she hurried into the kitchen. Her son Roy was watching "Speed Racer" on television. He was fourteen. She heard loud music in the background: Jennifer; Blondie—"Dreaming, dreaming is free."
>
> Her daughter came in, sucking a Starburst. She had on a pink blouse Mrs. Harrington didn't much care for. "How was it?" she asked, beginning to scrub the pots.
> "Fine," said Mrs. Harrington.

"What's for dinner?" Roy asked again.

"Chicken. Broiled chicken."

"Again?"

"Yes," Mrs. Harrington said, remembering the days when chicken hadn't mattered. Those days took on a new luxury, a warmth to match Christmas, in this light—the four of them, eating, innocent.

"Can I make some noodles?" Roy asked.

"Noodles!" Ernest shouted....

"Dad called," Jennifer said.

"Was he at home?"

"He and Sandy are in Missoula, Montana."

"Ha," said Mrs. Harrington. "One minute in Trinidad, the next in Missoula, Montana."

(David Leavitt, *Family Dancing*)

Or this:

The rain has stopped. Charles turns on the radio. Elvis Presley is singing "Loving You." Elvis Presley is forty. Charles turns off the radio. Susan wipes tears out of her eyes.

. . . Charles goes into the kitchen, looks through the cabinets to see what there is for dinner. Susan is right; he thinks about food too much. He picks up a package of dried peas, drops them back on the shelf. There is a large bottle of vanilla, a package of dried beans, a box of Tuna Helper, no tuna, a can of baby clams, two cans of alphabet soup, a canister with four Hydrox cookies (what happened to them? They used to be so good. Sugar. No doubt they're leaving out sugar), a package of Cheese Nabs, and a can of grapefruit juice. There is also a package of manicotti shells. They will have to go out for dinner.

(Ann Beattie, *Chilly Scenes of Winter*)

"So what?" one wants to scream. If all this obsessive detail were actually leading somewhere, one's reaction might be different. But no such luck. These flat little kitchen scenes are *it*—they're not lead-ins, not quiet domestic interludes between chunks of more compelling, dramatic stuff. They are the whole enchilada. Of course, we are meant to understand, amid all the meal preparation and television viewing, that our heroes are suffering in one way or another—facing divorce, disease, "relationship" problems, the passage of time, death. But we don't ever get very close to this emotional turmoil; the approach is elliptical throughout, and one gets the idea that, to these writers' way of thinking, a fuller, more direct treatment of human suffering would somehow be unbearably vulgar, *démodé*. It would certainly be more difficult to carry off.

Such, then, are the ways of the "Hey-I-Can-Do-That" school of fiction. Between the flat dialogue, the persistent allusions to Kool-Aid and "General Hospital," the endless descriptions of meaningless movement and insignificant activities, and the tepid little plots (often obviously autobiographical) that revolve around troubled relationships, cancer victims, and family tensions, it is hard to tell the work of one of these young writers from that of another. In the American fiction of the Eighties, unhappy families are all unhappy in pretty much the same way.

There are some standard variations on this formula, of course. In the work of some of our very newest writers, the detail-heavy, lightweight workshop prose is allied with what might best be described as a kind of knee-jerk, new-wave nihilism. More ambitious than their domestically oriented contemporaries to take on The Age, these young writers have transformed the profound, embattled despair of the major prewar novels into something very superficial, solipsistic, and modish; but then it is ridiculous even to speak of them in connection with the prewar novel, for they seem to be less influenced by writers like Hemingway, Fitzgerald, Faulkner, and Dos Passos—let alone Shakespeare and Swift —than by the mindless, self-indulgent anarchism of the new-wave scene. Their novels tend to take the form of slim, disjointed little tributes to East Village chic or Los Angeles decadence and to have titles like *It Was Gonna Be Like Paris* and *Less Than Zero*. (Even a good novel like Jay McInerney's 1984 *Bright Lights, Big City* flirts with nihilistic chic nine-tenths of the way through before throwing it over decisively.)

Just as nihilism, then, has become a Campy diversion, a "lifestyle," for legions of upper-middle-class young Americans, so it seems poised to become a literary conceit for many members of a generation of writers whose lack of understanding of the history and possibilities of the genre in which they are working is exceeded only by their lack of interest in honestly representing the depth and variety of human life in the closing decades of the twentieth century. In this, they have, sad to say, succeeded only in taking their elder and better-known colleagues' depredations of the novel form one step further. The American novel, to state it plainly, seems headed for some very grim times indeed.

The Novel in the Academy:
A Paean to Perplexity

MAY 1984

Until recently, if you wanted to know all about contemporary American novels without actually having to read any of them, you went to the library and paged through a dozen or so critical studies, among them Tony Tanner's *City of Words,* Leslie Fiedler's *Waiting for the End,* and Ihab Hassan's *Radical Innocence.* These were all nice, manageable books, tightly organized, neatly argued, their theses lucidly expressed in their opening sections and reasonably well developed thereafter, through the course of eight or ten chapters that dealt briefly and precisely with fifteen or twenty major novels. Some were better written than others, some more incisive or entertaining; but each had a clear reason for existing, for each had a somewhat different way of looking at things. These were *civilized* books, which co-existed peacefully in the same territory, and their authors nodded at each other every once in a while, acknowledging each other's work genially and accepting their unavoidable differences with equanimity. To read through them, one after another, was to walk from window to window in a single house, looking out at the same landscape from a series of different perspectives.

Enter *American Fictions 1940–1980: A Comprehensive History and Critical Evaluation* by Frederick R. Karl. Several times the size of most of its predecessors, it is patently designed to eliminate the need for Tanner's and Fiedler's and Hassan's window views (which, according to Karl, "all fall short . . . of being sufficiently inclusive") and to replace them with a single magnificently detailed aerial photograph of this rich, if inadequately charted, stretch of literary terrain. For every novel covered by Tanner or Fiedler, *American Fictions* covers ten: not only *The Naked and the Dead* but *Guard of Honor* and *The Young Lions* and *Dog Soldiers;* not only *The Adventures of Augie March* but *The Adventures of Mao on the Long March;* not only *Dangling Man* but *The Ginger Man* and *My Life as a Man* and *The Man Who Cried I Am.* There is no question but that Professor Karl wants us to look at this massive object—with its two columns per page of small print, its dust jacket on which the title is spelled out in imposingly serifed one-hundred-point crimson caps, and its comprehensive-looking list of contents on the back cover—and decide at once that this is *the* definitive study of the postwar American novel, the only book substantial enough to consider all the novels, to draw all the connections, to consolidate all the perspectives.

As it turns out, however, *American Fictions* is a foolishly conceived and poorly executed book that adds virtually nothing to Tanner, Fiedler, and the rest of the crop. Karl establishes his thesis (not to mention his penchant for nebulous abstractions and clumsy turns of phrase) in the book's first paragraph:

> The American novel since the Second World War is, obviously, that fiction which came after 1945; but it is also more than a body of work in chronological sequence. In attitudes, recognitions, ideologies, disturbances, and techniques, it is a fiction that molded itself to post-atomic ideas and responses and reached out to become something new. We have an era, really sustained for the first time, of what we may broadly call "American modernism," the rough equivalent in fiction of abstract expressionism or action painting, of the *nouvelle vague* in cinema, of the post-Pound-Williams era in poetry, of serial and electronic music, of increasing forms of abstraction which have characterized all the arts. On the stage, where our cultural ideas are visualized more directly, the bare, abstract, symbolic look is part of this general movement. Theater manifested the perfect expression of the era in Beckett's *Waiting for Godot*—in language, characters, themes, staging, even clothes. In all its diversity, the postwar novel has striven for precisely this achievement: to defamiliarize the world, and while moving the human experience to the margins, to move the margins toward the center.

Though, to me at least, parts of this paragraph are meaningless, the essential message is clear: "Make it new." This is, of course, Ezra Pound's phrase, and Karl seems to see himself as something of a Poundian figure, encouraging literary experiment wherever he finds it. But F. K. is no E. P. His philosophy of literature simply doesn't go very far *beyond* "Make it new." "We must never forget," he writes, "that Gide found Proust unintelligible, a poor writer of French; that early readers of *Ulysses* reeled without guidelines; that 'The Waste Land' remained impenetrable for years." True enough, and the lesson these facts teach us is that we should not dismiss the unfamiliar out of hand, that we should always remember that great literature can turn up in all sorts of places. But Karl draws another lesson entirely: he thinks that the more impenetrable a novel is, the greater the likelihood that it's *real literature*. Difficulty, in other words, is the cardinal sign of great contemporary literature.

Most of us, I suspect, have known English professors whose sentiments tended in this direction. They are academics through and through, who consider a novel to be, above all, its author's contribution to a symbiotic relationship with the academic community. This is how it works, if the relationship is successful: the academic critic publishes a paper about the novel, he gets promoted, he does a book, he receives tenure, he dies happy; the novelist, on his part, gets recognition in the groves of academe, his own entry in the *MLA Bibliography,* and his own session at the MLA Convention, and eventually becomes part of the "canon"—an immortal. Now, if this symbiosis is to function smoothly, what the novelist owes the academic more than anything else is a novel that contains enough material to work with. It has to be complicated. It has to require *figuring out.* And this, of course, is where the academic's half of the bargain comes in: he must crack the code, find the solution to the jumble. Not, note well, because he truly understands and is devoted to modernist ideals, or to any ideals that involve a conception of literary art whereby a given work may be difficult to apprehend because it seeks to represent with complete fidelity the magnificent complexity of life. No, it's pure pragmatism. Publish or perish.

Presumably, Professor Frederick R. Karl of New York University (whose list of publications reaches back a quarter of a century) is past the stage at which he must publish or perish. Yet his attitude is very much that of the enigma-happy junior scholar. To him, the novelist who writes something that puzzles the bejesus out of everybody is a hero, and the one who writes something lucid and lovely and moving is a viper. But Karl isn't merely another academic looking for something to analyze. No, Karl is now one of those newest-of-the-new academics who pride themselves on writing a lot of words, but who say very little of substance about the work of literature under discussion. A great contemporary novel, to him, is not simply one that requires figuring out, but one that *defies* figuring out—at least by him—so that to discuss it is not to analyze it but simply to admire, in a redundant and superficial manner, the way its chaotic text manages to reflect the anarchy of our age. To Karl, the superhero of the past four decades is indubitably William Gaddis, and the finest American novel of our day is Gaddis's supremely enigmatic megabook *JR,* which Karl reverently refers to as an "inaccessible triumph." Its importance is manifest from the very first page, apparently, for its beginning "is one of the most deliberately confusing in literature," and the confusion—to Gaddis's credit—"continues for pages, with names slipped in that mean nothing, the speaker unidentified. The reader struggles not only for identification of the speakers, or for the information, but for some thread of argument which connects these discrete pieces of material." After a few pages of this sort of thing, "without warning, different speakers appear. Words and voices, however, seem disembodied. Location, direction, content are unclear."

This, apparently, is what a "maker of literature" in the postwar period makes. According to Karl, we have had only a handful of these fellows during the past four decades, and their names are William Gaddis, Thomas Pynchon, John Barth, John Hawkes, Donald Barthelme, William Burroughs, and Joseph McElroy.[1] The quality that these novelists seem to share above all others, at least as Karl sees them, is their insistence upon talking not to their readers but to themselves. For this, Karl congratulates them warmly. "In *JR,*" he enthuses, "Gaddis is so unbending, and, one must add, obsessive, that the reader is forgotten." In *Letters,* John Barth engages in nearly unparalleled "self-indulgence" and "probe[s] new modes of perception, however tedious the process." And in a novella by John Hawkes,

> words pour out, as though the writer has forgotten us or assumes we know where he is heading, where he came from. There is none of the traditional information or linkage, as in Bellow, Mailer, or Malamud. . . . By way of disconnections and disruptions, the novelist—and the reader by implication—is doing no more than experiencing Emerson's dictum: "the *all in each* of human nature," the universal residing in each individual, by way of intuition. The novelist must move along lines of that intuition, even when it leads toward disaster.

Yes, it is a fine thing for the novelist to tap away at the collective un-conscious, to follow his instincts; but Karl is altogether too thrilled by the disasters into which the tedious, self-indulgent, deliberately confus-ing "instincts" of certain contemporary novelists have led them, and too deprecatory of the genuine achievements of novelists who have made masterly uses of conventional methods of exploring character and culture, or whose experiments have taken more modest or subtle or successful forms than those favored by Karl's ruling deities. This is a critic who does not hesitate to praise something by Hawkes for its "re-sistance to clarity" —as if clarity were some dread disease that infects lit-erature with mediocrity—and who shouts his admiration of Hawkes's ability to create "a dim outline, like the lines of a palimpsest."

It takes a while to get the hang of the topsy-turvy philosophy of this book, but one eventually does, and when one reads that Flannery O'Connor "resembles John Hawkes, although she is far less experi-mental or daring in her arrangements and in her demand upon the reader" (and that is as subtle and probing an analysis as any writer gets in this book), one knows immediately that the verdict is in—O'Connor is a lesser writer than Hawkes. The formula is simple: less daring plus less demanding equals less distinguished.

Virtually the only consistent thing about *American Fictions* is Karl's mania for muddle. It ruins the book, and causes one to hope fervently that *American Fictions* does not become general issue in undergraduate English classes. To teach students to admire effective works that are the product of modernist experimentation is one thing; but to instruct them in the perverse belief that incoherence is the surest sign of literary dis-tinction is quite another. If one wishes to believe that *JR* and *Gravity's Rainbow* are among the best novels of our day, very well; but they are not great because of their inaccessibility. A great novel succeeds by rising above the impediments to understanding that the composition of a deeply and comprehensively conceived work has forced upon its au-thor; it does not succeed as a result of those impediments. Karl's prob-lem is that he is impressed by reckless literary risk-taking whatever the circumstances—no matter whether it happens to have a purpose, no matter whether it pays off or falls flat. He ridicules the members of a *Commentary* symposium for thinking themselves "too fine" for the "not so brave new world" of contemporary letters in which they've awakened, but he goes ridiculously far in the other direction, eagerly running after anything that strikes him as "the rough equivalent in fiction of abstract impressionism or action painting, of the *nouvelle vague* in cinema." He calls to mind the poetry editor of an undergraduate literary magazine who described the sole standard by which he selected poems for publication as follows: "I pick the ones that are *weird.*"

American Fictions is itself, of course, a good example of *nouvelle vague* criticism. Granted, it *looks* well organized, with its chapters on "American Space and Spatiality," "The Persistence of Pastoral," "The War and the Novel—Before and After," "Growing Up in America: The 1940s and Thereafter," "The Counterfeit Decade," "The Possibilities of Minimalism," "The Nonfiction Novel," and so forth. These are, for the most part, understandable subdivisions for a study of contemporary American literature. But the framework results in anarchy. The discussions of a single writer's novels are likely to be spread over several chapters, depending on (a) when they were written, (b) which form (minimalist, nonfiction novel) they supposedly exhibit, and (c) which theme (counterfeiting, politics, etc.) Karl thinks of as dominating each book. Thus, of Saul Bellow's nine novels, the first (*Dangling Man*) and second (*The Victim*) are examined in Chapter Four; the third (*The Adventures of Augie March*) in Chapter Five; the fourth (*Seize the Day*), sixth (*Herzog*), and seventh (*Mr. Sammler's Planet*) in Chapter Eight; the fifth (*Henderson the Rain King*) and ninth (*The Dean's December*) in Chapter Seven; the eighth (*Humboldt's Gift*) in Chapter Eleven. Because of this format, Karl is unable to develop a coherent, accurate picture of any postwar novelist's *oeuvre* and must pepper his text with clumsy cross-references. For example, a footnote to a discussion of a James Purdy novel tells us, "In the section 'Growing Up in America,' I discuss his two earlier works, *Malcolm* and *The Nephew.*" And a passage about Jerzy Kosinski's recent novels begins, "*The Painted Bird* and *Steps* (see 'Growing Up in America' and 'The Possibilities of Minimalism') are the two coordinates of Jerzy Kosinski's fiction."

Such crudities would be acceptable if Karl's chapter divisions were especially useful. But they're not. Besides the fact that he adds almost nothing to what other critics have said about such subjects as space and spatiality, the pastoral, and the American political novel, Karl exaggerates the decade-to-decade thematic modulations to an absurd extent, expecting us to accept the notion that a wide variety of writers were all concentrating in the 1940s upon the theme of growing up, and that the same writers switched in the 1950s to the counterfeiting motif. He makes too many such black-and-white distinctions. For example, "The major problem of the novelist in the 1960s was that there seemed to be too many realities. In the 1970s, the problem has shifted, in that it has become too difficult to determine what, if anything, reality really is; where it lies; what shape it takes; where, if anywhere, it is heading." And:

> [*Native Son*] has many lives. It has its 1930s life as a novel about class, caste, and race; it has its reverberations in war novels of the late 1940s, so that we can look back at *Native Son* as Wright's version of a combat novel; it has its life in the 1950s and 1960s as a book that says critical things about black-white relationships and the victimization of poor blacks; it has its parallel cultural life in the attacks made on Wright by blacks themselves—Baldwin, among others.

In the first two or three thousand words of a typical chapter in *American Fictions,* Karl discusses the theme, mode, and/or period with which the chapter is concerned; the remainder of the chapter is a series of mostly unconnected one- to three-thousand-word segments about individual novels. Every so often, Karl takes a stab at tying a novel thematically into the chapter in which he has placed it. This is usually not very effectively done, even when there is a legitimate reason for the placement. Karl places *Lolita,* for instance, in Chapter Six, "The Counterfeit Decade," which is about novels of the 1950s. "Everything about *Lolita,*" writes Karl, "is parodic, a celebration of the counterfeit; its methods based on mirrors and reflections." Reading this, one cries out for examples; but there are none. Indeed, it is often the case that a two- or three-thousand-word-long passage on a novel will contain only a sentence or two of quotation from the novel. Thus, unless one has already read *Lolita* and perceived the genuine significance of mirror images in the novel—in which case, of course, one doesn't need to hear about it from Karl—the mention of these reflections in *American Fictions* is meaningless. Even when Karl does support his observations, he almost never answers the obvious questions they raise. Why, for instance, is Nabokov concerned with the theme of the counterfeit? How does it function in *Lolita*? What does it contribute to the structure, the meaning, the beauty, the human force of the novel? None of these questions is of much interest to Karl. To him, his job is not to elucidate the purpose of the counterfeiting motif in *Lolita,* but to impress upon us (somewhere in his swarm of generalizations about the novel) that *Lolita* is "a celebration of the counterfeit" and, in turn, that the 1950s were a "counterfeit decade." If one really wants to understand *Lolita*, one must turn to the novel itself or to another book of criticism, such as Tony Tanner's *City of Words*, which offers a fine discussion of Nabokov's symbolism.

Karl himself would have done well to turn now and again to *City of Words*, or to any of several other critical studies. But he hasn't. Somehow he sees no urgent need to take the work of other critics into account. If he quotes from the novels rarely, he quotes even less often from his fellow critics. The few critics whose work he does make use of are not the best, either: they seem to be trendy, gimmicky ones, such as Sandra Gilbert and Susan Gubar, whose *The Madwoman in the Attic* (like *American Fictions*, an attempt to force a number of authors into a highly contrived view of things) keeps cropping up in Karl's chapter on "The Female Experience."

With a few exceptions, then, Karl's critical comments are entirely his own. This one can hardly doubt, for they all strike one, with great force, as the products of a single mind. For example: "It is unlikely that a woman could write a novel of combat." "Bullfighting and big-game hunting are not ordinarily accessible to a Jewish writer." "While high art in the 1950s was identified with the Eastern Seaboard, lifestyles were the prerogative of the West Coast." "[Jazz's] lack of verbal content was essential to its impact as a purely aural form of experience." Karl disputes at length Elizabeth Hardwick's bleak description of Automat food in her novel *Sleepless Nights*, contending that "the Automat was quite different [from the way Hardwick portrays it]; the macaroni, actually, was a superb dish for the price." And he ridicules the "proliferation of designations" among writers:

> Among black writers alone, we have black Americans, Afro-Americans, Negroes, then subdivisions for each sex; among Jews, we find Jewish-Americans, Jewish novelists, subdivisions into male and female, occasionally further subdivisions into the particular Jewish orientation — German, Eastern European, Sephardic, and eventually we can expect South American Jews, North African Jews, Israelis, and so on.

There is, Karl states flatly, no such thing as a "Jewish novel"; yet he is constantly talking about "Jewish writers," and refers at one point to the "Jewish violence" that he finds in their work.

Bullfighting, jazz, Automat macaroni—sometimes it seems as if Karl will go off on any tangent to avoid writing about literature. He draws his prime example of 1950s schizophrenia, for example, not from literature but from rock and roll: "Elvis Presley, whom many Americans in the 1950s epitomized [*sic*] as dissolute, crummy, and shabby, saw himself as clean-cut, patriotic, indeed, supernationalistic." Oddly enough, Karl develops this trifling observation at greater length than he does some of his most important ones, devoting more than two paragraphs to Presley's antipathy toward the Beatles, the Smothers Brothers, and Jane Fonda, and the singer's affection for J. Edgar Hoover, to whom he offered his services as an informer. To help support his notion of the Fifties as a decade dominated by the themes of counterfeit (as explored in Gaddis's *The Recognitions*) and invisibility (Ellison's *Invisible Man*), Karl writes that "Presley reaches back to Whittaker Chambers, early in the 1950s, and works the line of counterfeit and invisibility." This is, by the way, hardly the most bizarre connection drawn in *American Fictions*; at various points, Karl manages to see what he thinks of as illuminating symbolic links between Patty Hearst and *Native Son*, Senator McCarthy and Mike Hammer, the Reverend Jim Jones and *Cat's Cradle*.

Perhaps Karl's favorite form of critical analysis is name-interpretation. In some novels, such as *Lolita*, the characters' names are indeed significant. But whereas Karl comments briefly on the name of John Ray, Jr., Ph.D., the "editor" (actually a creation of Nabokov) whose name is appended to the novel's preface, and on the name of Humbert Humbert, he doesn't bother to interpret the names of Lolita, Quilty, or Mrs. Haze—all of which are an integral part of Nabokov's scheme. But, again, Karl isn't interested in fitting the elements of *Lolita* together to see the grand picture; he's merely concerned with making random points about the novel, enough to justify classifying it as a work concerned with the theme of counterfeiting. Most of his name-interpretations seem off-the-cuff: "Augie is not Augustus or august, but *Augie,* a name for a man of the people; he must march." "Alexander (not the Great, not the son of Philip) Portnoy must somehow escape his House Beautiful scene to become his own person. This is the primal theme of growing up fiction." All right, though; the insights may not be anything to write home about, and the prose may make one squirm, but this sort of name-play is tolerable enough. Unfortunately, Karl doesn't stop at interpreting the names of characters; he interprets the names of *authors*. He makes a point of saying that Jerzy Kosinski has "a name like Joseph K." And he doesn't even stop there. Buried in the notes at the back of the book is a reference to Bert Parks, who, "with his Thoreauvian name . . . MC's Miss America contests!"

That Karl can be so comfortable using the word "MC"—as a *verb, yet*—brings us to another problem with *American Fictions:* namely, that Karl doesn't choose his words as well as he might. He overuses the word *compelling* and describes virtually everything, at one time or another, as *archetypal* or *prototypical* of everything else. But the main problem is simply a clumsy style. Karl wants desperately to be verbally agile, but he keeps tripping himself up. He refers to the 1950s as "a difficult time to grow up, but an excellently manured garden for fiction to develop in." On *Cat's Cradle:* "Once we get past some of the charming words Vonnegut has conceived, Bokononism is a sentimentalized belief full of the author's sweetness and generosity." On *Catcher in the Rye:* "Puking is a source of fun, or male genitals." On Saul Bellow: "In his *Paris Review* interview, Bellow stated his preference for nineteenth-century realism, of which Dreiser is a major American proponent. Favoring this kind of novel, which includes the Russians, has pre-empted Bellow's development in the post-war years." On God knows what: "The ordinary magnified can be the stuff of a life experienced on the edge of a precipice." On *Why Are We in Vietnam?:* "In a passage as if written by William Burroughs in a drug-induced hallucinatory state, Mailer binds old and new America." On Alan Friedman's *Hermaphrodeity:* "We have a not so mild pornographic stress to the book."

Not that Karl minds pornography. Indeed, as I am now regrettably compelled to demonstrate, he goes out of his way to prove that he is not afraid of vulgarity. He refers to Norman Mailer's hero Rojack as a "cocksman," speaks of the middle-class concern with "the perfect fuck" (which he then compares unfavorably with Eldridge Cleaver's desire to "rape white woman," as described in *Soul on Ice*), says that a character in Lisa Alther's *Kinflicks* "screws like a piston rod," observes that in *Gravity's Rainbow* "the environment is shit," suggests that Henry Miller "tried to set a literary fucking record," describes the "sense of past beshitting future" in Barth's *Letters,* and discusses Bellow's attitude toward "blacks, with their big cocks." The first sentence of the first chapter of *American Fictions* throws all inhibitions down the chute: "America as shit, America as shit-producer, America as be-shitten, America as a gigantic asshole out of which energy and waste pour, Texans as the biggest assholes of them all—such are the ways of explaining why we were in Vietnam." And such are the ways of all too many academic critics these days, who think that the best way to be "relevant" and "in touch with the times" is to fill their ivory towers with ordure.

The simplicity of Karl's philosophy, and the less-than-illuminating quality of his commentary, are perhaps well demonstrated by his remarks on that novel of novels, *JR*. Karl's thirty-five-hundred-word discussion of Gaddis's book begins with the statement that

> the key part here is the method: interrupted conversation, incomplete lines of thought, a shorthand language; language that no longer serves its traditional functions. Gaddis has tried to put gesture and expression into the written word. But it is, also, the language we feed into computers, set phrases programmed for rapidity, where our interest lies only in the printout.

Questions: (1) If Gaddis's language doesn't serve its traditional functions, what functions *does* it serve? (2) What's so special about trying to put gesture and expression into the written word? Doesn't every writer try to do this? (3) Why is the language of computers appropriate to novels? Karl does not answer any of these immediately, but after a two-paragraph digression he looks as if he is about to. Gaddis, he says, "has found a form, a language as well as a focus for his view of postwar America." *Terrific,* we think, *here comes an answer.* But no. Rather than develop this theme, Karl gives us another impromptu paean to perplexity: "Many devices from *The Recognitions* remain. The withholding of vital information is crucial; for the retention of material creates a pressure on the reader. We are caught, in a guessing game, a suspense drama, a purely dramatic action. Postponement, as in drama, is the key; we push against unknowns."

And for the next two paragraphs, Karl continues to pay tribute to the intentional confusion of *JR,* to the magnificent fact that its "location, direction, content are unclear." Eventually, he says, the reader becomes aware of the title character, bobbing now and then out of Gaddis's fog of prose. But Karl is quick to reassure us that JR, far from the fully realized individual that the hacks would give us, is instead a "shadowy schoolboy" who "rarely comes clearly into focus. He is a sixth grader, and a full-faced portrait, Gaddis realized, would be of little interest. Moving in shadows, however, he can be a giant, the mastermind of a vast corporate enterprise, something it takes us hundreds of pages to identify." What we are dealing with in *American Fictions* is a critic who finds the depiction of "a vast corporate enterprise" more interesting than the depiction of a human being, and who considers the magnitude of a fictional character to have less to do with the precision and comprehensiveness with which the author has evoked him on the page than with the position in the world of business that his creator has accorded him.

Karl goes on to explain that the gold in *Das Rheingold,* a production of which figures importantly in the novel, reminds one of the shares of stock mentioned at the beginning of *JR,* and that when we notice this connection, "we begin to perceive a theme [*sacre bleu!*], although unassociated with any particular characters. [What a relief!] Just as in *Das Rheingold* the Gold of the Rhine will dominate the opera and the entire Ring, so money will open and close the cycles of *JR.*"

Fine. So tell us, what does Gaddis have to say about money? How does it affect the characters' thoughts and feelings and lives and relationships? Karl appears to be on the brink of telling us. "About 75,000 words into the novel," he writes, "we have our first clear indication of what is going to be significant." Wonderful. *What?* But Karl's not going to stick even his tiniest toe beneath the surface of these waters, if he can help it. Instead he quotes JR's speech about his idea for a "selling outfit." The purpose is not to give us an insight into the thematic underpinning of *JR* but to set up yet another chorus of approbation. "This is one of JR's few long speeches," Karl says,

> and it is interspersed with interrupted sentences, a printout or shorthand method. The long sequences are fluid and of a conversational ordinariness which is remarkable. Gaddis's execution is merciless; more than satirical, the style strikes at the heart of every type of communication. Later, a radio plays because the turn-off knob cannot be reached. It catches our attention in small bursts, then fades. Our speech patterns are similar: people listen, then stop, then are caught up in their own speech, interrupt, are interrupted, and the cycle renews itself on human self-indulgence. We hear, ultimately, our own thought patterns, which we attempt to relocate in a language that is strangled before it reaches fulfillment. Counterfeit thoughts become part of an oral tradition.

Karl moves on to the subject of Gaddis's humor, but the litany of praise continues. "There are scenes [in *JR*] that are among the most hilarious in American fiction, despite this being a doom-filled vision." In a rare attempt to support an opinion, Karl offers a quite unfunny bit of *JR,* in which the humor is apparently supposed to derive from the mention of cartons containing "24—One Pint Mazola New Improved 36 Boxes 200 2-Ply" and "Wise Potato Chips Hoppin' with Flavor"— exactly the sort of thing that the most humorless sort of English professor perceives as humorous. Needless to say, Karl doesn't entertain any of the important questions suggested by his discovery of humor in *JR,* among them: (1) What part—structurally, thematically—does humor play in this "doom-filled" novel? (2) At whose expense—a character, an institution, a philosophy—does the humor take place? (3) Essentially what sort of humor is it—social satire or political farce? Shavian? Shakespearean? Does it bear any resemblance to the "American humor" described by Constance Rourke in her book of that title? Is it a humor of jokes or character or situation? Rather than answer any of these questions, Karl recapitulates his main theme. "This is incomparable comedy," he opines, "although for the reader to reach it, he much come through a verbal and narrative obstacle course." So what else is new? Once more, Karl congratulates Gaddis for his lack of interest in his readers, for "carrying on an extended, obsessively detailed dialogue with himself; he is the programmer and he receives the printout. All voices echo, a true universe of words, a parallel phenomenon to *Gravity's Rainbow.*" (Interesting, how you can be such an original experimenter and still be doing pretty much the same thing as somebody else.)

After a few more sentences praising *JR*'s self-directed prose, the lack of dimension in the title character, and the novel's "remarkable" central concept ("that with the telephone and mails, money can be made by any marginal operator, by a sixth grader, through a self-perpetuating system") Karl again begins to tell us, in a memorably bad sentence, what all this is supposed to add up to: "Gaddis stresses the depersonalization of moneymaking as part of the waste land in which people operate and thrive." But rather than develop this observation, Karl tells us that this sense of depersonalization is conveyed most effectively by—and, yes, here he goes again, telling us for what seems the hundredth time about Gaddis's difficult, disordered prose, his demonic way with conversational gambits: interrupted speech, run-together names and statements, broken-off phrases and barely uttered words, an oral shorthand. As in *The Recognitions,* we must pick up speakers from the situation and their words; but here the torrent of language pouring over us makes identification more difficult. In terms of language, Gaddis has tried to do for the oral American idiom what Joyce did for the written English—rediscover it as a literary voice, defamiliarize it so it seems fresh. His is the poetry, flow, and rhythm of routine speech, as much code as communication.

And (as a novelist whom Karl considers infinitely inferior to Gaddis might say) so it goes. Karl commends *JR* for its lack of a "sense of direction," and for its "verbiage [which] permits no clear definition." The climax comes when Karl brings in Pynchon, Gaddis's runner-up in the *American Fictions* sweepstakes, and tells us that both writers "do not use language to enter an interior world where all is self, narcissism, or indulgence; but as a way of exploring the outer reaches of language where it blurs into disorder. Their verbal construct is not a hiding behind words as a shield but the forcing of words outward, where language and things merge into each other." I'm not sure what some of this is supposed to mean, but it sounds as if Karl may be trying to suggest that the reason he refuses to take us beneath the jumbled surface of *JR* is that in the second half of the twentieth century neither critic nor novelist should be concerned with probing beneath surfaces, that the contemporary American novel at its best is a word game, pure and simple (or, rather, polluted and murky), which reflects the frenetic nature of the contemporary American relationships that really matter—not those between people, but those between corporations. Yes, corporations. Gaddis and Pynchon may well be "social and political novelists," but what that means to Karl is that they are "quite concerned with external worlds, whether America itself as a corporate empire, in *JR,* or as part of a multinational cartel, as in *Gravity's Rainbow*." He goes on:

> Their barrages of words, like Pynchon's rockets, are centrifugal, not centripetal forces. The impersonality of *JR* results from Gaddis's construction of a huge "outer world" with an existence of its own; in that world, which spans two decades, we find an entire value system, not a retreat from it.... For both Gaddis and Pynchon, the corporate empire embodies tremendous energy.... Both may parody finance, capitalism, the corporation, but they see in that a form of existence which gives real

meaning to individual lives. While it may, in its multiplicity and energies, bury the individual, it also engages him.

The remark about corporations "bury[ing] the individual" must be ironic, coming from a critic to whom "a full-faced portrait" of a real human being holds far less interest than "a small, impersonal title character" who takes his identity from "a vast corporate enterprise."

Karl's admiration for Gaddis, Pynchon, and company is matched only by his disdain for writers like Kurt Vonnegut, John Updike, Norman Mailer, and "even Bellow," who "have capitalized on the fact that a few others have kept the novel alive while they fiddle and garner prizes."[2] Karl seems to feel that Pynchon has been neglected by academic critics largely because he has avoided the limelight, while Mailer has been over-praised because he has courted fame. (Considering that Pynchon, the author of three books, is listed in the 1981 *MLA Bibliography* as the subject of forty critical and scholarly studies, and Mailer, the author of twenty-odd books, is the subject of only seven such articles, this charge of neglect is a peculiar one.) Vonnegut, the writer on Karl's blacklist whose work is marked by the greatest clarity and cult popularity, is predictably the victim of Karl's deepest digs. "With others doing the real work, Vonnegut can continue to publish his fictions under the protective mantle of the novel without really writing anything but 'prose fictions.'" Translation: Vonnegut is inexcusably readable. Or, as Karl puts it in his discussion of *God Bless You, Mr. Rosewater,* "The problem with the novel is obviousness." That is, to Karl's way of thinking, all that need be said. He seems to harbor a real hostility toward writers like Vonnegut, whom he sees as failing in their responsibility to create truly difficult fictions and thus to give academics something to do.

Karl condemns John Irving for a related offense: his narrative line is too strong. "We should not confuse ourselves," Karl says, "that narrative is necessarily the place where literature is located." The trouble with current academic criticism, of course, is not that too many critics think narrative is necessary to literature, but that too many of them, like Karl, think its presence a hindrance to literature and its absence a boon. (Elsewhere in *American Fictions,* Karl congratulates John Barth for recognizing that "storytelling belongs to a fictional type that no longer reflects who and what we are." Of course, he never gets around to explaining exactly who and what we are; that would be too centripetal of him.) Karl damns *The World According to Garp* as a "good read," and to him this means it cannot possibly be anything else as well. He assumes the book to be simpleminded because of the form it takes, and so gives it a simpleminded reading. He sees no thematic *raison d'être* in this novel whose thematic *raison d'être* is embarrassingly clear, and thus resorts to describing it as a "crazy quilt," a more or less random job of "moving eccentric characters around on a board." Ironically, Karl, a lover of ambiguities, complains about *Garp*'s ambiguities: why, he carps, are there so many tragic events in a novel that is, in large part, so jocular in tone? Unable to figure this out, Karl is forced to write off these tragic events —which are central to the book's plot and theme, and which include the violent deaths of the hero, his mother, and his son—as "isolated instances of terror," and to sum up *Garp,* whose second half is imbued with numbing existential despair (and whose last sentence is, "In the world according to Garp, we are all terminal cases"), by saying that "most of all, it conveys good feeling." Question: If Karl is so obtuse about such a simple, undeceptive book as *The World According to Garp,* how can we even begin to take seriously his judgments regarding such shady customers as *JR* and *Gravity's Rainbow?*

Predictably, Karl has little regard for a fine prose style, and when he does notice good writing he finds some reason to complain about it. No sooner does he describe William Styron's *The Confessions of Nat Turner* as "a beautifully crafted and written novel" than he suggests that, thanks to the gorgeous writing, "authenticity is lost. . . . Turner drowns in another man's language." The complaint is defensible, but that this is one of Karl's most visible comments on style speaks volumes. He comments similarly upon Updike, whose prose in *The Coup,* though it "has rarely been better . . . works at cross-purposes with the need for wit, or lightness. The prose takes the high road." The simple truth is that Karl is uncomfortable with fine prose. It bothers him. It indicates, on the part of the writer, an unpleasant awareness that somebody is going to read him, and an ugly determination to make sense, rather than chaos, of contemporary life. And most of all it signifies the writer's feeling that he is *not* a computer producing a printout, but a human being speaking to other human beings about what it means to be a human being. Than which—to Professor Frederick R. Karl, who unfortunately is not alone in his opinion—there is no greater literary crime in America today.

Criticism

in Extremis

SEPTEMBER 1985

In the past fifteen years or so, the world of academic literary criticism—heretofore dominated by humanists, with their view of literature as an aesthetic enterprise, a life study—has begun to fall into the hands of new-wave theorists with quite different perspectives. Some are deconstructionists, who maintain that all words are impersonal signs, that all texts are purely self-referential, and that literature, consequently, is not about life but about language; others are Marxists, who perceive literature as neither a life study nor a language game, but as political testimony.

Meet Charles Newman. Alumnus of Yale and Oxford, founder and editor of the literary magazine *TriQuarterly*, sometime professor at Northwestern, Johns Hopkins, and Washington universities, and recipient of Fulbright, Guggenheim, Rockefeller, and National Endowment for the Humanities grants, he is perhaps best known for the unabashedly Marxist anthology, *Literature in Revolution* (1972), which he edited with George Abbott White, and which one notices, these days, masquerading as a collection of literary criticism on many an English professor's office bookshelf. The book, whose title and guiding philosophy both derived from Trotsky's *Literature and Revolution* ("Artistic creation springs from the same sources as social rebellion"), featured an introduction in which Newman insisted that only some of its contributors were Marxists; the others "would simply say they find Marxist methodology 'useful.'"

That is for certain. Among the "critics" collected in the book were Noam Chomsky, the famed linguist and political extremist; Paul

Buhle, editor of *Radical America;* and Todd Gitlin and Carl Oglesby, erstwhile presidents of SDS. What critics—what criticism! Oglesby's essay on *Moby-Dick* quickly turned into a technophobic save-the-whales tirade; Hugh Fox's piece on Abbie Hoffman's Yippies (and what were *they* doing in a book on literature in the first place?) celebrated their "awakening in the Beast [i.e., America] a moral sense." And so it went. Whether the purported subject was Yeats, Milton, TV cop shows, or counterculture comic books, Newman's "critics" religiously tossed the question of aesthetic value onto the ash heap of history, and with fundamentalist zeal carried out a dedicated, narrowminded search for Marxian "political significance." As literary criticism, *Literature in Revolution* was—and is—worthless, but it remains valuable, for there can be few other books that so epitomize the unintentionally self-parodic lengths to which 60s mushmindedness could go.

Alas, Newman's latest contribution to the Republic of Letters is nowhere near as entertaining. Though he remains devoted to the preposterous critical stance that made *Literature in Revolution* so inadvertently humorous, and though he shows no sign of developing anything so perspicuous as an interest in literature *qua* literature, *The Post-Modern Aura: The Act of Fiction in an Age of Inflation* is quite a different kettle of fish. Not different fish, mind you, just a different kettle. What Newman has done is to throw over the lowbrow collective flavor of *Literature in Revolution* and opt for highbrow individualism—or at least the illusion thereof. Patently, he wants us to perceive his new book as a profound personal statement on the times we live in, a daring and *sui generis* dissection of postmodern America and its literature.

But you cannot pass yourself off as *sui generis* and still admit to being a Marxist; so, though he acknowledges his tendency "to see cultural and aesthetic conflicts as explicably social and economic," Newman now talks about this approach as if he had come up with it all by himself, and rejects the Marxist label. Or, rather, Gerald Graff does it for him, telling us in a preface to the book that Newman's study does not constitute "a Marxist analysis, though its argument owes something to the Marxist recognition that art has a social basis, for it accepts the fact that consumer capitalism is not likely to disappear in our lifetime."

Consumer capitalism: that, and not literature, is the obsession at the heart of this book. Newman looks at the unprecedented rate of growth of the post-World War II American economy and decides that we Americans have, in this era, been experiencing what he calls "climax inflation." Expansion and prosperity have been not a boon but a bane; they have led us into a habit of "irrational consumerism," not only of consumer but also of intellectual goods, and the consequence has been "cultural incoherence of the most destructive sort." The way Newman sees it, this is the worst of all possible fates: thanks to "cultural incoherence," the postwar American way of life is, without exaggeration, the most abominable in the history of mankind.

This inane but chic assumption (which Newman shares with Christopher Lasch, author of *The Minimal Self,* who has given this book a wildly enthusiastic blurb) forms the basis of Newman's entire argument. Americans of the 1980s "are suffering unspeakably," and our novels are suffering with us. For, in exactly the same way as money, estimable books—and even language itself—have, in these expansionary postwar years, been devalued by steady increases in their rate of production. This, in a nutshell, is "climax inflation."

There is an important truth at the core of all this. Good books are, as Newman suggests, always in danger of getting lost in the shuffle, and never has the possibility been more acute than in the present era, when, as he points out, "more books have been published than in any comparable period in history." This, indeed, is where the literary critic is supposed to come in. It is his job to make judgments, to separate the good from the bad, to keep the best that has been thought and written from passing out of sight. In a time when more books than ever are appearing, the critic's role is especially vital, his responsibility to high literary standards more serious than at any time in history.

But critical responsibility is not Newman's bag, and this book, as Graff observes approvingly in his preface, is most decidedly *not* "a call for 'moral fiction' or for the shoring up of cultural traditions or for 'humanistic values.'" Rather, it is a meditation upon the effects that climax inflation and its attendant phenomena—the absorption of publishing houses by corporate conglomerates, the ubiquity of the "media" (television)—have, in Newman's view, had on the postwar American novel.

Now, when a new-wave academic critic speaks of postwar American novelists, he is almost invariably referring to a handful of academically-oriented writers like John Barth and William Gaddis, who—taking their cue from the anti-traditional tenor of the 60s counter-culture—have turned out avant-garde "fictions" (as they like to put it) of an increasingly dehumanized, nihilistic, and reflexive bent. Intended both to reflect the supposed disorder of contemporary American life and to exemplify the post-modern "breakdown" of language, these novels—though they have proved of little interest to nonacademic readers—are precisely what the deconstructionists ordered. They are mainly language games, in short, and therein lies the cause of Newman's dissatisfaction with them.

In his view, the persistent attempts of these "Absolutist" writers (as he calls them) to outdo one another's avant-garde gamesmanship is a clear and unfortunate case of climax inflation at work. He calls this process the "rotational dynamic." Newman does not hold the Absolutists themselves responsible for the "rotational dynamic." As a "dynamic," it is an inevitable cultural phenomenon, a cut-and-dried case of the literary "velocity of change" keeping pace with the upward-spiraling economy. Nor are the Absolutists to be blamed for their novels being dismal, dehumanized, and disordered; they are like that not because the Absolutists are bad novelists but because the "inflationary commodity culture" in which we live is dismal, dehumanized, and disordered, and the Absolutists, admirably refusing to treat literature as "an illusory preserve within the ravages of our technology and the absurdity of our politics," insist in their work upon reflecting the state of the nation.

Newman considers this approach to be honorable in its adversarial motives, but pathetically misguided; for, in his view, the Absolutists have doomed themselves to ineffectiveness by "chang[ing] all *politics* into *mystiques*"—that is, they construct mirror images of America's technocratic impersonality when they should be attacking the technocracy directly—and by paying too little attention to the "literary elements" of their novels. Not that he cares about "literary elements" *per se;* he simply feels that politically-centered, socially "aware" novels, with more going for them aesthetically than the usual Absolutist fare, would be more likely to gain an audience and would thereby serve their polemical ends more effectively.

But in order to succeed with the reading public where the Absolutists have failed, the authors of such novels would have to act decisively upon the recognition that American publishing is behind the times: far from being "a conservative, print-oriented culture" of the sort that spawned modernism, American culture in 1985 is "based upon instantaneous pattern recognition, not delayed analytic decoding." Unfortunately, what Newman expects the new novelist to do about this supposed state of affairs—write comic books? create holograms?— he does not attempt to say.

W hich is, to be honest, par for the course. Far from presenting his argument as straightforwardly as my synopsis might suggest, Newman's book is in fact a masterpiece of muddle, a tour de force of tautology. What he offers is less a coherent argument than a loosely bound wad of assertions—usually unsupported, often vague, and frequently redundant—many of which seem directly to contradict one another. For instance, the statement (crucial to Newman's apparent thesis) that postwar Americans have had too much money to spend would appear to conflict with his contention that inflation has made it difficult to afford serious novels, and has turned us all into *de facto* victims of censorship. ("A classic totalitarian society," he explains, "censors at the production point. An oligopolistic democracy censors at the distribution point.") Likewise, Newman's assertion that Americans are no longer "print-oriented" contradicts his own observation that more books have been sold in postwar America than ever before, anywhere. And his presupposition of a chaotic contemporary America would seem to be incompatible with the belief, which he sometimes appears to profess, that the U.S. is far too stable and homogeneous these days for its own good.

But such inconsistencies do not disturb Newman, who blithely advertises his chronic disinclination toward coherence and clarity as if this were the best attribute a literary critic could have. "As befits its subject," he brags at the outset, "this will be a brief account of an incomplete idea; nothing so juicy as a sensibility, only a dim pathology of the contemporary, which amounts to Art is everywhere and Life is vague." In postmodern America, in short, life is chaotic and murky, literature is chaotic and murky, and so criticism has to be chaotic and murky too. Newman lives up to this pledge in spades.

Thus, even though he takes the Absolutists to task for their sloppy writing, Newman seems positively to revel in his own awful prose, in his tense shifts and agreement errors, in his nearly wholesale refusal to clarify or strengthen an assertion by providing an example, and in his habitual treatment of the word "media" as a singular noun. Though he ridicules the Absolutists' apocalyptic rhetoric, he indulges in it himself at every turn. ("The Apocalypse is over," he announces. "Not because it didn't happen, but because it happens every day.") And though he japes at postmodern writers' love of jargon, he flings it with the worst of them, describing language as a "reorientive enterprise," speaking of "routinized disturbances," "seminal idea structures," and the "writer/reader system," and turning out bushels of sentences like the following: "Youth culture offed literature as the dying privatized irrelevancy of a privileged class, only codifying existing forms of established power, inviting cultural repression, paternalism, and elitism."

The ultimate irony of this book on language and literature is that no one who truly cared for language or literature could have written it. Newman does not even pretend to care all that much. He makes no bones about his suspicion of art and culture; to him, language is manifestly hostile and alien territory, the uncomfortable but unavoidable route over which one is obliged to travel if one wishes to communicate a political position to one's fellow man. So disagreeable an entity is it, in fact, that at times he sees it more as a barrier between writer and audience than as a connecting highway. "Language," he grumbles, "is what veils the truth." He longs for something more raw, less refined. He admires, in the Absolutists, the way their novels "function very much like the primitive brain"; he sympathizes with their supposed feeling that language has been "exhausted" in the postwar era, perhaps beyond redemption; and he identifies with their "nostalgia for . . . prelingual paradise" (toward which his book appears to be a deliberate giant step). Why, in heaven's name, is a man with such an attitude in the business of literary criticism? It makes no more sense than a Christian Scientist becoming a surgeon.

One can only marvel at Newman's assumption that the best way to talk about literature is to talk about economics; at his view of the American economy as a tragedy not because it has failed (as the Marxists claimed in the 30s) but because it has been too successful; and at his blaming of that economy for the slovenly state of a species of fiction whose lack of discipline and love of aimless excess can be traced directly back to 60s radicalism. One must marvel, too, that a critic so preoccupied with Marxist economics and so impervious to the grandeur of language and literature can have received so many prestigious foundation grants, and that such an unqualified mess of a book can have been published by a reputable university press and reviewed admiringly in such venues as the *New York Times* and the *New Republic*. The whole scandalous story stands as testimony to the eagerness with which certain highly respected American institutions feel obliged to smile warmly upon "literary" and "intellectual" works that deal in irresponsible radical rhetoric—however insignificant such publications may be as works of art, however insipid their ideas.

Reading
Denis Donoghue

NOVEMBER 1987

Denis Donoghue is one of that small company of transatlantic men of letters who have established reputations as distinguished critics of both English and American literature. An Irishman by birth, Donoghue has taught at University College, Dublin, at Cambridge University, and (currently) at New York University, where he occupies the Henry James Chair of Letters, and since 1959 has published a dozen volumes, including studies of Yeats, Swift, Emily Dickinson, modern verse, drama, modern American poetry, and "the poetic imagination"; he is professionally concerned with the subject of Irishness (his last book, a selection of essays on his native land and literature, was entitled *We Irish*), and his new collection, *Reading America* —a gathering of twenty-seven reviews and essays about American writers from Emerson to Ashbery—testifies to his equally serious interest in the question of just what it is that makes American literature American.

This question is most explicitly engaged in the book's opening essay, "America in Theory," in which Donoghue discusses some of the more familiar critical conceptions of the nature of "the American experience" as it is rendered in the national literature. Examining the writings of such diverse critics as Tocqueville, D. H. Lawrence, Henry James, V. L. Parrington, Perry Miller, F. O. Matthiessen, W. H. Auden, Richard Chase, Leslie Fiedler, Leo Marx, Alfred Kazin, and Harold Bloom (Donoghue is nothing if not a compulsive scholar), he attempts to formulate a sort of unified field theory of American literature. But he never settles down quite long enough to state this theory succinctly and with finality; he seems unwilling to commit himself to any particular formulation, and thus throughout the essay is continually bringing in new quotations, new authorities.

For instance, Donoghue paraphrases Irving Howe to the effect that "the deepest desire in American literature is to be rid of every authority except that of the individual self," quotes Quentin Anderson's suggestion that American literature is designed to help readers "to fantasize a guiltless possession of the world," and apprises us of Nina Baym's argument that "the myth of the American experience . . . sets the hero free to disengage himself from a society he regards as embodied in women and the responsibilities of domestic life." At one point Donoghue seems to be subsuming all of these theories into the single (and well-put) observation that "[i]t is the moral and rhetorical aim of American literature. . . to separate essence from existence, and to protect essence—or call it selfhood—from the vulgarity imposed by mere conditions." In other words, American writers are more likely than their European counterparts to be essentialists, more likely to consider inner (or spiritual) existence to be separable from—if not more important or more interesting than—outer (or physical) reality. Having suggested this much, however, Donoghue proceeds to declare that "[a]n essentialist theory of American experience is . . . implausible," and to argue that "the American difference . . . arises from the incongruity between, on the one hand, a continent given over to commercial expansion and aggrandizement and, on the other, the promise of individualism and selfhood implicit in the once open expanse of virgin land."

What Donoghue seems to be saying here is that American literature tends to depict a tension between the forces of society and history and the lure of freedom, of unrestrained "selfhood." Many critics have observed this tension, though no two of them have described it in quite the same way, and different critics have convincingly emphasized different aspects of it; it is variously manifested as a conflict between city and wilderness, corruption and innocence, licit and illicit sexuality, marriage and bachelorhood, the company of women and the company of men, Europe and America, East and West, acquisitiveness and affection, the temporal and the eternal, intelligence and ignorance. (Which of these elements proves to be stronger, more virtuous, or more attractive than the other, however, varies from author to author.) This characterization of American literature is a wonderfully catholic one: it embraces everything from *The Scarlet Letter, Daisy Miller,* and the Leatherstocking novels to *Main Street, The Great Gatsby,* and *The House of Mirth.* Yet Donoghue does not do an effective job of setting forth this version of his theory; indeed, he barely nods in its direction before moving on to the somewhat different observation that American literature is concerned with "self and space, or self and nature," and that it represents an "attempt to understand man as such, free of social and historical contingencies." "Free"? Suddenly it seems as if Donoghue has given up the notion that American literature depicts a tension, and has decided instead that social and historical contingencies—far from existing in conflict with the urge toward freedom and "selfhood"—are to all intents and purposes nonexistent in American literature. Even this is not his final word on the subject, however. At the end of the essay—when he approvingly quotes Trilling's declaration that, Parrington to the contrary, a nation's culture "is not truly figured in the image of current," but that (in Donoghue's paraphrase) "the form of its existence is struggle"—Donoghue seems to return to the notion that American literature tends to portray, not freedom from "social and historical contingencies," but a struggle between a longing for such freedom and a helplessness in the face of such contingencies.

In short, Donoghue's essay does not come to anything resembling a clear conclusion in regard to a theory of American literature. On the essay's penultimate page, in fact, he speaks with apparent disdain of "the ferocious lucidity of a theory," as if to say that it is fun to play around with theories, but to settle down with one—and to declare plainly one's allegiance to it—is positively beastly. This position, to the present critic's mind, seems a bit too close for comfort to the gamesmanship of Derrida & Co.

What is no less lamentable than Donoghue's theoretical tergiversation is his deviation into politics. He begins the essay's concluding paragraphs by posing a question that seems to appear—in more senses than one—from out of left field: "to what extent does our professional interest in American literature, and our participation in State Department cultural enterprises, commit us to general sympathy with the aims of an American administration?" Donoghue says that at the 1975 Salzburg conference on American Studies which inspired the piece, this question was not entertained, but adds that "[i]t would have to arise if we were to assemble at Salzburg now: April 12, 1986." The remaining sentences of the essay are so remarkable that I feel obliged to quote them in their entirety:

> We would have to find some courteous method [he continues] of indicating that while we remained professionally concerned with American lit-

erature, and therefore with the society it expresses, we do not feel bound to approve this official policy or that. It is clear that President Reagan's foreign policy, in its bearing upon Nicaragua, El Salvador, Libya, and other countries, arises with appalling directness from a vision of America's destiny in the world. It is impossible to distinguish a vision from a theory in this context. The President's private war with the duly elected government of Nicaragua is his version, righteous and unquestioning, of the theory of America as Redeemer Nation. It is not even necessary for him to say that he regards America's destiny as one of saving the world from Communism: it is a matter of course. His more immediate problem is to convince millions of Americans that their security is threatened by the existence of one form of government rather than another in Nicaragua.

The easiest way, for a student of American literature, is to keep literature separate from a President's missionary zeal. I have no gift to set this statesman right. Perhaps it is enough to keep the political consequences of an inherited vision in mind, and to let it darken one's lucidity from time to time.

There are many things about the above passage that deserve comment, but I will confine myself to marveling at Donoghue's astonishing contradiction. If he genuinely does believe in keeping literature separate from politics, then what in heaven's name is this political jeremiad doing at the end of an essay on literary theory? The smug self-righteousness that is manifest here surfaces elsewhere in *Reading America* —and, for that matter, has surfaced not infrequently in Donoghue's other books. "I don't disavow an occasional inclination to set statesmen right," he admitted (note the similar phrasing) in the introduction to *We Irish,* but went on to claim that "[p]rofessionally, I am concerned with politics only when it invades literature and prescribes the gross conditions under which poems, plays, stories, and novels are written." May one be forgiven for finding this hard to believe?

But enough about "America in Theory," which after all is only one of ten pieces included in the first of *Reading America*'s two sections, under the rubric "Essays." (As distinguished, that is, from the "Brevities" —a euphemism for "reviews" —that are collected in section two.) The other nine pieces in the section—one of them previously unpublished, two of them originally included in the *Times Literary Supplement,* and the remainder first published in *Festchriften* and in such small-circulation journals as *Salmagundi, Nineteenth-Century Fiction,* and the *Sewanee Review* —take as their topics some of the major figures in American literature: Emerson, Thoreau, Whitman, Dickinson, Henry Adams, Henry James, T. S. Eliot, Wallace Stevens, and Lionel Trilling. As a rule, these pieces are overlong, stuffy, dull, pretentious, and a great deal more confusing than they need to be. "Emerson at First," for instance, is a twenty-page, chapter-by-chapter synopsis of *Nature* in which Donoghue manages to work in references to Valéry, Stevens, Coleridge, Wordsworth, Schiller, Henry James, Yeats, Hegel, Winters, and Swedenborg, among others, most of which references seem designed less to illuminate Emerson (whom Donoghue, by the way, has discussed more interestingly, and more briefly, in his book *Connoisseurs of Chaos*) than to throw all but the most industrious, sympathetic, and intellectually agile readers off the track. (Donoghue is the sort of critic who likes to behave as if his readers are intimately familiar with materials that he *knows* they aren't intimately familiar with.) "Thoreau" (which appears to be an expanded version of a review of the Library of America's Thoreau volume and Sharon Cameron's 1985 study *Writing Nature: Henry Thoreau's Journal*) seems, for most of its length, to be little more than a collocation of biographical facts and critical quotations; it is not until the last paragraph that Donoghue makes it clear that he has indeed, in a roundabout way, been developing a thesis—namely, that "[i]t is only in language, and not even in Nature, that Thoreau is content to reside." It is typical of Donoghue not to have put this sentence earlier in the piece, and saved us all a good deal of puzzlement.

"Whitman" is better. Though Donoghue devotes much of this thirty-page essay to a largely incoherent attempt to make Whitman's various metaphysical pronouncements cohere, he has some worthwhile things to say about Whitman's poetry. For example: "Whitman's favourite subject is movement, process, becoming: no wonder he loved bridges and ferries, which kept things moving while defining relationships, one thing with another." And: "To get the beauty of Whitman's poetry hot, one must read it in long, rolling stretches. No poet is less revealed in the single phrase, the image, or even the line. The unit of the verse is indeed the phrase, a loose-limbed structure of several words easily held together and moving along because the cadence goes with the speaker's breath." Yet Donoghue grouses altogether too much about Whitman's self-centeredness, anti-intellectuality, and lack of interest in history and form—which is rather like complaining that Kareem Abdul-Jabbar is too tall to make a good jockey.

The remainder of the "Essays" section is a mixed bag. "Emily Dickinson" is a competent review of Richard Sewall's biography; "On 'Gerontion'" is an intelligent explication of Eliot's poem. In "Henry Adams's Novels," however, Donoghue takes sixteen pages to make the admittedly correct but extremely simple point that Adams was too much of an ideologue on the subject of identity and power to be a good novelist; and in "Henry James and *The Sense of the Past*" he spends eight pages describing the various possible attitudes toward the past that one might assume, and then eight more pages describing the attitude that James adopts in his last, unfinished novel. This is provocatively if somewhat ploddingly accomplished, and the essay offers several examples of the way that Donoghue can at once impress with his insight and irritate with his manner of expressing it. Consider the following two sentences, for instance: "I assume, then, that James regarded 'the historic' as what pretends to be knowable, given a little rummaging around the archives and nothing much in the exercise of imagination. His chief sentiment, faced by the pretension, was resentment at the implication that there is a form of reality that makes the imagination redundant." This is very good, but badly put.

As for "Stevens's Gibberish" (published here for the first time, apparently), it is an extremely peculiar piece. It takes its cue from a couple of provocative lines in "Notes Toward a Supreme Fiction"—"The poem goes from the poet's gibberish to/The gibberish of the vulgate and back again"—but never settles upon anything resembling an intelligible thesis. At first Donoghue seems to be interested in demonstrating that "[i]n 'Notes Toward a Supreme Fiction' the poet seeks a complete poetic speech by bringing together . . . 'the imagination's Latin' [and] 'the gibberish of the vulgate.'" But then he proceeds to twist the meaning of gibberish in all sorts of perverse and obscure ways, so that the essay eventually seems less a study of gibberish than an exercise in it. For instance, he speaks of a sort of gibberish "which corresponds not to words that fail but to words that drive meanings beyond their rational forms into a void or a vertigo," describes rhyme (for reasons that never become clear) as a form of gibberish, refers to "the gibberish of syntax," and wanders (critically speaking) into French airspace:

> If we transfer to the reader the faculty of gibberish hitherto ascribed to the
> poet, we offer him the latitude of reading which Roland Barthes pro-

posed; not the duty of interpreting, moment by dutiful moment, the words on the page, but the pleasure that goes its own playful way. Barthes urged readers to act wilfully, running to excess in whatever directions they chose; anything, rather than accept the official rhetoric evidently enforced by a poem or novel. According to Barthes, there is no single privileged interpretation: the text is an occasion for being wilful.

In this respect, Barthes's recommendation coincides with Derrida's. . . .

It takes a while, after this detour, for Donoghue to get back (or, as he puts it, "revert") to Stevens, and when he does, the discussion of Derrida and Barthes appears not to have gotten us anywhere. But then Donoghue's principal purpose in this essay seems to be to work in as many high-powered names as possible; consequently he leads us through references not only to Barthes and Derrida, but also to Valéry, Rimbaud, R. P. Blackmur, Frank Kermode, Harold Bloom, Hugh Kenner, Kenneth Burke, Alain Robbe-Grillet, C. S. Peirce, E. M. Cioran, Anthony Hecht, and Michel Foucault, *et al.,* without ever making it very clear what our destination might be. What is frustrating is not that Donoghue is trying here to communicate some complicated ideas about language in poetry, but that rather than set these ideas forth as lucidly and coherently as possible, he presents them in unclear prose that abounds in gratuitous digressions and baffling transitions. This essay is followed by "Trilling, Mind, and Society," a tiresomely elaborate examination of Lionel Trilling's attitudes toward the two subjects named in the title and his notion of their proper relation to one another.

The key word here, it should be noted, is *attitude.* For it might fairly be said that, in all of the essays in *Reading America,* Donoghue is concerned less with the literary value of these authors' productions than with their points of view; his is not a criticism of aesthetics, or even of ideas, but a criticism of attitudes—attitudes toward, say, life and literature, mind and matter, nature and man. Such attitudes are, of course, a legitimate field of critical inquiry, but Donoghue is so preoccupied with them, in the first section of *Reading America,* that these supposedly literary essays read like studies in philosophy. He discusses the poetry of Whitman and Stevens in much the same way as he discusses the theories of Emerson and Trilling; to Donoghue, the *way* in which Stevens, say, wrote—the style, the form, the voice—seems to matter less than the attitudinal content of his poems.

It is no coincidence that the author whose name appears most frequently in these pages is Kenneth Burke—a man whom it does not seem quite proper to describe as a literary critic, a man of whom Donoghue himself observes, in a reverent review that appears in the second section of *Reading America,* that "[i]t is still not clear what kind of writer Burke is: it doesn't seem adequate to call him a literary critic, a poet, a novelist, a short-story writer, a sociologist, or a philosopher of history." Donoghue's solution: "[p]erhaps we should simply call him a sage, and think of the latitude traditionally taken by such a mind." He proceeds to compare Burke—favorably—to Emerson ("No comparison nearer home suggests itself"), and to provide a useful summary of Burke's approach to literature—which, because it sheds light on the background of Donoghue's own method, seems worth rehearsing here.

Donoghue explains that during Burke's "second phase" (apparently his most important phase by far, at least to Donoghue), Burke proposed "to read literature 'as equipment for living'. . . . Poems, plays, and novels were approached as strategies for dealing with particular situations. One might find in a poem 'the dancing of an attitude.'" During this phase Burke worked out the theory of dramatism, which is based upon the notion that the most useful way to discuss human actions, whether in real life or in literature, is to do so in terms of five key words—act, scene, agent, agency, and purpose. "What Burke is offering," Donoghue writes, "is both a poetics of social life and a way of reading as an epitome of a way of living." What he is also offering, one might add, is a critical method that is impersonally clinical, that threatens to reduce literature to a blueprint of behavior, that slights the importance of style and ignores the obligation to make a critical judgment. It is a method whose influence is apparent on every page of Donoghue's essays, with their relative lack of attention to aesthetic questions and their virtual preoccupation with the concept of attitude—Emerson's and Thoreau's attitudes toward nature, Thoreau's and Stevens's attitudes toward language, Whitman's attitude toward self and history, Henry Adams's attitude toward identity and power, and Lionel Trilling's attitude toward mind and society.[1]

Burke's influence can also be observed in the frosty, abstraction-ridden style of Donoghue's essays. Like Burke's, moreover, Donoghue's diction is often perplexing (Hart Crane, he writes, "had misgivings about the exemplary figure of his poetry"), inexact (he describes Dickinson's withdrawal from the world as "a gradual sequence"), or just plain awkward (Marianne Moore "didn't regard herself as a critic in any systematic sense: for her, Kenneth Burke was superbly enough in that category"). He complains that R. W. B. Lewis, in a discussion of Crane's poem "Chaplinesque," "does not encourage the reader to think of other poems that might measure that poem's achievement": what he means, I think, is that Lewis does not encourage the reader to measure the poem's achievement against that of other poems. This passage about the quotations in Marianne Moore's reviews is typically infelicitous in its phrasing:

> She never doubts that the quoted words have a valid adjectival relation to the personality from which they have issued; nor does she concern herself with values embodied in the linguistic medium rather than in a personality deemed to precede it. Many theorists would deny the merit of positing a personality separate from its linguistic form. But Moore resorted to words to assure herself of a personal force as if behind them.

Donoghue is, furthermore, partial to highfalutin but murky phrases such as "[h]istory as the narrative form of meaning." He often seems to prefer to say something confusingly and at length when he might say it clearly and concisely. In his essay on Henry Adams, he perpetrates several baffling and pretentious sentences the whole point of which (as becomes clear after two or three readings) is that Adams was interested in writing novels not as a means of understanding patterns and forces but as a means of conveying an understanding of them which he'd already come to. And Donoghue has a fondness for "explaining" quotations by paraphrasing them in more elaborate language and then bringing in a gratuitous quotation from some critic. For example:

> In *The Dolphin,* Elizabeth Hardwick is quoted as saying to Lowell, "Why don't you lose yourself/and write a play about the fall of Japan?" I take this as meaning: "Why don't you forget about yourself for a while, suppress yourself, and write something 'objective,' remote from your private interests and circumstances?" Or, in Char's terms, why don't you expel yourself, in all your incompleteness, from the scene, and expel all the other people whom you are in the habit of dragging into your poems as functions of yourself; and wait, trust in the Lord, until you will all be ready, combining in genuine presence?

Finally, Donoghue employs the words *revert* and *advert* to distraction and has an unfortunate affection for such precious vocables as *prescind* and *betimes;* also, over the course of the book he describes a number of things as exorbitant, and misuses the noun form of the word at least once, writing that Eliot wrestles with "the exorbitance of emotion to any object that supposedly provokes and justifies it."

Donoghue is not, then, one of the major prose stylists of our time. Yet he is a man of considerable critical talents—which are, as it turns out, manifested far more engagingly in the second section of *Reading America* than in the first. This section consists of seventeen reviews—which originally appeared between 1967 and 1986, most of them in *The New York Times Book Review* or *The New York Review of Books*—of volumes by or about Conrad Aiken, Marianne Moore, Stevens, Ransom, Tate, H. D., Crane, Auden, Burke, Berryman, Lowell, Plath, and Ashbery. On the whole, these reviews are shorter, livelier, sharper, less abstract, and a good deal more witty and readable than the essays that precede them. Indeed, Donoghue's tone, in these pages, is often downright colloquial. He writes that Aiken's "narrative poems are interminable, as if Aiken wanted to get into some *Guinness Book of World Records* for the longest something-or-other in American poetry." In this section Donoghue is less blatantly concerned with the subject of attitude (though it does rear its head now and again; he carries on at length, for instance, about Lowell's "patience" and his attitude toward history). Nor does he lead us, in these reviews, on interminable detours through the thickets of theory. "Olson," he writes, "had a theory about space, that Space rather than Time is the American category. Enough of that." (Enough for a "brevity," perhaps, but not enough for a Donoghue essay; in section one of *Reading America* he devotes two paragraphs, no less, to Olson's eccentric theory of space.)

Patently, the review format obliges Donoghue to do something that he can avoid doing in scholarly essays: namely, to render critical opinions, and to do so succinctly. These opinions are often both cleverly phrased and wonderfully sensible. Of H. D., for instance, Donoghue says that her "theme was all she had, except for a small rare talent and a pale Greek face." Crane, he observes, "cultivated intensity at the expense of every other poetic value, as if he numbered only the hectic hours." Donoghue describes Plath's "Lady Lazarus" as a "big striptease, Lady doing her number and singing the blues"; and he remarks wisely of Plath's "Daddy"—with its Nazi death-camp imagery—that "the thrill we get from such poems is something we have no good cause to admire in ourselves."

He observes at one point that Auden "is gifted in comparison and contrast, for the energy they release." So is Donoghue. If, in section one, his tendency to overindulge this talent—a talent, by the way, that he shares not only with Auden but with Burke—is responsible for many an irrelevant digression, in section two this same talent, more strictly disciplined, yields a number of provocative connections. Donoghue speaks, for instance, of Aiken's "night on the town with Edwin Arlington Robinson, another sprawling poet, incidentally, given to long narrative poems but a far more powerful because more dramatic poet than Aiken." And though his preoccupation with attitude is unfortunate, he does make an interesting distinction between Lowell's attitude toward history and Pound's. Needless to say, Donoghue more often thinks to compare writers' attitudes than their stylistic or formal choices; in "Trilling, Mind, and Society," he writes that, in "Hawthorne and Our Time," Trilling "distinguished not so much between Hawthorne, James, and Kafka as between our diverse understanding of their tempers and achievement." This is much the sort of distinction that Donoghue tends to make, often—one must say—quite well.

Yet to read *Reading America* is to be woefully aware of Donoghue's relative indifference to the sort of distinctions—namely, aesthetic distinctions—that ultimately matter the most when one is speaking of a work of literature. To be sure, there are times—as I have indicated—when Donoghue does discuss aesthetic matters, and does so with a commendable discernment; but all too frequently, especially when one is reading the first section of the book, one feels the urge to remind him that a writer is not merely a bundle of attitudes, that a great novel or poem is something more than a document in behavioral psychology. All too frequently, in other words, Donoghue simply seems uninterested in the music of poetry, the rhythms of prose, all those ineffable aspects of literature that cannot be reduced, as it were, to one of the five categories of dramatism. To echo his own remark about Kenneth Burke, in short, it sometimes doesn't seem quite correct to describe Donoghue as a literary critic; in his more solemn, heavy-duty essays, he is really more of a textual diagnostician, a sort of NMR-spectrography technician in the laboratory of literature. If it is sad to have to say this sort of thing about a man of letters, it is particularly frustrating to have to say it about Denis Donoghue. For this man who at times doesn't look at all like a literary essayist has produced a small body of "brevities" which demonstrate that—all his studied efforts to the contrary—he can be a very fine critic indeed.

Derrida's Dullards, Woolf's Womyn

FEBRUARY 1984

Once every two or three years, between Christmas and New Year's Day, the sidewalks of New York are filled with bearded men in corduroy jackets and crewcutted women in polyester pantsuits loudly pronouncing the words *metataxis, logocentric, paralogic, non-referential,* and *hermeneutics* at one another. There can be no surer sign that the holiday is over and the MLA has descended.

Any organization capable of publishing an almost completely unreadable journal can be relied upon to mount an intolerably dreary annual conclave. The MLA did not disappoint. For dullness with a difference, or (as Derrida would put it) *différance,* few of the six hundred ninety-three sessions listed in this year's convention program could have topped number 47, "Representation and its Discontents: Philosophers, Poets, and the Stories They Tell," on Tuesday evening, December 27. At this gathering—which might better have been titled "Masters of the Obvious: Or, It Seems to Me I've Heard that Song Before"—three of the top-seeded players on the contemporary critical circuit served up everybody's favorite paraquestion, namely, whether words correspond in some way to reality. The fun twist this time around was that, although everybody was, in his own little way, a Derrida disciple, the correspondence view won two sets out of three. David L. Bromwich of Princeton began the proceedings with a talk entitled "Why Authors Don't Give Us Their Own World," in which he announced his discovery that many novels, stories, and poems describe something which bears an uncanny resemblance to real life. Of course, he said, there are many authors who present relatively unfamiliar worlds, worlds that seem to be completely of their own invention. With this in mind, Bromwich invited us to imagine a spectrum of writers, and to place at one extreme Kafka,

> an author of strange texts which compel our attention for reasons not plainly connected with our world. At the other extreme, Tolstoy, who has impressed critics from Arnold to Leavis as extraordinarily lifelike. As applied to him, the defense that he creates his own world would seem to be beside the point. But what if we complicate the scheme just a little and put Jane Austen on the Tolstoy side as a moderate case of lifelikeness, more matter than Tolstoy, that is, working with less transparent convention but still comfortably of our world; and on the Kafka side, as a more moderate case of strangeness, put Dickens. Now if we tried to run through this group, from Tolstoy to Austen to Dickens to Kafka, where would we draw the line and say that there the author had begun to give us his or her own world? It seems to me that if books have mattered to you, you can't in fact draw the line at all because no text is ever completely strange. . . .

Thus Bromwich was able to conclude that all literature is, at least in some sense, concerned with the real world. (What a relief!) He did not, however, take the seemingly necessary next step of renouncing a critical parasystem that sees words as meaningless and language as a game.

The same goes for Gerald Graff, who began his paper by telling us that the "crudity" of representational theories makes him uncomfortable. On the other hand, it occurred to him that there may be a question of

> whether we can renounce the correspondence view [i.e., the view that language has some connection with something else in the world] without renouncing intelligibility. It is certainly salutary to reject crudely positivistic picture theories or copy theories of correspondence. But it's another thing to reject the concept of correspondence itself. In the process of seeking to discard the correspondence view of language, philosophers like Rorty may have had to presuppose it. At least this point could be argued from within the Wittgensteinian framework used by Rorty and others to discredit the correspondence view. A good Wittgensteinian, I think, could argue that the power of language to correspond with a prior object world is already presupposed in the practice of our conventional language games. The assumption that our interpretations can be motivated by a prior object world, in other words, is a condition of engaging

in discourse at all. [What a surprise!] I hope what I'm saying won't be confused with what Rorty would call a foundationalist philosophy of language, one which aims to find a ground for language outside it. Rorty is right in pointing out that we can't hope to ground language in a correspondence with something if we have to presuppose such correspondence in order to begin any such project of grounding. . . . What we can observe, however, is that the social practice of discourse involves believing that our utterances are independently motivated. It would make no sense to go on talking, much less engaging in philosophical and literary quarrels, if we didn't believe we could talk about objects to which talk refers.

And so on, into the night. The point, obviously, was not to say anything original or perceptive, or (God forbid!) both, but to repeat a single embarrassingly self-evident statement endlessly, in language so convoluted that many a listener might well have been fooled into believing that ideas were being exchanged. Graff's "conclusion" was that "the correspondence view of language is both philosophically uninteresting and inevitable." Which is to say, words do have a relation to reality, and it's a damn shame, because the whole idea of representation is so tacky; how much more intriguing words could be if they didn't mean anything. (If it's any consolation to Graff, I found a lot of his words to be meaningless.)

Richard Rorty came on last, with a talk entitled "Philosophy without Principles," and managed by the very swagger of his walk and the authority of his delivery to get across the idea that he was the old hand here, the dean of this sort of stuff, and that his two fellow panelists were neophytes. He was, indeed, the best of the three, in that the haze of banalities with which he obscured his lack of something to say was a lot thicker than theirs. His distinguishing marks were a refusal to accept the correspondence view at all, and the blunt self-importance with which he declared his allegiance to the pragmatic deconstructionist camp. Rorty was clearly not a believer in language as a means of communication, and perhaps he was right, at least about himself and his cronies. For there had been precious little communication here, in this paralogical paraparadise. There had only been circuitous language games, paragraphs of paraprose designed to hide a bankruptcy of meaning. With every disdainfully drawled word, and every supercilious question, the three panelists proclaimed the inferiority of all coherent systems of thought to their paramethod—while at the same time at least two of them recognized that words do mean something. This should have mattered, this implicit admission that the Derrida detour had reached a dead end, but it didn't. Nothing mattered. The whole exercise, in fact, was all so free of import, so stunningly illusory, that one almost expected Rorty, at evening's end, to quote Puck:

> If we shadows have offended,
> Think but this, and all is mended,
> That you have but slumber'd here
> While these visions did appear.
> And this weak and idle theme,
> No more yielding than a dream,
> Gentles, do not reprehend:
> If you pardon, we will mend....

Two nights later, in session number 620, "Teaching Virginia Woolf in the University," the present custodians of Woolf were on the rampage. This is not to suggest that the tone of the session was disagreeable; on the contrary, whereas "Representation and its Discontents" was deadly serious, this session had the cheery, gung-ho, palsy-walsy verve of a television game show. There was, too, a decidedly religious aspect to the proceedings. Woolf was the local deity, her writings the scriptures, her chief prophet "the brilliant Jane Marcus" (not present). James McGavran, Jr., in his paper, "Teaching Virginia Woolf in the University: A First Dose for Unwilling Undergraduates," spoke of introducing students to Woolf "with high hopes of making converts." Marcia Folsom, in her paper, "Gallant Red Brick and Plain China: Teaching *A Room of One's Own* in 'Women in Literature,'" explained that she uses *A Room of One's Own* as a sort of class Bible, requiring that her students carry the book to class throughout the term and use it to interpret the other works studied in the course—novels by the Brontës, George Eliot, Jane Austen, Zora Neale Hurston, Margaret Drabble, Kate Chopin, and so forth. All four panelists quoted long passages, mostly feminist rah-rah material from *A Room of One's Own,* their voices all creepily tinged with reverence. Folsom even testified to the audience that after her students have been studying *A Room of One's Own* for several weeks, they begin to sense that "Virginia Woolf is speaking directly to them." (If she is, she is probably saying, "Please read one of my other books.")

The papers, as befitting texts at a religious ceremony, all took essentially the same line. To summarize the contribution of Folsom—editor of an anthology called *By Women* and author of critical studies of Doris Lessing and Sarah Orne Jewett—is to give a pretty good sense of the offerings of all four. Folsom's aim was to describe how she uses *A Room of One's Own* to show her students at Wheelock College how deprived they are. To be sure, her students don't realize at first that they are deprived, or that Woolf was. But, using *A Room of One's Own,* Folsom manages to raise their consciousnesses. She explained to her audience how bad off Wheelock is:

> The first American university was Harvard, founded in 1636 and described in the current college catalog as "the oldest, the richest, the freest of American universities." American colleges for women, like those around Boston, are about one hundred years old. Wellesley, the richest of women's colleges, was founded in 1870. . . . Wheelock was founded in 1888 as a one-year school opened by Miss Lucy Wheelock, an American pioneer in the kindergarten movement. . . . The contrast between the noble old buildings of Harvard, the schools of law and business and medicine, the splendid gyms, the dozens of libraries, and staggering endowments, and Wheelock, where every tuition goes straight into operating budget, and the graduates who teach young children are lucky to earn twelve thousand dollars, is sufficiently instructive. The same contrast exists everywhere.

Worst of all, whereas the Harvard students (like those of Woolf's Oxbridge) get to eat off fine china, the poor girls at Wheelock must make do with plain china. (As a person of the male persuasion who spent four undergraduate years eating off plates made of paper, plastic, or styrofoam, I'm not too moved by this.) *A Room of One's Own,* Folsom continues, explains to her uninformed students the connection between "women's poverty" and childbearing, between childbearing and the suppression of the woman's voice, between patriarchy and fascism, etc. To Folsom—and to all of the panelists—Woolf is, above all, the author of *A Room of One's Own,* and *A Room of One's Own* is, above all, a piece of inspirational writing that

> offers valiant encouragement to all young Mary Carmichaels who may be daunted by headmasters with ornamental pots or bishops and deans and doctors and professors who say, "You can't do this!" "You shan't do

that!" *"Ladies not admitted."* They are given spirit and hope when she addresses them directly: "Now is the time," she says, "for the poet who died young to live again, the poet who never wrote a word and was buried at the crossroads. She still lives in you and me and in many women who are not here tonight." The opportunity to live and write the poetry of Judith Shakespeare, the novels of Mary Carmichael and essays to and for the common reader is exactly what Virginia Woolf offers to our students, young women who live in battled red brick and eat off plain china.

What does all this have to do with Virginia Woolf? you may ask. Ask you may in the comfort of your favorite reading chair, but you would not have risen to ask it up there in the Madison Suite of the Hilton, any more than you would stand up at a revival meeting to present an argument for rational humanism. Spirit and hope for young women? Valiant encouragement to the gender-oppressed? O ye of little faith, that is Virginia Woolf.

"The Story of English" on PBS

DECEMBER 1986

This fall, television viewers in both America and Britain were presented with a nine-part series entitled *The Story of English,* co-produced by MacNeil-Lehrer Productions and the BBC. Though the series was purportedly a joint American-British endeavor, was hosted by the anchorman of an American news program, Robert MacNeil, and was funded principally by an American corporation (General Foods) and an American foundation (the Andrew W. Mellon Foundation), *The Story of English* had a decidedly British flavor. This should not be surprising, for it was conceived and co-written by an Englishman, Robert McCrum, the editorial director of Faber and Faber and a graduate of Cambridge University (the series' other writer of record was MacNeil, who is Canadian by birth), and was produced and directed by William Cran, an Oxford-educated journalist who has created documentaries for public television both here and in Britain. McCrum, Cran, and MacNeil are, furthermore, the authors of a companion book—also entitled *The Story of English*—which was published to coincide with the airing of the television show.

The first episode of the series, entitled "An English-Speaking World," was less than promising. Its chief purpose seemed to be to tell us as many times as possible that English is "a language without frontiers," "the language of the global village of communication," "everybody's second language," "the indispensable language of progress for the Third World." MacNeil's cameras took us to Italy (where the multinational Iveco Corporation transacts all its business in English), to France (where the French-speaking countries, in general congress assembled, attempted to stem the tide of "Franglish" by coming up with French equivalents for *Walkman* and *compact disc*), to India (where young men want their brides to be fluent in English), to China (where the most popular television series is an English-language instructional program), to Japan, West Africa, Singapore, and so forth. This material started out by being fascinating and ended up by being very monotonous. The program dwelled in particular on California, whose "huge energy," MacNeil told us, "has overflowed into the language." He showed us surfers gabbing in "surf talk" ("check it out, dude"), Silicon Valley people using words like *on-line* and *high-tech,* and San Fernando Valley girls explaining "valley talk" (*grody, awesome*). An extremely unamusing homosexual comedian delivered a long routine that yielded exactly two examples of "gay slang" ("coming out of the closet," *queens*). Then, while we watched a group of women in sweatsuits practicing self-defense techniques, MacNeil rhapsodized about how "California has led the way in chopping sexism out of the language," and about how the elimination of words like *chairman* and *mankind* spells "the end of linguistic male chauvinism." Finally, MacNeil spoke ominously about "Pentagon language" ("predawn vertical insertion") and explained that it was the "ordinary fighting man" who had enriched military English, by coining words like *snafu.*

MacNeil explained, near the beginning of this first episode, that the series would speak of *varieties* of English, not *dialects,* for the latter "is often a loaded word." He said:

> Our story is not about the correct way to speak English but about all the different varieties and how they came to be. Why a MacNeil from Nova Scotia sounds different from a MacNeil here in Scotland or one in North Carolina or New Zealand. . . . In fact the idea of a correct or proper way to speak is surprisingly recent. There is such an idea, of course. It's often referred to as the Queen's English or BBC English or Oxford English or public-school English.

Whereupon *The Story of English* took us to Winchester, where a few high-toned teenage boys told us about the pressures public-school boys are under to speak the Queen's English. What's important here is that MacNeil, in pronouncing his refusal to endorse a "correct" brand of English, failed to distinguish between accent, on the one hand, and grammar and vocabulary on the other. To endorse one accent as correct would of course be out-and-out snobbery; to suggest that the grammatical rules of Standard English should be followed, and the received meanings of the words in its vocabulary respected, is something else again. *The Story of English,* for what its creators patently considered (in their ineffable Oxbridgean way) to be noble and egalitarian reasons, consistently blurred this fundamental distinction. Accordingly, MacNeil insisted at the conclusion of the first episode that, for all the scholars and writers and poets who have written memorably in English, "the making of English is not imposed from above. It bubbles up from below, from the speech of every man and every woman." Despite such ringing populistic declarations, however, the series had an unmistakable *de haut en bas* tone; though I didn't know when I saw this first episode precisely who had created the series, it was obvious from the program's strange preoccupation with public-school English (no matter what MacNeil actually happened to be saying about it), as well as from its desperately misguided stab at egalitarianism, that *The Story of English* was, in large part, the product of the Oxbridge mentality, with its perverse combination of snobbism and *nostalgie de la boue.*

Fortunately, the series was not as consistently offensive as the first episode suggested it would be. At its best, *The Story of English* presented a respectable simplified course in the history of the language. Episode Two ("The Mother Tongue"), for instance, effectively summarized the story of the language's beginnings. It covered the Indo-European background; the fifth-century invasion of Celtic Britain by the Anglo-Saxons, who brought with them their language, Old English, and borrowed relatively few words (*crag, tor, Avon*) from the Celts; the introduction of Christianity, with its Greek and Latin vocabulary (*angel, disciple, martyr, shrine*), in AD 597; the coming of the Vikings, with their Norse vocabulary, between the eighth and eleventh centuries (thanks to which speakers of English can either *rear* or *raise* a child, the former word arising from Old English, the latter from Old Norse); and the Norman invasion in 1066, which added a huge French vocabulary to the language (giving us a choice between the Anglo-Saxon *kingly* and the French *royal, regal,* and *sovereign*) and resulted in the development of Middle English. The episode took a deep bow in the direction of Chaucer, the language's first great writer, and of William Caxton, its first printer, who played a major role in establishing the language's spelling conventions; and it ended with an excerpt from the fifteenth-century play *Mankind,* whose language "is thoroughly and recognizably English."

The succeeding program, "A Muse of Fire," picked the story up from there, celebrating the English of the Renaissance, during which time between ten and twelve thousand new words were added to the language—words like *detail* (which was adapted from the French), *cupola* and *stucco* (Italian), *desperado* and *embargo* (Spanish), *smuggle* and *reef* (Dutch). From Latin, writers adapted words like *retrograde, reciprocal, defunct,* and *inflate,* which were widely regarded as pretentious and were known as "inkhorn terms." Sir Thomas More took the Latin word *communicare* and turned it into *communicate,* and Sir Philip Sidney combined the Greek words for "heat" and "measure" and created *thermometer.* The individual most responsible, however, for the enrichment of Renaissance English is Shakespeare, whose *Folio,* MacNeil told us, exerts a "direct influence on every one of us who speaks English today." Shakespeare, whose works contain a vocabulary of thirty-four thousand words (the greatest of any writer), "invented more words than anyone that ever lived," including *obscene* and *assassination;* a single line of *Macbeth* contains two new words, *multitudinous* and *incarnadine.* Shakespeare also made the language more flexible, using nouns for verbs (e.g. "grace me no grace"), and coined numerous phrases that have entered the language—which the program illustrated by a list of famous lines from *Hamlet* on the order of "Frailty, thy name is woman!" and "Alas, poor Yorick!" (The series' companion book does better by Shakespeare's phrase-making; it quotes a clever piece by Bernard Levin that is composed entirely of phrases originated by the Bard.) The program thereupon presented us with brief clips from the BBC's *Shakespeare Plays,* the purpose of which apparently was to remind us that Shakespeare wrote such lines as "Friends, Romans, countrymen, lend me your ears," and "The quality of mercy is not strained."

The episode moved on from Shakespeare to cover the King James Bible of 1611 (whose vocabulary consists of an austere eight thousand words) and the colonization of America—whose variety of English was founded, as MacNeil put it, upon the English of Shakespeare and the King James Bible. The majority of the settlers at Jamestown, we were informed, came from the West Country of England, whose stressed "r" sound, which is uncharacteristic of most English speech, became a notable characteristic of American English; the Puritan settlers of Massachusetts, on the other hand, came mostly from East Anglia (where one can find the original towns of Boston, Lincoln, Braintree, Cambridge, etc.), thus accounting for the fact that the New England accent, with its flat "a" and unstressed "r" (among other things), bears a strong resemblance to the East Midlands dialect. These accentual similarities were demonstrated—as such things were throughout the series—in longish sequences that took us into neighborhood pubs and shops on both sides of the Atlantic to listen to the natives chat each other up. In spite of the occasional inane detour, then, the second and third episodes of *The Story of English* were mostly fine, and one was able to imagine them being used profitably in conjunction with a high-school English course.

The same was true—but to a somewhat lesser extent—of Episode Four ("The Guid Scots Tongue"). When the Normans invaded England, they sent many Anglo-Saxons fleeing into Scotland, thus giving rise to the Scots dialect. Episode Four told us that the Scots—whose variety of English, but for the seventeenth-century union of the two kingdoms, might well have developed into a separate language—nonetheless have played an important role in the dissemination of English. (Incidentally, in one of the many discrepancies between the series and the companion book, the series told us that Scots—not to be confused with Scots Gaelic, the all-but-extinct Celtic language of the Highlands—might under different circumstances have become as distinct from English as Danish is from Swedish; the book tells us that Scots did indeed become as distinct from English as Danish is from Swedish.) Many Scots-Irish, MacNeil explained, emigrated to Philadelphia, and from there travelled westward through the Cumberland Gap, where their descendants speak the Appalachian dialect. That dialect's characteristic pronunciations (*bar* for *bear, cheer* for *here, hit* for *it*), in particular its open vowels, betray its Scottish origin. MacNeil maintained that not only the Appalachian accent, but the accents of the American Midwest and Southwest, all derive principally from Scots-Irish.

This episode—which was the first in the series to deal extensively with American English—had several notable failings. For one thing, like many of the episodes to follow, it sometimes fastened upon matters that seemed to have little or nothing to do with the topic at hand—truck drivers' CB-radio nicknames, for instance. More important, there was no mention that Charleston, South Carolina, received nearly as many

Scots-Irish immigrants as did Philadelphia, and that the largest concentration of Americans of Scots-Irish ancestry is in the southern states. One expected to see this oversight repaired in a later episode, but it never was.

Indeed, the very next installment of the series compounded the confusion on this matter. This episode, interestingly enough, began in Charleston, but didn't so much as mention the Scots-Irish—or, for that matter, the French Huguenots, who also migrated in large numbers to Charleston and exerted a considerable influence upon the speech of white people in that part of the country. Entitled "Black on White," the segment was concerned rather with the influence of American blacks on world English. It was, one should add, probably the most disturbing episode of the series, the one that most plainly demonstrated the perverseness of many of the attitudes and assumptions upon which the entire series was constructed. "White American language and culture owe much to the blacks," MacNeil said by way of introduction. Whereupon he introduced us to an obnoxious pair of upper-class white Charlestonians—a pompous young man preparing for a game of polo, a snooty belle parading around in a crinoline dress suggestive of Scarlett O'Hara—whose English, MacNeil explained, was a direct descendant of the Plantation Creole once spoken by Southern slaves, which had in turn developed out of the makeshift English of the African slave coast. The implication was that the English of all white Southerners is as strongly dependent upon Plantation Creole as is the English of Charleston; but the program failed to point out that the dialect of that city—the one-time center of the slave trade—is unique in the South, easily distinguishable from the English spoken in towns as close as fifty miles away.

This was not the episode's only peculiar omission. White Southern plantation children, we were told, learned to speak English from their black mammies, their black playmates, and their black house and field workers—who, significantly outnumbering the whites on the plantation, exerted a greater influence upon their language than did their parents. Well enough. But what of the great majority of white Southerners who were not plantation dwellers, outnumbered by their slaves? The program failed to take such people into account. (Those wealthy Charlestonians, with their aberrant accent and anachronistic way of life, were the only white Southerners featured in the whole series.) Nor, once again, did MacNeil distinguish between accent and grammar or vocabulary; certainly the grammar and vocabulary of most white Southerners were less influenced by Plantation Creole than were their accents.

MacNeil also introduced us to a community of blacks who live on the Sea Islands of South Carolina (and whose down-to-earth charm formed a distinct, and apparently intentional, contrast with the snootiness of the rich white Charlestonians). These blacks speak Gullah, a language peculiar to the Sea Islands, which is, in MacNeil's words, "one of the missing links between American and African civilization" and the "basis of black American English." From South Carolina, the program leapt across the ocean to the coast of West Africa where, two and three centuries ago, white and black slave traders communicated in West African pidgin English (a "pidgin" being a language with a simple grammar and limited vocabulary, and no native speakers, which is created so that people with different primary languages can talk to one another). This pidgin contained elements of a number of European and African languages (the pidgin word *pickaninny* derived from the diminutive of the Portuguese word *pequino,* "small"; *savvy* came from the French *savez-vous*). Because the captured slaves came from tribes that spoke a hundred and sixty different languages, pidgin English became their principal means of communication, not only with their captors but with another; thus it developed, in time, into the English Creole of West Africa and the West Indies (a "creole" being a pidgin that has become the first language of a speech community) as well as into Plantation Creole—which, in turn, developed into Black English.

One aspect of Black English is "jive talk," which was spread to the white community by black musicians early in the twentieth century. Jive talk added an abundance of slang and colloquial words to the language—*uptight, jazz, groovy, lingo*—and gave new meanings to many old words, among them *cool, joint, square, chick, beat,* and *jam.* The program explored this phenomenon responsibly enough, but then wasted several minutes on "Mr. Spoons," a black Philadelphian shoeshine man who writes "poems" like this:

> Step up on the stand
> And get the best shine in the land.
> If you don't like your shine, you get your money back

> But if you don't pay, you get your head cracked.
> That's the business of the boot-black.

While Mr. Spoons recited "one of his finest poems," a less-than-impressive meditation on civil rights ("There just ain't no justice here for the Black man. / How then can that be but wrong. / You see they closed most of the schools to us down here, / And we pay taxes but afraid to vote."), we watched some Sixties-vintage film of white cops and dogs terrorizing black protesters. For a while, the supposed topic of the series got lost in the shuffle; the creators of *The Story of English* clearly felt obliged to remind us that (a) black people had a rough time in America for several centuries and (b) MacNeil, McCrum, and Cran felt just sick about it. So they took us on a little detour from the story of English and instead we got to see, for the hundredth time, the March on Washington and Martin Luther King's "I Have a Dream" speech, and got to hear MacNeil noting triumphantly that in the twenty years since that speech, "Blacks have gradually taken their rightful place in American life."

We then met one of the country's more successful blacks, Mayor Wilson Goode of Philadelphia, who, MacNeil informed us, once took a speech course in order to lose his North Carolina accent. In yet another of its habitual refusals to distinguish between differences in accent and differences in grammar and vocabulary, the program seemed to equate Mayor Goode's deliberate change of accent with the attempts of American educators to help black students learn Standard English. The program purported to take no sides in the controversy over Black English, but in actuality it came down strongly on the side of Black English, suggesting that one "variety" of a language is as good as another, and even implying that the street kids who speak Black English are more vitally involved with language than are the English teachers who would have them adopt Standard English. After a black woman judge spoke eloquently against Black English, explaining that young black people need to master Standard English in order to compete equally in American society, MacNeil and company appeared to do their best to make her look like a reactionary, a traitor to her people and her culture. "Major changes in the language," MacNeil insisted, "don't happen because of educators and writers but on the street. The streets of the ghetto have been one of the great recent phrase- and word-factories of English."

And so MacNeil, in the last fifteen minutes or so of this episode, took us slumming on the ghetto streets, where "the traditions of Black English are alive and well." We met a gang of young blacks and listened to them converse with each other in their severely limited vocabulary (*funky fresh, wack, bad,* etc.) about a fight that one of them had almost gotten into with a dude from another gang; then we met a young street rapper named Perrey P who, MacNeil told us, has "made street talk into an art form all his own." Sample:

> Synthetics, genetics, command your soul,
> Trucks, tanks, laser beams
> Guns, blasts, submarines,
> Neutron, B-bomb, A-bomb, gas
> All that stuff will kill you fas'.

That their lack of fluency in Standard English all but guarantees that these street kids will grow into street adults seems not to have disturbed MacNeil, McCrum, and Cran; they displayed not the slightest hesitancy in celebrating the artfulness, the "vigor" and "zest," of these young people's language. One could not help but ask oneself: would MacNeil and company want their own children to talk this way, to be "artists" like Perrey P? Would William Cran hire a Perrey P to write one of his documentaries? Would MacNeil take him on as a reporter for *The MacNeil-Lehrer NewsHour?* Would McCrum give him a Faber and Faber book contract? Of course not. There is no question but that the facile, modish praise of Perrey P and his brethren represented *The Story of English* at its most hypocritical, irresponsible, and condescending.

The next few segments of the series were considerably less worrisome. Episode Six ("Pioneers! O Pioneers!") covered the development of English in the American West, including the contributions of Mississippi riverboat gamblers ("up the ante," "deal me out"), the Forty-niners ("hit pay dirt"), the Indian pidgin ("no can do," "long time no see"), cowboy jargon (*lallapalooza, absquatulate,* "bite the dust," "hot under the collar"), frontier Spanish (*stampede, sombrero, loco*), and the railroads (*sidetrack, whistlestop,* "make the grade," "one-track mind"). The episode afforded MacNeil the opportunity to refer to the encounter between whites and Indians as a "tragic culture clash" and to deliver the following sentence, which was typical of the series at its most fatuously rhapsodic: "Railroads found a special place in America's heart, putting the country's energetic spirit on wheels, sweeping its people and their language to the remote corners of the Union, stirring the melting pot of American English." (This was almost as impressive as a sentence from the first episode, which made MacNeil, for a moment at least, sound strangely like *Star Trek*'s Captain Kirk: "In this series we will take an extraordinary journey from an obscure Germanic tribe to the ends of the universe. . . .") There was also an apparent contradiction with Episode Four, which had maintained that the Scots-Irish were mostly responsible for the middle-American accent; now, MacNeil told us that the accent of the Midwest resulted from a merging of the accents of the eastern states.

But no matter. At this point—with a bow toward Whitman, who "celebrated the pioneer spirit of America," and toward Mark Twain (whose achievement was summarized by that all-purpose transatlantic authority, the redoubtable Alistair Cooke)—the episode turned to the contributions of non-English-speaking immigrants of the post-Civil War period. While we viewed the requisite film of huddled masses at Ellis Island, MacNeil read some purple prose about "this melancholy gateway to the New World"; then the program cut to New York's skyscrapers (with, somewhat disconcertingly, Copland's *Appalachian Spring* serving as the background music). We watched a parade in New York's Little Italy while MacNeil explained that the Italian language gave us words like *spaghetti* and *manicotti;* we watched a Steuben Day parade while MacNeil saluted Germany for giving us *kindergarten, cookbook,* and *delicatessen.* (At times, *The Story of English* made one downright hungry.) Finally MacNeil talked about how Jewish radio and television comedians spread Yiddish words (*chutzpah, schmaltz, kosher*) and phrases ("You should live so long," "Enough already") to the American public—apropos of which Leo Rosten, one of the many celebrated figures interviewed in the course of the series, offered a genuinely interesting observation about why Yiddish may well be (in MacNeil's words) "the most influential of immigrant languages." "Yiddish," he said, "lends itself to a remarkable range of psychological discriminations. It's steeped in sentiment and it's loosed with sarcasm. It knows that only paradox can do justice to the injustice of life. It adores irony because it knows that the only way Jews could retain their sanity was to view a dreadful world with ironic and astringent eyes."

But such moments of perceptiveness were few and far between in *The Story of English*. Episode Seven ("The Muvver Tongue") took a rather superficial, if diverting, look at the language of Cockneys and its influence upon Australian English (which also, the program informed us, preserves English localisms—Warwickshire's *larriken* for rowdy, rural Norfolk's *wowser* for killjoy—that are long since extinct in the mother country). Episode Eight ("The Loaded Weapon") was about Ireland and the Irish; it discussed the English language's borrowing of words like *smithereens, galore,* and *tantrum* from Irish Gaelic, the world's debt to Irish writers like Yeats and Joyce and Synge, and the Irish influence upon the New York accent in general and the coinage *yous* (as in "yous guys") in particular. Most of all, however, the episode seemed preoccupied with extremely familiar political matters—namely, with the centuries-old struggle between Ireland and England, in which the English language has of course played an important role. Accordingly, the program's final moments found MacNeil delivering an unsurprising conclusion to the effect that the Irish, their pipe dreams to the contrary, won't ever be able to shake off the English language and go back to Gaelic, but may yet "find in the accents of their English an escape from the prison of their history."

The series' closing installment, "The Empire Strikes Back," posed the question, "Will English, like Latin before it, gradually break up into separate languages?" MacNeil took us to Sierra Leone, Barbados, and Jamaica, where the natives speak English creoles. In Jamaica, activists expressed their desire to eliminate Standard English (which they look upon resentfully as "the language of authority") as the official state language, and to replace it with Jamaican Creole ("the language of the mass of the people"), so that street signs reading "No parking between signs," for instance, will be changed to read, "No paak betwiin dem sain ya." These activists—who referred to Jamaican Creole as the "nation language"—spoke of it in blatant political terms, encouraging its use not only on the island of Jamaica but among blacks, Jamaican and non-Jamaican alike, in Great Britain. Jamaican Creole, argued the Jamaican "dub" poet Desmond Johnson, is a unifying force among young blacks in London who "need to feel separate from a society that rejects them.... Caribbean patois gives them a language that's all theirs, and, when they imitate Jamaican Creole, a special sense of identity." MacNeil's contribution to all this, predictably enough, was to show us some Caribbean immigrant youngsters playing soccer in a

London neighborhood and—apropos of their lively chatter, which was full of exotic soccer-related terms—to offer the observation that Jamaican Creole is "more expressive" than Standard English. (And what, one wondered, if these kids want to grow up to talk expressively about something other than soccer?) We watched snippets of a black riot in London while listening to a reggae protest song, then—as the song continued—saw a mural of a prone black man with a white man's foot pressing down upon his head. Ah, the joys of language!

MacNeil then took us to India, where, we learned, more and more words from the various Indian languages are creeping into Indian English. "Local energies," he said, "are driving people away from Standard English." And apparently, as far as he was concerned, this was all just hunky-dory. "Our language thrives on change," MacNeil proclaimed, and quoted Anthony Burgess to the effect that English is "gloriously impure." Which indeed it is; but neither he nor the other creators of this series seem to have understood the real meaning of Burgess's observation. Indeed, the entire series appeared to be founded upon the principle that *every* sort of linguistic impurity is unquestionably glorious, that *any* change that takes place in a language is by definition a sign of "vitality." The series made no distinction between the changes in English introduced by Shakespeare, who broadened and deepened the language's expressive range, and those introduced by street kids, say, or surfers, whose jargon renders them incapable of discussing anything more subtle or complicated or abstract than a street fight or a good wave. That there can be both good changes in language (changes that make it more precise, majestic, and profound) and bad changes (those that make it more fuzzy and simpleminded) seems never to have occurred to MacNeil and company.

The *Story of English* companion book is so attractively designed, illustrated, and produced that one wishes it were more wisely and beautifully written. To be sure, it is, in many respects, superior to the television series. Though it covers essentially the same material, with each of its nine chapters corresponding to an episode of the series, it manages most of the time to be less tedious and pointless than the program. Whereas Episode Seven, for instance, paid inordinate attention to an Australian comedian named Barry Humphries, who likes to dress up as a woman, the coverage of Humphries in the corresponding chapter of the book is mercifully limited to a single photograph of him in drag. (Ah, the British sense of humor!) Likewise, one of the weaker aspects of the series was the excessive amount of time it devoted to interviews with quaint, aged speakers of archaic dialects (an unusual number of whom, as it happened, were fishermen); the reader of the book is spared all that. Yet, like the series, the book has its flaws. It is the sort of volume in which the authors offer, as testimony to the importance of English, the fact that it is "the official language of . . . the Miss Universe competition," and, twenty-three pages later, having somehow arrived back at the same topic, remind us that English is the language of the Miss World contest as well. Errors abound. In Chapter Three alone, the geographical areas indicated on two maps of the eastern United States don't jibe with their description in the captions; the territory covered by New Spain is misidentified; the English word *chocolate* is said to be derived from a South American or Caribbean Indian language, when in actuality it comes from the Aztec language, Nahuatl; and Puerto Rico is referred to as a "neighbor" of the United States.

The book's prose (most of which is, reportedly, the work of Mr. McCrum) is often quite awkward. Chapter Three tells us, for instance, that Tangier Island in Chesapeake Bay "forms one of the most vivid parts of the fossilized English language on the eastern seaboard of the United States." From Chapter Seven: "Unlike the Germans, the less-educated Italians made a more complete adoption of American English." And from Chapter Eight: Australian society "contrasts its classlessness with Britain's."

That the book is principally the work of an Englishman is especially clear, to an American anyway, in the passages dealing with the United States. McCrum and his colleagues write that "Thomas Jefferson, with his usual prescience, had seen that when the slave states of the South and the free states of the North competed to join the Union, there would be trouble." (Certainly the word *territories* would have served better than *states*.) The authors refer to Emerson, Thoreau, and Hawthorne—in contrast with Mark Twain—as "the men of the eastern districts." And, speaking of the European immigrants of more than a half-century ago, McCrum and company write that "in the schoolroom, and especially the playground, there were fierce pressures favoring the use of the American standard. The schools were the places where the immigrant children were rapidly Americanized by their playmates, and life was made intolerable, one imagines, for the child who had to use a foreign word rather than the English." On the contrary, most European immigrant children, living as they did in Jewish or Ukrainian or Italian ghettos, went to school with other European immigrant children; if they were rapidly Americanized nonetheless, it was because they and their parents *wanted* them to become Americans, to learn English and to make meaningful and productive lives for themselves in the New World. (In those days they didn't have Robert MacNeil to tell them, in his impeccable mid-Atlantic accent, how wonderful broken English could be; they didn't have Robert McCrum around, writing about "Americanization" as if it were some transatlantic counterpart of the Third Reich's Lebensborn program.)

The *Story of English* book manages to be at least as condescending as the television series. At the end of the "Black on White" chapter, for instance, the authors quote Walt Whitman to the effect that the English language has "its basis broad and low, close to the ground," and remark that "This is a sharp reminder that the best of English comes from a wide range of sources—Black and White." Pretty slick writing, that: the authors manage to praise black Americans and patronize them at the same time. (What's more, the sentence appears above two photographs of Martin Luther King and James Baldwin. Do the writers mean to suggest that King and Baldwin are in some way "low, close to the ground"?) In much the same vein, Chapter Eight tells us that "Italian Australians behave like Italians (promenading the street and ogling the girls)," while the book's epilogue, "Next Year's Words," describes Africans as "gifted linguists." (Are they also good tap dancers?)

Like the series, too, the book tends to wander into politics—and, when it does, tends not to find its way out for a good long time. Indeed, many of the political attitudes that are implicit in the television program are expressed more blatantly in the book. For example, McCrum and his colleagues mention with obvious dismay that "African governments, anxious in every other respect to throw off the shackles of imperialism, still show a genuine enthusiasm for speaking 'proper.'" The authors maintain that whereas the visits of Presidents Nixon and Reagan to Ireland were contrived for political purposes—with Nixon's visit, in particular, displaying "the element of chicanery so often associated with him"—President Kennedy's visit, by contrast, was "a genuine (though politically astute) pilgrimage, which drew huge crowds on a scale that his successors never matched." And the book complains that "gurus of grammar" like John Simon, William Safire, and Edwin

Newman grouse too much about the possible dangers of English-Spanish bilingualism in America. The creators of *The Story of English*, naturally, don't worry about the consequences of American bilingualism. They've got it all figured out. "Black Power, Hispanic Rights, Feminism, Gay Liberation, anti-Americanism: these are some of the issues of our time, and the English language will always be used by conservatives as a stick with which to beat the opposition." According to *The Story of English*, it's as simple as that: the only problem connected with bilingualism, Black English, and so forth is that there are reactionary fuddy-duddies out there who persist in talking about these things as if they *were* problems. If your next-door neighbor tendered such a misguided opinion of Safire, Simon, and Newman—a group of writers whose principal offense, apparently, is to take a responsible attitude toward their language and their society—it would be ridiculous, nothing more. But for the creators of a high-profile property like this one to propagandize for such a point of view is nothing less than outrageous. In the end, this sneer at linguistic standards tells us all that we need to know, really, about the sensibility behind *The Story of English*.

The *Pushcart Prize* Story

OCTOBER 1984

Every year in the United States the editors of hundreds of little magazines produce thousands of issues containing tens of thousands of stories, essays, and poems. Somewhere in this frightening abundance of reading matter is the very finest and the very worst that the writers of America have to offer. And there's the rub—for although nobody, Lord knows, wants to miss out on this year's "Waste Land," it would be all but impossible for any one of us to poke through all those magazines to find it. That's where *The Pushcart Prize: Best of the Small Presses* is supposed to come in. Issued yearly since 1976 by the Pushcart Press (with a well-distributed paperback version by Avon following hard upon), the series is intended, in the words of its founder-editor-publisher Bill Henderson, "to rescue some of the wonderful writing appearing in small presses from oblivion."

The Pushcart Prize, VIII is the 1983–84 edition, which means that it contains pieces originally published during 1982, republished in the hardcover *Pushcart Prize* volume in 1983, and distributed in the Avon paperback edition in 1984. Gail Godwin, in her introduction, quotes Henderson's words about rescuing wonderful writing from oblivion, and the back of the dustjacket quotes her quoting him. The front flap of the same jacket features a quotation from *Publishers Weekly* praising the book's "openness to new talent." Henderson wants to make absolutely certain, obviously, that we get the message that his book is not just another best-of-the-year anthology—he wants us to be convinced that it's a genuine attempt to preserve excellent but unheralded work written by relatively obscure writers and published originally by relatively obscure presses.

Unfortunately, the *Pushcart Prize* series is not what it cracks itself up to be. The majority of the writers and presses represented in the collection are far from obscure. Why, then, does the series exist? Mainly, one gathers, to save *Henderson* from sinking into oblivion. But we don't need to speculate. To our good fortune, Henderson has, in more than one essay, written candidly about how he came to establish the Pushcart Press, and, in turn, the *Pushcart Prize*[1]; to read these essays—and to read between a few lines—is to understand distinctly how the *Pushcart Prize* series came into being, and how it came to be exactly the sort of entity that it is today. With the ninth edition of the series due to be published soon, there could be no better time to explore the *Pushcart Prize* story.

The story began when Henderson, a teenager on Philadelphia's Main Line, decided that he wanted to be a writer. Well, it wasn't so much that he wanted to be a writer as that he wanted, in Dorothy Parker's phrase, to have written. And to have been published. In short, he dreamed "of the New York Pub Day Cocktail Party Girls," dreamed of re-enacting the "intoxications and fornications" of Norman Mailer, Ernest Hemingway, and Dylan Thomas, dreamed of the day when "all those literary groupies would tumble for me with my first Bill-Faulkner straight bourbon on the rocks. Like thousands of Great American Novelists, I sought truth, beauty, fame, fortune, and immortality. But what I really wanted was literary stallionship." So, at college, Henderson "jotted down the seven crucial facts of the age" and turned them into a novel.

> The facts were: (1) There is no sense of permanence in America. (2) Americans are rich. (3) Americans are lonely. (4) Americans are greedy. (5) The Bomb may drop. (6) The old American values are dead. (7) There is no sense of community in America. This final no–community fact was imitation Paul Goodman. I had just read Goodman's *Growing Up Absurd* and was overwhelmed by him. I was overwhelmed by most good writers.

As one might imagine, the unconventional novel that sprang from this list of assumptions (it was essentially about "a Vassar girl . . . who had jilted me") did not impress the publishing house to which Henderson submitted it. Disgusted by the refusal of the greedy American marketplace to cut him in for a share, Henderson tossed his manuscript into a drawer and resigned himself to the cruel circumstance into which Fate had forced him: a graduate fellowship at Harvard. "I loitered for two weeks at Harvard, then got Bill-Faulkner drunk on the train home. My parents were upset. I smashed a glass on the kitchen floor and yelled, 'I want to be a writer!'" He then went back to Harvard and wrote short stories. "I tried the usual *Atlantic-Esquire-Harper's* circuit and received all the usual form rejections. When a friend suggested the little literary magazines, I snapped it was the big time or no time."

He went to Paris. He attended the Sorbonne ("to keep the draft board happy") and drank lots of wine and reworked his unconventional novel and "refused to read books, since I didn't want to be influenced" and put on a "dipso, soulful writer act." He went back to America and continued to work on the novel. He put in several levels of meaning, so that English professors would declare it a classic. When the work was finally done, he submitted it to the Harper & Row Prize Novel Contest. He lost. He tried it on Knopf. They rejected it. So did Farrar, Straus & Giroux and Little, Brown and McGraw-Hill and Doubleday. Henderson found an agent, and the agent sent it around. No luck. Finally, after two years of turndowns, the agent gave up and returned the manuscript to Henderson.

For most aspiring novelists—even those from the Main Line, by way of Harvard and the Sorbonne—this would have been the end of the line. But Henderson had something inestimably valuable that few other rejected first novelists can boast of: a "big-hearted, adventuresome" uncle with lots of money. This uncle, when apprised of the frustration of his young nephew's ardent desire to become a literary stallion, recognized that there was only one thing to do: set up his own publishing house, install Henderson as editor-in-chief, and present Henderson's novel, *The Galapagos Kid,* to the world. Henderson found this plan agreeable and added his own twist: in order to keep this vanity operation from looking like a vanity operation, he decided to publish his novel under a pseudonym—Luke Walton. (The name came from a Horatio Alger novel.) Under his own name, Henderson made arrangements for the printing and distribution of *The Galapagos Kid,* and invested his uncle's money in advertisements for the book in *The New York Times Book Review, The New York Review of Books,* and *Publishers Weekly.* Nautilus—for such was the name of the one-man publishing house—gave Henderson his education in self-publishing.

And what did he get out of all this? Not much. Some fair to good reviews in the Miami, San Antonio, and New Brunswick, New Jersey, papers; a not particularly favorable review in *The New York Times;* and not particularly spectacular sales. "In all," Henderson writes, "I sold about 500 copies and figured my losses at $10,000 for a decade of unpaid labor." (Meaning that ten years had passed since he'd decided that he wanted to be like Dylan Thomas. He was twenty-seven.) Some might reckon this a defeat, but not Bill Henderson. Five hundred copies were "respectable enough for the serious, underground sort that Luke Walton now imagined that he was." Besides, even if he hadn't won fame and fortune and groupies, "I had made a few friends. I'd been reviewed in the *Times.* I'd tasted the bitch goddess and wasn't very impressed. And I had discovered the secret of publishing. Publishers exist to make money and make money to exist. [He was cutting class, one assumes, the day they taught that at Harvard.] My novel, and many like it, was rejected not because it was of poor quality or unloved, but because it would not contribute to profits. I knew that now from my own profit-and-loss sheet."

Henderson's vigorous promotional work on behalf of his author, Luke Walton, had attracted attention in the land of the bitch goddess—otherwise known as Publishers' Row—and Doubleday offered the plucky young man a job. Henderson leaped quickly enough into the goddess's lap. Apparently he had decided that if he could not become the great American novelist, he would become the great American editor. He was determined, he writes, to do all that he could to reform, from within, the crass system that had rejected him—to fight the mediocrity of commercial publishing by digging up some "fine literature" for Doubleday's list. Resolutely, he plowed through the firm's Himalayan slush piles in search of a masterpiece that he might rescue from the oblivion to which the avaricious, art-hating commercial publishing world had condemned it. Oddly enough, however, Henderson didn't come across anything he considered good enough to publish. It was unsettling. Here he was ready to play Spartacus, and there weren't any slaves to free. So much for being a crusading editor! But wait—he had an inspiration. It occurred to him that

> perhaps the reason so little good work was arriving at houses like Doubleday was not only that most commercial firms didn't want to publish it, but also that so much junk was being issued with big-bucks sound and fury that authors had stopped writing good books. Perhaps many of

them had succumbed to the despair I felt after years of rejection. [N.B. Two years.]

Writers had to be wised up, I thought. They should know that they didn't need commercial publishers of any sort. And they needed a book to tell them that.

The book, which Henderson soon began compiling, was *The Publish-It-Yourself Handbook: Literary Tradition and How-To.* In its pages, Henderson and a number of other self-published writers recount their inability to secure contracts with commercial publishers, describe how they had managed to get their work between covers anyway, and explain to the reader how he might do the same thing. The book allowed Henderson to become a crusading editor after all. He was, to be sure, hardly performing a public service: if one reads through the *Handbook,* one soon discovers that none of the contributors could claim to have made a living from self-publishing; most of them, in order to turn a profit, ended up handing their works over to commercial publishers or selling reprint rights to the usual paperback houses. Those few self-published works that went into the black without any help at all from commercial publishers—perhaps the most notable example is Barbara Garson's 1967 play *MacBird*—were clearly flukes. Henderson certainly hadn't gotten anything from his own self-publishing experience except a huge debt, a handful of reviews (mostly in the back pages of backwater papers), and skimpy sales. Nonetheless Henderson's *Handbook* trumpets self-publishing as *the* thing to do when "the moneymakers" (commercial publishers) turn you down.

Indeed, Henderson implies that self-publishing is a more honest, clean, and noble way of getting into print than signing a contract with . . . *them.* When, in the course of an interview with Henderson, Barbara Garson mentions the possibility of having her next book published by Doubleday, Henderson replies (one can almost hear him gasp): "Do I hear you right? You would actually consider another publisher-published book?" Garson (obviously feeling a sudden stab of guilt) rejoins, "Well, to be honest, yes." Henderson can't believe it: "Why, after all the good things that happened with *MacBird* and your less than pleasant experience with *All the Livelong Day* [published by Doubleday]?" Garson's answer is that, unlike *All the Livelong Day,* "*MacBird* was the product of a movement. . . ."

And at that word, *movement,* one can imagine Henderson calming down. Smiling, nodding. For the *Handbook* takes exactly that approach to self-publishing: it's a movement, supposedly (like Garson's *MacBird*) an outgrowth of the Sixties counterculture movement. It's idealistic. Selfless. Far from being a desperate, futile, time-wasting, money-wasting course to which a pathetically egoistic author is driven against his better judgment, it's a noble political action — a heroic act of defiance against the profit-mad conglomerates that run publishing in America. The self-publisher is the heir of Walt Whitman, the comrade-in-arms of the Russian *samizdat* publishers (and *The Publish-It-Yourself Handbook* is dedicated immodestly to both). For a self-publishing writer to pack up his presses and move on to a commercial publisher is to sell out to the bitch goddess.

Despite all this anti-Publishers' Row rhetoric, however, Henderson tried the manuscript of the *Handbook* out on several commercial publishers — only to be universally rejected — before deciding to publish it himself. The name of the house this time was Pushcart Press. Again Henderson became his own salesman and shipping clerk. And this time it paid off: *The Publish-It-Yourself Handbook* was an immediate success. Finally Henderson had the attention he had craved. Reviewers (many of whom, as Henderson has noted, are themselves rejected novelists) were intrigued by the book, and gave it extensive — and quite favorable — publicity; and the orders poured in. Nearly everyone, it seems, who had ever written an "unconventional" novel like *The Gala-pagos Kid* and who had, like Henderson, made the rounds of the publishers without any luck, wanted the book. Sales of the *Handbook* were as fast as sales of *The Galapagos Kid* had been slow; so it was that Henderson learned an important fact of life: "Many authors, while quite willing to buy a book about how to publish their own stuff, are far too reluctant to buy the works of other authors." The explanation, of course, is that the sort of "writer" who buys a book called *The Publish-It-Yourself Handbook* is likely to be a lot more serious about fame, fortune, immortality, and literary stallionship than about literature. And this, of course, was the big secret of Henderson's ultimate success — he knew how desperately, childishly, selfishly ambitious so many unpublished self-styled "writers" are. He had been there himself. The way he finally realized his dreams was by capitalizing on *their* dreams.

In 1978, the Pushcart Press published a book that might be fairly described as a companion volume to *The Publish-It-Yourself Handbook*.

Like the *Handbook, The Little Magazine in America: A Modern Documentary History,* edited by Elliott Anderson and Mary Kinzie, is mostly a collection of how-I-did-it stories—in this case, by people who founded and edited their own literary magazines. Though published in association with *TriQuarterly, The Little Magazine in America* takes a distinctly Hendersonian line; the attitude toward magazine publishing that runs through the majority of its forty-two chapters is identical to Henderson's every-angry-young-man-his-own-publisher attitude toward book publishing. In the first chapter of *The Little Magazine in America,* "Of Living Belfry and Rampart: On American Literary Magazines Since 1950," Michael Anania describes the different types of literary magazines that have been published in the United States in the past few decades. As he sees it, the field is divided up into

> university-based reviews with eclectic interest; quarterlies with distinct critical frameworks; independent eclectic magazines that have invariably served the centric literature nobly and well . . . ; and adversary magazines, those quicksilver enterprises that hold much of the romance of the little magazines in their invariable insistence that everybody in print is wrong about nearly everything literary and cultural except the few people published in their thirty-two saddle-stitched, untrimmed pages.

The emphasis in *The Little Magazine in America* is clearly on (and the sympathy clearly with) the latter sort of venture—the saddle-stitched, untrimmed "adversary magazines." After devoting the requisite chapters to *Poetry* and to the *Kenyon, Partisan,* and *Southern* reviews, *The Little Magazine in America* settles down, kicks off its shoes, and for the next several hundred pages offers us the histories of (among others) *Neon, Kulchur, Yugen, Trobar, Dust, Caterpillar, Io, Blue Suede Shoes,* and *Big Sky.* Like Henderson's "On Pushcart Press" (which appears on page 614 of the book), most of these chapters are stirring first-person tales of selfless, unstinting, Herculean labor in the service of—well, supposedly in the service of literature, although, strangely enough, the editor-chroniclers often talk about themselves a good deal more than they do about the material they published in their magazines. Keith Abbott's essay on *Blue Suede Shoes* is so illustrative of the type of unabashed solipsism that clogs so much of this book that the temptation to quote from it at length is hard to resist. Here is a taste of Abbott—and remember that this is in a reference book about American literary history:

Because I had received a huge grant for *BSS* from CCLM [the Coordinating Council of Literary Magazines], I planned to produce two novels as *BSS*: *Gush* by myself and *The California Papers* by Steve Carey. But what to do while I waited for them to be done? Easy. I began the Decimal Series, taking *BSS* backward in time. The few libraries I had as subscribers became upset.

But then *BSS* had a history of library problems. Opal L. Nations and I switched issues once. He did number 11 of *BSS* and I did number 9 of his magazine, *Strange Faeces*. This created a wonderful amount of confusion among our library subscribers. But the Decimal Series was the last straw for some of my libraries. It was reported to me that at one library they refused to recognize my Decimal Series and were hand lettering each issue as it came in: No. 16, No. 17, etc. [Oh, those philistines!]

I lost another library because they became hysterical when the .3141596265 issue came out; the number was too big to put on their index cards. (Alert readers will notice that this is the number for *pi,* only the decimal point has been placed incorrectly. This did not deter me, though, from calling it the *Pi* issue.)

. . . The Decimal Series, besides providing a way out of the *Gush* problem, was an attempt to revive what I felt to be a flagging focus. . . . I knew that I had to use as much reason as possible in order to smooth over the transition to the Decimal Series, so I tried to use *famous* decimals, such as Ted Williams' batting average, .406, the last time anyone hit over .400 in the major leagues, and Rogers Hornsby's equally celebrated .424, the highest batting average ever recorded. . . .

The word *self-indulgent* seems ridiculously tame in such a case. Not once in his entire essay does Abbott say anything interesting about the work that appeared in *Blue Suede Shoes. That* seems to be incidental. He does name some of the writers whose work he published, and he makes a few general statements about the nature of their contributions ("One genre interested me: the prose poem"), but one really gets no sense at all, from Abbott's essay, of what sorts of things one might have read in his magazine. What Abbott seems to consider most important about *Blue Suede Shoes,* if the emphasis in his essay is any indication, is the puerile issue-numbering pranks he played on librarians—the literary equivalent of short-sheeting the governess's bed. For the Pushcart Press to present this sort of sophomoric nonsense as part of American literary history is irresponsible beyond belief.

But that's the way it goes in this book. Too many of the editor-chroniclers in *The Little Magazine in America* dwell extensively on their own beloved quirks, caprices, and pointless outrages against good taste and literary value; too many describe their disorganization as if it were something to be admired; and too many devote too little space to questions of substance. Henderson and his editors appear to feel that the shoddier the product, and the more frivolous and egocentric the approach, the more virtuous the magazine. Throughout *The Little Magazine in America,* such solid, enduring literary magazines as *The Hudson Review* and *Poetry* are raked over the coals by one editor-chronicler after another—*Hudson* for being intolerably "highbrow" and "snobbish," *Poetry* for being too "pure," too "homogenized, antiseptic, democratic and dreary." Hardly anybody in these pages has a bad word, however, for such amateurish monuments to conceit as *Blue Suede Shoes.*

The central idea of *The Little Magazine in America,* indeed, seems to be that there's something noble and brave—something *politically virtuous* —about being one of these unconventional, Keith Abbott-type editors. They describe themselves and each other as if they were freedom fighters. Example: Jonathan Baumbach's contribution to the book, titled "Who Do They Think They Are? A Personal History of the Fiction Collective." The title communicates the main point of the piece: that the great thing about the Fiction Collective is not the quality of its product, but its awesome willingness to stand up to the "devils of greed" (yet another synonym for the commercial publishers) by putting out its own books.[2]

G iven Henderson's rhetoric about the avarice of commercial publishers, his purported admiration for the nobility of the writers and editors who turn their backs on Publishers' Row, and (most important of all) his own keen desire for a permanent niche in the New York literary establishment, it was only a matter of time before the *Pushcart Prize* series was born. "In order to give some sort of recognition to the more outstanding authors encouraged by the *Handbook* and by today's small press movement," Bill Henderson has written, "in 1975 I asked several distinguished editors to help me start an annual prize anthology: the Pushcart Prize series." One is meant to get the distinct impression that the *Pushcart Prize* exists largely for the purpose of reprinting work published originally by small presses—in particular, by the writers' own presses. Such, at any rate, is the image Henderson covets for the Pushcart Press: that of a homely-but-heroic one-man operation, reaching out to help other homely-but-heroic one-man operations. The dust-jacket of *The Pushcart Prize, VIII* carries the following blurb:

> In 1973 Pushcart Press was started with a minuscule budget and a single book dedicated to the writer's spirit of independence—*The Publish-It-Yourself Handbook,* edited by Bill Henderson. That title, typeset on an IBM selectric typewriter and decorated with homemade graphics in Letra-set press-on type, was so successful that Pushcart was able to undertake the first edition of *The Pushcart Prize* a few years later with the help of our founding editors.

From the revolutionary rhetoric about the "writer's spirit of independence" to the boastful references to the "minuscule budget," the improvised typesetting, and the "homemade graphics," this passage is an ideal example of Pushcart publicity. The emphasis is not on the literary quality of the book's contents (although that is certainly trumpeted loudly enough) but—as in so many of the essays in *The Little Magazine in America*—on the spunky, grassroots rebellion against the tyranny of mainstream publishing that the book purports to represent. The front matter of *The Pushcart Prize, VIII,* in fact, reminds us that the name of the Pushcart Press derives from Project Pushcart, George Plimpton's "independent book-selling march" down Fifth Avenue in 1973. One can admire and respect Plimpton and still find the political and military overtones of the word "march" (The Long March? The March on Washington?) a little ludicrous when Henderson applies it to a bunch of well-to-do New York bookmen parading their wares past Bonwit Teller, Saks, and the Sherry Netherland. The same goes for his use of the expression "small press movement": the phrase conjures up a picture of some sort of small-press *Solidarnosc,* with Henderson as Lech Walesa. And that's just a bit much.

One might be able to respect all this hyperbolic rhetoric if it were sincere—if Henderson really seemed to believe that the *Pushcart Prize* is doing for neglected small-press writers what medieval knights did for damsels in distress. But it's not. A cursory glance inside the covers of the last edition belies the book's image. The contents of *The Pushcart Prize, VIII*—which is in every way typical of its predecessors—bear astonishingly little resemblance to what one has been led to expect by Henderson's description of it as a place where fine writing is "rescue[d] from oblivion." Simply to list the names of some of the authors represented in the collection is to give a sense of what sort of book we are dealing with: Robert Bly, Andrei Codrescu, Cynthia Ozick, W.D. Snodgrass, Stanley Plumly, Richard Wilbur, Joyce Carol Oates, Raymond Carver, Amy Clampitt, Richard Howard, Philip Booth, Wayne C. Booth, William Dickey, Gordon Lish, Maxine Kumin, Lincoln Kirstein, Richard Hugo, Mary Oliver, Alan Dugan, Bobbie Ann Mason, Thomas McGrath, Ann Stanford . . .

This is rescuing from oblivion? What's the gag? Yes, there is a handful of token unknowns here, and their work is certainly not among the worst. But going systematically through the table of contents of *The Pushcart Prize, VIII,* one finds the great majority of the fifty-six names to be familiar ones. Either they are famous writers who have been winning National Book Awards and Pulitzers and Guggenheims for decades, or they are among the handful of hot young writers whose names are all over the place these days, who have won some minor awards and who have their feet firmly planted on the road to the major ones. Of the hundreds—thousands?—of people writing for the small presses and little magazines, these are exactly the ones who do *not* need a *Pushcart Prize* anthology to keep their work from passing into nothingness.

Indeed, after a look at the table of contents, one might suppose that, far from being intended as a rescue mission for worthy small-press publications threatened with eternal obscurity, the *Pushcart Prize* anthology was designed as a sort of academy of the highly celebrated. That most of the stories, poems, and essays in the 1983–84 book will, within the next few years, certainly be published, as a matter of course, in collections of their authors' works issued by major commercial publishing houses, makes the *Pushcart Prize* series a rather redundant act. Not to mention a hypocritical one. Gail Godwin, in her introduction to *The Pushcart Prize, VIII,* condemns commercial magazines for their notion of "targeting," of homing in on a specific demographic segment of the public by means of a pragmatic selection of material. Small presses don't do that, she says. They're free of crass commercial considerations. Art is their only criterion. But the contents of *The Pushcart Prize, VIII* are just as pragmatically selected as anything in *McCall's* or *Redbook.*

A close examination of the contents, in fact, reveals a bias not only in favor of name writers, but in favor of certain types of writing. It cannot be a coincidence, for example, that with so many interesting and diverse subjects being written about in the United States these days, five of the eight essays in *The Pushcart Prize, VIII* are somber considera-

tions of profound theoretical questions about the experience of literature. Granted, the experience of literature is a fascinating topic. But
there is such a thing as editorial balance; and there are wonderful es-
sayists around who do not go near such topics. This is not to suggest
that these five essays are not worth a look. Take them for all in all, they
are probably the most interesting things in the book. The briefest of the
five is Cynthia Ozick's "What Literature Means" (from *Partisan
Review*), in which she reminds us that "literature is the recognition of
the particular. . . . Literature is for the sake of humanity." Such truths
may seem self-evident, but it is best to repeat them every now and then.
Particularly when there are critics like Thomas LeClair going around
writing pieces like "Avant-Garde Mastery" (*TriQuarterly*), a tribute to
the use of systems theory as a structural foundation in the novels of John
Barth, Donald Barthelme, Don DeLillo, and others. An excerpt:

> The avant-garde of mastery is summarized by Barth's *Letters,* a system of
> systems that is and is about reconstruction, or what Barth has named
> "replenishment": the remaking from alphabetical letters a language both
> artful and referential, the remaking of mind through the information and
> reciprocity of mailed letters, the remaking of the book from "exhausted"
> forms in belles lettres. Barth's definition of plot—"the incremental
> perturbation of an unstable homeostatic system and its catastrophic re-
> storation to a complexified equilibrium"—suggests in a sentence the per-
> vasive presence of systems theory in the book, especially in its formative
> principles. As an epistolary novel, *Letters* accepts print as its medium and
> takes full advantage of two meanings of "correspondence," making it
> refer both to the processes of communication exchange and to the ho-
> mologous relations with reality emphasized in systems theory. As a se-
> quel to Barth's first six books, the novel recycles their disparate materials
> into an ecological whole, a large, collaborative, literally open system in
> which entropy is everywhere mentioned and everywhere combatted by
> the negentropic patterns of order and growth Barth formulates.

Most of these essays are in fact better than this. It's just a shame that the
editorial bias is so clearly in favor of the well-known writer who ponti-
ficates solemnly about an imposing theme, and against familiar essays,
social and political homilies of relatively modest scope, and even literary pieces about specific works or writers.

The fiction in *The Pushcart Prize, VIII* is as homogeneous as the essays, and to far drearier effect. The fiction writer who wants to get into

one of the *Pushcart Prize* books is hereby advised to make his characters and their actions as uninteresting as possible; to write a cold, clipped, noncommittal prose that makes Mickey Spillane look like Francine du Plessix Gray; and to fill his sentences with the names of fast-food outlets, television shows, celebrities, and the brand name of every household product he can think of. The theme that emerges from all this, of course, should be that the faceless, heartless, consumer-oriented American is so enthralled by the phony world of TV shows and the fantastic promises of TV commercials that he is a stranger to genuine emotion and sensible values, and moves through his banal life like a robot. The plot should turn on the protagonist's confrontation with the fact of human mortality and his consequent temporary awakening from this spiritless, robotlike stupor—an awakening which only serves, of course, to emphasize the essential deadness of his soul. One would think that six stories of this sort in the world would be at least five more than necessary, but apparently the marketplace is still hungry for them, and the writers who produce them are quite celebrated for it. Indeed, as Bill Henderson's own career demonstrates, one of the fastest ways to break into the literary establishment is to embrace a trendy anti-establishment ethos.

As for the poet who wants to make it into the Pushcart pantheon, here are a few tips: write poems about words; write poems that consist of numbered lists; write poems about works of art or your mother's body. Your style should be so prosy, flat, and torpid that when you put a word in italics in the middle of the sixth line, the relative excitement of the event should make your reader bolt out of his seat. (There is, of course, the Amy Clampitt option of making every poem impenetrably baroque, but remember that *there is no middle ground:* aim either for the painfully plain or the ridiculously rococo.) But don't hold your breath, writers: unless you've got a name, your chances of getting into the *Pushcart Prize* series are slim indeed.

What's more, it's not only the cachet of *your* name that matters when Pushcart Prize-picking time comes around; it's the cachet of the venue in which your work was originally published. Or, at least, so it seems: for the presses represented in *The Pushcart Prize, VIII* are hardly the sort that Pushcart's publicity would lead one to expect. Henderson's goal in founding the Pushcart Press was purportedly to disseminate some of the fine work issued by small presses, and (in particular) the best work of worthy self-publishers; but no self-publishers appear to be represented in the 1983–84 edition at all, and only three items in the book originate from small presses (as distinguished from magazines). Those presses are Copper Canyon Press, Blackwells Press, and Micah Publications. Everything else in the 1983–84 edition comes from magazines: four items apiece from *Poetry, Ploughshares,* and *The Iowa Review;* three apiece from the *Paris* and *Kenyon* reviews; two apiece from *Antaeus, Ironweed, TriQuarterly,* and the *Mississippi, Georgia, Hudson,* and *Threepenny* reviews; and one apiece from *Conjuctions, Daedalus, Raritan, Salmagundi, Chelsea, Cutbank, Grand Street, MSS, Kayak, Crazyhorse, Open Places, Frontiers, Ascent,* and the *Partisan, Ohio, Northwest, Missouri, Bellingham, Agni, Seattle,* and *American Poetry* reviews. Yes, exactly the sort of solid, enduring magazines, for the most part, that are ignored or insulted in *The Little Magazine in America.* One could hardly suggest that reprinting a story or poem or essay from any of these magazines in *The Pushcart Prize, VIII* represents a "rescue... from oblivion." *The Pushcart Prize* is simply not so much better known or better distributed than any of these magazines that its publisher can make such a claim convincingly. Indeed, so well established are some of these magazines that their editors are among the "distinguished editors" whose help Henderson enlisted in launching the *Pushcart Prize* in the first place, and who to this day are—along with eleven of the writers included in *The Pushcart Prize, VIII*—on the series' board of editors.

What one is left with, then, after examining the *Pushcart Prize* story, is a rather Bosch-like series of mental images. One pictures Bill Henderson, for example, standing in the bow of a lifeboat shouting encouragement while a boatload of distinguished editors reach into the churning sea to rescue... *themselves.* One imagines Henderson leading an army, composed of the crème de la crème of establishment writers and editors, in a frontal attack on... the crème de la crème of establishment writers and editors. Honestly, the man has done something remarkable. For nearly a decade he has published an annual anthology which, though almost claustrophobically entrenched in the literary establishment, is nonetheless shrilly and self-righteously dedicated to the principle that the literary establishment is corrupt and corrupting, and that the writer who wishes to be true to his art had best shun its shabby corridors. That this series of books—filled with the already overexposed works of the literary establishment's most overpraised writers —does not represent a sincere counterculture movement on behalf of writers left out in the cold by commercial publishers, but exists, rather, to serve the ambitions of the publisher, is embarrassingly obvious. The *Pushcart Prize* series has manifestly given Bill Henderson nearly everything he always wanted: a permanent seat on the lap of the "bitch goddess"; well-forged connections with every grubby, greedy "moneymaker" on Publishers' Row; and a respected position among the Oateses and Carvers and Plimptons. He has, in short, fulfilled his boyhood dream—he has promulgated a great fiction, and the literary world has given him its rewards.

II

The Music of Gatsby

FALL 1981

Chapter Three of *The Great Gatsby* opens in this way:

> There was music from my neighbor's house through the summer
> nights. In his blue gardens men and girls came and went like moths
> among the whisperings and the champagne and the stars. At high tide in
> the afternoon I watched his guests diving from the tower of his raft, or
> taking the sun on the hot sand of his beach while his two motor-boats slit
> the waters of the Sound, drawing aquaplanes over cataracts of foam. On
> weekends his Rolls-Royce became an omnibus, bearing parties to and
> from the city between nine in the morning and long past midnight, while
> his station wagon scampered like a brisk yellow bug to meet all trains.
> And on Mondays eight servants, including an extra gardener, toiled all
> day with mops and scrubbing-brushes and hammers and garden-shears,
> repairing the ravages of the night before.

Music is thus associated with Gatsby. By contrast, as far as we can see,
the life of our narrator, Nick Carraway, is without music until he
moves in next door to Gatsby—for, in the first two chapters of the
novel, there is no mention of music whatsoever. Note that the music
coming from the great mansion is undifferentiated, uncharacterized;
there is no talk of jazz or slow waltzes or string quartets, just the single
word "music," which could stand for anything from Bach to Berlin.
The paragraph quoted above, which begins with the novel's first reference to music, covers a gamut as well: there is the magic of the summer
nights at Gatsby's house—the girls like "moths," the "whisperings,"
the "champagne," the "stars"—as well as the reality of the morning
after—the "mops" and "scrubbing-brushes" and "hammers" and

"garden-shears" of the morning that repair the "ravages" of the previous night. So it is that the music from Gatsby's house is associated with a wide range of impressions—from champagne to scrubbrushes—which make up the atmosphere of a Gatsby party.

Indeed, Fitzgerald takes care to establish music as a key imagistic device in the depiction of the Gatsby party atmosphere. The description of the party that occupies the first few pages of Chapter Three continually reverts to the music metaphor. The bar is not simply busy; it is in "full swing." There are "floating rounds of cocktails," and an "opera of voices" that "pitches a key higher." The Britishers out for easy American money are "convinced that it was theirs for a few words in the right key." Thus drinking, talking, conniving are all presented through a musical image.

All the time of course there is real music playing: "a whole pitful of oboes and trombones and saxophones and viols and cornets and piccolos, and in low and high drums." It is an interesting assortment of pieces, not a mere jazz band nor even a typical orchestra; to the instruments one might expect at a fashionable twenties party (trombones, saxes, cornets, even an oboe) are added the viol and the piccolo—significantly, the pieces which reach the lowest and highest notes respectively in the canon of instruments. This image of extremes is reinforced by the mention of "low and high drums." If music is a metaphor for the Gatsby party, then clearly Fitzgerald is characterizing the party—and life at the East Egg mansion in general—as one that will have its highs and lows.

The music is not all of an ilk. There is "a celebrated tenor" singing in Italian, and a "notorious contralto" singing "in jazz": Fitzgerald puts the serious alongside the flippant, the ponderous alongside the joyful. Vladimir Tostoff's *Jazz History of the World* is played, and again there is an odd affiliation: the mention of "Carnegie Hall" in the same breath as the word "jazz," which in 1925 would have been a much stranger fusion than it is today. The very phrase "Jazz History of the World" is peculiar, because of the juxtaposition of jazz—a thing of the moment, the key to which is improvisation—and history. Fitzgerald is playing with time, in reminding us that there are things that are timeless and things (like improvisational music, jazz) that are not—things that must be enjoyed for the moment, and cannot be duplicated. Thematically, this juxtaposition has an obvious function: to foreshadow Gatsby's failure to revive his relationship with Daisy on a permanent basis after six years. (Recall that later in the book Nick will tell Gatsby, "You can't repeat the past," and Gatsby will reply: "Why, of course you can!")

As Chapter Three began with music from Gatsby's house at night, so Chapter Four begins with the sound of bells from the church on Sunday morning. The contrast between Gatsby's house and the church is intensified in the second paragraph of the chapter:

> "He's a bootlegger," said the young ladies, moving somewhere between his cocktails and his flowers. "One time he killed a man who had found out that he was nephew to Von Hindenberg and second cousin to the devil . . ."

Second cousin to the devil: the intended antithesis between Gatsby and God could not be more straightforward. And note that Fitzgerald has used music to bring Jay and Jesus together—Gatsby with his wild night music, God with his morning church bells. Again, there is a sense of foreshadowing in having Gatsby's wild party night followed by a delicate reminder of the Enduring Things, in the form of church bells that have rung every Sunday for generations. God is eternal, Fitzgerald reminds us, and Gatsby is not. Even before he has renewed his affair with Daisy, the musical metaphors have presaged his failure to make it endure.

And why will the affair fail to last? Further musical references illuminate a flaw in Gatsby's personality in which may lie his ultimate doom. For example, when Jordan and Nick are riding through Central Park, little girls are heard singing:

> I'm the Sheik of Araby.
> Your love belongs to me.
> At night when you're asleep
> Into your tent I'll creep—

The lyric of course recalls Gatsby and Daisy. But the irony emerges from the contrast between the two situations thus brought together: Gatsby is not creeping into Daisy's tent; he wants her to creep into *his* tent. One is reminded of the unnaturalness of Gatsby's attitude, his perhaps excessive romanticism alongside the realistic attitude of the times (the universality of the song's practical view of man-woman relationships is suggested by Fitzgerald's placement of the song lyrics into the mouths of babes—even the innocent have a more realistic view of sex than Gatsby!).

Gatsby's overly romantic perspective is re-emphasized by Klipspringer's playing of "The Love Nest" on the piano while Gatsby shows Daisy through his house. The room in which Klipspringer is playing is referred to by Nick as the "Marie Antoinette Music Room," and the huge room serves as an analogue for the entire house. Again, Gatsby's romantic opacity is thrown up alongside reality: his East Egg residence is no nest (not even a tent), but a sprawling mansion. The disparity between the ideal and the actual reinforces the effect of the "Sheik of Araby" lyric. Further, when Klipspringer plays "Ain't We Got Fun," the background is a loud wind outside and

> a faint flow of thunder along the Sound. All the lights were going on in West Egg now; the electric trains, men-carrying, were plunging home through the rain from New York. It was the hour of a profound human change, and excitement was generating on the air
> 'One thing's sure and nothing's surer
> The rich get richer and the poor get—children.'

Alongside the profundity and gloom of the scene, the lyrics of the song ("In the morning, in the evening, ain't we got fun—") seem frighteningly ominous in their simple, idealized view of life. Indeed, we are reminded, there *is* "nothing sure" in life, and the stark truth rises out of the deceptively cheerful lyric to play the hopes of Gatsby off against the hopelessness of the real world.

Another such juxtaposition is effected when, at the Plaza Hotel, Gatsby and his party hear the Mendelssohn Wedding March playing downstairs. The "portentous" tones of the march remind the reader of Daisy's wedding ties and suggest the doom they will spell for Gatsby's romantic dream. Though the wedding march is followed by some hot jazz, Daisy doesn't want to dance; she would, she says, "If we were younger." The wedding march has perhaps reminded her of her bond to Tom; and the victory it thereby wins over the dance music is a telling augury. There is an interesting if subtle differentiation in Daisy's voice quality before and after the wedding march, in both cases referred to in musical terms: before hearing the March, her voice is "a cymbals' song"; afterwards it "drops an octave lower." Again, it is a subtle but significant pointer in the direction that Gatsby's romantic fortunes will go.

The last song mentioned in the book is "The Rosary," a religious song, which someone whistles "tunelessly" in New York on the morning of Gatsby's funeral. The song recalls the antithesis that was set up earlier between Gatsby and God, between Gatsby's house and the church, through the use of music. We are reminded, subtly, that the Eternal Powers have prevailed over Gatsby, the fleeting and temporal.

The last reference to music hearkens back to the opening of Chapter Three, to Nick's (and the reader's) introduction to Gatsby. "I could still hear the music," Nick reflects, sitting in his again silent house after Gatsby's death. As music came into his life with Gatsby, so it is gone now that the star-crossed lover is dead; thus the identification of Gatsby with music is carried through to the end. With Nick, the reader remembers Gatsby the more sharply, in his highs and lows, by recalling the spectrum of music that has filled the great man's house; moreover, with that one line, "I could still hear the music," Fitzgerald evokes the entire structure of musical metaphor that has worked throughout the book to contrast Gatsby's romanticism with the world's reality. As we read the line we recall Gatsby's sense of triumph at the same time as we realize the inevitability of his tragic end.

Behind the Images:
Fitzgerald and Cheever

MAY 1985

Scott Fitzgerald—who was renowned in his lifetime as much for his escapades with Zelda as for his contribution to literature—would doubtless be gratified to know how profoundly most literate citizens of the English-speaking world now admire *The Great Gatsby, Tender Is the Night,* and a number of his short stories. Yet one wonders how he would react to the news that, in 1985, the world continues to be even more fascinated by his magical, misguided life than by his fiction. Certainly there cannot be many who are unfamiliar with the outlines of the Scott Fitzgerald story: the early years in St. Paul as the humiliated son of a failed businessman (and as the inordinately proud descendant of Francis Scott Key, author of "The Star-Spangled Banner"); the glorious salad days at Princeton University, which he left without a degree; the wartime courtship of Zelda Sayre, the belle of Montgomery, Alabama; the sudden fame—and the marriage to Zelda—that followed the publication of *This Side of Paradise* in 1920; the wild, drunken parties in New York and Maryland, on Long Island and the Riviera, during the roaring Twenties; the flapper stories for the *Saturday Evening Post* which set the tone of the "Jazz Age" while paying the Fitzgeralds' bills for a decade; the friendships with Edmund Wilson, Ring Lardner, Gerald and Sara Murphy, and above all with Hemingway; the insanity that crippled Zelda during the Thirties, and the alcoholism that devastated Scott; the prolonged composition and demoralizing failure of *Tender Is the Night*; Zelda's institutionalization in North Carolina and the attempted resuscitation of his career by means of a scriptwriting stint in Hollywood; the affair with the gossip columnist Sheilah Graham, who helped him climb back on the wagon and encouraged his return to novel-writing with the never-completed but extremely impressive *The Last Tycoon;* and, finally, the heart attack at the age of forty-three.

It's a legendary American story, a beautiful and damned American dream turned nightmare, and in the past five years alone three biographers have seen fit to tell it yet again. In 1981, Matthew J. Bruccoli, archetype of the preposterously prolific modern American literary scholar (in the past decade or so, he has not only collected Fitzgerald's letters, screenplays, notebooks and minor stories, but written Brobdingnagian lives of John O'Hara and James Gould Cozzens), produced a sloppy, simple-minded, adoring doorstop of a biography entitled *Some Sort of Epic Grandeur*. André Le Vot, a French scholar, followed in 1983 with a graceful English translation of his stately, sensitive and painstakingly researched *F. Scott Fitzgerald*. And now James R. Mellow—who in a brief period has turned out gargantuan lives of Nathaniel Hawthorne and Gertrude Stein (and is at work on Hemingway)—has weighed in with *Invented Lives: F. Scott and Zelda Fitzgerald*.

The most noticeable distinction between Bruccoli and Le Vot, on the one hand, and Mellow, on the other, is that the latter is not a scholar but a "writer," a literary journalist. Most of the facts in *Invented Lives* have been cheerfully glommed from those who got there before he did—not only Bruccoli and Le Vot, but the earlier Fitzgerald biographers, Andrew Turnbull and Arthur Mizener, Zelda's biographer Nancy Milford, and Sara Mayfield, author of *Exiles from Paradise*. Mellow relies so heavily upon his predecessors, in fact, that Fitzgerald fans who have only recently read the Le Vot book may find passages in *Invented Lives* bringing on attacks of déjà vu.

Why, then, is Mellow offering this third Fitzgerald biography in five years? His answer: *Invented Lives* isn't just another biography. It has a thesis. What thesis? That Scott and Zelda Fitzgerald struck out into life seeking, not so much to "find themselves," as to create themselves. That they were protagonists in a novel of their own creation, actors who saw the whole world as a stage. One problem with this thesis, of course, is that "playing a part" is not a rare phenomenon. Just to skim the index of *Invented Lives* is to come across the name of one person after another who did this: Tallulah Bankhead, T. S. Eliot, Sheilah Graham, Ernest Hemingway. To be sure, Mellow is undoubtedly correct in asserting that the Fitzgeralds had it worse than most. But this is hardly news. Their relentless self-dramatization is by now a cliché of American literary history. We all know that, for Scott and Zelda, it was not enough merely to be happy and successful: they had to be the happiest, kookiest, most in-love, most beautiful couple on earth, the very personification of the youthful, buoyant age they lived in. Unfortunately, Mellow does not have much that is new to say about this.

It would be misleading, though, to suggest that *Invented Lives* is devoted in any large part to the defense of its unspectacular thesis. Rather, it is, like *Some Sort of Epic Grandeur,* a monster of a biography—into which, every so often, Mellow remembers to interpolate a token sentence or two touching on his thesis. Chatty, diffuse, unencumbered by any finicky concern for stylistic elegance, *Invented Lives* often seems to be little more than a mammoth, mechanically compiled collection of every known Fitzgerald anecdote, strung together in (more or less) chronological order.

Yet *Invented Lives* has its virtues, among which is a sturdy skepticism. If Le Vot, for instance, appears to accept as gospel truth Hemingway's devastating "reportage" in *A Moveable Feast* concerning his first encounter with Fitzgerald, Mellow, noticing the little inconsistencies in Hemingway's memoir, does not hesitate to suggest that it is, at least in part, an act of dishonesty, "a masterly exercise in retrospective revenge" designed to expose every fault in Fitzgerald's character and make Papa shine by comparison. Mellow's argument is convincing. Likewise, while Le Vot admiringly describes Fitzgerald's devotion to the Princeton honor code (expressed in a letter to Maxwell Perkins) as "idealistic," Mellow juxtaposes Fitzgerald's letter with some pretty impressive bits of evidence that, honor code or no, would appear to suggest that Fitzgerald cheated on tests while at college. Time and again, then, Mellow provides a refreshingly cynical corrective to his perhaps excessively reverent predecessors.

Mellow is well-advised, too, I think, in placing more importance than previous biographers on the outrageous superficiality of Fitzgerald's attitude towards romance. To Fitzgerald, the ritual of courtship was, fundamentally, not a matter of love between man and woman but of competition between man and man. He always wanted the most popular girl in town—whether Ginevra King in St. Paul or Zelda Sayre in Montgomery—simply because she was the girl all the other men were after. To win the love of such a woman, and eventually secure her hand in marriage, was to triumph over one's rivals, to be recognized publicly as the victor in a great competition.

What made Fitzgerald adopt such a strange, artificial view of the relations between the sexes? Mellow comes closer than Bruccoli, Le Vot, and company to giving this question a satisfactory answer. Though he carefully avoids making any explicit claims in this direction, his book is full of evidence suggesting a strong homosexual component in Fitzgerald. This is hardly the first time that has been intimated, but Mellow has mustered the evidence more thoroughly and convincingly than any previous biographer. Though edgy with homosexuals, consistently disparaging of them in his fiction, and convinced, as Mellow writes, that they "were the enemies of life, the enemies of promise," Fitzgerald became, in time, "more and more inquisitive about such sexual habits." He was compulsive about "tallying 'fairies.'" He could write to Edmund Wilson—as a "joke," of course—that "I long to go with a young man . . . for a paid amorous weekend to the coast." He chased strange boys at parties, asking, "You're a homosexual, aren't you?" and, drunk in Paris, asked Morley Callaghan: "You thought I was a fairy, didn't you?" Zelda accused him regularly, for a time, of having an affair with Ernest Hemingway, and in fact Scott *was* obsessed with Hemingway; one cannot help getting the impression that his disgust with the stereotypical "fairy" image made it impossible for him to admit (to himself or anybody) the true nature of his feelings for the younger novelist. The closest he came to acknowledging these sentiments was in an oblique, rather enigmatic reference in his private notebook. "I really loved him," he wrote (obviously alluding to Hemingway), "but of course it wore out like a love affair. The fairies have spoiled all that."

One does not immediately think of Scott Fitzgerald and John Cheever as having much in common, but the more closely one scrutinizes the lives and works of these two writers, the more similar they look. Like Fitzgerald, Cheever watched his father fail in business, saw his family come down in the world, resented his father because of it, and developed an inordinate regard for wealth and respectability. He even had his own version of Francis Scott Key, the all-purpose respectable ancestor, in the form of Ezekiel Cheever, who arrived in the Massachusetts Bay Colony from England in 1637 and begat several generations of Boston society. If Fitzgerald made it to Princeton only to leave without a degree, Cheever didn't even get that far: he left prep school and, like the young author of *This Side of Paradise,* sought literary success in New York, not pursuing his Muse so much as fame, fortune and respect.

Cheever went on, as Fitzgerald had, to make his living by churning out formula stories. If Fitzgerald's hack jobs for the *Post* were invariably cloying chronicles of flapper romance, Cheever's generally more estimable contributions to the *New Yorker* concentrated, as a rule, on the travails of the upper bourgeoisie on New York's Upper East Side. (Later, when the Cheevers moved from Manhattan to the northern suburbs, the settings changed accordingly, to the fictitious commuter burgs of Bullet Park and Shady Hill.) Like Fitzgerald, Cheever was, in his early novels (*The Wapshot Chronicle, The Wapshot Scandal*) and in stories like "The Enormous Radio" and "The Pot of Gold," concerned with the fragility of material success and of social status—which is to say, he was fascinated by money, by those who had it and those who coveted it, by the *nouveau riche* and the "shoestring aristocrats"; and his stories are thus peppered (as are many of Fitzgerald's) with the names of the Holy Places of the New York wealthy—Sutton Place, Tiffany's, the Plaza. Cheever, like Fitzgerald, was something of a hypocrite on this topic: he could moralize in his fiction about the vapidity, phoniness and corruption of the moneyed class even as he labored to insinuate himself into it; he could satirize social climbers even as he dreamed—so Susan Cheever tells us in this memoir of her father—of marrying his daughter to "a Vanderbilt, a Biddle, a Cabot."

Eventually, Cheever's literary focus shifted. As Fitzgerald had, in the Thirties, alienated the *Post* by submitting gloomily honest stories like "Babylon Revisited," Cheever incurred the disapproval of his editors in the Fifties and thereafter by turning out stories like "The Swimmer" and "The World of Apples" which in the words of one editor, William Maxwell, "collided with the *New Yorker* idea of fiction." Meanwhile Cheever was, as his daughter reveals, colliding, too, with the *New Yorker* idea of Cheever. For one thing, he was, beginning in the 1950s, an alcoholic—who, like Fitzgerald, heroically kicked the habit toward the end and resuscitated his talent in an impressive way (producing two intense, offbeat short novels, *Falconer* and *Oh, What a Paradise It Seems*). For another, he was a closet homosexual, who did not come to terms with his inclinations until his last decade. Like Fitzgerald, "he feared and despised what he defined as the homosexual community: the limp-wristed, lisping men who are sometimes the self-appointed representatives of homosexual love in our culture." Even when he accepted his impulses and initiated affairs with young men, Cheever continued to hide behind an image of himself as "a patrician, old-fashioned country gentleman."

These revelations of Cheever's long-suppressed homosexuality go a long way toward explaining his fixation, in life as in literature, upon appearances. Characters in his stories—the early ones, at any rate—are defined by whether the clothes they wear are stylish, the streets they live on fashionable, the jobs they hold down prestigious. He was the same way in life, according to Miss Cheever. "We were told that appearances were not important," she writes, "but no one believed it for a minute. My father described everything in terms of appearances." One can hardly help seeing this systematic superficiality as a form of psychological camouflage, designed to keep his unexpressed longings buried as long as possible. The phrase "invented lives" was never more appropriate.

Because of these disclosures of alcoholism and homosexuality, Miss Cheever's book provoked controversy when it appeared in America last year. The critics formed two neat ranks. One faction maintained that Miss Cheever had written a loving, heartfelt tribute to her late father; the words "sensitive" and "honest" were frequently invoked. The other faction felt that the book was an act of spite: Miss Cheever had exploited her father, had made unfair use of his private journals, had produced a tasteless, sensationalistic book. The latter group of critics have a point. Cheever is so recently deceased—1982—that his daughter's rush to print does seem indecorous, her eagerness to advertise his painful secrets unsettling. And yet the book is no *Daddy Dearest*. It does not hurt Cheever. On the contrary, Cheever comes off as a rather sympathetic character. His personal torments give a human dimension to a man whom many considered something of a cold fish, a snob. The main problem with *Home Before Dark,* in fact, is that it doesn't give him quite as much human dimension as one might have expected.

What causes this disappointment to rankle is that there was clearly an abundance of promising material at Miss Cheever's disposal. Some of it, to be sure, has found its way into *Home Before Dark*. Miss Cheever's inside stories about the *New Yorker,* like all inside stories about that most peculiar of publications, are fascinating. Cheever, as it happens, grew dissatisfied at one point with the magazine's "Byzantine system" of payment (the complex pay-rate formula, according to Miss Cheever, involved a minimum word rate, a bonus system that "rewards the writer for the quantity of stories published in the magazine each year," a "Cost of Living Allowance," and the editor's top-secret "grading" of each story "from A down to C minus"). On the day he delivered "The Swimmer" to Maxwell at the *New Yorker* offices, Cheever hit him for a raise, and Maxwell replied that there was nothing he could do. Cheever thereupon left the building, walked down the street to a pay phone, called agent Candida Donadio, and told her his problem. "Stay right there," she said, and called back within minutes to relay a munificent offer from the *Saturday Evening Post*. Cheever went back to the *New Yorker* with the news. "Hurried conferences" ensued. Cheever was offered "bonuses" such as "the key to the men's room and all the bread and cheese he could eat"—and, ultimately, he elected to stay with the *New Yorker*. Afterwards, he wrote in his journal: "The *Post* has offered me twenty-four thousand; the *New Yorker* has offered me twenty-five hundred and I will take the latter. I'm not sure why." But of course we all know why, and so did he.

The glimpses of Cheever's mind that such anecdotes give us are, in the last analysis, frustrating. They're just not enough. Miss Cheever brings to mind one of those nervously self-conscious film directors who, desperate to avoid being taken for mere storytellers, make a habit of cutting away just when a sequence begins to get interesting or enlightening. The deliberately disordered, patchwork-of-memories structure of *Home Before Dark*—unobjectionable in itself—makes it easier for Miss Cheever to carry off this systematic superficiality. So does the style. Miss Cheever has the *New Yorker* in her blood, and she has chosen, in *Home Before Dark,* to write in a plain, impersonal manner, rich with maddeningly irrelevant detail, that is almost a parody of *New Yorker* style. The last thing this story needs is a plain, impersonal manner. Nor does it need so many pointless particulars—Miss Cheever gives us, for instance, enough addresses to fill a small-town telephone book.

Both books force us to think seriously about—even if, more often than not, they fail to help us to a better understanding of—their subjects' obsession with wealth and social status, their pessimism about marriage, their all too often one-dimensional characterization of women, their bleak view of bourgeois family life, and their reluctance, in many a short story, to venture very far beneath the surface of things.

Hemingway's Prelude
to Paris

October 1985

Many of us are curious about the lives that great writers led when they were young, but some are curious for different reasons than others. There are those who are genuinely interested in the personal circumstances that give rise to great art, who are captivated by the spectacle of a young person discovering his talent, deciding what use he will make of it, and developing a mature and triumphant creative vision. Then there are those who, being indifferent to the germination of genius, are diverted by the inside gossip, by the sexy tidbits, by the miraculous metamorphosis of a nobody from Dublin, Dorset, St. Louis, or St. Paul into an immortal—and the closer it all comes to a Judith Krantz novel, the better. Alas, the biographers and memoirists who have chronicled Ernest Hemingway's fitful and flaming youth in the wake of Charles A. Fenton's pioneering study, *The Apprenticeship of Ernest Hemingway: The Early Years* (1954), have tended to provide more sustenance for the Judith Krantz fans than for the bona fide admirers of the literary art.

Now a scholar named Peter Griffin has furnished us with yet another account of Ernest Hemingway's boyhood and young manhood, entitled *Along with Youth: Hemingway, the Early Years*. The book—whose title is that of an unfinished 1925 novel about Nick Adams as well as of an unremarkable poem that appeared in Hemingway's first published book, the 1923 *Three Stories and Ten Poems* ("Yesterday's Tribune is gone/Along with youth," etc.)—covers Hemingway's life until 1921. That was the year when Hemingway, aged twenty-two, left America for an eight-year residence in Paris, where he would meet, befriend, and learn from Ezra Pound, Gertrude Stein, Ford Madox Ford, and F. Scott Fitzgerald, and write his two best novels (*The Sun Also Rises* and *A Farewell to Arms*) and all but two or three of his best stories. As the prologue to these years in Paris, then, the years chronicled in *Along with Youth* are of great interest to every admirer of Hemingway.

They are of interest for other reasons, too. The more one reads about these early years, for one thing, the more one finds oneself thinking about a contemporary of Hemingway's whom many would consider his opposite: T. S. Eliot. The parallels and contrasts between the two men's lives and literary methods are intriguing and instructive. Like Eliot, his senior by eleven years, Hemingway was a child of the urban Midwest, the pampered scion of a well-to-do, socially prominent, and insufferably proper family of high Victorian temper. This Victorianism notwithstanding, however, Hemingway's mother (Grace Hall-Hemingway, as she signed herself) was, like Eliot's mother, "liberated," ambitious, pious, possessive, and emotionally demanding, which may help to explain why both writers developed such a detached, hostile attitude toward women.

The paths that Eliot and Hemingway took from these unorthodox-yet-proper homes to literary distinction diverged early: whereas Eliot left St. Louis for the Milton Academy and Harvard College, Hemingway departed the Chicago suburb of Oak Park at eighteen to receive his higher education as a cub reporter on the seamy streets of Kansas City and as an ambulance driver in Italy during World War I (where he became, by some accounts, the first American to be wounded on the Italian front). Yet both Eliot and Hemingway—who, after the war, returned to Chicago to work as an advertising copywriter—felt the need, as their literary careers loomed before them, to take their talents, and their considerable ambitions, to Europe. (After which, except for a handful of brief visits, neither would return to his hometown.) It was there that both of them—Eliot in London in 1911, Hemingway in Paris a decade later—began, with the assistance and encouragement of Ezra Pound, to make significant (and extensively imitated) contributions to the modern movement, and to establish elaborate public images that seemed designed, at least in part, to proclaim how far they had come from their middle-American origins.

But how different those images, how antithetical the ways in which the two writers embodied the modern spirit! Each modeled his celebrated persona, to an extent, upon one of the two great masters of late nineteenth-century American fiction. Whereas Eliot's prototype was the elegant, hypercivilized Henry James, Hemingway's was the plain-spoken, ungenteel Mark Twain (whose *Huckleberry Finn* he saw as the ancestor of the modern American novel). And whereas Eliot, in his increasingly symbolistic poetry, attempted to build a structure of meaning around the "void" at the center of his soul by employing high-flown abstractions and recondite vocables, Hemingway took the opposite approach. In his positivistic prose, he sought to combat the "nada" at the heart of existence by banishing what he saw as the brittle fabrications of the intellect and relating, in language as pared-down as possible, the purest and simplest of sense impressions. These methods shared a single purpose: to isolate Truth—which, to Eliot and Hemingway alike, was the most valuable and elusive of commodities—in a world of doubt and confusion. It was, to a degree, this acute consciousness of the evasiveness of knowledge that inspired both of them to cultivate a semblance of authority—one as pedagogue, the other as Papa.

Of the two great writers, Eliot is invariably considered the more difficult. Yet somehow his achievement has always seemed easier to describe and to appreciate than that of Hemingway. Like the armies of second-rate, imitative American novelists who, in the middle decades of the century, behaved as if a terse, tough-sounding style was all one needed to emulate *The Sun Also Rises,* all too many of Hemingway's critics have been guided by the assumption that his achievement can be explained by one simple formula or another. Leftist critics such as Malcolm Cowley, for example, have long insisted upon reading Hemingway's *oeuvre* as a nihilistic "criticism of society"—specifically, of modern Western society—and as a wholesale condemnation of that society's imperialistic wars. The conservative critic Kenneth Lynn, for his part, while justly taking Cowley to task for his "critical extravagances," has imprudently attempted to downplay the importance of war as a theme in Hemingway's work. This is a difficult task indeed, for war is clearly at the center of all but one of his novels. *A Farewell to Arms* (1929) takes place during World War I, *For Whom the Bell Tolls* (1940) during the Spanish Civil War; *The Sun Also Rises* (1926) details the lingering postwar effects of Jake Barnes's battle injury; *Across the River and into the Trees* (1950) is grounded in Richard Cantwell's memories of the First World War; and *Islands in the Stream* (1970) traces Thomas Hudson's gradual movement toward involvement in World

War II. Significantly, the sole Hemingway novel that is not concerned with war is *To Have and Have Not* (1937), which is widely—and correctly—regarded as Hemingway's major departure from his characteristic manner, the result of a temporary, and aesthetically lamentable, capitulation to the fashionable socialism of the mid-Thirties.

It is, then, unreasonable to deny that Hemingway's fiction is preoccupied with war; but it is equally unreasonable to assume, with Cowley, that this preoccupation necessarily implies a criticism of twentieth-century Western civilization or an endorsement of socialism. On the contrary, in Hemingway's most enduring and representative fiction, war is not an ideological but an anthropological phenomenon—not a darkly revealing manifestation of twentieth-century Western society but an inescapable consequence of human character. To Hemingway, human life, at its richest, represents a shuttling back and forth between two distinct states of being: on the one hand, the order, stability, and discipline of civilization; on the other, the primitive, often mortal, rituals (such as bullfighting, boxing, fishing, and hunting) by means of which one maintains one's connection with the elemental foundation upon which civilization is erected. And war, as the ultimate ritual, is an inevitable part of life. As such, it is neither good nor bad—or, if one prefers, is both good *and* bad. At any rate, it abideth forever, like the earth, occasioning meaningless death and meaningful heroism alike.

It should be no surprise, then, that Hemingway's narrators and characters are frequently drawing parallels between war and other rituals. In *For Whom the Bell Tolls,* Pablo compares the perils of combat to those of bullfighting: "Within the danger [of war] there is the safety of knowing what chances to take. It is like the bull fighter who knowing what he is doing, takes no chances and is safe." In *The Sun Also Rises,* Robert Cohn asks, "Can you bet on bull-fights?" and Jake answers: "It would be like betting on the war. You don't need any economic interest." In *Islands in the Stream,* Hudson's son David, after a bloody, hours-long struggle with a big fish, describes the curious feeling that all these rituals engender in the soul of a true-blue Hemingway character: "In the worst parts, when I was the tiredest I couldn't tell which was him and which was me. . . . Then I began to love him more than anything on earth. . . . Really love him. . . . I loved him so much when I saw him coming up that I couldn't stand it. . . . All I wanted was to see him closer."

In these paradoxical sentences resides the essence of Hemingway's ethos: to his mind, sex and war, bullfighting and deep-sea fishing, are life-giving as well as life-taking, enriching as well as depleting, possessed of a dark virtue and a terrible beauty. Each of these rituals is at once a contest of individual wills, a way of strengthening oneself, and a means of reasserting the bonds of common existence. And the art with which Hemingway treats of these matters is one not of unmitigated despair or of shrill condemnation but, rather, of stoic resolution; it is an art that accepts as a given both the difficulty and the value of human life, an art that honors the qualities of character that make it possible for a man not only to endure but, by sheer force of will, to give life order and infuse it with meaning.

How did Ernest Hemingway happen to grow into such a writer? That's the question Peter Griffin claims to be intrigued by, and he insists that *Along with Youth* came into being precisely because previous Hemingway biographers failed to answer this question adequately.

> On October 28, 1977, I wrote a six-line note to Mary Hemingway. I told her I wanted to write my dissertation at Brown University on her husband because his works had meant a lot to me during the hardest times of my life. I said I knew most scholars agreed that Hemingway had been "done." But I said I could not find the author of *In Our Time, The Sun Also Rises,* and *A Farewell to Arms* in the biographies I had read.

So Griffin tells us at the beginning of his preface. And so far, so good. But what sort of person does Griffin think wrote *In Our Time* and *The Sun Also Rises?* What nuances of character does he believe eluded his predecessors in the Hemingway-biography game? He doesn't say. He *never* says. If he has a clear vision of Hemingway, he has kept it to himself. One might suppose his epigraph, from *Sons and Lovers,* would provide a clue: "He was the sort of boy that becomes a clown and a lout as soon as he is not understood, or feels himself held cheap, and again is adorable at the first touch of warmth." We are, one assumes, supposed to understand that this is what the young Hemingway was like; but there is hardly a single sentence in Griffin's book that would seem to support it. Nowhere does he suggest that a tendency to alternate between clownishness and adorableness was the young Hemingway's signal trait, or that this trait is, somehow, the key to comprehending the man or his work.

It is difficult, in fact, to figure out, from Griffin's diffuse, impercep-

tive, and directionless book, *what* he makes of the young Hemingway.
In reaction, one imagines, to Carlos Baker's surefooted standard biography, *Ernest Hemingway: A Life Story* (1969) — and with misguided
reverence, perhaps, for Hemingway's own reluctance to inject inter-
pretative remarks into his novels and stories — Griffin makes a point of
offering very little in the way of analysis or commentary. He concen-
trates, rather, upon the accumulation of details. But since he is not
Hemingway, his tireless (and ludicrously unselective) gathering of
minutiae adds up to a good deal less than one has a right to expect from
such a book as this. To be sure, there is new material in *Along with
Youth,* drawn from letters that have only recently come to light, and
this new material appears to be the biography's principal *raison d'être* as
well as its chief selling point. Thanks to this material, the book has received considerable advance publicity. A recent *New York Times* article
by Edwin McDowell, for example, announced to the world that Griffin's book would be "based upon a number of previously unpublished
documents, including some 2,000 pages of unpublished letters," most
of them between Hemingway and his first wife, Hadley Richardson,
and his friend Bill Horne. But what McDowell neglected to add was
that this body of correspondence, for all its bulk, is surprisingly unrevealing. Griffin seems to have found it easy to ignore this fact; he is
apparently starstruck by Hemingway, is thrilled to have met the great
man's surviving friends and relatives, and — however useless these letters may be — is overwhelmed by the fact that he is the first scholar to
have been permitted to use them.

And use them he has. Indeed, while the first half of his book, cover-
ing Hemingway's first eighteen years, draws for the most part upon the
same sources as Baker's biography, the second half, which deals with
Hemingway's nineteenth through twenty-second years, consists almost entirely of paraphrases of and quotations from the letters. This is
unfortunate, partly because most of the letters are not from Hemingway but from Hadley, partly because they were written during a relatively brief period (eight months or so), and partly because this period
(the first part of 1921, when Hemingway was working at his despised
copywriting job) was arguably among the most uninteresting of the
writer's adult life. But it is unfortunate most of all because, like most
billets-doux, Hadley's letters to Ernest, when quoted from in such abundance, make very dull and unenlightening reading for a third party. If
these letters prove anything at all, it is that Hadley was indeed very
much enamored of her "Nesto." To this end, of course, two or three

quoted sentences would have more than sufficed; instead, Griffin gives us fifty or so pages, the highlights of which read more or less as follows:

> I think you are the nicest lover a person ever had, really. I feel matched up and appreciated and taken care of the way I did the night I rolled so fast and scaredly down the sand dune in the dark and you whirled me up and kissed me. . . . I want to be picked up now Ernest. I want you here tonight around me. I feel small and lovely and lonely (but happy) 'cause I know that if you were here you would be around me and domestic and needing to be necessary. Do you ever feel that way about me. Big and lonely, only, and needing?

That's on page 150; on 153, we get this:

> I'm so terribly in need of just such an adorable warm-hearted sweet and tender darling to love me. But even more than that I need someone to give my lots and lots of lovingness to. . . . It's probably very prehistoric in me but I do think I can't get along without awfully much worshiping the goodness in a man I'm to love for always. I have such an initiative, healthy, put the other fellow first, kind of goodness and you have a heart that I undoubtedly adore!

And on it goes. On the next page, Hadley assures Ernest that "There isn't any arms in the world I want around me as much as yours. There's no heart like yours for me." She explains that she loves him "so highly and lowly and like a boy and girl warmly," and that she finds it "so hard to mail these letters. It's like putting yourself in the mailbox." She wants "to be walking with you in a forest. A very soft dark green. There would be things to do there that would be more beautiful than anywhere else."

Unarguably, it's all very sweet and lovely—but to include every word, unedited, in a literary biography is absolutely ridiculous. This is not to say that Griffin confines himself to Ernest and Hadley's declarations of love; he also offers us reams of miscellaneous material that is perhaps best classified as Amazingly Trivial. We learn, for example, that on a certain evening Hadley went to a Douglas Fairbanks movie, that on another occasion she met a man (unnamed) who slouched and smoked a pipe, that at a party somebody named Dick "flirted with Pete Rowland's girl," that Hadley played "Malagene, Jeux d'Eaux, and a Brahms ballad" on the University Club's piano. In letter after letter, we find out what Hadley had for dinner, whom she played tennis with, what streets her various friends lived on.

Throughout all of this, Griffin hovers far in the background, comporting himself less like a biographer than like a humble medieval scribe, dutifully copying out his sacred texts, word for prosaic word, reverently preserving for posterity each redundancy-choked passage, each trifling anecdote, each obscure allusion. When, every so often, a letter actually raises an interesting question or two, Griffin almost invariably refuses to take it up. In many of Ernest's letters to Hadley, for instance, he goes out of his way to drop the names of women that he has been seeing in Chicago. In particular, there is one Kate Smith, who is in love with him, and with whom he socializes a great deal. (And who, years later, will marry John Dos Passos.) Instead of being upset, though, when Ernest throws Kate's love for him in her face, Hadley is strangely saint-like, suggesting in all seriousness that Kate is "[w]orth about three of me... and [would] probably be a better lover and worker for you, and everything. My but it's queer the way things happen, and if you didn't want me pretty hard, as I think you do, I'd make you throw me over and do yourself justice." A letter or two like this is enough to convince one that Hemingway's relationship with Hadley had its intriguing aspects, all right, and if only Griffin had chosen to select a few key passages from these letters for rigorous examination and intelligent discussion, he might have produced an enlightening book and actually added something worthwhile to the burgeoning storehouse of Hemingway scholarship. But that's not his style. Like Matthew J. Bruccoli, the literary scholar who has made a name for himself by writing gigantic biographies and compiling obscure documents of dubious value (among his productions is a collection of the articles young Hemingway wrote for the Oak Park High School newspaper), Griffin seems to believe that the best way to understand a great writer is to accumulate every word he ever wrote and to publish it, with unscholarly fanfare, under one's own name.

I have not yet mentioned that *Along with Youth* contains, in addition to all those letters, the complete texts of five short stories—"The Mercenaries," "Crossroads: An Anthology," "The Ash-Heel's Tendon," "Portrait of the Idealist in Love," and "The Current"—which Hemingway wrote in 1919 and 1920, when he was twenty and twenty-one. For reasons that should be obvious to anyone, but that are not obvious to Griffin, Hemingway never published any of these stories in his lifetime.

Griffin has remedied this situation, and doubly so: aside from printing them in *Along with Youth,* he has cooperated in their publication in *The New York Times Magazine,* where they appeared in the issue of August 18, 1985, along with an introduction by Griffin himself. In *Along with Youth,* since Griffin is not the type to relegate anything by Hemingway to a mere appendix, the stories appear, peculiarly enough, as part of the text; when the appropriate chronological point arrives, Griffin interrupts his biographical narrative, gives us a story, then resumes the biography without so much as a word of comment about the interruption. It's a very peculiar format, reminiscent of Hemingway's *In Our Time* (1925), wherein the chapters of the original *in our time* (1924) were separated by short stories. The difference, of course, is that in *Along with Youth* the format makes no sense, logical or aesthetic or otherwise, and therefore doesn't work. Nor does it help that the stories are far inferior to those collected in *In Our Time.* Although they are written, for the most part, in a streetwise vernacular that recalls many a later Hemingway story (and that, incidentally, betrays the influence of Sherwood Anderson and Ring Lardner), these five early works lack both subtlety and depth. One misses, in all of them, the agonizing restraint, the calculated repetitions, the profound vision of the mature Hemingway, not to mention that crucial feeling that seven-eighths of the story is hidden beneath the surface. To see such primitive works as these, in fact, splashed across the pages of *The New York Times Magazine,* and accorded places of honor in a biography published by Oxford University Press, is, for any sincere admirer of Hemingway, a truly depressing experience.

Griffin, to be sure, acknowledges the inferiority of the early stories; but he argues, nonetheless, that they show Hemingway "discover[ing] a voice that soon would speak for a generation." The stories, he claims, disprove Gertrude Stein's contention that "she and Sherwood Anderson had 'formed' Hemingway." Insists Griffin: "What ended with 'The Old Man and the Sea' began with 'The Mercenaries,' 'The Ash-Heel's Tendon,' and 'Crossroads.'" This is pure hype. What "The Mercenaries" and its brethren show, on the contrary, is that at the age of twenty-one, only a couple of years before producing such excellent pieces of short fiction as "My Old Man" and "Cat in the Rain," Hemingway was still perpetrating juvenilia. If anything, then, these early works tend not to disprove but to support Stein's contention that she helped mold a crude Kansas City journalist into a great author.

So skewed is Griffin's judgment in this matter, in fact, that at times one has the distinct suspicion that Griffin really does not recognize how bad these stories are, and that his much-vaunted admiration of Hemingway has at least as much to do with the magnitude of the novelist's current reputation as with the actual value of this work. What's more, for a man who claims to be so enamored of Hemingway's work—and therefore, one would assume, reasonably sensitive to the nuances of well-crafted prose—Griffin is an exceedingly unimpressive stylist. He is one of those writers who commit all the classic, avoidable errors. For example: "Shortly after Agnes left, Ernest wrote two stories he would never publish on Red Cross Headquarters stationery." He has an uneasy way not only with the English language but with punctuation marks, a failing which often causes his sentences to be clumsier than they have to be: "At supper, 'Abba' the biblical word for father as he insisted on being called—gave the blessing. . . . " And then there are the little awkwardnesses, the instances of inappropriate diction that occur a bit too frequently for comfort. On a single page (152), for example, Griffin refers to Carl Sandburg and Sherwood Anderson as "nightlights of the Chicago renaissance," tells us that Anderson "had accomplished *Winesburg, Ohio* in 1919," describes Anderson as having rejected "the kind of life Ernest believed Clarence Hemingway [his father, a physician] had cowardly embraced," and refers to Anderson's belief "in the salvific power of a 'good woman.'" Twice Griffin describes people as getting "purposively drunk." And sometimes he comes off as just plain addlepated, alluding several times (as if this were a most impressive statistic indeed) to the fact that Hemingway had size-eleven feet and mentioning no fewer than four times, in the course of a five-page preface, that Bill Horne's black dog is named Lena (Lena Horne, get it?)—this apparently being, to Griffin's tastes, sophisticated wit.

We are informed that *Along with Youth* is the first installment of a multiple-volume biography. A bit of arithmetic: since Baker devotes 83 of the 564 pages in his biography—or approximately one seventh of the total—to the twenty-two years covered in *Along with Youth,* we may reasonably expect, it would seem, that Griffin's masterwork has at least five, perhaps six, more volumes to go, for a grand total of about fifteen hundred pages, before it reaches that sunny morning in July of 1961 when the Hemingway story came to an end. Fifteen hundred pages: that's an average of about thirty words of biography for ever single day that Hemingway lived. Think of it. And think, too, of the as-yet-unpublished documents that Griffin may quote and paraphrase at hundreds of pages' length; think of all the important facts that he may choke to death in a fog of inconsequential details before he's through. It's unsettling. One cannot help but be reminded, again, of the remarkable Professor Bruccoli. Unsurprisingly, it is Bruccoli himself whom Griffin cites, in his *New York Times Magazine* introduction, by way of defending his publication of the early Hemingway stories: "As the Hemingway scholar Matthew J. Bruccoli has written, 'Everything Ernest Hemingway wrote is of importance because he wrote it.'" Yes —it is of importance to scholars, as background information which may or may not provide insights into Hemingway's life and character. But important as literature—important to readers of biographies and of major newspapers? Certainly not.

What it all comes down to is that Peter Griffin is less interested than he should be in the question of how Hemingway's early years helped make him the sort of writer he was. And he is more interested than he should be in some matters that many would consider the stuff of gossip—in the fact that Hemingway and Hadley apparently slept together before their marriage, for instance, or in the revelation that Hemingway's wartime romance with his nurse Agnes von Kurowsky (the prototype of Catherine Barkley, the heroine of *A Farewell to Arms*) was somewhat hotter and heavier than many critics have assumed. The simplemindedness and sensationalism of this approach is particularly regrettable because there is, manifestly, a significant story to be told about Hemingway's first twenty-two years and their impact upon his mature writings. Among other things, the writer of a responsible and useful book about these years would have made a greater effort to understand Hemingway's hostility toward his mother, his ambivalent feelings about his father (who, like Ernest, committed suicide), his fascination with the Indian life of upper Michigan (which plays such a large role in his earliest Paris stories as well as in *The Torrents of Spring*), and the complicated ways in which his war experience (which was clearly both traumatic and liberating) contributed to his development as a man and young writer and set him on much the same road as Eliot— toward self-exile in Europe and the advancement of literary modernism. If *Along with Youth* is such a disappointment, then, it is not because Griffin has, like many literary scholars these days, chosen for himself a ridiculously arcane topic, but because he has taken a subject so worthy of exploration and has failed to take it seriously enough. The authoritative book about the young Ernest Hemingway has yet to be written.

Hemingway:
The Meyers Version

NOVEMBER 1985

What is the relationship between a writer's life and his work?

That's the primary question raised by the genre of literary biography, and—as it happens—it's also one of the major questions raised by the case of Ernest Hemingway. For he was not only one of America's greatest novelists but one of its most prominent celebrities. Though he spent most of his life far from the madding crowd, in places like Key West, Cuba, and Idaho, his face was familiar to everyone and his swaggering persona and military and athletic exploits were legendary; rightly or wrongly, Americans felt they knew him, and this impression colored their reading of his work. Readers could not help but notice that his protagonists—Jake Barnes in *The Sun Also Rises,* Frederic Henry in *A Farewell to Arms,* Robert Jordan in *For Whom the Bell Tolls,* and so forth—bore more than a passing resemblance to Hemingway himself. Likewise, critics, recognizing a "code" of stoic endurance and bravery that seemed to underlie both his conduct and that of his heroes, could not be prevented from reading the novels as some form of thinly disguised autobiography. Yet readers and critics alike, in the course of their attempts to connect the word with the life, tended to confuse the life with the legend. And Hemingway's self-mythologizing books of "nonfiction"—*Death in the Afternoon, The Green Hills of Africa* and *A Moveable Feast*—encouraged them to do so.

Though more than a dozen memoirs (including widely publicized books by A. E. Hotchner, Gregory Hemingway, and Mary Hemingway) have followed in the nearly quarter-century since his death, the first book to succeed extensively in separating the life from the legend was Carlos Baker's much-pilloried but invaluable 1969 biography, *Ernest Hemingway: A Life Story.* Now Jeffrey Meyers, the author of biographies and studies of T. E. Lawrence, Wyndham Lewis, and Katherine Mansfield, among others, has given us *Hemingway: A Biography,* a quite worthy successor to the Baker. Meyers's biography is, to be sure, significantly different from Baker's. If Baker's strengths were his sense of authoritativeness, his restrained, evenhanded manner and his apparent scholarly thoroughness, Meyers's prime virtues are his lucidity, his liveliness, and his willingness to draw and support conclusions, many of them debatable, all of them provocative, none of them irresponsible. Baker told the Hemingway story chronologically; Meyers follows a roughly chronological pattern, but moves from topic to topic rather than from week to week, so that if you want to read about Hemingway's friendship with F. Scott Fitzgerald, for instance, you can find most of what Meyers has to say on the subject in a single chapter.

Hemingway was born in 1899, in the highly conventional Oak Park suburb of Chicago, to a neurotic, overbearing musician mother and a tense, henpecked physician father (who would commit suicide in 1928). The town was his mother's world. His father's world, as Meyers observes, "was in the open countryside just west of Oak Park and in the wilds of Michigan" where Ed Hemingway "incited Ernest toward an endless destruction of fauna: if it moved, they killed it." At home, Ernest was under his mother's domineering thumb; in the woods, with his gun and his reel, he was not only free but exercised a godlike omnipotence. After his graduation from high school in 1917, Ernest, who already knew he wanted to write, worked briefly on the Kansas City Star; but, eager to participate in the war in Europe and prevented by bad eyesight from getting into the army, he joined the Red Cross as an ambulance driver on the Italian front and was wounded during an act of heroism.

That wound has been the center of much controversy. Some critics have attributed his novels' obsession with war to his trauma over that wound; others have blithely denied that he suffered any trauma at all and insist that his wound made him feel happy, proud, invincible. Meyers seems to see things more clearly than most. He denies the simplistic trauma theory but recognizes that in some way, all of Hemingway's mature fiction does arise from that wound: "The wound made him aware not only that he could die, but also that he could survive. It made him feel invincible, made him live intensely, made him want to challenge fate rather than submit to it." It also, one might add, made him aware of the formidable nature of what he was challenging—the horror of war, the magnitude of death. "Like Jake Barnes and Frederic Henry," notes Meyers (who is good at recognizing such parallels), "his later heroes are wounded men: Harry Morgan has an amputated arm, Robert Jordan has a fractured leg, Robert Cantwell has a misshapen hand, Santiago has Christ-like wounds in his body. Hemingway . . . saw most clearly when he lived most intensely. He believed you 'have to be hurt like hell before you can write seriously.'"

For the remainder of his life, Hemingway sought to recover the intensity, the danger, the violence of the Great War. He traveled to Spain during the Civil War and to Paris during World War II; in both cases he was accredited as a correspondent but managed to take part (sometimes very heroically and selflessly) in the fighting. (Said Martha Gellhorn, his third wife: "I think [the Spanish War] was the only time in his life when he was not the most important thing there was.") When there were no wars to go to, he went to Pamplona to watch men kill bulls, or himself took on wild game in Africa or marlin in the Caribbean. Life itself, in fact, was a battleground to Hemingway. He fought with his mother, his siblings, his four wives, his three sons, alienating many of them forever. When he had safely outstripped the fame of such friends as John Dos Passos, F. Scott Fitzgerald, and Archibald MacLeish, he drove them out of his life as well, after which he never again had a close literary friend. Rather, he assumed the role of "Papa Hemingway," treating everyone around him as a dependent. Instead of writers, the companions of his last couple of decades (when his prose grew slack and self-parodic) were Cuban millionaires, international sportsmen, Hollywood actors, and the like.

Despite all this, Meyers's Hemingway is a good deal less of a loud-mouthed, imperious, double-crossing, macho phony than one might have expected. For all his flaws, as a matter of fact, he comes across, at times, as wonderfully brave, humorous, and well-liked. He is, perhaps, the most believably human Hemingway we have yet been given. Among other things, he is less of a political naif than most of the Hemingways of yore. Meyers reminds us that the novelist "never swallowed and then recanted Communist ideology, as Dos Passos, Edmund Wilson, and Max Eastman did, nor became reactionary in middle age." On the contrary, Hemingway could be quite sophisticated in his political dealings: of all the colleagues who rushed to Ezra Pound's defense after his post-World War II incarceration, it was Hemingway — not Eliot, Frost, Archibald MacLeish, or William Carlos Williams — who thought up the idea of an insanity plea.

Meyers offers a number of fascinating details of which I, at least, wasn't aware before reading the book. I learned, for example, that the bitchy wife in "The Short Happy Life of Francis Macomber" was based on one Jane Mason, Hemingway's mistress during the years in Cuba (who later married Arnold Gingrich); that Pauline Pfeiffer, Hemingway's wife during the Spanish Civil War, was a Franco supporter (and after the divorce had an affair with Elizabeth Bishop); that Mary Welsh, before becoming Hemingway's fourth wife, was Irwin Shaw's mistress and the prototype for a major character in *The Young Lions;* that Hemingway's younger brother, Leicester, who spent his life trying to copy Ernest, committed suicide in 1982 and was not taken seriously even then because "everyone thought it was just another imitation of Ernest."

Meyers's picture of Hemingway's broken-down last years, when this exuberant, vivacious sportsman declined rapidly in health and became, in the words of one observer, the "saddest man I ever met," is more detailed and evocative than anything I've read on the topic. This is especially true of the description of Hemingway's final weeks, when shock treatments (intended to cure his depression) erased his memory and turned his life into "an overwhelming void." As Meyers discloses, Hemingway's suspicion that the FBI was spying on him during his 1960–61 stay at the Mayo Clinic was more than just the symptom of paranoia that his family assumed it to be; as FBI records show, agents of the intelligence organization *were* following him around at the time, questioning his doctors and filing reports to J. Edgar Hoover.

Hemingway killed himself on July 2, 1961, his mind and body both devastated beyond repair. Meyers observes: "His code — formulated in youth, based on toughness and stoicism — was not suited to old age and failed him at the end." But one may well argue, to the contrary, that suicide is a Hemingway code hero's final act of courage. This, at least, would seem to be the view of the bullfighter Juan Belmonte, who, when told "Don Ernesto has just committed suicide," slowly and clearly replied: "Well done."

On the whole, Meyers's critical judgment is solid, and many of his observations arresting and perceptive. He recognizes that Hemingway's works of the '20s—among them, his first two novels, *The Sun Also Rises* and *A Farewell to Arms,* and such stories as "Cat in the Rain," "My Old Man" and "Big Two-Hearted River"—are, as a rule, far superior to his later writings. Meyers is, of course, amply justified in praising two stories of the 1930s, "The Short Happy Life of Francis Macomber" and "The Snows of Kilimanjaro." To my mind, however, he wildly overrates *For Whom the Bell Tolls,* which he deems "a great novel." Though his discussion of the novel is illuminating—he convincingly argues for the influence upon it of *Seven Pillars of Wisdom* and of *War and Peace,* and draws some intriguing parallels between the relationship of its hero and heroine and that of Frederic Henry and Catherine Barkley in *A Farewell to Arms*—he fails to disabuse this reader, for one, of the feeling that *For Whom the Bell Tolls* is less than a magnificent artistic achievement. It lacks, as a rule, the leanness and vitality, the agility and naturalness, of Hemingway at his peak; its protagonists are too often one-dimensional, its prose too frequently possessed of a forced and ponderous simplicity.

If Meyers is excessively generous in his praise of *For Whom the Bell Tolls,* his judgment of Hemingway's last major work, *The Old Man and the Sea,* strikes me as a bit harsh. Its weaknesses, he insists, "are radical. There is pervasive sentimentality and self pity. . . . The stoicism . . . has become simpleminded." He criticizes the book's "inspirational theme" and condemns the story's final irony as "crude and obvious." This is, I think, an overstatement. It is difficult to avoid feeling that one reason, at least, why Meyers rates *For Whom the Bell Tolls* so much more highly than *The Old Man and the Sea* is that the former book is downbeat, the latter uplifting.

This is not, then, a perfect biography. It has other flaws, too. Its style is more often workmanlike than truly elegant; there are awkward patches and repetitions. Meyers offers, quite unnecessarily, dozens of capsule biographies of peripheral figures, and a few pointless anecdotes. And the unorthodox structure, predictably enough, sometimes causes confusion. But, taken as a whole, the book is an impressive one. "The most complicated subject that I know," wrote Ernest Hemingway, " . . . is a man's life." Jeffrey Meyers has taken on a complicated subject and made it a good deal clearer for all of us.

Hemingway:
The Lynn Version

August 1987

The Hemingway industry is booming. Two years ago in these pages, I reviewed Jeffrey Meyers's biography of the author; last year, I passed judgment on Ernest Hemingway's new novel-from-beyond-the-grave, *The Garden of Eden*. But these two books were only the tip of the iceberg. Within the past three or four years there have been prominent biographies of Hemingway's early years by Peter Griffin and Michael Reynolds, a book called *The Hemingway Women* by Bernice Kert, memoirs by Hemingway's sister Madelaine and his son Jack, and numerous critical studies. Now Kenneth S. Lynn, a professor of history at the Johns Hopkins University who has written widely on American literature, has gotten into the act. Lynn's *Hemingway* is the third full-scale biography of the author, following Carlos Baker's *Ernest Hemingway: A Life Story* (1969) and Meyers's *Hemingway: A Biography* (1985).

Meyers's biography, which made some rather startling revelations about Hemingway's sexual psychology, established that much of the reason for Hemingway's obsession with manliness had to do with his feelings about his domineering mother Grace; his entire life, in a sense, was a declaration of his independence from her. Lynn has taken this Freudian observation even further and built his book around it. His thesis, plainly stated, is that Grace—the woman Hemingway often referred to as "that bitch"—was the single most potent influence on Hemingway's life and work. Or, as Lynn puts it with somewhat greater melodramatic force: "All his life, his mother would remain the dark queen of Hemingway's inner world." To Lynn's mind, it was Grace's habit of dressing her baby boy in "girls' clothing" that resulted in a lifelong crisis of sexual identity on Hemingway's part, and was responsible for, among other things, his famous obsession with masculinity. Yet, as many critics have pointed out, small boys of Hemingway's generation often wore dresses. Lynn's attempts to establish that Hemingway was kept in such garb for a significantly longer period than the average boy are unconvincing. That Lynn rests so much of his argument upon this shaky hypothesis is probably his book's greatest weakness.

Yet he does succeed in proving that Grace's influence was considerable. For instance, it was Grace's conceit that Hemingway and his sister Marcelline—his elder by a year and a half—were twins of the same sex. Both children, up to the time they entered kindergarten, were dressed in identical dresses and bonnets. Lynn draws a convincing connection between this circumstance and the fact that there are many twins in Hemingway's fiction—as well as many men and women who pretend to be, or are thought to be, twins. Twinhood, indeed, came to be symbolically associated in his fiction with the extreme closeness that can develop between lovers or married couples. In "The Battler," for instance, Ad's wife "looks enough like him to be his own twin." And in *The Garden of Eden,* a honeymooning couple are taken by observers to be brother and sister. Likewise, Lynn makes a point of the fact that Grace sometimes had Ernest's and Marcelline's hair cut the same way (although sometimes, he admits, she did not), and that she repeatedly extolled "the beauties of blondness." He connects these maternal enthusiasms to Hemingway's own preoccupation with hair, haircuts, and hair color—a preoccupation most noticeable in *The Garden of Eden,* wherein Catherine, just married to David, has her sun-bleached hair cut short and declares that she is not Catherine but Peter, and that he is Catherine. She says, "Will you change and be my girl and let me take you?"

Such fantasies of sexual transference, Lynn notes, were common not only in Hemingway's fiction but in his life. Hemingway and his first wife, Hadley, took turns "being the passive lover"—a relationship that was in part the inspiration for the astonishing sex scenes in *The Garden of Eden.* About his fourth wife, Mary, Hemingway wrote in a diary that "she has always wanted to be a boy and thinks as a boy without ever losing any femininity. . . . She loves me to be her girls [sic], which I love to be. . . ." He enjoyed the notion of exchanging identities with women, and in his letters to Adriana Ivancich, a young woman he met in 1948 and to whom he developed a strong attachment, Hemingway addresses her as "Hemingstein" (one of his nicknames) and signs himself "A. Ivancich."

Related to Hemingway's fascination with sexual transference, according to Lynn, was his interest in lesbians. Hemingway was attracted to a number of them, including Gertrude Stein; his second wife, Pauline, had affairs with women after their divorce. Yet when Lynn tries to draw a direct cause-and-effect relation between Hemingway's attraction to lesbians and his childhood cross-dressing, it seems a bit simplistic. "It surely was his firsthand experience of knowing how it felt to look like a girl but feel like a boy," writes Lynn, "that was the fountainhead of [Hemingway's] fascination with the ambiguities of feminine identity." Many a strict Freudian, I suspect, would be made uncomfortable by that "surely."

Though there are, to the naked eye, no lesbians in Hemingway's best novel, *The Sun Also Rises,* Lynn finds one, after a fashion, in the person of the hero, Jake (Jacob) Barnes, whose war wound makes him unable to consummate his love for Lady Brett Ashley. Lynn argues that the key to recognizing Jake's similarity to a lesbian is in his name — which, far from being randomly chosen, was (Lynn suggests) based upon the names and addresses of two lesbian friends of Hemingway's: Natalie Barney, who lived on the rue Jacob, and Djuna Barnes, who resided at the Hotel Jacob. "From these two associations," writes Lynn, "Hemingway derived the name of a man who is passionately in love with a sexually aggressive woman with an androgynous first name and a mannish haircut, a man whose dilemma is that, like a lesbian, he cannot penetrate his loved one's body with his own." This argument is convincing and fascinating.

Lynn has a sharp eye, then, for esoteric connections between life and fiction. Yet his well-nigh fanatical tendency to seek such connections leads him, time and again, to reduce some of Hemingway's best works to mere records of the author's experiences or parables of his deepest psychic conflicts. Though some Hemingway experts, for example, are certain that the author lost his virginity to a waitress in Michigan, Lynn disagrees with this notion, mainly because in the story "Up in Michigan," the waitress's "importunate partner appears to have had a fair amount of practice." After admitting that "it is altogether likely . . . that the story departs from the truth," Lynn turns around and says that the story nonetheless "casts a shadow of doubt across the genteel assumption that until he was twenty Hemingway's body was the unprofaned temple his mother had always hoped it was."

If in the case of "Up in Michigan" Lynn implies that a story can be used as biographical evidence, in the case of *The Sun Also Rises* he makes it clear how unwise such wholesale biographical readings can be. In Paris in 1924, he tells us, Hemingway punched out a physically unimposing fellow writer, Nathan Asch, only to break into Asch's hotel room later, mouthing a drunken, tearful apology. But when Hemingway incorporated this incident into *The Sun Also Rises,* the details were craftily shifted around: the onetime Princeton boxing champ Robert Cohn (a character based largely on Harold Loeb, who had stolen the heart of Hemingway's beloved Lady Duff Twysden) knocks out Jake Barnes (a character largely based on Hemingway), and that night Barnes enters Cohn's room to find Cohn weeping contritely on his bed. Lynn concludes that it was to make Cohn—and, therefore Loeb—look bad that Hemingway made Cohn, not Jake, the weeping bully. Yet can we really believe that when Hemingway departed from the literal truth in writing this episode in *The Sun Also Rises,* he did so not because he thought this departure best served the novel's dramatic and thematic purposes, but simply because he wanted to wreak revenge on an erstwhile friend? This is not the way great novels are written.

Lynn takes the same odd view of the making of fictions in his discussion of "Big Two-Hearted River." This story, he claims, "raises more tantalizing questions than any other Hemingway story." Hemingway himself noted on many occasions—for instance, in the posthumously published memoir *A Moveable Feast*—that this story was about "coming back from the war but there was no war in it." Indeed, there was not even any mention of the war. In the story the young Nick Adams goes into the Michigan countryside, leaving "everything behind, the need for thinking, the need to write, other needs." Lynn, eager to read the story as an implicit comment not on the wages of war but on Hemingway's own family problems, balks at the notion that Nick's motivations have anything to do with war. Instead he proposes that, because Hemingway wrote it after having spent several months "in bitter contention with his mother," the story is really about the aftermath of a mother-son conflict.

"Perhaps," Lynn writes, "the 'other needs' Nick feels he has put behind him include a need to please his mother, while his talk of his tent as his home may represent a reaction to being thrown out of his parents' summer cottage. Perhaps, too, the burned-over country and the grass-hoppers that have turned black from living in it constitute tacit reminders to him of his mother's penchant for burning things. And finally, the activity of his mind that keeps threatening to overwhelm his contentment could be rage." Perhaps, in short, the story is nothing but a gloss on Hemingway's own private life.

As for the fact that Hemingway himself affirmed that the story was about war, Lynn suggests that readers who believed such a thing, when they first read it in *A Moveable Feast,* "would have been better advised to wonder if a master manipulator was not making fools of them from beyond the grave, as he so often had in life." But Hemingway's tendency to boast about his exploits and lie about his friends had nothing to do with his attitude toward his fiction. His fiction was the most important thing in the world to him; he respected and cherished his art, and would never have prevaricated about the theme of one of his most important stories simply to "make fools" of people.

But then for some reason Lynn finds it necessary to soft-pedal the importance to the teenage Hemingway of being wounded in World War I. The biographer even claims that Hemingway's war poems—which were written around 1921, and which presented war "as a colos-sally mismanaged butchery"—were influenced not by the young man's own experience but by various negative books about the war that had been published since the Armistice. Lynn offers no evidence for this as-sertion, aside from his own sense that the darkness of the poems could not have derived from Hemingway's experience but "surely"—again, that surely—"had to do with a larger pessimism about human life." And Ernest's pessimism was founded, no doubt, upon his family prob-lems.

At the end of his discussion of the Cohn-Loeb-Asch nexus in *The Sun Also Rises,* Lynn quotes some words that Jake speaks in his role as narrator: "Somehow I feel I have not shown Robert Cohn clearly."

Lynn's comment: "Perhaps it was Ernest Hemingway that he was unable to show clearly." In this remarkable statement Lynn sums up the fundamental flaw in his approach to literary biography: namely, that he seems hardly to realize that it is not, and should not, be the intention or obligation of a fiction writer to "show" himself "clearly," at least not in the simpleminded sense that Lynn's words imply.

To be sure, Lynn's *Hemingway* has many virtues. Aside from offer-ing many valid and valuable insights, only a few of which I have been able to mention here, it is written with intelligence, enthusiasm, and style. (Indeed, it is probably the best written of all Hemingway biographies.) But the book is seriously weakened both by Lynn's excessive devotion to his thesis and by his regrettable attitude toward Hemingway's greatest fictions—by his tendency, that is, to discuss them as if they were the transparent effusions of a crippled mind, rather than the supremely crafted works of a complex genius. Which they are, of course—for, if they were not, precious few of us would be interested in Hemingway's life in the first place.

Hemingway's
Garden of Eden

Y ou've got to hand it to him. Even though he's been gone for almost a quarter of a century, Ernest Hemingway keeps turning them out. He's more prolific dead than many other celebrated writers are alive.

Since his death in 1961, Scribners has brought out no fewer than ten new Hemingway books. Many have been accompanied by hyperbolic press releases apparently designed to create the impression that a masterpiece has been unearthed. The best of all these posthumous books was the taut, vivid memoir *A Moveable Feast* (1964). Other items, however—such as the novel *Islands in the Stream* (1970) and the previously unpublished short works included in *The Nick Adams Stories* (1972)—have been less deserving of attention.

The past five years have been especially productive ones for the late Mr. Hemingway. In 1981, Scribners issued a nearly thousand-page volume of his selected letters, edited by Carlos Baker; the year 1984 saw the publication of a pocket-sized compilation—apparently intended for gift-giving—called *Ernest Hemingway on Writing;* and in 1985 came *Deadline: Toronto,* a collection of Hemingway's news dispatches of the early '20s, and *The Dangerous Summer,* a copious bullfighting memoir that seemed designed only for hard-core fans of the *corrida.*

Hemingway's latest posthumous opus is a novel entitled *The Garden of Eden.* Like *The Dangerous Summer,* it was, in manuscript, very rough and overwritten and had to be extensively pared down by the people at Scribners before it could be considered at all publishable. The 120,000 words of *The Dangerous Summer* were reduced to 44,000 for publication; *The Garden of Eden,* which originally contained 200,000 words, was cut down by Scribners editor Tom Jenks to one-third of that.

Would Hemingway have approved of the sculpting of published novels out of his piles of left-behind manuscript? The folks at Scribners, of course, say yes. So does Peter Griffin, author of the inept 1985 biography, *Along with Youth: Hemingway, the Early Years.* In a recent *New York Times* article by Edwin McDowell, Mr. Griffin is quoted as saying that Hemingway "made lots of indications on the manuscripts of things to be changed, and when he went bad he would often interject signs in his writing to indicate he didn't like it. If someone really knows his stuff, he can tell where Hemingway should be cut."

I submit that only an obtuse "authority" on the order of Peter Griffin could come out with such a cocky, audacious remark. Even Hemingway himself, who labored over *The Garden of Eden* for the last fifteen years of his life, could not decide where the thing should be cut. But of one matter he was certain—namely, that editing Hemingway's prose was *his* job, and nobody else's. He regarded with contempt Thomas Wolfe's excessive reliance upon their editor Maxwell Perkins, who had to cut Wolfe's mammoth, incoherent manuscripts down to a small fraction of their size for publication. Hemingway patently felt that if an author could not bring a manuscript to its final shape, the book should not be published; it was not for an editor to try to carve books out of an author's failures. To this reader, at least, it seems obvious that Hemingway would have regarded what Scribners has done to his books as little short of dishonorable.

This is not to suggest that *The Garden of Eden* is without merit. Highly readable and often diverting, the book tells the story of a successful young novelist named David Bourne and his wife, Catherine, who are on an extended honeymoon in France and Spain. Their union, which at first seems utterly idyllic, soon proves disastrous, for Catherine, a wealthy and willful young woman who is rather unbalanced mentally, resents David's fame, talent, and preoccupation with his work. When a beautiful girl named Marita enters their life, their *pas de deux* gives way to a grotesque *ménage à trois,* which precipitates Catherine's breakdown. Through all this, David sticks stoically to his writing schedule, producing several *cahiers* full of stories about his childhood in Africa (these passages, by the way, contain the best, tightest prose in the book). We are meant to understand from this that

David is not a lousy, self-pitying, undisciplined writer like Robert Cohn in *The Sun Also Rises,* but that he is, on the contrary, a good writer who respects his vocation and who suffers the quiet tortures of creation without complaint. He is, in short, Hemingway.

Like many of Hemingway's novels, then, *The Garden of Eden* is in large part autobiography. There are unmistakable parallels between its story and that of Hemingway's first and second marriages, to Hadley Richardson and Pauline Pfeiffer. (There are also, as the reader may already have gathered, numerous echoes of Fitzgerald's *Tender Is the Night.*) Indeed, *The Garden of Eden* is more interesting as self-revelation than it is valuable as literature. Though Hemingway's intention seems to have been to mourn the ephemerality of life and love and to celebrate the ability of the writer to recapture the events and feelings of the past, he is ultimately more interested in contrasting Catherine's mental fragility, moral corruption and self-indulgence with David's strength of character. The novel seems, in other words, to celebrate Hemingway more than anything else. And it does so, alas, at nearly intolerable length. Even though two-thirds of the original manuscript has been excised, the book is still astonishingly slack; its scenes of eating, drinking, showering, and hairdressing—though vividly described—are redundant and (finally) tiresome.

But the publication of this book does not reflect badly upon Hemingway, who recognized the shortcomings of the manuscript out of which it was carved and would never for a moment have countenanced its appearance in print. On the contrary, the book discredits only the powers that be at Scribners—who must realize how its author would have felt about all this, and who apparently could not care less.

No Angel

MAY 1987

L iterary greatness is one thing; icon status is another. Consider the major American novelists of the 1920s and 1930s. The lives and personalities of Thomas Wolfe, Ernest Hemingway, and F. Scott Fitzgerald have long since become a cherished part of American literary folklore; those of William Faulkner and Willa Cather, for whatever reason, have not. Every year the books keep coming: either a new biography of Tom or Scott or Ernest, or a journal by one of them, or a collection of letters, or some sort of book (usually autobiographical) which an immoderately ambitious editor has carved out of the scrap heaps in the Wolfe, Fitzgerald, or Hemingway archives. Every year, consequently, for what seems the hundredth time, we find ourselves reliving one or another of those tempestuous, tragic lives. Indeed, it doesn't seem too much of an exaggeration to suggest that, for Americans of a literary bent, the lives of Tom, Scott, and Ernest are (for better or worse) our great national legends—our answer, if you will, to the Greek myths, the Icelandic sagas, and *Beowulf*—which, partly for inspirational and partly for cautionary purposes, we feel religiously compelled to rehearse periodically, the way Jews, each spring, recite among themselves the story of Passover.

So familiar are the general outlines of Thomas Wolfe's life that it is surprising to be reminded that, prior to the publication of *Look Homeward,* by the distinguished Harvard historian David Herbert Donald, there were only two full-scale biographies of the North Carolina novelist—Elizabeth Nowell's in 1960 and Andrew Turnbull's in 1967. Though both of these books were commendable in many ways, both had considerable flaws. Nowell, a fine writer who had been Wolfe's agent, was too close to her subject; Turnbull, who was also the author of a celebrated Fitzgerald biography, often seemed less interested in comprehending Wolfe than in retailing juicy anecdotes. It is pleasant, then, to report that *Look Homeward* represents a notable improvement over both its predecessors. Lively yet thoughtful, scholarly yet lucid, Donald's book strikes an admirable balance between attention to the life and to the work, between an ironic and a deferential attitude toward its subject.

And what a subject: a highly regarded American writer whom John Dos Passos described as "a gigantic baby," whom Hemingway called "a glandular giant with the brains and guts of three mice"—a man whose self-absorption rendered him so incapable of functioning like a normal adult that his publisher was forced to handle his money for him, so cowardly that he brought his mother north to help him dump his mistress, so irresponsible that when one of his bed partners informed him that she was pregnant, he told her, "Why don't you telephone Miss Nowell: she's my agent; she takes care of everything for me." His warmth, candor, and humility—to which many of Donald's sources testify—could turn in a flash to suspicion, hostility, and egotistic rage. As for his literary taste, he was indifferent at best to the work of Henry James, T. S. Eliot, and Proust, but loved Sinclair Lewis and Sherwood Anderson. Donald keeps telling us that Wolfe had "the best formal education of any American novelist of his day" (he attended both Chapel Hill and Harvard), but to my mind Wolfe is vivid proof that there is a difference between going to school and being educated. Curiously, after strongly denying (on page xvii) that Wolfe was "a literary naif," Donald (on page 399) uses precisely that phrase to describe him. And though Donald makes an elaborate case for the influence upon Wolfe of his favorite professors' systems of thought, it is clear that, though he certainly did parrot each of these professors for a time, none of them really taught him to *think,* taught him how to process ideas, helped him develop breadth or subtlety of mind. Indeed, throughout his life he was fervently anti-intellectual, suspicious of logical, consecutive, coherent thought, convinced that the purest and truest sort of literary artist didn't go in for such things.

When he did express an intellectual opinion, it was an embarrassment. In the 1930s, unable to stay off the political battlefield, he spoke up in turn for both German fascism and American Communism, neither of which he understood in the slightest. Regarding Nazi Germany, for instance, he said in 1936 that Americans should bear in mind that "in Germany you are free to speak and write that you do not like Jews and that you think Jews are bad, corrupt, and unpleasant people. In America you are not free to say this." Later that same year, he described himself in a letter to his editor, Maxwell Perkins, as a "Revolutionary," "a brother to the workers," and proclaimed his apparently newfound belief "that this system that we have is evil, that it brings misery and injustice not only to the lives of the poor but to the wretched and sterile lives of the privileged classes who are supported by it." (Two interesting facts: Perkins cut a good deal of Marxist rhetoric out of *Of Time and the River;* Wolfe took the title of *You Can't Go Home Again* from a remark made at a dinner party by Lincoln Steffens's Communist widow, Ella Winter.)

But Wolfe was too full of himself to be sincerely devoted to any political idea. While reading proofs of his first novel, *Look Homeward, Angel,* at Scribner's, he wrote to John Hall Wheelock that "there are moments when I feel that no one else has a quarter of my power and richness. . . that, one way or another, I am a fine young fellow and a great man." He bragged to his mistress Aline Bernstein that she would be remembered in death because she would be "entombed in his writing" (a favorite image; perhaps Wolfe was identifying with his father, a carver of gravestones). As he loved himself, so he loved his own prose: his famous inability to edit himself manifestly derived not only from his lack of discipline and of editorial training but from his mindless adoration of every sentence, good or awful, that came out of him. "Every time he began a revision," writes Donald, "his incredibly tenacious memory recalled every word that he had included in all the previous drafts, and he could not bear to dispense with any of them." His short list of twentieth-century novelists included two names: his own and Hemingway's. One of his countless lady friends observed (with a rather Wolfean wordiness) that "he didn't really care about and care for other human beings in the way that most of us as human beings do."

Certainly Wolfe was capable of treating other people—even those closest to him—with remarkable cruelty and utterly unfounded distrust. This is especially true of his behavior toward Aline Bernstein, with whom he periodically severed all ties; not above hurling ethnic slurs at her, he brought their final encounter (in 1938) to a close by denouncing the Jews, wishing for them to be "wiped off the face of the earth," and calling for "three cheers for Adolf Hitler." In the end, however, his systematic alienation of everyone who cared for him hurt Wolfe more than anybody, and one cannot help but feel sorry for him. Time and again, one finds oneself reading a painful anecdote that brings to mind Scott Fitzgerald and Delmore Schwartz at their most pathetic. Early on Christmas morning of 1937, for example—having recently left his beloved editor, Max Perkins of Scribner's, for Edward Aswell of Harper & Brothers—Wolfe arrived at Aswell's home with a large stuffed toy dog for Aswell's little boy. But both man and dog were in horrible condition: "Gift-wrapped when Wolfe bought it, [the stuffed dog] had been used to wipe up the bars he had visited; the wrappings had come off, the box had disintegrated, and the tail was attached by only a few threads. 'Sorry to be late, Ed,' Wolfe greeted him. 'I hadn't meant to do this, but I got something here for your boy for Christmas.'"

Essentially, the story of Wolfe's life is a story of excess: too much liquor, too much impersonal sex (among his conquests was the wife of Soviet diplomat Maxim Litvinoff), too much disordered prose poured onto too many blank pages. Just as he loved America (of which, until the last years of his life, he actually saw very little) largely for its great size, and was very impressed by his own mammoth physical dimensions, so he seemed to regard sheer bulk as the prime characteristic of a great work of literature. You weren't a great writer, he believed, unless you produced a big, hefty book.

Donald does a good job of explaining, as far is as possible, how this disorganized, eternally dependent, incredibly puerile individual came into being. Interestingly, literature figured in his parents' first meeting. In 1884, in Asheville, North Carolina, Julia Westall, recently jilted by the love of her life, called on the newly widowed W. O. Wolfe to try to sell him the *Golden Treasury of Poetry and Prose*. The two fell into a literary discussion, a friendship developed, and within the year they were married. It was not a love match, however, but a practical arrangement: W. O. "needed someone to look after him and to cook for him," and Julia "needed someone to provide for her." As it turned out, though, Julia was the sort who likes to fend for herself, and Tom (born in 1900), the youngest of her seven children, grew up with both an unromantic image of marriage and an unusually chaotic view of family life. In 1904 Julia dragged most of her children to St. Louis, where she ran a boardinghouse that catered to World's Fair visitors; two years later, back in Asheville, she opened a boardinghouse called "The Old Kentucky Home" a few blocks from the Wolfe residence and took Tom to live with her there, leaving the other children with W. O. "For Tom," writes Donald,

> the move . . . marked a recognition that the turbulent disorganization of his family was not some transient phase but a permanent condition. . . . Constantly shifted from one room to another, obliged to eat his meals in a little pantry that Julia had scooped out in order to make more room for the boarders in the dining room, Tom was never sure whether his mother would caress him or neglect him. Growing up as an appendage to Julia, he did not develop a full sense of autonomy, the feeling that he was an independent person in his own right. For the rest of his life he felt obliged to attach himself to a stronger, older, wiser person, on whom he could lean, in order to feel complete.

Likewise, the extreme emotional shifts of his parents and siblings — affectionate toward Tom one minute, cruelly insulting the next — helped give rise to his own considerable talent for mood swings.

For the most part, Donald does not make excessive claims for Wolfe's writing. He admires Wolfe's fiction because "it offers a remarkably full social history of the United States during the first four decades of the twentieth century," and because it is "a barometer of American culture," reflecting the national temper of the Twenties and Thirties. While deploring the novels' formlessness and bad writing, moreover, Donald applauds Wolfe for his "unforgettable characters," "strong and crisply defined" individual episodes, and above all his "unique literary voice," particularly as manifested in his frequent outbursts of lyricism. These distinctions impress one as sensible and just. After all, for all the tons of chaff in Wolfe's novels, one cannot help but be moved by occasionally lyrical passages such as the following (which Aswell placed at the end of the posthumously published *You Can't Go Home Again,* and which affirms that the most felicitous influence upon Wolfe's style was the King James Bible): "Something has spoken to me in the night, burning the tapers of the waning year; something has spoken in the night, and told me I shall die, I know not where. Losing the earth we know for greater knowing, losing the life we have for greater life, and leaving friends we loved for greater loving, men find a land more kind than home, more large than earth."

Oddly, on the dustjacket of *Look Homeward,* Gore Vidal writes that "It is Professor Donald's discovery, or insight, that Thomas Wolfe was to prose what Walt Whitman was to poetry, but thanks to two editors, Perkins and Aswell, he was cut up into conventional 'novel-length' sections—as if *Leaves of Grass* had been reshaped by John Greenleaf Whittier." But Donald, though he does take Aswell to task for his high-handedness, never says any such thing. And of course Vidal is all wrong about Wolfe being another Whitman, or Perkins and Aswell being Philistines who mangled his beautiful work. If Wolfe had not the remarkable good fortune to happen upon Maxwell Perkins—whose reshaping of *Look Homeward, Angel* made it publishable (or, in Donald's view, "transformed it from an imperfectly executed American *Ulysses* into a first-rate novel about a boy's growing up") and who helped Wolfe carve *Of Time and the River* out of a mountain of disordered manuscripts —he would almost certainly never have become a published novelist, let alone one of the most celebrated authors of his time. The difference between Wolfe and Whitman—both of whom, admittedly, were capable of writing very, very badly—is that, whereas Whitman had an exquisite sense of form (notwithstanding the fact that he usually eschewed conventional forms), and revised his poetry numerous times in an attempt to perfect it formally, Wolfe was incompetent when it came to such things. In order for the words that he poured out in torrents to find any shape at all, he desperately needed an editor.

This is not to suggest that Wolfe's editors performed magic. Indeed, for all of Perkins's reorganization of the first two novels, Aswell's shaping and editing of *The Web and the Rock, You Can't Go Home Again,* and *The Hills Beyond,* and Nowell's meticulous condensation of his magazine pieces, Wolfe's *oeuvre* remains severely flawed. Though his books are at times charming and mesmerizing, to read them in sequence is, ultimately, to find them childish and tiresome in the extreme. There will always, perhaps, be those who fervently disagree: in death as in life, Wolfe is notorious for his ability to polarize readers. (Donald tells us of a *Saturday Review of Literature* poll conducted in 1935, in which *Of Time and the River* received the greatest number of votes for both best and worst novel of the year.) Besides, whatever the course of his literary reputation, one has the feeling that the legend of his life is here to stay, a romantic, compelling, strangely resonant chapter in the annals of American literary folklore. David Herbert Donald, in *Look Homeward,* has chronicled the life behind this legend—in all its craziness, fatuity, and chaos—with admirable intelligence and equipoise.

A Naked Wolfe

In 1936, Thomas Wolfe published a small book called *The Story of a Novel,* in which he described the composition of his second novel, *Of Time and the River* (which had been published the year before), rhapsodized about the history and mystery of his creative gift, and, in general, sang himself. Two years later he returned to the same vineyard and emerged with a somewhat smaller pressing of the same vintage. He called this second exercise in self-celebration "Writing and Living," and—in what turned out to be his last public appearance—presented it as a lecture at Purdue University in the summer of 1938. More than two decades afterward, in 1962, professors William Braswell and Leslie Field of Purdue added an introduction, copious textual notes, and two extensive appendices and published the lecture as a book to which they gave the flat but accurate title *Thomas Wolfe's Purdue Speech: "Writing and Living."*

Now, the same Professor Field has brought these two small books together, omitted the scholarly apparatus, and formed yet another small book, to which he has given the catchy if rather misleading title *The Autobiography of an American Novelist.* Granted, these *are* works of personal reminiscence, and *The Story of a Novel*—by far the better known and more interesting of the two pieces—is in part an American success story in the manner of Moss Hart's *Act One* and Norman Podhoretz's *Making It.*[1] In classic small-town-boy-makes-good style, Wolfe describes the longing to create that came to him in his childhood among "the working class of people" in Asheville, North Carolina; he recalls the education in playwriting which he received from Professor

George Pierce Baker at Harvard; he offers a diverting account of the writing, publication, and stunning success of his first novel, *Look Homeward, Angel,* the massive, chaotic manuscript of which did not impress anyone overmuch till it reached the desk of Maxwell Perkins, who found it worthy, made order of it, and gave Wolfe a hand up to a seat at the table of the immortals.

But all of this personal history is merely prefatory. The emphasis in both pieces in *The Autobiography of an American Novelist* is not on Wolfe's life but on his art. *The Story of a Novel* may be cousin to *Making It* but it is brother to such essays as Orwell's (and Joan Didion's) "Why I Write," William Stafford's "A Way of Writing," and Jacques Barzun's "A Writer's Discipline." It is the kind of piece that all writers must at one time or another feel tempted to write: writers, after all, aim to make sense of a mystery, and the mystery with which they come into contact most often is the writing process. It is when Wolfe attempts to penetrate this mystery, in *The Story of a Novel,* that he becomes most Wolfean. Seeking the best way of telling us what it felt like to write *Of Time and the River,* for example, he jumps nervously from one excessive metaphor to another. He begins by observing that the book was conceived, like the universe, "in a whirling vortex and a creative chaos." But the cosmic image does not seem to satisfy him, and he switches to meteorology: the book, he writes, was "a huge black cloud" inside him, "loaded with a kind of hurricane violence that could not be held in check much longer"; when the cloud finally opened, the book "came in torrents." But this image doesn't seem to do it either, and Wolfe turns to geology (the book came "like burning lava from the crater of a volcano") and to diabolism (the book, like a demon, "took hold of me and possessed me") and then back to meteorology: "it was exactly as if this great big storm cloud I have spoken of had opened up and, 'mid flashes of lightning, was pouring from its depths a torrential and ungovernable flood."

And so forth *ad infinitum,* or at least so it seems when you read it for the first time. Wolfe's grandiloquent tone is terribly grating, his verbosity appalling, his self-fascination tiresome, his un-self-conscious Cecil B. DeMille-izing of his experiences with pencil and paper embarrassing. But his worst defect is his pride in his defects. He tries to sound modest, but is quite unconvincing. He confesses: "I don't know how to write a story yet. I don't know how to write a novel yet. . . . I am the last, the worst, the least prepared to tell anyone how to write a story in such a way that it will sell to anything, no matter what." Humble? No. Translation: I am not a commercial writer; I don't know any hack tricks; I am a true *artiste,* acting completely on instinct, personal vision, call it what you will; *je suis dans le vrai.* Like many an artist, Wolfe enjoys thinking of himself as a divinely inspired boob, a country boy touched by the hand of God. Such a self-image makes it possible for him to construe his faults as virtues. He wears his indiscriminate copiousness, for instance, like a badge of honor; he is constantly reminding us how many millions of words he poured out while composing *Of Time and the River,* and how many thousands of pages they filled. He is equally boastful about his inability to carve a novel out of this formless mound of manuscript, and about his reliance upon Maxwell Perkins in this regard. He writes that "When a man's work has poured from him for almost five years like burning lava from a volcano . . . it is very difficult suddenly to become coldly surgical, ruthlessly detached." Thus it is a very good thing for a man to have a Doctor Perkins to call in for major surgery: scene transplantation, chapter excision. Although Wolfe pretends to be admitting a lamentable deficiency on his part, it is precisely his incompetence as a word surgeon that, to his way of thinking, separates him from all the Grub Street types, whose slick prose does *not* rise like lava from the hot core of the soul. Thus Wolfe's inability to give focus, balance, and structure to his work is not, according to his philosophy, a failing at all, but rather a mark of his special genius.

Clearly, Wolfe's understanding of the writing process was severely flawed. Somehow he never grew beyond the happy fecundity of the clever adolescent. He was mesmerized by his power to create but did not realize that being a writer means being able not only to surrender to the Muse but, at the same time, to be victorious over her—to master her, and press her into the service of some governing design. Wolfe never learned that what you do after you finish writing is the most important part of writing. In his cavalier attitude toward the part of writing that takes place after the lava has settled, and in his religious devotion to the small voice of truth within him, Wolfe was of course most American—a descendant of Thoreau and Whitman, an ancestor of Kerouac and Ginsberg. And indeed, if there is any reason for critics to dwell excessively on Wolfe, it is that he was one of the most American of writers. He is more of an expansive and spontaneous celebrator than Whitman, more of a transcendentalist than Emerson, more of a fabulist than Washington Irving, more of a confessional poet than Lowell or

Berryman or Plath, more a painter of grotesques than Sherwood Anderson or Frank Norris. Like Twain, Lewis, Dreiser, and Mencken, Wolfe is a self-proclaimed atheist, sinner, and exposer of Babbitts who is at heart a Puritan, a moralist, and a booster. Like William Carlos Williams he is fascinated by the characteristic rhythms of the American language; like Wallace Stevens he considers writing not a literary but a vital activity—to write is to give life, to edit is to kill.

In what was by far the most famous (or infamous) review to greet *The Story of a Novel* upon its appearance in 1936, Bernard DeVoto, writing in the *Saturday Review,* expressed his disgust at Wolfe's idiot-savant approach to writing. Regarding *Of Time and the River,* DeVoto wrote that "such organizing faculty and such critical intelligence as have been applied to the book have come not from inside the artist, not from the artist's feeling for form and esthetic integrity, but from the offices of Charles Scribner's Sons." Wolfe "has mastered neither the psychic material out of which a novel is made nor the technique of writing fiction." Although DeVoto was doing little more than reporting what Wolfe had written, many members of the literary community were outraged at his remarks. What is more, Wolfe was deeply hurt (though he did not admit it), and DeVoto's review planted in his psyche a seed of resentment toward Perkins that grew apace and led eventually to his departure from Scribner's.

One might suppose that Professor Field's *Autobiography of an American Novelist* is, at least in part, meant to combat the DeVoto-ism that has (as Wolfe might put it) taken hold of and possessed the critical establishment in the decades since Wolfe's death. Whatever efficacy the book might have had in this direction, however, has been entirely (and, I am sure, inadvertently) neutralized by Professor Field. For, rather than reprinting the competent version of *The Story of a Novel* published by Scribner's in 1936, which was the result of a major editing job by Wolfe's agent Elizabeth Nowell, Field has used instead Wolfe's twice-as-long, never-published-before, absolutely terrible original draft. In his preface Field mentions Nowell's editing, but makes it sound as if she thoughtlessly mutilated a masterpiece in order to get it published and collect her ten percent; the truth is that Nowell, a very fine and sensitive editor, improved greatly on a miserable mess. Her version is not, as Field describes it, an "incomplete form" of *The Story of a Novel,* but the authorized final draft. Her work, after all, was done under Wolfe's aegis; he looked her revision over before its book publication, restoring a few passages she had deleted but for the most part approving her cuts.

She tossed out only chaff, never wheat; she gave Wolfe focus, balance, concision, authority; she straightened out Wolfe's often mangled syntax, corrected his grammar and diction, and made sense of aimless, unbelievably redundant paragraphs in which he circled around and around an idea without expressing it clearly and of pointless sentences which he had actually forgotten to complete. Her expert blue-penciling clothed Wolfe to his best advantage; Field, on the other hand, has chosen for some reason to show the public a completely naked Wolfe, with his defects mercilessly exposed. Here, for example, is a passage from the original draft—the "complete form"—of *The Story of a Novel,* in which Wolfe discusses the period following the publication of *Look Homeward, Angel:*

> My name was known and I was being talked about. I would read about myself, for example, as one of the "younger American writers." I was the person who, some of the critics said, was to be watched. They were looking forward to my future book with interest and with a certain amount of apprehension. Here, too, my education as a writer was increasing all the time. Now, indeed, I could read about myself as a young American writer, and somehow the fact was more formidable than I had dreamed that it could be. I would read about my virtues and my defects as a writer and whether I showed promise of improving in the future or declining or whether I would ever produce another book. . . .

Very well. Point made. But Wolfe has only begun to make it. Later in the same paragraph he is still saying the same thing:

> Now I was a young American writer, discussed and talked about, and I would read about myself and hear doubts and hopes expressed about my second book and my future work and get letters and advice and criticism from friends and strangers, some of which asked me in a friendly way if I could go on, if I had shot my bolt or not, if I thought I had any more to write about, if I was done for, finished, emptied out, or if the seeds of life were in me, if the power was in me which could make me keep producing.

Eight synonymous expressions in one sentence: now the lava is really flowing. Wolfe goes on to a new paragraph but not a new idea:

> I was a young American writer, and they had hopes and fears about my future, and what I would do, or would it be anything, nothing, much, or little? Would the faults which they had found in my work grow worse

and would I conquer them? Was I another flash in the pan? Would I come through? What would happen to me?

Three paragraphs later—believe it or not—the song is still the same.:

> I was a young American writer; my first book had done well. The critics had begun to ask questions about the second book, so now I had to think about the second one as well.

The passage in which these sentences occur illustrates an unpleasant Wolfean habit: when he was unable to figure out immediately what to say next, he did not, like any other writer, pause and think about it; instead he just kept moving his pencil along.

There are in the original draft of *The Story of a Novel* numerous passages of this sort. When one turns to Nowell's revision—from which all such redundant ramblings have been expertly expunged—one wonders why Professor Field chose to use the original text in his book. For *The Story of a Novel,* as he presents it, is no service to the reader, and certainly no service to Wolfe. It may be thought a service to the science of textual scholarship, but I'm not so sure about this either. To work out the precise original text of *Hamlet* is a worthy goal; for each word of that text is part of a brilliantly shaped work of art. However, Wolfe's originals—as Wolfe himself admitted—were unshaped rough drafts; not until his pages had been reworked by others (in consultation with him) was the vision truly achieved, the approved text established. It may, then, be of historical interest to establish a first-draft text of *The Story of a Novel,* but to accept it as the definitive text, and to package it in a slim, attractive volume designed for the general reader, is absurd. By publishing this unpublishable rough version of *The Story of a Novel,* Professor Field is ignoring everything that is implicit in *The Story of a Novel.* He is doing something that Wolfe himself, who knew better, would never have done.

Glenway Wescott:

1901 – 1987

MAY 1987

To most literate Americans these days, the name probably means nothing. To some, who haven't read him but are aware of his reputation as an American expatriate writer contemporary with F. Scott Fitzgerald, Ernest Hemingway, and Gertrude Stein, it may conjure up vague images of Paris, the Riviera, and the transatlantic literary scene *entre deux guerres*. To those select few who are acquainted with his best writings, however, the name of Glenway Wescott, who died on February 22 at the age of eighty-five, doubtless recalls a number of very fine things: sensitively drawn characters; a witty and perceptive eye for detail; a prose of wonderful, almost Flaubertian, control, elegance, and penetration; and, above all, a rare delicacy and honesty of feeling—but feeling that has been digested, disciplined, transfigured into art.

Like Fitzgerald (who was five years his senior) and Hemingway (two years), Wescott was a son of the Midwest—a Wisconsin farm boy, to be specific—who began publishing at a very young age. His twenties —which were almost congruent with the 1920s (he was born in 1901)— were extraordinarily productive. By the time he was thirty-one, Wescott had published two books of poetry, *The Bitterns* (1920) and *Natives of Rock* (1925); three novels, *The Apple of the Eye* (1924), *The Grandmothers* (1927), and *The Babe's Bed* (1930); a collection of stories, *Good-Bye, Wisconsin* (1928); numerous book reviews (written in his very early twenties for *Poetry, The New Republic,* and *The Dial*); and two idiosyncratic books of non-fiction, *Fear and Trembling* and *A Calendar of Saints for Unbelievers,* whose failure on their publication in 1932 brought to an end this prolonged period of productivity. All of this writing was accomplished under the most unsettled of conditions. From the age of thirteen—when difficulties with his father forced him to leave home, and to live with his uncle and others—Wescott led a rambling life; after dropping out of the University of Chicago during his sophomore year, he spent periods in New Mexico, Wisconsin, Chicago, the Berkshires, New York, England, and Germany, finally settling in 1925 in France, where he remained until 1933.

The striking difference between Wescott's fiction of the Twenties and that of Fitzgerald and Hemingway is that Wescott's draws more explicitly on his family background. Compared to those two great contemporaries, Wescott seems to have felt more comfortable with himself and his parentage, more willing to accept—or, at least, to explore in his work—the overwhelming importance of his family, his Midwestern heritage, in the formation of his own character. While Fitzgerald was romanticizing his college days in *This Side of Paradise* and hinting elliptically at the depth of his feeling about his Minnesota upbringing in *The Great Gatsby,* and while Hemingway was writing about hunting and fishing in Michigan—but never about Mother and Dad in Oak Park— in numerous stories, Wescott was elaborately, almost compulsively, exploring his roots. Both *The Apple of the Eye* and *The Grandmothers* are based in large part on family stories that Wescott had heard, and on family events and situations that he had experienced.

The Apple of the Eye begins with a narrative of the rough and dreary life of Hannah Madoc, a rural Wisconsin spinster who, after her lover Jule Bier throws her over to marry Selma Duncan, becomes a bar girl, and then a broken-down hermit, old before her time, whose racy history has earned her the nickname "Bad Han." And yet Hannah's "badness" has provided her life with its only joy. "To her simple eye," Wescott writes, "nothing was degrading, nothing evil; everything formed a single difficult pure coil—moralless and pure." Years after Hannah's death, her story becomes a local legend to such young folk as Jule's daughter, Rosalia, and his girlish, moody fifteen-year-old nephew, Dan Strane (based on Wescott), who is devoted to sexual purity and to his deeply religious mother. Mike Byron, the Stranes' hired man, tries to change the boy's ideas about the impurity of sex, telling him that "everything is pure, everything is good that doesn't hurt somebody else." Dan becomes very attached to Mike, and when Mike and Rosalia fall in love and have an affair, Dan feels himself to be a part of it. But when Mike leaves, and Rosalia—suddenly horrified by the sins they have committed—kills herself, Dan blames Rosalia's death on Mike's "exaltation of sensuality, his evil love of life." Yet by and by, he discovers that even his uncle Jule doesn't blame Mike; instead, Jule suggests that "what is taught people, religion and morals and so on, are mostly to blame," and tells Dan the story of Hannah, who "knew the way to live." Hannah's life becomes a beloved myth for the boy, and at the end of the novel he goes away to college, his mother "praying for the perfection of his life, " Dan knowing that there can be no perfection, that his "business was to go on, just to go on," and that there is nothing wrong with taking pleasure where he finds it.

The Apple of the Eye is a peculiar hodge-podge of a book. It reads at the beginning like a Midwestern cross between *Maggie: A Girl of the Streets* and *Ethan Frome,* segues after Hannah's death into an all-white variation on *Their Eyes Were Watching God* (with Rosalia's mad scenes briefly evoking *Hamlet* IV:v), and ends up, after Rosalia's death, as a sort of minor-league Willa Catherish *Portrait of the Artist as a Young Man.* But *The Apple of the Eye* is not as good as any of these works, and Wescott, in 1924, was not yet as skilled as any of their authors. Especially in the opening chapters, the novel's style is extremely stiff; every word seems an effort, and not a sentence flows naturally. Wescott's descriptive chapters, and his metaphors and similes—many of them relating to nature, for he manifestly wants this to be a book of sensations, of sensuality, in which human sexual cravings and consummations and the smells and breaths and sounds of nature are intimately bound together —feel particularly forced and overdone: he cannot mention Hannah's barns without referring to their "bitter scent" or "fragrant gloom," cannot mention the cows inside the barns without speaking of their "profound mottled eyes and brutal lips" and "pure plush voices" or describing them as "[s]hadowy cattle [that] creaked in their wooden stanchions." Wescott hardly lets a noun into the book without gratuitously or clumsily modifying it ("the tawny marshes and harsh grasses," the "infrequent hairs" on Hannah's father's head and the "capable, fat hands" of the local doctor), hardly mentions an object without ingeniously comparing it to something else ("the herds of waterfowl in insubstantial letters on the sky," the crows with "their square notched wings like ragged sails"). In short, he tries too hard. For all the talk of passion, moreover, *The Apple of the Eye* is for the most part an inert object. We have to take Hannah's sensuality and Rosalia's sexual conflict—both of which are central to the novel—entirely on faith; the only truly believable character is in fact Dan Strane, and the only believable attraction that between Dan and Mike.

Wescott's second novel, *The Grandmothers,* subtitled "A Family Portrait," established him as one of the major American novelists of his generation. It is in every way an improvement over *The Apple of the Eye;* its style is assured and natural, many of its characters are three-dimensional, and it is quite affecting in the way that Wescott intended it to be. The book's focal character, Alwyn Tower—whose first and last names are quasi-anagrams for Glenway Wescott, as well as emblems of the boy's ambition and idealism (*all win tower*)—is, like Dan Strane, a version of Wescott himself; like Dan, too, with his devotion to the myth of Hannah Madoc, Alwyn is a student of his family's legendary past. *The Grandmothers,* indeed, is about the history of the Towers in Wisconsin, as that history exists in the consciousness of the young Alwyn Tower.

The book begins with two chapters entitled "The House" and "Alwyn's Knowledge of America and His Family," in which Alwyn —now a very young man moving in high-toned European circles—remembers being surrounded, during his Wisconsin childhood, by

> grandparents, and their friends, and old cousins, and great-aunts, and uncles; and behind each one a life had extended into the past like a corridor—poorly lighted, long corridors winding away in every direction, through reticence and forgetfulness, to their youth; and in the ring of rocking-chairs, the child for whose existence all the corridors had come together, had shivered in the gusts of emotion which blew vaguely down them, and tried to understand the strange syllables which echoed from one life to another.

Growing up, Alwyn "had noted every word of sentences he was not expected to understand, and added each detail, in his memory, to its proper nucleus. Little by little he had uncovered the life of his elders; little by little he had grown up. . . ." And throughout his adolescence and early manhood he had continued "[t]rying to understand, for his own sake, [the] shadowy men, women, and children [of his family]," for he felt that if he could come to understand the lessons of his forebears' lives—the lessons of their loves and hates, tragedies and failures —his own future would be less of a riddle, and he would be less likely to devote himself to "useless ambitions" or to be hampered by "unreasonable aversions." And gradually the story of his family did take shape in his mind, a story of solemn and pious people who had worked hard and never prospered as they deserved to, a story of a "long series of passions which had in the end produced himself." He discovered that their lives had ended in regret, a regret "which weakened and then strengthened his will: regret that the time for laughter and ease, even for him, seemed never to come, while work never came to an end."

The opening chapters of *The Grandmothers* are succeeded by a dozen chapters with titles like "His Mother's Girlhood and Marriage" and "His Great-Aunt Nancy," each telling the story of a different member of Alwyn's family. The first of these chapters is about his grandfather Tower, a small man whose early years had been exciting and tragic: he brought the family from New York to Wisconsin, suffered great hardship, fought in the Civil War, lost his first wife to a fever, and married his brother Leander's abandoned sweetheart, Rose Hamilton. As with Bad Han, things settled down after those early adventures, and "[t]he rest of his life seemed unimportant." Subsequent chapters tell the stories of Grandmother Rose Tower; Alwyn's bachelor uncle Leander (who as a young man was adored not only by Rose but by his younger brother Hilary, a relationship that closely echoes Mike and Dan's in *The Apple of the Eye*); of Uncle Evan (an Army deserter); and so forth. What is interesting about all these chapters—these lives—is the way in which they fit together, and at the same time do not. The lives of the Towers are like facets of a gem; however close they may be to one another, each views the world from a different window. The profoundest passions and longings of one remain a secret to most of the others for decades; events which assume cataclysmic significance in one life are mere footnotes in another; one person's trifling action changes another's life forever. The lives of the Towers, then—like the lives of all families—are at once elaborately interwoven and utterly separate.

There are many similarities between *The Apple of the Eye* and *The Grandmothers*. Both reject the notion that a novel should concern itself throughout with the adventures of a single protagonist. (Indeed, Wescott's practice, in *The Grandmothers,* of shifting from one character to another as a means of telling a family's story is reminiscent of *To the Lighthouse,* which was published in the same year.) Both novels trace the events of a young man's life as well as events—which to him are no less than mythic—in his family's past; in both novels, what the young man learns about those past events helps him to decide upon the course he will take in life. There are also several more specific parallels. Dan and Alwyn, for example, both have mothers who are "saint[s] on earth," eager for their sons to live purely; both boys have unsympathetic fathers who love to hunt and are not very cerebral.

As in *The Apple of the Eye,* moreover, there is sometimes too much needless description of landscapes and animals in *The Grandmothers;* lists of farm chores and house furnishings and the like abound. It is as if Wescott wants to preserve every impression he remembers from childhood, every anecdote he has heard; as if he wants to provide as thorough an account as possible of the way these people lived. Despite this occasional tendency to go overboard with detail, however, on the whole the book works marvelously. There is something wonderfully mature about it, about its quiet recognition that we are all the products of our families, and that the better we understand them the better we can understand—and create—ourselves. At the end of the novel Alwyn opts for a life different from those his antecedents have lived, and Wescott applauds this decision, and wants us to do the same; but this does not prevent him from regarding the lives and choices of the other members of the family with awe and humility and respect. Indeed, it is in large part Wescott's tacit but powerful respect for the past that makes the book so affecting. To be sure, there are tedious passages, and it might be argued that the book is less than the sum of its parts—for the "lessons" that Alwyn has learned from his examination of the family history are never spelled out very plainly. Wescott does intimate, however, that Alwyn is in some way like his old bachelor uncle Leander, and that the lessons he has learned—like Dan's—have a good deal to do not only with choosing not to be a Wisconsin farmer but with defying the conventional Tower attitudes toward sexual behavior. *The Grandmothers* is in a sense an *apologia pro vita sua* —a declaration by Wescott of his great loyalty and affection for his country, state, and family, along with an attempt to account for his departure from them and their traditions. It is certainly the best of Wescott's full-length novels.

In both *The Apple of the Eye* and *The Grandmothers,* however, Wescott's explanations of his young heroes' motivations are less than completely candid; to read either of these books is to have the sense that something of consequence is being dealt with but never explicitly acknowledged. That subject is homosexuality. The fact is that Wescott was homosexual; his longtime companion was Monroe Wheeler, at one time a curator at the Museum of Modern Art, whom Wescott met in his teens and lived with into his old age. The otherwise puzzling events of Wescott's early years—the difficulties with his father that forced him to leave home at age thirteen, and a suicide attempt at age eighteen (at which time he was engaged to be married to a young woman), followed by his withdrawal from college—seem to make more sense if one knows that he was homosexual. So, for that matter, does the eight-year silence that followed the publication of *A Calendar of Saints for Un-believers* in 1932. In his early novels and stories, Wescott—who was plainly, at that point, an autobiographical writer—had exhausted the material of his childhood and youth. What was left for him to write about? *The Grandmothers* reads like a prolegomenon to a body of autobiographical fiction, a series of novels centered on Alwyn Tower's adult life—and for Alwyn Tower, of course, read Glenway Wescott. But in the 1930s Wescott could hardly write about the life he was leading with Monroe Wheeler. In *The Grandmothers* he had written a book about a family, a book that almost anyone could identify with; but few readers, at that time anyway, would have regarded an equally sensitive and candid novel based on Wescott's adult domestic life with anything other than horror.

The publication of *Fear and Trembling* and *A Calendar of Saints* at the very end of his long period of productivity suggests that Wescott may have been contemplating a switch to non-fiction. If so, the dismal reception of those books must have killed that idea. This is not to suggest that the reception was undeserved. Indeed, whereas Wescott's best novels and stories were masterpieces of restraint, some of his non-fiction was downright undisciplined and self-indulgent. The deliberately outrageous *A Calendar of Saints* may be the most egregious instance of this; it consists of sardonic versions of the saints' lives, the overall point being that the saints' unyielding idealism, far from being admirable, was tragically self-defeating. (This rejection of the concept of perfectibility is reminiscent, incidentally, of the end of *The Apple of the Eye*.) *A Calendar of Saints* strikes one as a book that Wescott—obviously raised in a pious environment—had to get out of his system; that it was published in a limited edition indicates that Wescott knew it would have extremely limited appeal.

By contrast, the ignominious failure of *Fear and Trembling*—a longer

and far more ambitious book—seems genuinely to have shocked him
(and continued to embarrass him decades later). The book—which is
based upon the observations made by Wescott and three of his friends
(including Wheeler) while touring Europe by car in 1931—attempts not
only to understand, but to provide a set of solutions to, the dauntingly
complex international crisis that was then taking shape in Europe. But
the book has little to offer aside from unsupported overstatements, wild
poetic surmises, and euphuistically rendered impressions. It is naïve
and facile, redundant and self-contradictory; Wescott behaves as if
everything he notices, and each inchoate conclusion that pops into his
head, is worth our attention. This would be an unfortunate posture under any circumstances, but given the dreadful solemnity of his principal
subject, it is truly offensive. Indeed, for all its supposed seriousness, the
book contains many flippant passages, campy asides, tongue-in-cheek
quips, irreverent anecdotes, discussions of where in Europe he'd most
like to live, and the like. It is tasteless to mix such material in with
sentences like the following:

> We passed under a tree laden with green apples, also bearing in its bran-
> ches at the moment two brown hungry boys who, when they have
> ripened a little, will make very good eating for one of those new short
> guns with wide mouths.

Placed in its context in *Fear and Trembling,* this sentence strikes me as
stupefyingly callous. If Wescott really believed these boys would die in
a war within the next few years (as perhaps one or both of them did) he
shouldn't have written about their fate so glibly, should have seen the
tastelessness of discussing his pleasure jaunt and these boys' tragic fate
in the same work. Wescott seems almost smug in his awareness that he
will be able to escape to America in the event of a European war,
whereas these boys will have to tough it out, perhaps fight, perhaps
even sacrifice their lives.

For all his impatience with idealism, furthermore, Wescott's supposed solutions to the European crisis are ridiculously unrealistic.
Here's his standard ploy: he names an obvious problem, and his "solution" is to say that the problem must be eliminated. Take the problem
of militarism and xenophobia. Solution: "The martial impulses must be
paralyzed, the national liberties must be taken away...." Another pre-
scription: the West needs "renewed faith in wealth"—or, to put it dif-

ferently, "[t]he better practice of luxury by a few persons on a larger scale." (The best that can be said for this opinion is that it must have taken a great deal of courage to hold in the literary and intellectual world of the Thirties.) Not that wealth is better than poverty. *Au contraire*, the poor are better off poor: if they were rich they'd be more sybaritic, less strong and healthy (for the "genuinely and purely poor," he writes, are *always* healthy). Indeed, "poverty may be merely an unforeseen sort of wealth." And besides, the workers are as a rule "a good deal handsomer than their masters." (Handsomeness, by the way, is a topic that the very handsome Wescott returns to frequently, and often disconcertingly, in *Fear and Trembling* —remarking, for example, upon the "wondrously handsome" faces in the photographs of the Bolshevik hordes.) Among Wescott's other prescriptions: the bourgeois have "made a mess of his world" and now it should be "the neurotic's turn"; children should be given the vote; inferior couples should be sterilized. Like many in the 1930s, Wescott pronounces democracy a failure. But unlike many, he seems not to have understood quite clearly that what was shaping up in Europe was a decisive confrontation between democracy and tyranny, and that for all the problems of democracy, its survival was essential to the maintenance of everything that he valued.

After his silence of the Thirties, Wescott produced two more long works of fiction, *The Pilgrim Hawk* (1940) and *Apartment in Athens* (1945). The former, a novella, is perhaps his most nearly perfect work —taut, subtle, and exquisitely ordered. It takes place on a single afternoon in May of 1928 or 1929—the narrator, Alwyn Tower, can't quite remember which, since so many years have passed—in a house at Chancellet, outside of Paris, where he then lived with his "great friend Alexandra Henry," also known as Alex, who would later marry his brother. On that May afternoon some friends of Alex's, a rich, foolish Irish couple named Larry and Madeleine Cullen, come to visit, bringing with them Mrs. Cullen's new pilgrim hawk, Lucy. Mrs. Cullen's affection for, treatment of, and remarks about Lucy (particularly her hunger) cause Alwyn to think about, and to see the hawk as a symbol of, a variety of things. For instance, Mrs. Cullen's observation that falcons feel hunger more intensely than people makes Alwyn reflect that "[a]lthough I had been a poor boy, on a Wisconsin farm and in a slum in Chicago and in Germany in 1922, I could not recollect any exact sensation of hunger, that is to say, hunger of the stomach." But he thinks of the other hungers he has known:

> For example, my own undertaking in early manhood to be a literary art-ist. No one warned me that I really did not have talent enough. Therefore my hope of becoming a very good artist turned bitter, hot and nerve-racking; and it would get worse as I grew older. The unsuccessful artist also ends in apathy, too proud and vexed to fly again, waiting upon with-held inspiration, bored to death.

He thinks about sexual hunger, too, about the fact that "[y]outhfulness persists, alas, long after one has ceased to be young. Lovelife goes on in-definitely, with less and less likelihood of being loved, less and less ability to love, and the stomach-ache of love still as sharp as ever. The old bachelor is like an old hawk." And as Alwyn continues to observe the hawk, his sense of identity with it intensifies, his emotions sharpen: "old bachelor hungry bird," he thinks, "aging-hungry-man-bird, and how I hate desire, how I need pleasure, how I adore love, how difficult middle age must be!"

And how difficult marriage. The novella is largely about the Cul-lens's marriage and about Alwyn's attitude toward it. It is not a perfect marriage, for although they are very much in love, Larry resents the hawk enormously; it's a terrible nuisance and an embarrassment, he tells Alwyn, and often comes between them in the most hurtful ways. Consequently, when Madeleine puts Lucy out in Alex's garden, Larry covertly cuts its leash, removes its hood, and lets it fly away. And yet, after the bird has enjoyed a few moments of freedom, it returns will-ingly to Mrs. Cullen—for it is still hungry. Alwyn, having been thrilled by the bird's freedom, equally enjoys "the little spectacle of her capture or surrender," and is surprised at himself for this. His reaction makes him aware "of my really not wanting Larry Cullen to escape from Mrs. Cullen either, or vice versa. Perhaps I do not believe in liberty, or I re-gard it as only episodic in life; a circumstance that one must be able to bear and profit by when it occurs; a kind of necessary evil. When love it-self is at stake, love of liberty as a rule is only fear of captivity."

What happens in *The Pilgrim Hawk,* in short, is that Alwyn Tower, now fortyish, remembers a day in his late twenties—the twilight of his youth—when the visit of a troubled married couple with a hungry hawk caused him to think about his own hungers, and to see clearly the future ahead of him: no marriage, no writing. But much remains un-spoken in the novella. What, for instance, is the relationship between Alex and Alwyn? Apparently they lived together for a considerable length of time—Alwyn, after all, can't remember what year it was in which the Cullens visited—but, judging from the way they talk to each other about sex and love, there is no romance between them, no physi-cal relationship. They are not lovers but *Doppelgängern,* two seemingly carefree young unmarrieds who in truth find themselves rather envying even a very troubled and tacky married couple and who fear a lonely, unproductive future full of unsatisfied longings. (Their likeness is sym-bolized, incidently, by the similarity of their names.) The difference be-tween them, however, is that Alex will eventually marry and Alwyn will not. As in *The Apple of the Eye* and *The Grandmothers,* the unmen-tioned subject here is homosexuality: it is not absolutely necessary, to be sure, that one assume Alwyn to be homosexual, but it makes his cer-tainty about his increasingly lonely, marriageless future far more un-derstandable.

The Pilgrim Hawk was not Wescott's first work to deal with mar-riage. The short stories that he published in *Good-Bye, Wisconsin* in 1928 are full of weddings, which invariably symbolize an end to possibility and the beginning of captivity. In a story called "The Wedding March," for instance, the wedding bell, in the mind of a young groom, becomes "a death knell," and the walls of the church in which the wedding takes place are described as being "the color of a tomb." Similarly, at the end of "The Whistling Swan," the story's young protagonist, who has been planning to go to Paris and become a great composer, decides instead to stay in Wisconsin and (probably) to "hold his peace—a dumb, whole-some, personal peace. Talk about Paris, who cared, who cared? . . . That night he accepted the offer of the college in the south of the state, and agreed with Muriel to be married at once." To marry, in these youthful stories, is to deny oneself, to repeat the mistakes of one's fore-bears, to head down the same bleak, well-worn, unsurprising path. In *The Pilgrim Hawk* Alwyn recognizes that, for all the grotesqueries and limitations of marriage, it may not, in truth, be the grimmest of all pos-sible fates. The things he avoided marriage in order to pursue—his writing, his love life—seem to him to have little future in them, and what will he have when they're gone completely? For the first time, perhaps, Alwyn sees that he will not win all.

The Pilgrim Hawk is an exemplary novella in the classic tradition, its manner stately and elliptical, its characters subtly and ironically etched. Wescott weaves together his various themes—art and love, freedom and captivity, desire and satiation—with great elegance. And yet, in this work that may represent the height of his achievement, he essentially accuses himself of having little talent and hints that his awareness of this failing is responsible not only for the preceding eight-year dry spell but for the dry spells that will follow. (Interestingly, in his entry in *Twentieth Century Authors,* published two years after *The Pilgrim Hawk,* Wescott echoed this self-evaluation: "I have had good luck in every respect but one; my talent has not seemed equal to my opportunities or proportionate to my ideas and ideals. . . .") William H. Rueckert, in his Twayne-series study of Wescott, even goes so far as to say that *The Pilgrim Hawk* is "Wescott's goodbye to fiction and to himself as a novelist."

Though Wescott was to publish one more novel after *The Pilgrim Hawk,* in a sense it does represent a leave-taking, for it was his last major fictional work in which the protagonist is plainly a variation on the author. *Apartment in Athens,* by contrast, is a completely fictional work—even, one might say, a completely impersonal book, an act of creative will. Described by Wescott at the time as his "war work," it tells the story of the Helianos family of Athens—Nikolas, a middle-aged publisher; his wife; their retarded ten-year-old daughter, Leda; and their sickly twelve-year-old son, Alex—during the German occupation, when a captain named Ernst Kalter is billeted in their house. Nikolas believes in cooperating with the cruel, insensitive Captain Kalter; it wouldn't do any good, he feels, to be heroic. When Kalter, having been promoted to major, returns from a brief trip to Germany a much sadder and kinder man, Nikolas is eager to take advantage of this change, eager to fan the flames of humanity in Kalter's soul; he becomes a sort of confidant, or at least sounding-board, for Kalter (who eventually explains his newfound gentleness and despondency by saying that he has recently lost his wife and two sons in the war). The two men discuss the war, and when Kalter confesses his weariness of it, Nikolas expresses his sorrow that two men, the Führer and the Duce, could bring such tragedy upon so many other men. And it is this remark that seals his doom. At once Kalter reverts to being the cold-blooded representative of an occupying power; summarily he has Nikolas arrested and imprisoned.

Up to this point *Apartment in Athens* seems nearly flawless. Unerringly structured and paced, it is the sort of meticulously wrought novel—with a Hellenic austerity and lack of sensationalism—that is criticized by some for being cold, artificial, fussy, labored; yet in truth there is not a single false note in it. After Helianos is sent to prison, however, the book changes abruptly. The story goes limp, and Wescott becomes tiresomely didactic. The closing pages of the book, indeed, are reminiscent of one of those World War Two-vintage movies whose conclusions dispense with the need for a proper dramatic climax and denouement and offer instead a non-sequitur pep talk directed at the audience. (Diana Trilling, in *The Nation,* was particularly hard on Wescott for taking this didactic turn, complaining that the book was not much different from dozens of other anti-Nazi novels she had read. "We don't expect a writer of Mr. Wescott's caliber," she complained, "to use his talents in the service of propaganda.") But to blame the weak ending on the wartime atmosphere would be misleading, for, as Edmund Wilson justly observed at the time, the endings of Wescott's works of fiction are generally their weakest parts. "The incisive beginnings," Wilson wrote, "are sometimes betrayed by a tendency to blur at the close; the sure hand, with its deliberate strokes, seems to falter when it comes to the point of drawing the action to a head and driving the meaning home."

Its ending notwithstanding, *Apartment in Athens* is a very fine book. Considering that Wescott was nowhere near Greece during the war, it is something of a tour de force, for it captures convincingly the Helianos family's sense of oppression, their painful conflict between pride and the instinct for survival. Why is the book set in Greece? Primarily, one has the impression, because in important ways the Greeks and the Germans form a sharp contrast to one another. First, in attitudes toward fate: "You naturally are afraid of fate," Kalter tells Nikolas. "We are not afraid, because we have identified with it, we are active in it, we are it. Whatever happens, yes, we have the satisfaction of knowing that we have helped it along, with all our might, with a whole heart. If it is not what we expected we care little—it is a change, it is creative! Nothing we have had anything to do with will ever be the same again." What's more, the Greeks consider "private life greater than public life, which [is] the opposite of German principle." Finally, Germans are utopians; they believe in the possibility "that one day at last the world will be well-governed, by those willing and able and worthy to govern it—not always in a mess as it is now." Greeks are more realistic. (This is one way, at least, in which *Apartment in Athens* can be thematically connected to Wescott's earlier fiction: just as *The Apple of the Eye* and *The Grandmothers* contrast the sexually realistic attitudes of Dan and Alwyn with the religious utopianism of their mothers, so *Apartment in Athens* contrasts the socially realistic attitude of Helianos with the Nazi utopianism of Major Kalter.)

During the more than four decades that followed the appearance of *Apartment in Athens,* Wescott published only one book, *Images of Truth* (1962). It is a collection of eight long, highly impressionistic critical essays about six writers—Katherine Anne Porter, Somerset Maugham, Colette, Isak Dinesen, Thomas Mann, and Thornton Wilder—all of whom Wescott admired greatly and most of whom he knew personally. (The book's subtitle is "Remembrances and Criticism.") The book is gracefully conversational, and demonstrates considerable critical acuity and—even more so—a charming gift for appreciation. But it is most valuable, perhaps, for what it tells us about Wescott's literary tastes. He is, to judge by his remarks, a foursquare anti-modernist and a lover of small, elegant, well-ordered books that attempt to illuminate a character or situation. Wescott confides that he dislikes Virginia Woolf for her "herculean minutiae of form and style," and that he doesn't care much for Henry James because—strangely enough—James was the first important writer to evade "the responsibility of omniscient understanding"; he cites *The Golden Bowl, Finnegans Wake, The Making of Americans,* and *The Trial* and *The Castle* as "arch-examples of the withering away or frittering away of the novelist's old authoritativeness, and general and objective knowledge, and firm grasp of human nature." There is no significant mention in the book of either Fitzgerald or Hemingway. Wescott admires Maugham and Colette because they "have systematized their novel writing and narrowed it down, in order to combine a measure of craftsmanship and fine finish with a desired expeditiousness and productivity." He calls Colette's *Le Pur et l'Impur* "a work of gospel truth" which "has greatly guided me in my own life and love life." (Certainly the notion that there is nothing impure about consensual sex is central to much of his fiction.)

His two favorite English-language novels published in his lifetime would seem to be Wilder's *The Ides of March* and Maugham's *Christmas Holiday.* Both are works of "political allegory," but neither is a "propaganda novel"; rather, both are concerned with the "human equation." Wilder's novel about the assassination of Julius Caesar appeals to him "more . . . than any other novel by a fellow American of my generation" because it gives an "extraordinary impression of a fate running its course." Maugham's is one of the best novels of the century because it "explains more of the human basis of fascism and Nazism and communism than anyone else has done." To read Wescott's encomia for these two books—one need not even be familiar with the novels themselves—is to recognize that at least one thing he was trying to do in *Apartment in Athens* was to explain, by focusing of the character of a single human individual, Major Kalter, the nature and workings of the Nazi mentality. (It is worth noting that Wescott has nothing to say about such larger, noisier novels of World War II as *The Naked and the Dead*.)

In the last twenty-five years of his life Wescott published next to nothing. Though he reportedly continued to write, he was presumably unable to complete a book—to his satisfaction, anyway. Until his final days he resided in the New Jersey farmhouse which he had occupied since 1943. But he was no Salingeresque hermit: he was very active in the American Academy of Arts and Letters (serving as its president from 1959 to 1962) and other writers' organizations, and was a familiar face at high-society soirees on both sides of the Atlantic. He also continued to keep a diary, which is said to be perhaps his most provocative production of all, with its commentary on his famous friends and its candid accounts of Wescott's own sexual exploits; a brief and intriguing portion of it, entitled "Paris 1938," appeared in the inaugural issue of *Grand Street*.

Until such time as Wescott's diary is released to the world, however, we have his fiction—a sophisticated body of work that is, alas, less appreciated than it should be. He was at once an accomplished stylist and a gifted observer of human behavior, good at manners and morals, at little details and little ironies; he observed the way people cheer themselves up out of momentary dark moods by being eloquent at small talk, observed the subtle interplay of suspicion and resentment and envy and love that takes place between a husband and wife in the course of a seemingly inconsequential dinner-party confrontation. He was, to be sure, intent upon knowing himself, and *did* know himself, but somehow managed not to be full of himself. There is in his finest work an appealing gentleness and humility for which, despite all their brilliance, many of the indubitably greater fiction writers of his time are not especially known. Somehow he seems to have been able to accept his failings more easily than they could accept theirs. He didn't play roles, didn't pretend to be better than he was, or to know things that he didn't know. He knew in fact that he was less than perfect, and he seems to have managed to have lived a relatively serene life with this knowledge. (This, come to think of it, may be why his stories don't end as decisively, as strongly, as they might: because he didn't want to pretend to be more certain than he was of what the final outcome of his heroes' decisions would be, what the future would hold, what the ultimate point was.) To read the body of work that he has left behind is not only to marvel at its charm and polish but to admire its probity and seriousness of purpose—a seriousness that is evident even in his most precocious fiction. That Glenway Wescott has fallen into near-obscurity is a measure less of his own failings than of the misbegotten values of the literary culture that has allowed him to fall.

III

Salinger's Arrested Development

SEPTEMBER 1986

> *When I was a child, I spake as a child, I un-*
> *derstood as a child, I thought as a child: but*
> *when I became a man, I put away childish*
> *things.* —I CORINTHIANS 13:11

Though his only novel, *The Catcher in the Rye*, is one of the sturdiest best-sellers of the post-World War II era—a staple of high-school English courses, and a standard according to which every newly published tale of tortured adolescence is inevitably judged—Jerome David Salinger is probably as famous for his elusiveness as for his work. He has been called "the Greta Garbo of American literature," and the more one thinks about it, the more appropriate the epithet seems to be. As Garbo's early retirement into seclusion was triggered by the disastrous reception of her movie *Two-Faced Woman*, so Salinger's decision to go into personal and professional hiding appears to have been provoked by the refusal of both the reviewers and the public to approve of the direction in which his last book—*"Raise High the Roofbeam, Carpenters" and "Seymour: An Introduction"* (two stories published together in 1963)—indicated he was developing. As in the case of Garbo, though, Salin-

NOTE: Random House was enjoined by the U.S. Court of Appeals from publishing *J.D. Salinger: A Writing Life*. In February 1988 Random House announced publication of a substantially revised book by Ian Hamilton titled *In Search of J.D. Salinger*.

ger's insistence upon being left alone served only to increase the public's curiosity about him, thus preserving his celebrity status throughout a long period of professional inactivity; indeed, it might reasonably be argued that his love of privacy has, in the years since his departure from the active literary scene, made him a "legend" in a way that his work alone could never have done. Four decades after Salinger vouchsafed *Catcher* to the world, *Gatsby*-like gossip about the master's past, present, and future activities continues to make the rounds, and curious folk still make the pilgrimage to his Cornish, New Hampshire, sanctuary in hopes of glimpsing him through a hole in the fence. In short—and herein lies the ultimate irony in this most bizarre set of circumstances— it is precisely his fanatically enforced privacy that, more than anything else, has helped to place J. D. Salinger's life and not his writing at the focus of public scrutiny.

Given this state of affairs, it seems likely that Ian Hamilton's forthcoming para-biography, *J. D. Salinger: A Writing Life,* will generate an enormous amount of interest. I call it a "para-biography" because to use the word "biography," in this instance, would be egregiously misleading. Mr. Hamilton, a distinguished English poet who brought forth a solid if somewhat fact-happy life of Robert Lowell four years ago, has simply been unable to gather enough material to produce a full-fledged biography of Salinger. This is not to say that the book lacks detail. Indeed, it is altogether too plentifully stocked with gratuitous trivia—with, for example, quotations from the movie reviews Salinger contributed to his college newspaper and bits and pieces of every letter (apparently) that Hamilton could get his hands on. What the book is short on, however, is detail that is illuminating and appropriate. Though Hamilton usefully summarizes Salinger's literary career—giving us synopses, reviews, contract arrangements—he does not even come close to providing a vivid, coherent rendering of Salinger's life. The subject never really comes into focus. And the scraps of personal material that Hamilton *has* been able to collect—most of which concern Salinger's life in military school, college, and the army (the three periods when he was forced, day and night, into the company of others)—are frequently either misconstrued or over-analyzed. (Most of this information has previously appeared in print anyway, notably in *J. D. Salinger* by Warren French, the revised edition of which appeared in 1976 from Twayne Publishers.)

Stylistically, the book is a disappointment. The prose lacks fastidiousness; grammatical errors abound. The most annoying stylistic feature is the constant and inexplicable—and often very awkward— shifting of tense. More important, Hamilton sometimes draws unwarranted conclusions from highly tenuous bits of evidence—a habit that he evinces in the very first lines of the book. "J. D. Salinger," he writes, "has often said that he 'started writing at the age of fifteen,' as if this was when, for him, real life began." That, to my mind, is a most peculiar "as if"; certainly most of Salinger's fiction suggests that, much to the contrary, real life *ended* for him at the age of fifteen. But Hamilton's reason for beginning his book with such a slippery piece of logic soon becomes clear: having discovered next to nothing about Salinger's first fifteen years, he wishes to justify that period's almost complete omission from the book by underrating its importance to Salinger's development. For Hamilton's coverage of Salinger's youth consists of little more than an assortment of vital statistics. We learn that Salinger's mother was Irish; that his father, Sol, an importer of cheese and ham, was a Jew, born in Chicago in 1888, apparently a willful sort, perhaps the son of a Cleveland rabbi; and that the writer's only sibling is a sister, Doris, fully eight years his senior. We gather also that the cheese and ham importing business flourished during the writer's boyhood, for the family kept moving, in those years, to increasingly affluent neighborhoods. When Jerome was born on New Year's Day in 1919, the Salingers lived far uptown, at 3681 Broadway; later that year they moved to 113th Street; by 1928 they were at 221 West 82nd Street and four years afterwards they took occupancy of an apartment on Park Avenue at Ninety-first Street. In his early years Jerome attended public schools; later he transferred to the McBurney School on West Sixty-fourth Street, where he accumulated a below-average academic record, reported for the school paper, and earned enthusiastic notices for his performances (invariably in female roles) in school plays. And that, essentially, is all that Hamilton gives us on the childhood of a writer whose fiction is enigmatically obsessed with the theme of childhood—whose entire *oeuvre* cries out for a biographer able to shed some light on the reasons for its strange fixation.

It is not till Salinger reaches military school that we begin to get a picture of him—albeit a fuzzy one. At age fifteen, Hamilton tells us, Jerome was suddenly plucked out of McBurney and enrolled in the Valley Forge Military Academy in Valley Forge, Pennsylvania, where he continued to write and act. (Because his application to the academy was "hastily filled out" by his father, Hamilton deduces that Sol was, for some reason or other, "out of patience" with Jerome; and he uses this conclusion, in turn, to support his hypothesis that father and son didn't get along well.) Salinger, who appears to have been the Oscar Wilde of Valley Forge, is remembered by former classmates for his "sardonic wit," "sizzling wisecracks," and "sophistication and humor." "He always talked in a pretentious manner," recalls one former cadet, "as if he were reciting something from Shakespeare." "His conversation," remembers another, "was frequently laced with sarcasm about others and the silly routines we had to obey and follow at school." To his friends at Valley Forge, most of whom were small-town Pennsylvania boys, Salinger was the "big city boy" who "knew about Broadway shows, and read *The New Yorker* and *Esquire*," and who dreamed of writing movies in Hollywood. A telling example of Hamilton's tendency to cover less-than-crucial material at excessive length is his discussion of the 1936 Valley Forge yearbook, of which Salinger was the literary editor. Hamilton devotes several pages to an overly ingenious analysis of the yearbook's utterly routine contents, which he assumes were entirely the work of Salinger. Hamilton purports to detect a subtle irony in the yearbook, and in his defense of this notion he seems (not for the only time, either) to employ circular logic. If, he argues, Salinger wrote the effusive Class History, the fawning tribute to the school's founder, and the pious Class Song, then surely they are meant to be, on their deepest level, parodic; if so, then surely they are by Salinger. Having thus established that the young Salinger was simultaneously sycophantic and insubordinate, Hamilton proceeds to draw a parallel between this apparently two-faced quality of the writer-to-be and the combination of nonconformity and submissiveness that characterizes Holden Caulfield, the boy hero of *The Catcher in the Rye*.

At times, it should be noted, Hamilton does make too deliberate an attempt to identify Caulfieldian traits in the young Jerome. Yet the fact remains that there *are* a surprising number of parallels between Salinger's life at Valley Forge and Holden's life at the fictional Pencey Prep. Hamilton informs us, for instance, that there actually was a boy at Valley Forge who, like James Castle in *The Catcher in the Rye*, fell to his death from a dormitory window; that at Valley Forge, Salinger, like Holden Caulfield, chronically used the expression "a prince of a guy" to describe people he disliked; that Salinger's roommate, Ned Davis, was apparently the model for Holden's narcissistic roommate Stradlater; and that one night Salinger "became so impossibly drunk and 'Holden Caulfield-ish,' vowing to break out of the school once and for all, that a close friend had to fell him with a knockout punch to prevent him from waking the militia."

Like Holden, too, Salinger was (to use a word that is nearly ubiquitous in his fiction) something of a "phony." Following his graduation from Valley Forge, a year at New York University (though he left "no trace of ever having been there"), a job entertaining the passengers on a cruise ship, and several months in Vienna on business for his father, Salinger entered Ursinus College, where he proceeded to behave like a full-blown snob. His purported reason for attending Ursinus—a science-oriented Pennsylvania school whose students were principally middle-class Pennsylvania Dutch locals—was that "he needed a quiet place to write." But why Ursinus? Hamilton surmises that it may have been easier for Salinger to get into than other colleges: since it was near Valley Forge, perhaps "some local strings were pulled" to get Salinger in. Yet one has the feeling that Ursinus—rather than, say, NYU or Columbia or some other Ivy League university—filled a crucial need for Salinger in that it provided a place where he could feel superior to, and easily get away with patronizing, his fellow students. Indeed, after several years of being the "big city boy" at Valley Forge, he may well have found it intolerable being just another cell in the NYU student body. At Ursinus, as the memories of his classmates demonstrate, he played to the hilt the part of the rich cosmopolite, the experienced world traveller, the gifted great-writer-to-be. He conducted himself, apparently, as if he were better than everyone and everything around him; in a school full of students who considered college education a privilege and who felt (in the words of one of them) that they "had to make the best possible use of it and had the obligation to pass on to others as much as possible," Salinger's arrogant indifference to such matters as classroom attendance (his arch, *New Yorker*-ish campus newspaper column was called "Skipped Diploma") was by itself enough to win him notoriety. If the girls admired him for his veneer of worldly sophistication (not to mention his height and good looks), the other boys envied him these attributes. Yet he kept his distance, and former classmates remember him primarily as a "loner," underneath whose flashy image one or two of them were insightful enough to perceive a boy who, like Holden, was at bottom confused and disturbed by the grown-up world and not quite certain how to make a place for himself in it. "When we knew Jerry," recalls Frances Glassmoyer (whose name inspired that of Salinger's character Franny Glass), "he *was* Holden Caulfield, although when *The Catcher in the Rye* burst in upon the literary world, he expressed surprise when I recognized him as Holden. I guess he never knew his adolescence was showing."

Plainly, Salinger's "phoniness," his supercilious air, was a sign of insecurity. But why was he so insecure? Born into a family that lived on a modest block of upper Broadway, did he feel out of place in the Park Avenue apartment that his family had moved into when he was thirteen? Did the other young men in his New York set, most of whom had presumably been born into their wealth, intimidate him? Did he refuse to take school seriously because he was secretly afraid of not doing well enough? Did he, indeed, play the part of the sophisticated New Yorker at Ursinus precisely because, when he *was* in New York, he felt relatively *un*sophisticated? One begins to think so. Hamilton, who appears to identify with Salinger's contempt for the Ursinus crowd, has little or nothing to say on these matters, except to observe that whereas "[o]utside New York the young Salinger could pose as a sophisticate," in the city itself "there must always have been a Scott Fitzgerald-style discomfiture about his college pedigree: who else did he, or anybody, know who had been schooled at Valley Forge and polished at Ursinus, Collegeville?" But one suspects that Salinger's discomfiture preceded his years at Ursinus and even at Valley Forge—that, in fact, a nagging sense of being inferior to the born-and-bred Park Avenue types may go some way toward explaining his calculated phoniness in the company of his Pennsylvania schoolmates.

Whatever the case may be, it is clear at least that leaving college and entering the literary world did not stop Salinger from looking down his nose at one and all. Though his first stories were obviously manufactured for a middlebrow audience and saw publication, to his delight, in such well-paying and widely circulated "slicks" as *The Saturday Evening Post, Collier's,* and *Esquire* (as well as *Story,* whose founding editor Whit Burnett was an early mentor), Salinger's thrill at being published in their pages soon gave way to haughty disapproval of every little detail of their *modus operandi.*[1] The *Post* in particular irritated him by changing his stories' titles and illustrating them with silly drawings; though this sort of thing was standard practice, a few such experiences were enough to make Salinger dispatch an angry letter to Burnett saying that he was no longer going to write for the "slicks." In later years, his disdain would continually attach itself, in like fashion and upon similar grounds —margin size, cover design, jacket photograph, typeface, advertising copy, binding—to one book publisher after another; so strong was his feeling about such matters that in several cases his objections to publishers' handling of his work caused Salinger to break off longstanding personal and professional relationships. (Similarly, after seeing the results of the sale of *Catcher* and "Uncle Wiggily in Connecticut" to—respectively—the Book-of-the-Month Club and Samuel Goldwyn, he forbade the future sale of his work to book clubs and film studios.)

Joining these institutions in Salinger's disesteem were those individuals whom he looked upon as "professional" readers—that is, English professors and literary critics. Referring to a controversy between Sinclair Lewis and the critic Bernard De Voto over the merits of Lewis's novel *Arrowsmith,* Salinger observed that De Voto was probably in the right but had "no right to be right"; in a just world, novelists like Lewis would be criticized not by "small-time" opinionizers like De Voto but "by men of their own size"—by, that is, writers of fiction. (In opposition to the professional reader, naturally, Salinger placed the "amateur reader," to whom, in part, he dedicated his last book.) Salinger also looked down upon women. According to Hamilton, "there were two kinds of girls: those he despised immediately and those he fell in love with and afterwards semidespised." Salinger's references to women in his letters are almost invariably patronizing: he describes them as "little girls" or "little numbers"; his girlfriend Oona O'Neill (who later married Charlie Chaplin) is referred to as "little Oona." Even his fellow servicemen, during his World War II stint in the Counter Intelligence Corps, did not earn his respect; he treated them with what Hamilton describes as a "sour or condescending aloofness."

There is, then, a long list of individuals, groups, and institutions that Salinger seems to have looked upon with scorn. Alas, so catholic was his contempt that it would probably be wrong to leave his own name off the list. For it seems probable that, in addition to everyone else, Salinger despised himself—and did so, in large part, for the same reason that Holden Caulfield despised himself: because, though he looked down upon the fashionable and phony, he couldn't resist the temptation to be himself a member of the fashionable and phony crowd. Holden speaks of his classmates at Pencey Prep as having "this goddamn secret fraternity that I was too yellow not to join." To Salinger, the Park Avenue set, Eugene O'Neill's daughter, and Harold Ross's magazine were, taken together, exactly this—a "secret fraternity" that he saw through but was too yellow, too insecure, not to strive to be (or, at least, to pretend to be) a part of. For him, it was somehow never possible to live normally, in equality and friendliness, among his fellow adults; he had either to move among them with a haughty superciliousness—all the while hating himself for doing so—or to keep apart from them altogether.

I t should hardly be surprising that a man who found it so hard to relate maturely to his peers should have created a body of work that is distinguished primarily by its nostalgia for childhood and its hostility toward the conventions and responsibilities of adult life. In "Franny," a college girl who can't cope with adulthood suffers a nervous breakdown; in "Uncle Wiggily in Connecticut," a woman collapses in anguish over her sweet, spent youth; in "Raise High the Roofbeam, Carpenters," a young man who is "too happy" to marry deserts his fiancée on their wedding day; in "A Perfect Day for Bananafish," the same young man, having married after all, has a wistful encounter at the beach with a small girl and kills himself immediately after in his hotel room, while his wife sleeps nearby; and in "For Esmé—with Love and Squalor," a soldier driven to a nervous breakdown by the horrors of the adult world is redeemed by a child's affection. And so it goes in Salinger's fiction: one protagonist after another finds communication with grownups difficult or unfulfilling and is drawn instead to children. Some of the resulting encounters (Holden and his sister Phoebe, Sergeant X and Esmé) are among the most poignant in Salinger's fiction; some are just plain weird.

None of these fictional episodes, however, is quite as odd as a story that Hamilton tells about Salinger. Within weeks after relocating, in 1953, to his present modest residence in the small town of Cornish, New Hampshire (a move that recalls Holden Caulfield's escapist dream of living in a cabin by a brook), Salinger befriended a number of high-school students; they were, it seems, not protégés or admirers so much as they were "pals" whom he regularly attended football games with, consorted with at a local coffee shop, and entertained frequently at his house. "He was just like one of the gang," one of these young people later remembered. (One immediately thinks of Holden's dream of being in a field of rye with numberless children: "Thousands of little kids, and nobody's around—nobody big, I mean—except me.") This most peculiar idyll was ended when two of Salinger's young friends interviewed him for the high school page of the Claremont *Daily Eagle* and the interview appeared not on the high school page but in the front of the paper, as an *Eagle* "scoop." Apparently feeling betrayed, Salinger proceeded, in a striking display of childishness, to sever his ties with all of the students; very soon afterwards, he had a high fence constructed around his house.

Why? One has the impression that Salinger's teenaged interviewers, by behaving too much like grownup reporters, violated his sentimental illusions about youth. His fiction makes it plain that Salinger enjoys thinking of young people as magically wise and innocent beings, immune from the phony erudition, the sneaky cleverness, and the moral corruption that plague adults. Not that the children in Salinger's fiction are Rebeccas of Sunnybrook Farm; on the contrary, they are almost invariably smart, fresh, precocious (sometimes quite improbably so), and just this side of obnoxious. Nevertheless, time and again it is children, in Salinger's work, that embody goodness and decency and a sort of great and simple cosmic knowingness. Consider, for instance, "For Esmé—With Love and Squalor," one of his two or three most accomplished stories, which was originally published in 1950 in *The New Yorker* and reprinted in *Nine Stories* (1954). The protagonist tells us that he is writing the story in honor of the forthcoming wedding of a young lady whom he met six years earlier, during World War II, when she was a thirteen-year-old English girl and he was a young American soldier stationed in Devon. He first saw her singing in a church choir, and met her a few minutes later in a tearoom; a titled and conspicuously well-to-do war orphan, she was friendly, forward, articulate, and rather snobbish ("You seem quite intelligent for an American," she said). After telling him about her dead parents, of whom she spoke in an extremely affectionate but formal manner, she asked him to write a short story for her—"I prefer stories," she said, "about squalor"—and then bade him goodbye, hoping he would return from the war "with all your faculties intact." The second half of the story finds the soldier (who now refers to himself as "Sergeant X") in Bavaria, a few weeks after V-E Day, headquartered in a house that once belonged to a Nazi woman. A book in the house contains the handwritten inscription (in German): "Dear God, life is hell"; the soldier, who has suffered a nervous breakdown and seems to be in desperate emotional straits, appends, in English, a postscript from Dostoevsky: "Fathers and teachers, I ponder 'What is hell?' I maintain that it is the suffering of being unable to love." Then, after he tosses a few disaffected, patronizing jokes at a dumb-but-amiable corporal named Clay (the same sort of jokes, by the way, that Zooey Glass will wound his mother with in "Zooey"), the soldier receives a sweet letter, delayed a year or so in transit, from Esmé, with which she encloses her late father's watch, its crystal broken. Suddenly, thanks to the letter, the soldier feels sleepy, "almost ecstatically" sleepy, for the first time; we are meant to understand that this turn of events is a hopeful one indeed, for "you take a really sleepy man, Esmé, and he *al*ways stands a chance of again becoming a man with all his fac—with all his f-a-c-u-l-t-i-e-s intact."

If "Esmé" is among Salinger's finer stories, it is largely because the protagonist's antipathy for adult life is understandable—he has seen, in the horrors of war, the evils of which the human soul is capable—and because the girl is charmingly drawn. But the change effected in the soldier by Esmé's affectionate letter, is, alas, less than thoroughly plausible. A widely overlooked detail in the story is that the soldier (unlike Salinger, who in many other ways is clearly his prototype) has a wife back home in the States—a wife who has, apparently, been unable to do for his emotional stability what this child, a virtual stranger, has accomplished with a single letter. Viewed from this perspective, the story seems to say less about the redemptive power of children's innocent love than (unintentionally) about the ability of intelligent and perceptive writers to deceive themselves with sentimental conceits.

"A Perfect Day for Bananafish" (1948), also reprinted in *Nine Stories,* similarly contrasts the heaven of children's love with the hell of the adult world. Like "Esmé," the story falls into two distinct parts. In the first, we meet Muriel, a young wife in a Florida beach hotel, who after reading a women's magazine article titled "Sex is Fun—or Hell," speaks by telephone to her mother in New York. Like most of the women in Salinger's fiction, both Muriel and her mother are superficial, insensitive, gabby, their dialogue peppered with references to fancy Manhattan stores. The subject of their conversation is Muriel's disturbed husband, Seymour Glass, who has been in a mental hospital, who has dubbed Muriel "Miss Spiritual Tramp of 1948," and who (the mother fears) "may completely lose control of himself" during the vacation. Her authority for this pronouncement is a psychiatrist with whom Muriel's father has consulted (like many obtuse and callous characters in Salinger, these women believe religiously in modern psychiatry). One thing that the women find particularly "awful" and "sad" about Seymour is his extraordinary enthusiasm for a certain twentieth-century German poet (unnamed, but indubitably Rilke). From Muriel's hotel room we move to the beach, where Seymour chats about olives and Little Black Sambo with a toddler named Sybil (who calls him "see more") and then takes the child into the ocean to catch "bananafish." "This is a *perfect* day for bananafish," he tells her, and proceeds to explain that bananafish "lead a very tragic life," chasing down bananas in bananaholes and eating so many that they can't get out again, eventually perishing of banana fever. Leaving Sybil in the water, Seymour returns to his hotel room, sees Muriel lying on the bed, pulls a gun out of a suitcase, and shoots himself in the head.

The story has considerable strengths: the style is vivid, the structure taut, the interlude with Sybil both charming and disquieting. (Note that "Bananafish" is, in a way, "Esmé" in reverse: the first half demonstrates the grim reality of adult life, the second presents a friendly encounter between an adult and a child.) But what are we supposed to make of it all? Apparently we are meant to recognize in Seymour a sensitive soul who can "see more" profoundly than the common herd into the heart of man's darkness, and who is consequently incapable of living comfortably in the crude and callous world of adults; like a bananafish, he has taken in too much—has, that is, overloaded his fragile psyche—and feels trapped, isolated, doomed. Yet the more closely one examines the story, the more one comes to recognize it as a facile (albeit very well executed) exercise in what may be called suicide chic. Salinger's empathy, one cannot help but notice, is not distributed as evenly as his attention: we are expected to understand and identify with Seymour—to take his side, as it were, against the phony adult world—yet Salinger is not at all concerned with having us understand or sympathize with Muriel's view of things. Though we are meant to forgive Seymour's considerable flaws (egocentrism, irresponsibility, cruelty, intellectual snobbery) as the understandable reaction of a helpless, delicate soul to the adult world, we are meant to see in Muriel's flaws an indication of how vicious and vapid that world can be. This blinkered vision is typical of Salinger's stories. Continually they suggest to us that it's Salinger, the protagonist, perhaps an innocent child or two, and we the readers (the *amateur* readers, anyway) against everybody else of voting age. That some children can be as reprehensible as some adults is never acknowledged. And there's hardly any indication in these stories that human frailties can not only divide us but bind us together—that they can, in fact, help make us look into each other and see ourselves, and take strength.

*T*he *Catcher in the Rye* (1951), Salinger's only novel, was a long time in the making. The name Caulfield (which the declared movie-hater Salinger borrowed from his favorite movie star, Joan Caulfield) appears in several early stories; Vincent Caulfield, in "The Last Day of the Last Furlough," published in *The Saturday Evening Post* in 1944, has a younger brother named Holden. Two Holden Caulfield stories that were forerunners of *Catcher* appeared during the 1940s. One was accepted by *The New Yorker* in 1941 but was never published in its original form; a revised version, titled "Slight Rebellion Off Madison," appeared there five years later. The other, "I'm Crazy" (consisting essentially of Holden's leave-taking of Mr. Spencer and the episode in Phoebe's bedroom), was printed in *Collier's* in 1945. (A descriptive tag billed it as "The heartwarming story of a kid whose only fault lay in understanding people so well that most of them were baffled by him and only a very few would believe in him.")

If *Catcher* is Salinger's single most effective published work, it is largely because in its pages he is more objective than usual, more distanced from and clear-headed about his protagonist's solipsism. It is also partly because, in this case, for once, the Salinger protagonist who despises adult life and longs for childhood is not a young adult with an acute case of arrested development; rather, he is himself a child (or, more correctly, a boy at the threshold of manhood) whose vanity, unreason, and unconscious hypocrisy—and whose anguish and confusion over his vanishing innocence—are more easily forgivable, and less severely psychopathic, than they would be in a young man a few years older.

The story of *Catcher* is perhaps the best known in postwar American literature. Holden Caulfield is sixteen, the middle child of a wealthy corporate lawyer and his wife whose family occupies half of a floor in an apartment building near Central Park; he's lately sprouted up very quickly to a height of six feet two-and-a-half inches and has just been expelled from his fourth prep school, Pencey Prep in Agerstown, Pennsylvania, for failing four out of five subjects. (He passed English.) Since he doesn't want to remain at Pencey for the last few days remaining in the autumn semester (he's "lonesome" there), and can't bring himself to face his parents before the news of his dismissal reaches them by mail, he leaves school abruptly on a Saturday night in December and spends the next two days and nights gadding around Manhattan. During this brief but intense odyssey he gets shaken down in a seedy hotel by a prostitute named Sunny and a pimp named Maurice; has drinks with a sometime school buddy (who describes his ex-girlfriend as "the whore of New Hampshire"); tries unsuccessfully to persuade his friend Sally Hayes to escape with him to some place far away where they can live simply and anonymously; and runs to an ex-teacher, Mr. Antolini, for refuge only to have the man put the moves on him. In the course of narrating the events of this lost weekend (or, as he puts it, "this madman stuff that happened to me around last Christmas"), Holden manages to describe nearly everything he comes across—and virtually everybody older than he is—as "corny" or "phony" or "depressing." He is, as his little sister Phoebe complains, down on everything: "You don't like *any*thing that's happening." The only people he really loves, or can even tolerate, it seems, are Phoebe and his older brother D. B., a Hollywood screenwriter. (His father is also in show business, after a fashion: he invests frequently in Broadway plays.) To be sure, he has a touching affection for the occasional odd, innocent, and seemingly insignificant memory. For example, when he discovers that his roommate, a make-out artist named Stradlater, is about to go on a date with a friend of his, Jane Gallagher, he remembers fondly how, when he and Jane used to play checkers, "She wouldn't move any of her kings. What she'd do, when she'd get a king, she wouldn't move it. She'd just leave it in the back row. She'd get them all lined up in the back row. Then she'd never use them. She just like the way they looked when they were in the back row." At sixteen he's already crippled by nostalgia.

Like Seymour Glass and other Salinger protagonists, Holden doesn't want any part of a world which seems to him an obscene place full of prevarication and pretentiousness. But he is a Salinger hero with a difference. Instead of painting him as some sort of mad, sainted isolato, Salinger makes it plain that Holden is an essentially normal teenager, temporarily disturbed, who is himself guilty of many of the things for which he faults others. Though he claims to hate movies, for instance, he has seen *The Thirty-Nine Steps* ten times; though he calls himself a pacifist, he physically attacks his Pencey roommate Stradlater for seducing Jane Gallagher; though he criticizes his schoolmates for their "lousy manners," he, for his part, is frequently rude and insulting; though he hates dishonesty, he admits himself to be "the most terrific liar you ever saw in your life"; and though he is repulsed by "big snobs," he acknowledges having chosen to room with Stradlater on account of his wealth and sneers at the provincial ignorance of three young Seattle women whom he meets at a seedy New York hotel. It is, in short, the obvious unreliability of many of Holden's negative impressions that gives the book a levelheadedness that many of Salinger's stories lack.

Holden is a boy possessed by memories; and the memory that haunts him most of all is that of his late brother Allie, whose death three years earlier appears to have much to do with his present emotional disturbance. Holden recalls that soon after Allie's death, his parents almost had him psychoanalyzed because, in his despair, he broke all the windows in the garage of their summer house in Maine. Though three years have passed, death—not only Allie's death but mortality itself—continues to prey upon his mind. Throughout *Catcher,* old people (Mr. Spencer; a visiting Pencey alumnus; the characters played by Lunt and Fontanne in *I Know My Love*) disconcert and depress him; on more than one occasion he mentions his own tombstone, upon which he imagines someone writing an obscenity. If Holden has no interest in becoming a responsible and mature adult, it seems to be largely because he knows that adulthood leads to death—and death is something with which he has simply not come to terms. Though it has been driven home to him in the past couple of years that he lives in a world of sinfulness and mortality, he has not yet accepted his inability to escape either of these things, and the force and fierceness with which childhood has been taken from him (his brother's demise, his speedy growth) have made it increasingly difficult for him to respond to life with anything but aimless panic, a desperate fear of the future, and an unmodulated, undifferentiated attachment to the past. At the end of the novel he says:

> D. B. asked me what I thought about all this stuff I just finished telling you about. I didn't know what the hell to say. If you want to know the truth, I don't *know* what I think about it. I'm sorry I told so many people about it. About all I know is, I sort of *miss* everybody I told about. Even

old Stradlater and Ackley, for instance. I think I even miss that goddam Maurice. It's funny. Don't ever tell anybody anything. If you do, you start missing everybody.

That is, for a Salinger protagonist, an unusual sort of despair; it is the despair not of a grown-up neurotic or psychopath who refuses to face adulthood, but of a troubled boy—a boy for whom we must feel sympathy and with whom (in some small way, at least) we cannot help but identify. It is, indeed, the poignant credibility of Holden Caulfield that is largely responsible for *The Catcher in the Rye*'s being not only Salinger's best single published work but also one of the few small classics of postwar American fiction.

Between 1954, when *Nine Stories* was issued, and 1965, when Salinger ceased publishing fiction, a total of five Salinger stories saw print. All five appeared in *The New Yorker,* and all five are about a family named Glass, the oldest of whose seven children, Seymour, had already been introduced—and killed off—in "A Perfect Day for Bananafish." Like Holden, the Glass children with whom Salinger is most concerned are emotional cripples, aloof and superior in their relation to the adult world. It's a situation which might be very compelling but for the fact that Salinger seems to identify much too strongly with them, and thus tends to present them not as pathetic, maladjusted misfits but as romantic egoists who are incalculably finer and more fascinating (not to mention more brilliant and beautiful) than regular folk. The first of these stories, the sharp, lively "Franny" (1955), takes place several years after Seymour's suicide and concerns the nervous breakdown that Franny Glass, a college student who is Seymour's youngest sister, suffers when she visits her boyfriend Lane Coutell on his campus the weekend of the Yale game. Like Holden Caulfield, Franny is mightily displeased by the human race—whose manifold uglinesses she'd apparently never had a good look at before going away to college. She tells Lane that she is "just so sick of pedants and conceited little tearer-downers I could scream"; her poet-professors aren't *"real* poets. They're just people that write poems that get published and anthologized all over the place, but they're not *poets*. . . . If you're a poet, you do something beautiful!" Like Holden, she has unreasonable and romantic expectations of her fellow human beings: "I'm sick of just liking people. I wish to God I could meet somebody I could respect." And: "I'm just sick of ego, ego, ego. My own and everybody else's. I'm sick of everybody that wants to *get* somewhere, do something distinguished and all, be somebody interesting. It's disgusting—it is, it *is*. I don't care what anybody says." (As should be clear by now, Franny even *talks* like Holden, peppering her conversation liberally with the expressions "you know," "I mean," "God," "goddam," and "and all.")

Franny, in short, is a noble-minded, idealistic young lady who is unable to accept the compromises and the imperfections—and, it should be added, the raw, ugly *sexuality*—of adulthood. Lane, neatly enough for the story's purposes, is her exact opposite, all untempered ego and sex: he brags obnoxiously about the possibility of publishing a paper he wrote for an English course (unlike Franny, he's more interested in publishing his ideas than in the ideas themselves) and complains pretentiously about Flaubert's lack of "testicularity." Like "Bananafish," then, "Franny" centers upon a contrast between the two leading characters, one of whom is a sensitive Glass and the other of whom is an unfeeling fool who likes to listen to himself talk; as in the earlier story, Salinger clearly wants us to sympathize with the former and see in the latter the personification of the world's obtuseness and insensitivity. But once again he has loaded the dice to a ridiculous extent, depicting his well-adjusted character as a self-important lout—as if to say that this is the only sort of person who can function smoothly in society. (As in "Bananafish," one cannot help but wonder what these two extraordinarily incompatible people ever saw in one another.)

The principal difference between Holden Caulfield and Franny Glass is religion. In *Catcher,* there are few explicit references to it; the most memorable one is Holden's coffee-shop encounter with a couple of nuns, whom, once or twice afterwards, he has a vague desire to see again. That's the extent of Holden's interest in religion. Franny is something else again. Running away from the world, she dives into the arms of God; fervently she tells Lane (who is, naturally, a devout Freudian) about the power of prayer, claiming that if you keep repeating the name of God, "You get to see God." She's been reading a book, she tells him, called *The Way of a Pilgrim,* about a man who walks "all over Russia, looking for somebody who can tell him *how* to pray incessantly." Eventually she goes to the ladies' room and collapses.

That is the end of "Franny," but not of the chronicle of Franny's nervous collapse. Salinger picks up the action the following morning in "Zooey" (1957), which is four times as long as its predecessor and was reprinted with it in *Franny and Zooey* (1961). The style of the second story represents a distinct falling-off from the crispness of the first; Salinger opens with a windy, self-indulgent passage in which the narrator introduces himself as the writer Buddy Glass, Franny's oldest living brother and apparently one of the more stable members of the seven-sibling Glass clan. (As we learn later in the story, Buddy, like Salinger, lives in the woods "like a *her*mit.") Apropos of the story's wordiness, Buddy explains that "We are, all four of us [Buddy, Zooey, Franny, and their mother Bessie], blood relatives, and we speak a kind of esoteric, family language, a sort of semantic geometry in which the shortest distance between any two points is a fullish circle." It is an apt warning, for "Zooey" and the stories that follow it are plagued by an increasingly bizarre, frustrating, and nearly pathological logorrhea; it is as if they were written not only of and by, but even exclusively *for,* the Glass children, as if Salinger/Buddy were trying to keep the rest of us out of the lives of this family that he has created for himself by erecting an all but insurmountable lexical fence around them.

The beginning of the story proper finds twenty-five-year-old Zooey, the youngest Glass boy, sitting in "a very full bath" in his parents' Manhattan apartment, where he and Franny still live; in this womb-like environment, he is reading a four-year-old letter from Buddy. Zooey, we are told, is a successful television actor, small, slight, and "surpassingly handsome," who has been fighting "a private war against narcissism . . . since he was seven or eight years old," and who as a child appeared regularly on a radio quiz show called "It's a Wise Child." Indeed, between 1927 and 1943, all seven of the Glass children were, at one time or another, regular panelists on the program; all won reputations as prodigies, but none was so impressive as the brilliant eldest son, Seymour, who, with Buddy, went on to play tutor to the family's two youngest members, Zooey and Franny. Buddy recalls in his letter how he and Seymour wanted them to "know who and what Jesus and Gautama and Lao-tse and Shankaracharya and Hui-neng and Sri Ramakrishna, etc., were before you knew too much or anything about Homer or Shakespeare or even Blake or Whitman, let alone George Washington and his cherry tree or the definition of a peninsula or how to parse a sentence." We are to understand that it is because of (a) that quiz show, (b) the army of "child psychologists and professional educators" who "voraciously examined, interviewed, and poked at" them (especially at Zooey) throughout their childhoods, and (c) Seymour and Buddy's offbeat metaphysical teachings, that Franny and

Zooey are unstable and alienated and even more obsessed with the past than the rest of the family. As Zooey tells his mother: "This whole god-dam house stinks of ghosts. . . . We're *freaks,* the two of us, Franny and I . . . and both those bastards [Seymour and Buddy] are responsible."

Indeed, though he's been dead for seven years, Seymour *is* rather responsible for Franny's breakdown. The books she's been reading (not only *The Way of a Pilgrim* but its sequel, *The Pilgrim Continues His Way*) are from Seymour's room; their aim, as Zooey explains to his mother, is "to wake everybody up to the need and *ben*efits of saying the Jesus Prayer incessantly. . . . The idea being that if you call out the name long enough and regularly enough and *lit*erally from the heart, sooner or later you'll get an answer. Not exactly an *an*swer. A *response.*" To be specific, the prayer, endlessly reiterated, brings enlightenment; one enters "the reality of things," achieves "pure consciousness"—which is to say that one utterly escapes the false reality of a world full of fools. This is a consummation for which not only Franny but Buddy and (in his time) Seymour have devoutly wished. Toward the end of the story, after Franny complains to Zooey (much as Holden does to Phoebe) about how despicable people are, he tells her—and this seems to be the moral of the piece, if moral there be—that if there aren't any people in the world for whose sake it is worth making an effort at life, she should live and work and strive for God's sake, because He's always out there watching. Obviously, we are supposed to admire and be moved by the Glass children's preoccupation with spiritual purity and incessant prayerfulness. But it's hard not to see it all as self-destructive, psychopathic, fanatical; hard not to be disturbed by Salinger's, and the Glasses', blithe equation of religion and misanthropy. It is also difficult not to be irritated by that precious, tiresome, and most labored piece of fictional machinery, the late lamented children's radio quiz show, "It's a Wise Child"—which is, after all, simply a facile contrivance designed to account, in one fell swoop, for an entire family's emotional delinquency. It demonstrates that Salinger is more interested in having a family of incurably childlike adults to play with on paper than he is in trying to figure out how people like that *really* get to be that way or how they might manage to become (horrors!) emotionally healthy adults.

I n "Raise High the Roofbeam, Carpenters" (1955), Salinger jumps back in time. The story takes place on the day of Seymour's wedding in

1942; Buddy is not only the narrator—providing yet more information about the Glass family and "It's a Wise Child"—but the protagonist. A twenty-three-year-old serviceman stationed at Fort Benning, Georgia, he travels to New York and appears at the Manhattan brownstone where the ceremony is to take place only to discover that Seymour has backed out. Shortly thereafter he finds himself in a car with a number of people from the wedding who are so unfavorably disposed toward Seymour that Buddy finds it more comfortable not to admit to being his brother. As a result he ends up hearing all sort of unflattering remarks about Seymour—that he's "a latent homosexual and a schizoid personality," that he's "either never *grown up* or is just an absolute raving maniac of some crazy kind," that having been on the radio as a child must have made it impossible for him to "learn to relate to normal people." Buddy ends up taking the people to his apartment, where his sister Boo Boo's been staying; there he comes across Seymour's diary, in which Seymour records his fiancée Muriel's (and Muriel's mother's) fears about his sanity, and his own theories: "Oh, God, if I'm anything by a clinical name, I'm a kind of paranoiac in reverse. I suspect people of plotting to make me happy." He quotes Vedanta: "Marriage partners are to serve each other. . . . How wonderful, how sane, how beautifully difficult, and therefore true. The joy of responsibility for the first time in my life." Eventually—to the ire of Buddy's guests—word comes that Seymour and Muriel have eloped; and it is suddenly clear that the quoted diary passage was meant to make us realize that it would be inappropriate for such a brilliant, self-searching paragon as Seymour to wed Muriel in the company of these vulgarians.

"Seymour—An Introduction" (1959), which was reprinted together with "Raise High the Roofbeam, Carpenters" in 1963, rehearses yet again the high points of the Glass family saga, and provides us with a few new facts on Seymour. We learn, for instance, that Seymour was five ten-and-a-half and that he loved sports and games; we learn what a magnificent Oriental-type poet he was, one of the "three or four *very* nearly non-expendable poets" America has produced (no samples); and we get pages and pages of description of Seymour's eyes and nose and mouth and skin. The ultimate purpose of all this is to communicate some notion, in that elliptical Glass manner, of why Seymour "was the only person I've ever habitually consorted with, banged around with, who more frequently than not tallied with the classical conception, as I saw it, of a *mukta,* a ringding enlightened man, a God-knower."

(That's Buddy talking.) The piece does not take the form of a short story because "his character lends itself to no legitimate sort of narrative compactness that *I* know of." And so what Salinger/Buddy gives us instead is an extremely eccentric series of wordy, highly self-conscious periodic sentences and transitional-sounding paragraphs—which, though they run on and on for nearly a hundred and fifty pages, manage to say very, very little about Seymour, or, for that matter, about anything else. (One of the more peculiar things about this story is that Buddy intimates that *he* wrote "A Perfect Day for Bananafish," and tells us the story was not "true," but was rather an imaginative reconstruction of the events of Seymour's last day based upon the available facts.)

Salinger's last published work, "Hapworth 16, 1924" (1965), is even more bizarre—indeed, virtually unreadable. It takes the form of a letter that Seymour writes home from summer camp at age seven; but no seven-year-old in the history of the world ever wrote anything remotely like this. The letter is thoughtful, introspective, and twenty thousand words long, its ornate vocabulary and elaborate rolling sentences suggestive (despite occasional awkwardnesses) of William F. Buckley at his most Buckleyesque. A large portion of the letter is devoted to Seymour's summer reading list, which consists of dozens of high-toned and esoteric (and both Western and Eastern) volumes of literature, theology, history, science, and philosophy—far more books than twenty literate adults would be likely to read in one summer. Is this Salinger's ideal child? (One recalls a line from a letter—quoted by Hamilton—that Salinger wrote his friend, Judge Learned Hand, upon the birth in 1956 of Salinger's daughter: by summer, he boasts, the baby will be able to explain some of the more obscure aspects of Vedanta to both of them.) Or is the story a wish-fulfillment fantasy—a chance for J. D. Salinger to be seven years old again, with nearly all the wit and articulateness of his grown-up self?

Throughout all of these Glass family tales, the consistent presence— whether as a living person or as an honored ghost—is that of Seymour, the child-man (and, finally, in "Hapworth," the man-child); he hovers over the stories the way that giant fetus hovers in the heavens near the end of *2001: A Space Odyssey,* the inescapable personification of all the qualities that Salinger held, and perhaps still holds, most dear. This obsessive deification of Seymour could never have happened, of course, had Salinger not been, to put it plainly, a child at heart—a writer who had difficulty establishing a memorable conflict that did not involve a childlike sensibility coming up against the "real world," who rarely, if ever, created a compelling character that did not end up with a nervous breakdown as a result of such a conflict, and whose imagination seems to have been constitutionally incapable of taking such a character past the breakdown and into a stable adult life, or some reasonable approximation thereof.

Like many other Beat and hippie-era American children in search of pure and sweet and simple keys to the cosmos, Salinger was, it is clear, drawn all too easily into the black hole of Oriental mysticism, where Western systems of aesthetic valuation have no place and where a Seymour Glass—child prodigy, Oriental poet, spiritual *Übermensch,* and tragiheroic suicide—could evolve posthaste into an all but godlike symbol, the typical Salinger protagonist taken to its illogical extreme. So fascinated did Salinger become with the idea of Seymour that he lost all interest in plot, pace, characterization, conflict, and other such irrelevancies; far from being recognizable works of contemporary American fiction directed at a literary audience, his last two published prose pieces are, rather, letters to himself—gospels, as it were, about the Glass family, that private pantheon of eternally puerile Olympians.

To be sure, generations of celebrated American writers have been nearly as devoted as Salinger to the theme of innocence and experience, to the exploration of characters who are extraordinarily pure in soul or who refuse to accept adulthood or whose characteristically American guilelessness is contrasted tellingly and tragically with the sophistication and corruption of Europe. One thinks—to select only a few representative names—of Melville's Billy Budd, Twain's Huckleberry Finn, James's Daisy Miller. (The writer as a child of sorts has also, in this century at least, become a peculiar American institution: one thinks of Fitzgerald, Hemingway, Mailer.) Leslie Fiedler wrote an entire book, *Love and Death in the American Novel,* demonstrating that the protagonists of American fiction since the time of Cooper had, to an extent unprecedented in Western literature, been notable for their aversion to adult relationships and responsibilities. But the writers—at least the greatest writers—of the works in question did not themselves *endorse* their characters' childish aversions; they did not see those characters' immature behavior as marks of superiority.

And that is where J. D. Salinger is different. For, despite its many virtues, its frequent charm and felicity of style, the bulk of Salinger's fiction is seriously weakened by the fact that he is congenitally less interested in getting to the bottom of his characters' emotionally retarded behavior than he is in celebrating it; less interested in creating a credible fictional universe than in sequestering himself within a private, privileged nursery with his child-heroes and childish heroes, a place from which he can look down upon those numberless masses who are not only less sensitive and intelligent, but less beautiful, sophisticated, and wealthy, than his protagonists. (And who, incidentally, unlike most of his central characters, neither have a connection to show business nor look down upon it as fervently as Salinger thinks they should.) For all his supposed spiritual enlightenment, then, Salinger manifestly remained, throughout his public writing career, as snobbish as he had been at military school and college. It is dismaying, but should not be surprising, that so contemptuous a man, however considerable his talent, was unable to produce a more consequential body of work than that which he has bequeathed us. Nor, alas—given the current literary climate, in which cultish devotions and sentimental attachments often count as strongly as sensible critical evaluation in the making of a literary reputation—is it surprising that the immense esteem in which Salinger is held by literate Americans should continue to stand in such remarkable disproportion to the actual level of his literary achievement.

Capote's Children

JUNE 1985

Truman Capote, who died last summer at the age of fifty-eight, was one of a handful of American novelists who became famous at a very early age in the years following the Second World War. Perhaps the three most celebrated of these writers were Gore Vidal (whose *Williwaw* appeared in 1946, when he was nineteen), Norman Mailer (whose *The Naked and the Dead* was issued two years later, when he was twenty-five), and Capote (who published *Other Voices, Other Rooms* in 1949, at the age of twenty-three). If Mailer and Vidal spent the early part of their careers climbing out of derivative ruts and attempting to find their own voices, Capote was an original from the start. This is not to suggest that he did not, in the manner of every young writer, learn from his antecedents. *Other Voices, Other Rooms* is riddled with Southern Gothic touches—grotesque characters, haunting scenes—that are reminiscent of Faulkner and Carson McCullers; its lyrical style and elegiac tone (a tone that was to stay with Capote forever, however radically his style might change) recall Willa Cather; and the situation and the contours of the plot bring to mind both *Jane Eyre* and *The Turn of the Screw*. For all this, to read *Other Voices, Other Rooms* is not to catalogue influences but to appreciate the way Capote makes these varied borrowings over into something entirely his own.

Other Voices, Other Rooms charts the path toward self-discovery of an intelligent, rather delicate thirteen-year-old, Joel Knox, who, as the novel opens, is finding his way to the grand, dilapidated back-country home of his invalid father, Mr. Sansom, and his stepmother, Miss Amy, neither of whom he has ever met. Joel has been sent for by these two, but, as he eventually discovers, the summons was really the work of the third member of the household: his odd cousin Randolph, who appears one day, ghost-like and dressed as a woman, at an upstairs window. Randolph's yen for Joel is obvious, and at the end of the novel Joel recognizes his own fate is, to put it delicately, bound up with Randolph's:

> His mind was absolutely clear. He was like a camera waiting for its subject to enter focus. The wall yellowed in the meticulous setting of the October sun, and the windows were rippling mirrors of cold, seasonal color. Beyond one, someone was watching him. All of him was dumb except his eyes. They knew. And it was Randolph's window. Gradually the blinding sunset drained from the glass, darkened, and it was as if snow were falling there, flakes shaping snow-eyes, hair: a face trembled like a white beautiful moth, smiled. She beckoned to him, shining and silver, and he knew he must go: unafraid, not hesitating, he paused only at the garden's edge where, as though he'd forgotten something, he stopped and looked back at the bloomless, descending blue, at the boy he had left behind.

Capote never stopped looking back at that boy. The innocence of childhood, the tragedy of having to trade it in for the sordidness and disillusionment of adulthood: these themes haunt all of Capote's major works. The heroes of his novels are invariably sensitive souls, aliens in the world of civilized, responsible adults, who are tortured by their inability to let go of childhood.

Critics have leveled many complaints against *Other Voices, Other Rooms:* that it hasn't got much of a plot, that it doesn't add up to anything, that it's intellectually barren. It's a mood piece, they complain, a stylistic tour de force. Perhaps. But what a mood, what a style! One marvels at the assured prose, at this young writer's ability to sweep one up and carry one, without a misstep, through a mysterious landscape which is to the real Deep South as Hardy's Wessex is to Dorset. One marvels, too, at his ability to defamiliarize—without a trace of self-consciousness—that most tiredly familiar of all first-novel genres, the *Bildungsroman.*

For almost a decade after *Other Voices, Other Rooms,* Capote produced one largish project per year. 1949: *A Tree of Night* (a story collection). 1950: *Local Color* (travel essays). 1951: *The Grass Harp* (a novel). 1952: the stage adaptation (unsuccessful) of *The Grass Harp*. 1953: the film *Beat the Devil*. 1954: book and lyrics (including the jazz standard "A Sleepin' Bee") for a Broadway musical, *House of Flowers,* with music by Harold Arlen. 1956: *The Muses Are Heard,* a journal of Capote's trip to the Soviet Union with the cast of *Porgy and Bess.* Clearly, in the early Fifties Capote was already developing the fascination with those glitzy extraliterary milieus (showbiz, café society, the jet set) which were to usurp much of his time and energy over the ensuing years, and evincing a remarkable willingness (and ability) to apply his talents to a variety of genres. Despite this dazzling (and, perhaps, dismaying) versatility, however, Capote continued to devote himself, throughout the 1950s, primarily to prose fiction.

Like *Other Voices, Other Rooms, The Grass Harp,* his major work of the period, offers a setting in the Deep South, eccentric relatives, grotesque neighbors, an intelligent yet delicate boy's confrontation with adulthood, a thinly veiled homosexual theme—and rich, romantic prose:

> When was it I first heard of the grass harp? Long before the autumn we lived in the China tree; an earlier autumn, then; and of course it was Dolly who told me, no one else would have known to call it that, a grass harp.
>
> If on leaving town you take the church road you soon will pass a glaring hill of bone-white slabs and brown burnt flowers: this is the Baptist cemetery.... Below the hill grows a field of high Indian grass that changes color with the seasons: go to see it in the fall, late September, when it has gone red as sunset, when scarlet shadows like firelight breeze over it and the autumn winds strum on its dry leaves sighing human music, a harp of voices.
>
> Beyond the field begins the darkness of River Woods. It must have been one of those September days when we were there in the woods gathering roots that Dolly said: Do you hear? that is the grass harp, always telling a story—it knows the stories of all the people on the hill, of all the people who ever lived, and when we are dead it will tell ours, too.

The speaker here is sixteen-year-old Collin, who lives in a small town with his father's cousins Verena (a tyrant) and the above-mentioned Dolly (the first of many endearing child-women in Capote's work). When Verena returns from a trip to Chicago with a vulgar man named Morris Ritz, who insists upon learning the formula for Dolly's secret herbal medicine—he and Verena want to patent it, market it, and reap the rewards—Collin, Dolly, and their black friend Catherine escape to a tree house in the woods. Complications ensue—some forced and farcical, some melodramatic: the town descends upon them, threatening legal action and physical harm; the local judge and Riley, the town hellion (and Collin's idol), join them in the tree; Ritz absconds with Verena's money; Collin and his companions abandon the tree house; Dolly dies of a stroke; Riley marries; Collin packs his bags and leaves town, "not foresee[ing] that I would travel the road and dream the tree until they had drawn me back." *The Grass Harp* demonstrates that Capote's aims had changed somewhat since his first book: he wanted to be not only moving but *funny,* to create a mood *and* tell a relatively involved story, and to concentrate less on his boy-hero and more on the people around him. But the style of this short novel did not, for the most part, depart markedly from the lyrical, meditative manner of *Other Voices, Other Rooms.*

Capote continued to develop, though, and in the same direction. By the time of *Breakfast at Tiffany's* (1958), he was even more concerned with developing a plot, being humorous, and looking beyond his protagonist (who had, by now, grown into a young man); and he had, fortunately, developed a style that suited these ends perfectly. That style, *New Yorker*ishly terse and precise, is reminiscent of J. D. Salinger, and so is the setting, "a brownstone in the East Seventies . . . during the early years of the war." The hero of the novella is a fledgling Southern (and, though he never says so explicitly, homosexual) writer who lives in that brownstone; the heroine, Holly Golightly, is a gorgeous, stylish playgirl in the apartment directly below, who peppers her conversation with French expressions, earns her living by dating middle-aged men and delivering coded messages to a "sweet" Mafia kingpin named Sally Tomato, and hopes to marry very, very rich. *Breakfast at Tiffany's* marks a switch in Capote's stylistic emphasis from evocative description to dialogue—which is, in its own way, equally evocative:

> "Be a darling, darling, rub some oil on my back." While I was performing this service, she said: "O. J. Berman's in town, and listen, I gave him your story in the magazine. He was quite impressed. He thinks maybe you're worth helping. But he says you're on the wrong track. Negroes and children: who cares?"
>
> "Not Mr. Berman, I gather."
>
> "Well, I agree with him. I read that story twice. Brats and niggers. Trembling leaves. *Description.* It doesn't *mean* anything."

The twist in *Breakfast at Tiffany's* is that Holly (who seems here, perhaps, to have been reading something very much like *The Grass Harp*) is
a hillbilly girl, real name Lulamae, the runaway wife of a horse doctor in
Tulip, Texas, who is old enough to be her grandfather. She is, at bottom, a scared, vulnerable Southern child, a self-exile, compelled by her
helpless fear of the responsibilities of adulthood to wander far from
home, binding herself to no one, trying desperately to lose sight of her
terror and loneliness among the bright lights and the nightclub crowds
of New York.

The more closely one looks at *Breakfast at Tiffany's* the more difficult
it is to avoid feeling that the novella is something of a schizophrenic act
on Capote's part. One side of him (the disciplined, mature writer) observes the other (the wild, frivolous partygoer, enthralled by criminals
and enamored of the very, very rich, who refuses to grow up). The ego
lives upstairs, the id downstairs. Not that this Freudian schema is at all
conspicuous; on the contrary, few contemporary novels provide as
good an example as *Breakfast at Tiffany's* does of Flaubertian economy,
elegance, and (seeming) objectivity. It is Capote's finest work—witty,
affecting, not a word wasted.

M any, of course, would accord that distinction to *In Cold Blood*
(1966). This study of the 1958 murder of the Clutter family of Hol-
comb, Kansas, is undeniably riveting, but Capote's lifelong tendency
to identify with the outsider led him, in this instance, to present the facts
in such a way that the reader has to struggle to avoid sympathizing with
the murderers, Perry Smith and Richard Hickock. As Capote describes
them, the Clutters are *Reader's Digest*-reading robots, fudge-baking
clones, church-going zombies, who have no great ambitions, no profound torments, no interest in pursuing anything other than the unexamined life. Contrasted with these card-carrying members of the
Bible Belt *booboisie* are the two killers. The Clutters' murderers—Perry
Smith especially—fascinated Capote. In Perry, a small, childlike man
with an I.Q. of 130, a carful of books, maps, poems, and letters, and a
preoccupation with his memories of boyhood, Capote appears to have
seen a sensitive soul—and, one suspects, yet another alter ego. Though
the tone of *In Cold Blood* is controlled and impersonal, the fact is that
Capote developed a warm friendship with the murderers during his
years of research; at the end, he accompanied them to the scaffold, wept

for days over their deaths, and even paid for their grave markers. One wishes, for the sake of *In Cold Blood,* that he had been as close to the Clutters. Even that, though, would probably not have been enough: Capote's fascination with murder and murderers (which by no means ended with *In Cold Blood*) was too profound, and his aloofness from moral considerations (in these matters, at least) too extreme, to allow for much authorial sympathy for the victims.[1]

Capote trumpeted that he had, in *In Cold Blood,* created a new literary form, the "nonfiction novel." Some critics hailed this "invention," others dismissed it. Norman Mailer suggested that Capote's swing to nonfiction bespoke "a failure of imagination," and then (as Capote spent the next eighteen years pointing out) wrote *The Armies of the Night,* a "novel-as-history," and won the Pulitzer Prize for it. *In Cold Blood* is, of course, no novel; but it is a very sophisticated piece of New Journalism, the sort of handsomely written, subtly partisan reportage that only a gifted author of fiction could have concocted.

After *In Cold Blood,* Capote continued to experiment with genre. He published less and less; during most of the nearly two decades between the publication of *In Cold Blood* and his death, Capote claimed to be working hard at a book called *Answered Prayers,* which he described as "a variation on the nonfiction novel." (The title "is a quote from Saint Thèrése, who said: 'More tears are shed over answered prayers than unanswered ones.'") Chapters from this work-in-progress appeared in *Esquire* during the mid-Seventies, and the information they disclosed about certain of Capote's café-society friends—who, by that time, seemed to have become far more important to him than his writing—supposedly turned all of them against him. (This rejection, in turn, reportedly drove him to the heavy drinking and drug-taking that brought on his death.) The excerpts didn't do Capote's literary reputation much good either. Critics saw *Answered Prayers* as gossip, not serious literature—the work of a man grown lazy and self-indulgent. And they were, unfortunately, right: the *Esquire* excerpts represent a surrender, on Capote's part, to those more puerile tendencies that were evident in—but did not, at any rate, tyrannize—his earlier work. To be sure, one can discern, in reading the excerpts (which *are* beautifully composed), that Capote did have at least a ghost of a serious literary intention here. He wanted to say the usual things about fame, wealth, and the wages of ambition, while doing for the New York society of the 1970s what Edith Wharton had done for the New York society of the

1870s. The excerpts do succeed in one sense: they prove beyond a doubt that most of the rich ladies who spend their afternoons at La Côte Basque and La Grenouille are dull and shallow. This, indeed, seems to be Capote's main point. But why, if these women *are* so dull and shallow, would anyone want to spend a decade of his life reproducing their silly chatter and collecting their gossip—or, for that matter, keeping them company? It is, to be sure, possible that *Answered Prayers,* as Capote envisioned it, would have added up to a profound, penetrating novel of contemporary manners. But the published excerpts, as they stand, do not penetrate very deeply.[2]

It appears likely that we shall never know precisely what *Answered Prayers* could have been. An article by Julie Baumgold which appeared last fall in *New York* magazine told the story. After Capote's death, his biographer, his editor, and his lawyer searched his Long Island house but failed to find a single page of the manuscript that he had claimed, for so many years, to be toiling over, and which (though he had never shown it to anybody) he had expostulated upon at length in countless interviews. After looking everywhere, Capote's friends faced what appeared to be the unpleasant truth: there was no *Answered Prayers;* Capote had seemingly been lying for years about his progress on it. It is, of course, possible that he had produced hundreds of pages of his intended *magnum opus,* but had found them unworthy and destroyed them in the course of attempted revision.

In the preface to his final book, *Music for Chameleons,* Capote indicated that he had stopped work on *Answered Prayers* as the result of "a creative crisis and a personal one" that came upon him at the same time. These crises, as it turned out, "altered my entire comprehension of writing, my attitude toward art and life and the balance between the two, and my understanding of the difference between what is true and what is *really* true." The upshot is that he began to rewrite *Answered Prayers* in an entirely new style. That style—which dominates *Music for Chameleons*—represents yet another step in the direction Capote had been moving all along: toward greater concision and "realism," a heavier reliance upon dialogue, and a more comprehensive combination of forms. The idea was to "combine within a single form . . . all [he knew] about every other form of writing. . . . A writer ought to have all his colors, all his abilities available on the same palette for mingling (and, in suitable instances, simultaneous application)."

The longest and most effective of the pieces in *Music for Chameleons,* a "nonfiction short novel" called "Handcarved Coffins," describes a bizarre-but-true series of crimes that Capote followed closely during the late Seventies; the new style works well here, and the story, though shorn of the depth and detail of *In Cold Blood,* has an immediacy, an emotional force, and a quality of genuine suspensefulness and terror that Capote had never achieved before. The "Conversational Portraits" that occupy nearly half of *Music for Chameleons* are somewhat less ambitious. As the collective title indicates, each of these short pieces consists of the record of a conversation between Capote and someone he finds interesting—Pearl Bailey, Bobby Beausoleil (of Manson Family fame), Mary Sanchez (Capote's cleaning lady). In the most celebrated of these pieces, "A Beautiful Child," Capote describes his cavortings on an April day in 1955 in Manhattan with Marilyn Monroe, whom he sees as a Holly Golightly-like child-woman, a beautiful innocent adrift on the corrupt seas of life. The cavortings end at twilight on South Street Seaport:

> M A R I L Y N: Remember, I said if anybody ever asked you what I was like, what Marilyn Monroe was *really* like—well, how would you answer them? (Her tone was teaseful, mocking, yet earnest, too: she wanted an honest reply) I bet you'd tell them I was a slob. A banana split.
> T C: Of course. But I'd also say . . .
>> (The light was leaving. She seemed to fade with it, blend with the sky and clouds, recede beyond them. I wanted to lift my voice louder than the seagulls' cries and call her back: Marilyn! Marilyn, why did everything have to turn out the way it did? Why does life have to be so fucking rotten?)
> T C: I'd say . . .
> M A R I L Y N: I can't hear you.
> T C: I'd say you are a beautiful child.

There is some lovely writing in the work that Capote published after *In Cold Blood,* and the mixed-salad style of *Music for Chameleons* is often surprisingly successful. But—as pieces like "A Beautiful Child" graphically illustrate—the appeal of much of this work has relatively little to do with its literary merits. Capote, in his zeal to write "nonfiction novels" and "nonfiction short stories," may well have thought that he was being faithful to "what is *really* true," but all he was doing, in actuality, was neglecting his obligation as a literary artist to create, to order, and thereby to serve not merely personal and superficial truths but universal ones. It is an obligation to which Capote was attentive for so long, and which he fulfilled with such distinction, that his ultimate renunciation of it (manifestly well-intentioned though it may have been) is particularly disheartening. Because of this renunciation—and for the other reasons I have suggested—it is, perhaps, easier to celebrate the fine literary talent Capote was gifted with than to applaud many of the uses he made of it. The Capote-like narrator of one of the published *Answered Prayers* excerpts, writer P. B. Jones, remarks at one point: "I knew I was a bastard but forgave myself because I was *born* a bastard—a talented one whose sole obligation was to his talent." This sounds exactly like Capote talking about himself, and it describes what may well have been Capote's tragic flaw: that throughout most of his adult life, he considered himself to be responsible only to his talent. It seems never to have occurred to him that his talent, in turn, might have its own responsibilities.

All About Norman

MAY 1985

Novelist, journalist, activist, narcissist, prisoner of sex, self-advertiser and American dreamer: is there any contemporary writer other than Norman Mailer whose life could keep us enthralled for seven hundred pages and more? "Please do not understand me too quickly," he pleaded, quoting André Gide, at the beginning of *The Deer Park* in 1955, and there has been precious little danger of that in the ensuing thirty years; among the few things Americans have been able to count on during the Age of Mailer, in fact, is that every so often the Republic's premier Existentialist would come hurtling out of his supercharged little corner of the globe—outrageous, offensive, and (with any luck) thought-provoking—and proceed once more to shake up both the cultural situation and the State of the Union.

It has not, in short, been a typical literary life. Nor has Peter Manso, in *Mailer: His Life and Times,* given us a typical literary biography. *Mailer*—a book so huge that it makes *Ancient Evenings* and *The Executioner's Song* look like pocket diaries—is, like Jean Stein's *Edie,* an oral memoir in symposium form, the literary equivalent of a week-long episode of *This is Your Life.* One after another, figures from Mailer's past (150 in all) trot onstage—everybody from Gene Kelly to Gene McCarthy, Midge Decter to Abbie Hoffman—and unburden themselves of anecdotes (chronologically arranged), literary opinions, psychological interpretations, personal tributes. And, of course, an occasional harsh word, though not so many as one might expect. (Gloria Steinem, voicing what seems to be a common sentiment, says, "I find it almost impossible to be angry at him.")

One consequence of this format is that *Mailer* is a good deal more gossipy, redundant, and packed with irrelevancies than the average biography; at times one finds oneself asking, "What does *this* have to do with literature?" But all in all, the book is interesting and the life just plain overwhelming. One soon loses count of the number of fascinating books, bawdy wives, dumb brawls, noisy controversies. If there is a figure in the carpet, it is Fanny Mailer, the writer's adoring mother, who recalls that even as a boy Norman "had a circle around him. . . . It was like he was a little god." His father would complain about Norman's messy room, but not her: "I'd say, 'Leave him alone. He's going to be a great man.'"

From Brooklyn, we follow Mailer to Harvard, then into the Army. We see him publish his Dos Passos-inspired naturalistic war novel, *The Naked and the Dead,* become famous, and go to Hollywood (where, according to Shelley Winters, he *did* meet Marilyn Monroe, whether he remembers it or not). We watch the failure of the naively Marxist *Barbary Shore* and *The Deer Park* lead Mailer to drug taking, hipsterhood, the founding of *The Village Voice,* and the compilation of the egocentric existential manifesto *Advertisements for Myself.* ("Unconsciously," he says now, "I was trying to take inventory . . . to end a certain part of my literary life and begin anew.") We relive the night Mailer stabbed his wife Adele, the day he stormed the Pentagon, the hectic writing and editing of the Pulitzer Prize-winning *Armies of the Night,* the filming of *Maidstone,* the race for mayor of New York, the 1968 conventions, the Town Hall debate over *The Prisoner of Sex,* the marriage to two wives in one week, the campaign to free convicted killer Jack Henry Abbott, who killed again shortly after being released. . . and so on. That a man could do so much living and yet manage to do so much writing is remarkable.

If there is a major problem here, it is that Manso gives us the pieces of the puzzle but leaves it to us to fit them together. How to explain a man in whom courtly charm vies with arrogance, family love with buffoonish sexual obsession, social responsibility with an attraction to violence? His macho code clearly derives from Hemingway, but perhaps D. H. Lawrence is an equally important influence. Like Lawrence, Mailer seeks truth in madness, identity in action; craves sex with women, scuffles with men; is a philosopher of primitive emotional states and the devoted son of a doting mother. Like Lawrence, he believes in being guided by instinct, by "vision": this is why his ideas are so often bizarre, his work uneven, his actions and public statements self-ruinous. He has mellowed with age, but for most of his career he behaved as if life was meaningless unless he was constantly engaging other human beings in hazardous sex or combat or argument (it hardly seemed to matter which) and thereby allowing himself, for better or worse, to be changed. To him war seems to be the ultimate experience, and a possible reason for the self-willed immoderation of his life, the deliberate attempts to antagonize, is that he has been trying all along to duplicate the risk and turbulence of war.

A contrived approach to life? Indeed. But even as Mailer has rejected the distinction between fiction and nonfiction, he has renounced the barrier between life and art, and persists in thinking of himself and his loved ones as characters to be shaped, developed, put through paces. At sixty-two, he continues to try on new masks, persists (to quote Norman Podhoretz) in "making a project of himself." But the man behind the image has yet to come completely into focus. Like his parents' homeland, Russia, which he recently visited, Mailer is a riddle wrapped in a mystery inside an enigma. Peter Manso has gotten the unwrapping under way in impressive fashion.

Talking Heads:
The Novels of Saul Bellow

SEPTEMBER 1987

We can't say he didn't warn us. On the very first page of his first novel, *Dangling Man,* Saul Bellow's narrator-protagonist complains that in present-day America

> the code of the athlete, of the tough boy . . . is stronger than ever. Do you have feelings? There are correct and incorrect ways of indicating them. Do you have an inner life? It is nobody's business but your own. Do you have emotions? Strangle them. . . . If you have difficulties, grapple with them silently, goes one of their commandments. To hell with that! I intend to talk about mine, and if I had as many mouths as Siva has arms and kept them going all the time, I still could not do myself justice.

Bellow has been talking ever since. In the past forty-three years he has published ten novels, and whatever else one might find to say about them, they have (with only a single exception) been remarkably talky. And the savvy reader always knew who it was, really, doing the talking: the protagonist might have happened to go by the name of Artur Sammler or Moses Herzog or Charlie Citrine or Augie March, but when he began carrying on about sorrow and love and the emptiness of the heart and the meaning of existence in modern America, it was patently Bellow, and nobody else, who was speaking. This is not to deny that many of the things Bellow has had to say have been worth listening to; on the contrary, he has almost invariably had highly intelligent observations to make about the life he leads and the world he knows. It is simply to indicate that one cannot imagine Bellow, in the heat of composition, coming up with a bit of social commentary or a tidbit of philosophical wisdom and saying to himself, "No, this observation isn't right for *this* novel's protagonist. Maybe the next one." (Or, "This discursive passage just doesn't go here; it slows down the action; it blurs the focus.") The truth is that, for all their differences, when it comes to range of reference and cast of thought, most of Bellow's protagonists are interchangeable; and all too often, alas, it seems as if range of reference and cast of thought are all that some of Bellow's protagonists amount to.

It is hardly surprising that Bellow has given his tenth novel the title *More Die of Heartbreak.* For throughout his career, both death and heartbreak have figured significantly in Bellow's fiction. They are, one might even say with little exaggeration, Bellow's stock-in-trade. Almost all of his novels contain a prominent *memento mori* motif. Over the course of *Dangling Man,* the protagonist's landlady grows ill and dies; in *The Victim,* Asa Leventhal's nephew Mickey takes ill at the beginning of the novel and passes away near the end; at the close of *Seize the Day,* Tommy Wilhelm, whose father continually speaks of his own imminent death, weeps at the funeral of a stranger; near the beginning of *Henderson the Rain King,* Eugene Henderson finds the dead body of a neighbor, and the realization that he too will die spurs him to escape the world he knows and go to Africa; at the conclusion of *Humboldt's Gift,* Charlie Citrine, who has been haunted by the memory of his late friend Von Humboldt Fleisher, witnesses Humboldt's reburial; and in *The Dean's December,* Albert Corde travels with his wife to Rumania to see her critically ill mother, who eventually passes away.

In *More Die of Heartbreak* it is a businessman–thug named Vilitzer—an uncle of the narrator, Kenneth Trachtenberg—who has an appointment with the Grim Reaper. Vilitzer's age and feebleness are discussed throughout the novel; his death is announced in the book's last brief section. "I don't see why you're broken up over that old crook," says Kenneth when he sees his Uncle Benn weeping. Benn's response: "[H]e was still a man, a person. Now he's just a packet of ashes, inside a black box." This is a constant theme in Bellow's work: that all human beings are our brothers and when they die they deserve our grief, for no other reason than that they were human. The reason that Bellow so often sets his novels against a backdrop of death is probably most succinctly summed up in the injunction that Tommy Wilhelm recalls in *Seize the Day:* ". . . love that well which thou must leave ere long."

None of the above-mentioned individuals, of course, dies of heart-break. But in Bellow's novels, many a character's heart, if it is not broken, is at least tormented in one way or another. At various points in the novels, hearts are heavy, hurt, quaking, aching, sore, soft, stirred, sinking, full, tender, troubled, torn, rent, pent, overflowing, passionate, suffocated, and even "shat on"; they swell and flutter and "feel sick" and pound "with dangerous thick beats." The protagonist of *Dangling Man* describes "the least penetrable part of me" as "the seldom-disturbed thickets around the heart." In *Humboldt's Gift,* Charlie Citrine (who suffers "uneasiness or heaviness of heart") tells his daughter that he loved his parents "[d]eep in the heart," discusses with Humboldt "the riches of the human heart," and is told by his friend Ulick that if living in Chicago "hasn't killed your fucking heart, you must be a man of iron." In *Herzog,* Moses Herzog dwells on "the American experience of the heart and the deepening of character in the modern age," wires the man who cuckolded him that "Dirt Enters At The Heart," and worries that if his daughter is not "educated according to the Herzog standards of 'heart' . . . she will fail to become a human being." And Herzog quotes Rousseau: *"je sens mon coeur et je connais les hommes."* When he wants to give a passage that special extra touch of emotional profundity, Bellow will often work in the word *heart.* Thus the heart figures in the conclusion of more than one of his novels. At the end of *Mr. Sammler's Planet,* Artur Sammler prays over the body of his dead nephew, observing that the young man "did meet the terms of his contract" with life, "[t]he terms which, in his inmost heart, each man knows." And at the close of *Seize the Day,* when Tommy Wilhelm attends the stranger's funeral, he "crie[s] with all his heart," sinking "deeper than sorrow, through torn sobs and cries toward the consummation of his heart's ultimate need."

Heart is not the only abstraction that recurs in this fashion in Bellow's novels. The words *soul* and *spirit* are perhaps equally prevalent. And the word *human,* often in combination with the word *being.* This is appropriate, because Bellow means for us to recognize his protagonists as human beings of heart and soul and spirit—sensitive intellectuals, almost to a man (and they *are* all men, and urbanites, and all but two of them are Jewish), trapped in an age and a society that, we are meant to understand, make it supremely difficult for one to be a human being of heart and soul and spirit. Because they are this sort of human being, Bellow's heroes suffer tremendously—and *suffer* is another favorite word of his. A friend of Herzog's, observing his grief over the collapse of his marriage, speaks of suffering in a strange, complimentary manner with which Bellow would seem to be sympathetic: "Well, when you suffer, you really suffer. You're a real, genuine old Jewish type that digs the emotions. I'll give you that." Later in the same novel, Herzog wonders whether he's "paid his debt to suffering," and speaks of "creative suffering" and "suffering in joy."

These words—and one or two others, such as *sorrow*—adorn Bellow's pages like merit badges or combat medals intended to testify to the depth of his protagonists' feelings, the degree to which they have been victimized by life. Gloom, world-weariness, and suffering; in the world of Bellow's novels these things are the order of the day. Indeed, Bellow often seems to believe that to be world-weary is to be sophisticated, to be gloomy is to be serious, to suffer is to be virtuous. (In *Humboldt's Gift,* Citrine speaks of "the graver, more important human feelings"—as if love and joy were less important.) The reader is supposed to be moved by this suffering, to feel for and identify with the hero-as-victim; for though the protagonist is more often than not an intellectual, living in either Chicago or New York, he is also clearly intended to be an Everyman figure, whose plight is recognizable to people who couldn't even *spell* Wittgenstein.

But Bellow's novels are not as effective, on this score, as he doubtless would like them to be. For one thing, since it is usually difficult not to identify Bellow's heroes with the author himself, all the talk of the greatness of their souls, hearts, humanity, and suffering—especially when other characters are dwelt upon so sporadically—quickly begins to look like mere self-absorption, self-glorification. For another thing, feelings in Bellow's novels are more often named than believably communicated, more often discussed than truly felt. As a rule, his fiction is as emotionally inert as it is intellectually intense. When such words as *heartbreak* and *sorrow* and *suffering* appear—especially (as they sometimes do) in pleonastic profusion—it is almost as if they are there by way of acknowledging the author's unwillingness to evoke the corresponding emotions. To read Bellow, in short, is typically not to be made to feel but to be made (or at least asked) to think about certain categories of feeling.

And not just of feeling: all of Bellow's novels are concerned, in a major way, with moral, philosophical, social, and political questions. A randomly chosen twenty-page passage from any of the novels will almost certainly touch upon several of the following questions: What responsibilities does a man have to himself? To his family? To his society? To the human race? What is the value of life? Of democracy? Of civilization? Of culture? Of money? Of sex? What does it mean to be an American? What are the proper limits of ambition? These are obviously important questions, and Bellow's thinking upon them is almost invariably of a high order. Indeed, the typical page of Bellow contains more evidence of a superior and serious mind at work than do the entire texts of most novels. This is no less true of *More Die of Heartbreak* than of any of its predecessors; Bellow's new book, in which the uncle of a young university professor marries an unsuitable woman and finds his entire way of life and system of values threatened, attests to Bellow's continuing fascination with such questions. Yet with this novel, as with all but one of Bellow's earlier novels, one's ability to become engaged by the characters' reflections on life and man and America—or, for that matter, to respond to their feelings, if not with empathy, then at least with understanding and pity—is frequently compromised by a certain lack of restraint on Bellow's part. Whether he is interrupting his narrative to expound upon his characters' private sorrows or to relate their reflections on American civilization and culture—or whether, as often happens, he is doing both simultaneously—he will generally either go on too long, repeat himself unnecessarily, or engage in hyperbolic rhetoric.

To read any of his novels (with, again, a single exception) is to be frustrated by his insistence upon suspending the narrative, at every turn, for yet another grand pronouncement—a pronouncement which may or may not have anything to do with the grand pronouncement on the previous page, but which, if one has read enough Bellow, will probably remind one of a dozen or so other pronouncements of comparable grandeur. Perhaps the most frustrating thing about reading Bellow is that these self-exploratory and discursive passages usually don't lead anywhere, don't add up to anything, don't connect with one another in any systematic way, and don't seem to have much impact (or, when they do, don't have a very *plausible* impact) upon the protagonist's state of mind or the direction of his life. Sometimes, for that matter, one bit of Bellovian wisdom contradicts another. It is obvious that Bellow recognizes all this, and that he thinks it is just fine. Yet it would be understandable for a reader to decide, after reading two or three of Bellow's books of fiction, that they are less novels, in any conventional (or even unconventional) sense, than intellectual grab-bags. Several times in Bellow's books, characters venture the fanciful opinion that human beings are mere shadows; alas, in most of his novels, they assuredly are. The publication of *More Die of Heartbreak*—which I will discuss presently—would seem to provide a splendid opportunity to examine this phenomenon at some length.

In Bellow's short first novel, *Dangling Man* (1944), for example, the protagonist—who gives his name only as Joseph—argues that in the twentieth century, and particularly in America, "we have been taught there is no limit to what a man can be." If, during the God-fearing Middle Ages, "a man was what he was born to be," in the modern world "the stage has been reset and human beings only walk upon it," and instead of God "we have . . . history to answer to." So far, so good. But as Joseph goes on his rhetoric grows excessive, and—although it is clear that Bellow expects the reader to identify with him—the state of mind he describes eventually becomes unrecognizable to anyone not suffering from clinical depression:

> We were important enough then [six hundred years ago] for our souls to be fought over. Now each of us is responsible for his own salvation, which is his greatness. And that, that greatness, is the rock our hearts are abraded on . . . we hate immoderately and punish ourselves and one another immoderately. The fear of lagging pursues and maddens us. The fear lies in us like a cloud. It makes an inner climate of darkness. . . .

Joseph's entire situation in *Dangling Man* is an instance of Bellovian excess. As the book opens, seven months have passed since Joseph quit his travel-bureau job "to answer the Army's call for induction"; but, because of bureaucratic red tape, the call hasn't come. So Joseph, supported by his wife, has been at liberty; his life is one of "narcotic dullness," but he won't get another job because "I am unwilling to admit that I do not know how to use my freedom." To be sure, he's tried his hand at some essays on the philosophers of the Enlightenment, but has thrown them aside to keep the journal that comprises the text of the novel. In the journal he writes about himself sometimes in the first person, sometimes in the third, and debates with himself—in the form of a "Spirit of Alternatives" that he addresses as *Tu As Raison Aussi*—the comparative values of regular employment and total freedom. He notes that "Joseph suffers from a feeling of strangeness, of not quite belonging to the world, of lying under a cloud and looking up at it." In short, he lives outside the respectable workaday world, and contrasts himself with his friend Myron, an insider who "has worked hard to reach his present position" and who, unlike Joseph, has learned to appreciate convenience and make compromises. Yet eventually Joseph determines that he, and modern Americans in general, find it difficult to govern themselves and are therefore afflicted with an "inability to be free" that causes them "weariness of life." When his notice finally comes, bringing his period of freedom to an end, Joseph is grateful to be "relieved of self-determination." The book ends with heavy-handed irony:

> Hurray for regular hours!
> And for the supervision of the spirit!
> Long live regimentation!

Bellow patently wants to suggest that real freedom is rare, and that American life is such that even when we are given freedom we feel oppressed by it, and prefer the regimentation of regular employment, however spiritually unrewarding it may be. But the book does not convey this theme convincingly. Joseph's anguish is excessive to the point of unbelievability; he speaks of his liberty as if it were the most horrible torture known to man. His self-absorption, moreover ("Shall my life," he wonders, "by one-thousandth of an inch fall short of its ultimate possibility?"), makes him less than lovable. Besides, he seems to be too much of an intellectual to have such trouble finding something to do with his time. This is, after all, a man who, in the name-dropping manner of almost all Bellow protagonists, speaks of his friend Abt as "Lenin, Mozart, and Locke all rolled into one," and whose friend Alf reminds him of Rameau's nephew, "described by Diderot as '... un (personnage) composé de hauteur et de bassesse, de bon sens et de deraison.'" Such a man certainly wouldn't find a gift of time to read and think and write such a cosmic tragedy. Even if he did, it would be up to the author to distance himself from the character, to try to give some sense of why such a fortunate individual might be so pathologically self-involved, so morbidly full of self-pity. But that is not Bellow's view of Joseph, and not his intention; he identifies with Joseph, and wants his readers to do so as well. The crux of the problem with the novel is that such identification is impossible; Joseph is not a man so much as he is an embodiment of Bellow's ideas about man—many of which, at the time he wrote *Dangling Man,* were strongly influenced by Existentialist philosophy. What Bellow does in his first novel, in short, is to try to pass off a Sartrean shadow puppet as Everyman—with the result that, although the book makes plain the impressiveness of Bellow's intellectual attainments, it is not much of a novel.

"How should a good man live; what ought he to do?" This is a question that Joseph asks himself in his journals, and it is one that Bellow has posed anew, in one way or another, in each of his novels since *Dangling Man. The Victim* (1947), a short, temperate novel in the third person, concerns a New York editor named Asa Leventhal, who has been an "insider" for only a few months. Before acquiring his job, he lived, like Joseph, on the fringes of the respectable world; when an acquaintance name Kirby Allbee arranged a job interview for him, Leventhal, with his outsider's lack of pragmatic restraint, insulted the interviewer and may unwittingly have lost Allbee his position. Now safe and comfortable, Leventhal begins to be pestered by an unemployed and emotionally unstable Allbee for some form of restitution. This turn of events provokes in Leventhal a number of unsettling thoughts. Profound generalizations fill his mind—about the cruelty of American society (he has "the feeling that he really did not know what went on about him, what strange things, savage things"), about the limitlessness of Americans' ambitions ("[e]verybody wanted to be what he was to the limit. When you looked around, that was what you saw most distinctly. In great achievements as well as in crimes and vices"), and about many other things.

As a novel, *The Victim* is an unarguable advance over *Dangling Man:* the protagonist is more believable, the supporting characters more rounded; though the oppressively dark and confined atmosphere seems at times too self-consciously (and almost monotonously) Kafkaesque, it is nonetheless very artfully evoked. What's more, Bellow is splendid at conveying a frightening sense of the financial precariousness of many middle-aged people's lives: one can *feel* (a rare experience in Bellow) Leventhal's insecurity over his job, his fear of falling between the cracks of society and becoming an outsider again. Yet, as with *Dangling Man,* the overt excursions into metaphysics and social analysis are plentiful to the point of distraction and annoyance; and for all the bad things that happen to him, the protagonist's gloom frequently seems excessive. All in all, *The Victim* is a promising small novel, stylish and well formed, which suffers considerably from its author's enchantment with doom and gloom, and his unfortunate tendency to *tell* rather than to *show*.

Both of Bellow's first two novels received considerable praise upon publication. But it was *The Adventures of Augie March* (1953) that established him as a major novelist of his generation, and, in particular, as a philosopher of sorts about the meaning of American life. For *Augie March* is a picaresque novel in the American naturalistic tradition of *U.S.A.* and Theodore Dreiser, and its hero is a Jewish cousin to Studs Lonigan as well as a descendant of Huckleberry Finn. Brought up in a poor Chicago family by his mother and by a boarder named "Grandma" who "wise[d] us up" with "animadversion[s] on the trustful, loving, and simple surrounded by the cunning-hearted and tough," Augie sets out on an odyssey that involves him in all sorts of enterprises of varying degrees of legality, including an outfit run by a shady but learned real-estate operator named William Einhorn, who quotes from *Hamlet* and refers in casual conversation to Alcibiades and Socrates. Augie is an energetic young man but doesn't know what he wants or where he is going. Yet he has an "ambition of something special and outstanding." Einhorn warns him, "You've got *opposition* in you" — i.e., he's a born outsider, a natural candidate, unless he watches himself, for "the clinks and clinics and soup lines."

The difference between Augie and the protagonists of Dreiser, Farrell, and company, needless to say, is that Augie is the naturalist hero as intellectual. Augie is introduced to books when he becomes involved in a book stealing scam; before long, he is reading—and, of course, reeling off the names of—all sorts of great writers: "Two volumes of Nietzsche's *Will to Power* I had a hell of a time swiping, for they were in a closed case at the Economy Book Store; I also got him Hegel's *Philosophy of Right,* as well as the last volumes of *Capital* from the Communist bookshop on Division Street, Herzen's *Autobiography,* and some De Tocqueville." Naturally, Augie devours all this stuff in record time, and before you know it he sounds like — well, like Saul Bellow. But he's not the only one. Wherever he goes in the seamy urban underworld, Augie somehow manages to find himself in the company of extraordinarily well read, articulate people with strong ideas about the nature of modern American civilization. Indeed, they all sound as if they're on their way to the same symposium. And they're all eager as hell to share their ideas with Augie: he barely says hello to these people before they start pontificating. A stammering millionaire, for instance, tells Augie that the rise of American democracy and American wealth represents "the greatest crisis in history," for once "the decrepit old civilizations" with their grinding poverty were swept away,

> we'd find out if there was going to be this earthly paradise or not. . . . M-machinery'll make an ocean of commodities. Dictators can't stop it. Man will accept death. Live without God. That's a b-brave project. End of an illusion. But with what values instead?

Bellow is so preoccupied here with what the millionaire is saying that he doesn't seem to consider that a reader might find it difficult to imagine a millionaire saying such things. So frequently does a reader have this sort of difficulty that it comes to seem as if Bellow incorporates such arguments and apothegms into the novel as they occur to him, and places them in the mouth of whichever character happens to be onstage at the time.

Augie March does have considerable virtues. Perhaps more successfully than any other Bellow novel, it evokes the rush, the complexity, the energy of American urban life. And the picaresque form is well suited to Bellow's own dialectical tendencies: simply by putting many of his discursive passages in the mouths of successive characters (each of them drawn with exuberance and a rare attentiveness to physical detail), Bellow gives *Augie March* a sense of movement that many of his books lack. Yet, like many of Bellow's other novels, *Augie,* taken as a whole, amounts to a good deal less than the sum of its parts—a failing more noticeable in this instance than in any other, if only because *Augie* (the longest of Bellow's novels) contains so many parts. For all the wonderful concrete details that this book contains (and it contains many), Bellow seems, in its pages, to labor under the impression that, for a novel to be truly impressive—truly *serious*—every concrete detail must lead to some abstraction, the loftier the better. Time and again, potentially powerful dramatic climaxes are blunted when Bellow makes a gratuitous shift into the didactic mode, and proceeds to spell out "truths" (e.g., "The power of an individual to act through his intellect on the reason of mankind is smaller now than ever") that would be more effectively conveyed through dramatic means. In the end, furthermore, despite all his reading and listening and observations and insights, Augie seems to have come to few firm conclusions, to have found no direction; as Norman Podhoretz wrote in his 1959 essay on the book, Augie "goes through everything, yet undergoes nothing." Indeed, for all the ideas about humanity that he kicks around, there is not much human substance to him; to exaggerate only slightly, he is six hundred generalizations in search of a character. And the book that takes its name from him is less the *Bildungsroman* that it seems indeed to be than it is a potpourri of *pensées*.

Bellow followed his longest novel with his shortest. *Seize the Day* (1956) is Bellow's most admirable work of fiction—concise, cogent, and finely controlled. Tommy Wilhelm is in his middle forties and is residing at the Hotel Gloriana on New York's Upper West Side, which is mostly occupied by elderly people, his physician father among them. Like Augie March, Tommy Wilhelm has energy—and it's done him nothing but harm. For years he tried to be a movie actor in Hollywood, but then "his ambition or delusion had ended," and he became a salesman, and now—that pursuit having failed as well, along with his marriage—another resident of the hotel, a shady character named Dr. Tamkin, has talked him into speculating in the commodities market. "Seize the day," Tamkin advises.

The book is unique among Bellow's works. The setting is meticulously described, and several of the characters are memorably developed. Most remarkable of all, though, is Bellow's restraint: with a few exceptions (e.g., the list of books by "Korzybski, Aristotle, Freud, W. H. Sheldon" in Dr. Tamkin's apartment), neither the narrator nor any of the characters feels obliged to drop the names of high-toned books and authors or to generalize about such matters as suffering, death, freedom, and the meaning of America—which are, nonetheless, among the themes of *Seize the Day;* and the book is all the more effective, of course, because of this avoidance of explicit theme-mongering. The novel's conclusion is especially powerful: in quick succession Wilhelm discovers that Dr. Tamkin has swindled him, is rejected by his father ("Go away from me now. It's torture for me to look at you, you slob!"), and has a painful telephone conversation with his estranged wife; he then finds himself in "the great, great crowd" on Broadway,

> the inexhaustible current of millions of every race and kind pouring out, pressing round, of every age, of every genius, possessors of every human

secret, antique and future, in every face the refinement of one particular motive or essence—*I labor, I spend, I strive, I design, I love, I cling, I uphold, I give way, I envy, I long, I scorn, I die, I hide, I want.*

A moment later he is in a funeral chapel, on a slow line filing past a coffin; the dead man's meditative look strikes him with "horror," then "heartsickness," and then finally "sorrow," but he cannot leave the corpse, and is soon crying over it, his sadness at the death of "another human creature" mixed with his continuing anguish over his own problems. It is an affecting ending, as much a reminder of the ubiquity of death (and of the fact that life continues, in all its equivocality, pettiness, and pathos, in spite of death) as it is an affirmation of human connectedness. One of the special things about *Seize the Day,* in fact, is that it seems more universal—less bound to its particular time and place, less concerned with facile social criticism, more sharply focused upon the eternal verities—than Bellow's other novels. Of all Bellow's endings, moreover (which are, as a rule, notorious for their inconclusiveness), the ending of *Seize the Day* is the one that feels most like a coherent, satisfactory, and earned resolution.

At the close of *Seize the Day,* the description of the crowd on Broadway seems life-affirming; at the beginning of Bellow's next novel, *Henderson the Rain King* (1959), a more self-referential catalogue has the opposite effect. The narrator is Eugene Henderson, a fatuous millionaire who wants to explain why he took his big trip to Africa, though "there is no quick explanation."

> When I think of my condition at the age of fifty-five when I bought the ticket, all is grief. The facts begin to crowd me and soon I get a pressure in the chest. A disorderly rush begins—my parents, my wives, my girls, my children, my farm, my animals, my habits, my money, my music lessons, my drunkenness, my prejudices, my brutality, my teeth, my face, my soul! I have to cry, "No, no, get back, curse you, let me alone!" But how can they let me alone? They belong to me. They are mine. And they pile into me from all sides. It turns into chaos.

He proceeds to give a quick résumé of his life: it consists largely of two marriages, five children, and a "ceaseless voice in my heart that said, *I want, I want, I want.*" Clearly this is a man who needs a Bellovian lesson in limits. In any event, somehow or another—he can't quite define how or why—this "disturbance in [his] heart" led Henderson to Africa.

Henderson the Rain King is, in many ways, the most uncharacteristic of Bellow's books: the protagonist is a Gentile, the setting rural. Yet there are parallels to other Bellow novels, in particular *The Adventures of Augie March*. For, like *Augie March, Henderson* is the exuberant yet strangely solemn story of an adventurer, a man in search of self-definition who at novel's end claims to have learned a thing or two about life but who has not really changed at all. Among the differences between them, of course, is that Augie is poor, young, and Jewish, and Henderson is rich, middle-aged, and WASPy. He has reason to identify strongly with America and its history: his great-grandfather was a secretary of state, his father a friend of William James and Henry Adams. But for him his native land does not seem, at the novel's beginning, to hold any promise; nor does it offer any reply to the obscure, persistent cry of his heart.

But Africa doesn't seem to answer his cry either. He seeks transcendence; but his encounters with the natives—he cockily tries to rid one tribe's water supply of frogs, for example, and his explosives end up destroying the water supply itself—teach him that he is no god. And herein lies a big problem with the book: the reader knows from the beginning that Henderson is no god, and cannot be overly sympathetic with him when he learns otherwise. There are some charming and funny incidents in the novel, and it is less clogged with distracting discursive passages than most of Bellow's books. But in the final analysis it is peculiar and unsatisfying; the African setting and characters are largely unconvincing, the ending inconclusive, and Henderson himself —by far the least intellectual of Bellow's protagonists ("I haven't ever been calm enough to read")—too unattractive and uninteresting to sustain one's attention for the length of the novel (which is not Bellow's longest, but reads like it). How, after all, can one care much about a conceited, obnoxious millionaire whose heart keeps crying *I want, I want, I want?* One's initial impulse is to tell him to grow up; and this impulse doesn't change much over the course of the book.

In *Herzog* (1964), Bellow returned to familiar territory. Moses Herzog is a middle-aged Jewish intellectual historian from Chicago, the author of a book called *Romanticism and Christianity* whose wife, Madeleine, has divorced him and become the lover of his best friend, Valentine Gersbach. Though Herzog—who has left Chicago for New

York, where he teaches a night course in "The Roots of Romanticism" —has as his consolation the sexual companionship of an attractive student named Ramona, his "heart has been shat on" and his sanity shaken. He insists that he's "not going to be a victim," but that's what he acts like: when he is not busy thinking about his ex-wife, his daughter, his Yiddish-speaking Russian parents, and everybody from de Maistre to Tocqueville, he is composing cranky letters to public figures and perpetrating a manic mélange of *mots* on the subjects of life, death, selfhood (" 'personal' life is a humiliation, and to be an individual contemptible"), the "destiny of Man," the nature of freedom in the modern world ("people can be free now but the freedom doesn't have any content. It's like a howling emptiness"), and of course America:

> The people who come to evening classes are only ostensibly after culture. Their great need, their hunger, is for good sense, clarity, truth—even an atom of it. People are dying—it is no metaphor—for lack of something real to carry home when day is done... what a responsibility we bear, in this fat country of ours! Think what America could mean to the world. Then see what it is. What a breed it might have produced. But look at us—at you, at me. Read the paper, if you can bear to.

But most of Herzog's dark socio-political musings, as well as his conviction that "the human spirit has poured itself" in recent years into a "program of destruction," seem intimately connected to his melancholy over losing Madeleine—and, perhaps, his guilt over having left behind the Montreal ghetto, where he'd had "[a]ll he ever wanted," and over having married a *shiksa*. This circumstance would seem to call the validity of his remarks, as social criticism, into question; but Bellow obviously doesn't think so. To him they are plainly not just the *disjecta membra* of a tortured soul, but valid observations worthy of our thoughtful consideration. Nor does Bellow ever appear to consider it ridiculous that Herzog intellectualizes absolutely *everything* (e.g., "It's possible that a man like Hoberly [a former lover of Ramona's] by falling apart intends to bear witness to the failure of individual existence").

For all the breadth of his social commentary, though, Herzog dwells mostly upon himself:

> Oh, what a thing I am—what a *thing!*... I fall upon the thorns of life, I bleed. .... What good, what lasting good is there in me? Is there nothing else between birth and death but what I can get out of this perversity—

only a favorable balance of disorderly emotions? No freedom? Only impulses? And what about all the good I have in my heart—doesn't it mean anything? Is it simply a joke? A false joke that makes a man feel the illusion of worth?

The self-absorption of some of these passages in *Herzog* is incredible; equally incredible is the degree to which Herzog wallows in dejection. Susan Sontag once called for an "erotics of art"; Bellow, in *Herzog,* perfects what might be called an erotics of melancholy:

> He was in pain. He should be. Quite right. If only because he had required so many people to lie to him, many, many, beginning, naturally, with his mother. Mothers lie to their children from demand. But perhaps his mother had been struck, too, by the amount of melancholy, her own melancholy, she saw in Moses. The family look, the eyes, those eye-lights. And though he recalled his mother's sad face with love, he couldn't say, in his soul, that he wanted to see such sadness perpetuated. Yes, it reflected the deep experience of a race, its attitude toward happiness and toward mortality. This somber human case, this dark husk, these indurated lines of submission to the fate of being human, this splendid face showed the responses of his mother's finest nerves to the greatness of life, rich in sorrow, in death. . . .

And so forth. At times Bellow seems determined to prove that he can carry on endlessly, hysterically, *sorrowfully,* about any aspect of himself (or Herzog's self). This is true not only of Herzog's thoughts but of his conversations, some of which are so pretentious that one can hardly appreciate whatever they may contain in the way of real self-understanding. Does anyone, for instance, actually talk like this to his beloved?

> ". . . You want to put me on a higher level and bring out the Orphic element in me. But I've tried to be a pretty mediocre person, if the truth be told. . . . On the side, I was just flirting a little with the transcendent."

And would a man who is sitting in a car, preparing to kill his wife's lover, actually think about the fact that "demographers estimate that at least half of all the human beings ever born are alive now, in this century. What a moment for the human soul!" If *Herzog* is a particularly frustrating book to read, it is because the novel testifies to the existence of so many feelings that are simply not evoked in its pages.

*H*erzog—Bellow's sixth novel—seems in retrospect to have been a sort of watershed. For all their thematic sameness, Bellow's first five novels vary relatively widely in size, form, and so forth: *Dangling Man* takes the form of a journal; *Seize the Day* is brief, taut, and Flaubertian, *Augie March* capacious, diffuse, and naturalistic; *Henderson the Rain King* is about a WASP in Africa. Bellow's second five novels, beginning with *Herzog,* constitute a more uniform group; it is as if, in *Herzog,* Bellow finally found a basic form and manner that he was willing to settle upon. These later novels are all rather long, and each focuses upon a relatively short period—a few days or weeks—in the life of a New York or Chicago intellectual with (usually) a professional interest in social history or the history of ideas. The novels are desultory, slow to establish a plot and slow to develop it; the narrators continually wander away from the story line, piling digression upon digression, shuttling from one time frame to another, creating a mixed salad of tangentially relevant anecdotes, cries of the heart, high-toned reading lists, and social and philosophical reflections. The principal conflicts are personal ones involving love, death, and crime, but they are all intended to convey larger truths about the nature of humanity and, of course, about the dreadful state of American society and culture in our time.

Mr. Sammler's Planet (1969) presents us with Artur Sammler, a man in his seventies who lives alone on New York's Upper West Side; the son of a once well-to-do European family, he is now forced to do "things that cooks and maids had once done" and takes this sorry state of affairs as a sign of "[h]istorical ruin." He spends a good deal of time at the Forty-second Street Library, and on the bus he takes home he has begun noticing a black pickpocket at work. The criminal fascinates him; he informs the police, but they can't do anything. So fascinated is Sammler, in fact, that he takes to riding the bus more than ever—until one day the pickpocket notices his interest, follows Sammler home, and exposes himself to him.

Like Herzog, Sammler occupies much of his time by coming up with broad generalizations about the human condition in our era:

> [Broadway] was aware of being a scene of perversity, it knew its own despair. And fear. The terror of it. Here you might see the soul of America at grips with historical problems, struggling with certain impossibilities, experiencing violently states inherently static. Being realized but trying itself to realize, to act. Attempting to make interest. This attempt to make interest was, for Mr. Sammler, one reason for the pursuit of

madness. Madness is the attempted liberty of people who feel themselves overwhelmed by giant forces of organized control. Seeking the magic of extremes. Madness is a base form of the religious life.

And he thinks a lot about the decline of civilization, especially in terms of race. To Bellow, Sammler and the pickpocket embody a number of contrasts: civilized *vs.* primitive man; mind *vs.* body; conventional *vs.* modern (circa 1970) sensibilities; good *vs.* evil; restrained dignity *vs.* "oceanic, boundless, primitive, neckfree nobility"; humankind's "old patience," now extinct, *vs.* "the peculiar aim of sexual niggerhood [sic] for everyone"; and, finally, Idea *vs.* Will—for, as Sammler recalls, Schopenhauer declared that "[t]he organs of sex are the seat of the Will" and that "only Ideas are not overpowered by the Will."

There is much to admire in *Sammler:* the old man is one of Bellow's most fully realized protagonists, and is compelling as well as endearing; both his fascination with the pickpocket and the contrasts between the two men are nicely developed. Moreover, the New York setting is vividly suggested. Yet the book has its troubling aspects, one of them being that there is something rather offensive about establishing an exhibitionist and a pickpocket as a symbol of the black race—or, to put it another way, about using the black race as an emblem of criminality. Furthermore, many of Sammler's observations about modern life would seem to be equally applicable to life in any period of human history; for instance, one would think, from the way this book laments the sexual hedonism of modern America, that sex was a late twentieth-century discovery. This would be a much stronger novel if only someone had persuaded Bellow to excise most of the discursive passages and allow the story to speak for itself.

Humboldt's Gift (1975) is, at least in part, the most plainly autobiographical of Bellow's novels. The protagonist, Charlie Citrine, is a Chicago writer, the author of a highly successful Broadway play and the winner of two Pulitzer Prizes, who (to the consternation of his publishers) has recently written a serious, quickly remaindered book called *Some Americans: The Sense of Being in the USA,* and is currently at work on a sequel. Citrine is haunted by his memories of his late friend and mentor Von Humboldt Fleisher, a poet whose book of ballads, published in the Thirties, was "an immediate hit." The character of Humboldt is based largely on Delmore Schwartz, who was a close friend of Bellow's in New York.

Humboldt's Gift may well be the best of Bellow's longer novels. If so, it is in part because, for once, a character besides the narrator—a character whom one does *not* identify with Bellow—is allowed to occupy center stage, allowed to become a symbol of virtue and knowledge, a role usually reserved only for Bellow's narrator-protagonists. The book also conveys more genuine feeling than the typical Bellow novel: Bellow's wistful affection for Schwartz, and for the lost youth and shared dreams that his memory represents, comes through clearly. Besides, Schwartz, like the typical Bellow protagonist, talked obsessively about philosophical and social issues, and peppered his conversations with the names of great leaders and thinkers. If the conversation of many Bellow characters seems contrived, then, Humboldt's conversation—based, as it is, on Schwartz's—is believable. And finally, *Humboldt's Gift* is eminently readable simply because one knows that, to an extent anyway, it is a roman à clef, and Delmore Schwartz was one of the most colorful literary figures of his time.

Yet the novel does not stray very far afield from Bellow's usual themes, for many of his obsessions were also Schwartz's:

> The noble idea of being an American poet certainly made Humboldt feel at times like a card, a boy, a comic, a fool. We lived like bohemians and graduate students in a mood of fun and games. Maybe America didn't need art and inner miracles. It had so many outer ones. The USA was a big operation, very big. The more *it,* the less *we.* So Humboldt behaved like an eccentric and a comic subject. But occasionally there was a break in his eccentricity when he stopped and thought. He tried to think himself clear away from this American world (I did that, too). I could see that Humboldt was pondering what to do between *then* and *now,* between birth and death, to satisfy certain great questions.

Humboldt had high hopes; he felt that with America's rise to world power, philistinism was finished. But Humboldt's pipe dreams of the empowerment of intellectuals fell through, and he eventually went mad. As his star fell, Citrine's was on the rise. Citrine became an insider, while Humboldt became more and more an outsider, living in fleabag hotels in the Times Square area. Citrine remembers Humboldt telling him "that poets ought to figure out how to get around pragmatic America." Citrine has gotten around pragmatic America by writing trash ("*Von Trenck* ran for eight months on Broadway. I had the attention of the public for nearly a year, and I taught it nothing"); Humboldt stuck by his guns to the end, and perished.

The passages in which Citrine recalls Humboldt have a vividness and empathy that are rare in Bellow. But, alas, the novel—especially the latter part—is devoted mostly to more recent events, notably Citrine's harassment by a flashy, gun-toting thug named Rinaldo Cantabile, who cheated him out of some money at cards. "I had gone out one evening to amuse myself in vulgar company," Citrine explains, "and I had fallen into the moronic inferno"—that is, into the perilous chaos of America. Like Sammler's black pickpocket, Cantabile has a "natural imagination," an instinctive desire to humiliate intellectuals by forcing them into situations of physical intimacy: instead of exposing himself, he forces Citrine to stand in a bathroom stall with him while he defecates.

The principal reason for the thug Cantabile's interest in Citrine, ridiculously enough, is that he wants him to help Mrs. Cantabile with her dissertation (yes, dissertation) on Humboldt. That Mrs. Cantabile is writing such a dissertation is, to Citrine's mind, a manifestation of the fact that "[t]he country is proud of its dead poets. It takes terrible satisfaction in the poets' testimony that the USA is too tough, too big, too much, too rugged, that American reality is overpowering. . . . So poets are loved, but loved because they just can't make it here." The novel's ultimate irony is that Citrine is enriched by a "gift" from Humboldt that Cantabile's wife unearths: a film script that Humboldt and Citrine wrote together years ago and that, thanks to Cantabile, goes into production. Compared to the parts of the novel in which Humboldt is remembered, these non-Humboldt portions are pallid and familiar; the situation is contrived, the ironies heavy-handed, the character of Cantabile hard to buy. The truth is that *Humboldt's Gift* comes alive, really, only when Citrine is remembering Humboldt. Perhaps this is intentional—a way of suggesting that the life has gone out of Citrine's existence—but it makes for a novel which, though very engaging at the start, becomes less and less interesting.

The first novel that Bellow published after winning the 1976 Nobel Prize in Literature was *The Dean's December* (1982). It is a weak novel, perhaps Bellow's weakest since *Dangling Man*. The dean of the title is Albert Corde, a professor of journalism at a Chicago university and, like Herzog and Citrine before him, the author of solemn tracts on American life—namely, two notorious articles for *Harper's* magazine about crime and punishment in Chicago, which have earned him a reputation as a racist. The novel—which concerns Corde's journey to

Bucharest with his Rumanian-born wife to see her dying mother—is concerned largely with comparing American society (which Bellow again refers to as a "moronic inferno") to the "penitentiary societ[y]" of Rumania. Or, more specifically, comparing the disadvantages of American life to the disadvantages of Rumanian life. The American phenomena to which Bellow pays the most attention in this novel are crime and pollution. Shortly before Corde's departure for Rumania, a student of his is killed by two black men, one of them a friend of his nephew Mason (as in *Mr. Sammler's Planet,* then, Bellow uses blacks to symbolize, in part, the horrors of contemporary American life). And a scientist named Beech describes to Corde the horrifying extent to which, according to his figures, the air, water, and soil of America have been poisoned by industrial deposits of lead; "[c]hronic lead insult," he concludes, "now affects all mankind." Needless to say, Bellow neither shows us the murder nor dramatizes the effect of "chronic lead insult": these horrors are just talked about.

So much for America. As for Rumania, Corde does not experience very much of life in that country and what does happen to him there is not of great interest. The novel's prime example of the horrors of life behind the Iron Curtain is the strictness of hospital visitation rules. Nonetheless, it is something of a relief to follow a Bellow hero around Bucharest, for a change, instead of doing another tour of New York or Chicago. Besides, given his obsession with the horrors of America, the few observations that Bellow does have to offer about life and death in the Communist world are of special interest; and the very act of placing his comments about American politics, society, and culture in the context of the Soviet bloc strikes one as something that he should perhaps have thought to do a long time ago. Yet on the whole *The Dean's December* must be counted as one of Bellow's slacker, more mechanical efforts. It reads like the work of a tired man; Bellow seems merely to be going through the motions, recycling the usual remarks about civilization and its discontents more out of habit than out of conviction.

Which brings us, at last, to Bellow's newest production, *More Die of Heartbreak,* perhaps the least satisfying of Bellow's later novels. Kenneth Trachtenberg, the novel's narrator, is a young assistant professor of Russian studies in an unnamed city that sounds very much like Chicago. His name is a combination of the German words meaning "to strive or aspire" and "mountain or hill." But his professional aspirations are modest; his career is less important to him than his relationship with his uncle Benn Crader, a distinguished botanist past his middle years whom Kenneth has come to the Midwest to be near. In the maddening way of many a Bellow speaker, Kenneth's narration meanders like the conversation of a barroom drunk from one anecdote or idea or putative witticism to another, and only after a hundred or so pages does it become clear what the novel is "about": Benn's ill-advised, and ill-fated marriage to a beautiful young WASP heiress named Matilda Layamon. Benn compares Matilda's beauty to that of Helen of Troy, as described in Poe's poem; the lines are quoted several times in the course of the novel. (The name *Layamon* may derive from the fact that the poem *Brut* by the medieval author Layamon is a historical chronicle that begins with the fall of Troy.) It is a marriage that the naïve, romantic scientist enters into behind Kenneth's back, and after the wedding he finds himself regretting it. Matilda's tastes are expensive, beyond what Benn can afford even on his generous salary; and Matilda's wealthy father, Dr. Layamon, is a sharp businessman who, having discovered that Benn once owned the land on which the city's tallest structure, the Electronic Tower, is built, tries to persuade him to sue his crooked cousin Vilitzer, who negotiated the sale and kept most of the several million dollars of profit. Yet Benn resists Dr. Layamon's pressure, and eventually asserts his independence and humanity in a decisive manner.

Readers of Bellow's previous novels may well feel that they have already met many of these characters and observed many of these situations. Vilitzer, for instance, is the latest in a long line of businessman-thugs in Bellow's fiction; and the financial conflict between him and Benn recalls a passage in *The Dean's December*, describing the way that Corde's cousin Max, having been given Corde's power of attorney, swindled him in a real-estate transaction. Like Corde, Kenneth is the son of a playboy; Benn, for his part, recalls a number of scientists in previous Bellow novels, including the eminent scientist named Beech in *The Dean's December*. Matilda is in many ways a retread of Madeleine, the beautiful young wife whom Moses Herzog married without his family's approval (and whose father, like Matilda's, expresses an abnormal, and vulgar, curiosity about her sex life). As in *Herzog*, we are supposed to sympathize with the no-longer-young man for finding himself tied to such a shallow, grasping *shiksa*; never does it seem to occur to either Bellow or his narrator that a man would have to be pretty shallow himself to marry a beautiful woman, many years his junior, without even noticing until after the wedding how incompatible her interests, tastes, and ambitions were with his.

Indeed, Matilda is yet another Bellow female who, for all her accomplishments (and often these Bellow females *are* highly educated), is patently meant to be seen, first and foremost, as a beautiful bitch—or, in the words of *Herzog,* a "frigid, middlebrow, castrating female." One Bellow novel after another characterizes women as disloyal, as unsatisfied with a single man. In *Mr. Sammler's Planet,* for instance, Angela Gruner, after several drinks, admits that "[a] Jew brain, a black cock, a Nordic beauty . . . is what a woman wants." In *More Die of Heartbreak,* Kenneth's cousin Fishl says that "candid women will tell you, I'd like some of this and some of that—a little Muhammed Ali for straight sex, some of Kissinger for savvy, Cary Grant for looks, Jack Nicholson for entertainment, plus André Malraux or some Jew for brains. Commonest fantasy there is. Unfortunately you have to limit your catch to one." How cruel these women can be! Toward the end of *Herzog,* when Madeleine looks at her ex-husband across a courtroom, her eyes "expressed a total will that he should die"; in *Seize the Day,* Tommy Wilhelm complains that his estranged wife "has fixed herself on me to kill me." So uncharitably does Bellow characterize the female of the species that it is almost as if he regards feminine pulchritude as a wile, a cunning means of ensnaring trustful men, of distracting them from their families, their responsibilities, and their allegiance to the true, the good, and the more spiritually beautiful.

One very noticeable fact in *More Die of Heartbreak* is that all the characters talk the same way: the young Paris-bred Russian scholar, the WASP doctor and his daughter, the aging Jewish botanist, and so forth. They're all egregiously vulgar, and indeed often sound like character actors playing thugs. For instance Kenneth—who is supposed to be sensitive and intelligent—describes his attraction to Treckie, the mother of his child, as follows: "This sexual kid, I went for her." (Kenneth is yet another Bellow protagonist who is estranged from his woman and child.) He speaks of himself as reading "Russian stuff," describes a woman as being "twigged out," says that "Uncle had whatchamacallit for me—charisma," describes Dr. Layamon as a "hotshot" and his own father as a "cocksman" and "such a dude," and says of Matilda that she is the sort of woman who "didn't have to futz around in Paris with all that postwar sleaze." Similarly, Dr. Layamon calls

Benn a "cocksman" and refers to "the way they fart around in these glitzy restaurants." Matilda too uses the word "glitz"; Benn, for his part, uses words like "stumblebum." Then there's Kenneth's cousin Fishl, who speaks of Layamon as a "creepo" and asks rhetorically, "[W]hat's so distinguished about letting people screw you?"; and Kenneth's friend Dita Schwartz, who says, "I don't understand this rage for titless broads"; and Treckie's mother, who says that ski instructors "have all the sack traffic they can handle."

They *all* talk this way. Indeed, part of the reason, I think, for everybody talking in the same lowbrow fashion is that Bellow labors under the delusion that it takes the sting off the pretentious things that people say to have them say it in gutterese. (As somebody says to Moses Herzog, "You're not like those university phonies. You're a *mensch*.") What's more, they all seem to have the same range of reference: Treckie's mother refers to Auden; Fishl, a crude operator, compares himself to Edgar in *King Lear*. Finally, the characters in *More Die of Heartbreak* all play what one might call the "synonym game"—they say the same thing two, three, four times in a row, in slightly different words, as if the author, unable to decide among the possible alternatives, decided to use them all. For example, at one point in the narrative Kenneth announces that "out of the troubled landscape there appears, takes shape, materializes, the somnambulistic form of Caroline Bunge."

All of these aspects of *More Die of Heartbreak* should be rather familiar to the reader of Bellow's previous novels; but in the present novel these elements of the Bellovian manner are even more noticeable—and more irritating—than in its predecessors. At times, indeed, Bellow seems to be wearing his less fortunate stylistic habits on his sleeve, to be making little wise-guy jokes about his characteristic manner. More than once, for instance, he has Kenneth apologize to the reader for allowing himself to be "sidetracked." When Kenneth plays the synonym game in the course of defining the word *arcanum* ("it's what you have to know in order to be fertile in a creative pursuit, to make discoveries, to prepare for the communication of a spiritual mystery"), he adds parenthetically: "Excuse the language; I'm in a hurry and I can't stop to pick and choose among the available terms." And at one point Bellow has Kenneth say, "I take very little pleasure in theories and I'm not going to dump ideas on you."

Au contraire, naturally. As usual, there's a new theory, idea, cultural observation, or philosophical *mot* trotted out on virtually every page of *More Die of Heartbreak*. Some of this talk is interesting enough:

> Death . . . while you enjoy a viewer's immunity from it, is entertaining, as it was in imperial Rome, or in 1793. As, today, Sadat is murdered, Indira Gandhi is assassinated, the Pope himself is gunned down in St. Peter's Square, while, personally unharmed, *you* live to see more and more and more, until after many deferrals death gets personal even with you. The jumpmaster says, "You bail out next."

But Kenneth's brief passage about his profession—to choose one from dozens of possible examples—strikes one as obvious, easy, tired:

> Being an academic is quite a thing. You can take my word for this because I'm an academic myself. I don't say that I'm sold on being one, only that I am one—for the time being, marginally—an assistant professor of Russian literature. Exciting to me, but how many are worked up over such studies—compared, say, to Bruce Springsteen or Colonel Qaddafi or the majority leader of the U.S. Senate?

Indeed, Kenneth himself, as a character, is rather obvious, easy, and tired. He resembles Bellow less than previous Bellow protagonists; but he is not very much like anyone else either. Alas, he's barely there at all. It's as if Bellow wanted to focus less on his protagonist than he generally does, in order to be able to accord greater attention to the secondary characters; he does so, however, not by strengthening the secondary characters but by weakening the protagonist. The fact is that we do not really know Kenneth, and we cannot believe in his supposedly powerful emotional bond with his Uncle Benn (an out-of-the-ordinary attachment that recalls, among other things, Herzog's unusually strong affection for his brother Will, Tommy Wilhelm's intense desire for his father's love, and the special uncle-nephew and uncle-niece relationships in various other Bellow novels). Nor do we know Benn well enough to understand why Kenneth might be so attached to him, or why Kenneth, from the very beginning, perceives Benn's marriage to Matilda Layamon as a terrible idea. And it is hard to understand Kenneth's conviction that it would be wrong for Benn to heed Dr. Layamon's pleas and sue the crooked Vilitzer. Alas, there are too many things, in this novel, that Bellow unreasonably expects one to understand intuitively.

Saul Bellow deserves admiration for many reasons. One can have nothing but respect for his ceaseless preoccupation with such serious themes as the "sacredness of life" (as he puts it in *Sammler*) and the interconnectedness of all humanity; what is unfortunate is that he explicitly insists on these things more often than he conveys a sense of them. It is praiseworthy, too, that Bellow's novels are so concerned with the making of one's soul, with the question of how one should lead one's life; but sometimes his protagonists seem to think of nothing else, and at such moments the novels read like exercises in solipsism. Bellow's love of ideas is admirable as well; one wishes only that rather than wandering capriciously (as he frequently seems to do) from idea to idea, he would make a greater effort to subsume his inevitable battery of sociological observations, metaphysical musings, and learned quotations to more rigorously structured plots and more thoroughly and realistically developed sets of characters. It is wonderful that Bellow is so determined to write novels of ideas; the problem is that he is usually more interested in the ideas than in the novel.

All too frequently, moreover, Bellow's discursive passages—especially those in which he attempts to characterize American life and the modern sensibility—strike one as remarkably misguided. For example, he speaks of such universal human qualities as ambition and carnal passion as if they were peculiar to the twentieth century or the United States; and he refers to the philistinism of the bulk of the American public as if it were some sort of gross historical anomaly, as if it were reasonable to expect most people in any society to be intellectuals. In his more than four decades as a novelist, Bellow has taken what may well be an unparalleled number of facile jabs at American life. (For instance, Herzog, in jail for a day, reflects that a prison cell "was not the sphere of his sins. . . . Out in the streets, in American society, that was where he did his time.") Bellow suggests that in America today the opinions and ideas of a single individual count for less than ever, when the fact is that nowadays articulate and intelligent people, who in previous centuries might have been mute inglorious Miltons, stand a far better chance than ever before of finding a suitable forum and a sizable audience for whatever they have to say. Bellow also suggests that individuals are more than ever forced to endure lives of bleak, mechanical routine, subordinated to things larger than themselves—big government, advanced technology—when in truth, as a result of the advancements of technology, fewer and fewer people are called upon these days to perform the sort of menial, dehumanizing tasks to which the majority of human beings, until this century, had to devote most of their waking hours. Bellow hammers home his dark pronouncements on the way we live now with such insistence that one often has the impression that he considers it his duty to find something uncheering to say about any topic that may happen to come his way; at times it even appears as if he is doing his best to squeeze some great general truth out of every episode that he writes, whether or not such a thing is actually hiding in there.

So distinct is Bellow's novelistic method that it does not seem excessive to describe his novels as a subgenre unto themselves—a subgenre of books that are "successful" only to the extent that they provide a framework within which he can talk about his favorite subjects with some semblance of formal justification. It is, moreover, because of this difference between Bellow's novels and those of other contemporary American writers that one cannot easily compare his achievement to theirs. Certainly he is one of the most intelligent—perhaps *the* most intelligent—of novelists working today; but the question of how distinguished his novels are, *as novels,* remains. It has been argued by many writers and critics, of course, that superior intelligence is not required to write even a great novel, and that, indeed, a brilliant mind can be a definite drawback for a novelist—when, presumably, it is not accompanied by an equally strong aesthetic sense. To be sure, *Seize the Day* demonstrated that Bellow is capable of writing something taut and beautifully focused, of reining in his tendency to talk his themes to death. Yet it somehow seems unlikely, at this stage of the game, that Bellow will produce another such book. What is far more likely, alas, is that—having long since settled into a mode that affords him endless opportunities to indulge his penchant for cerebral chatter—Saul Bellow will keep on talking.

John Hawkes's
Fan Club

NOVEMBER 1984

*H*umors *of Blood and Skin: A John Hawkes Reader*—the author's thir-
teenth straight book from New Directions—contains just about what
you'd expect: four short stories, excerpts from all nine novels, a frag-
ment of a novel-in-progress, brief autobiographical prefaces to each of
the selections. A fair enough overview. But the book's primary purpose, one senses, is not so much to provide the reading public with
snippets from twenty-year-old novels as it is simply to *exist,* and by existing to get us all a little bit more used to the idea that John Hawkes is an
important writer, a modern classic, an Author for the Ages. Indeed,
William Gass's introduction stops just short of proclaiming Hawkes's
divinity—and the man even signs himself "William H. Gass, Washington University, St. Louis," as if this were a scholarly document of
sorts, which in a way it is; for though Hawkes has achieved literary
eminence in the great world beyond the campus gates, the hotbed of
Hawkesianism is, was, and ever shall be the English department.

In fact, the Hawkes phenomenon was *born* in the English department—in English J, to be specific, a creative writing course taught by
Professor Albert J. Guerard at Harvard in the autumn of 1947. Hawkes,
an undergraduate, was a student in English J who had somehow discovered—quite on his own, apparently—that plot, character, setting,
and theme got in the way of "totality of vision" and were therefore "the
true enemies of the novel." Guerard was so impressed by the stories
that young Mr. Hawkes had written under the influence of this hypothesis that he took the precocious theorist and his work straight to the offices of New Directions, whose president, James Laughlin, was a Har-

vard alumnus and Guerard's friend. Laughlin was impressed too, so impressed that by the time Hawkes had his A.B. in hand, Laughlin had not only published Hawkes's novella, "Charivari," in *New Directions 11,* but had issued his first novel, *The Cannibal,* with an introduction by Professor Guerard.

And what an introduction it was! Singlehandedly, it set the schizophrenic tone—half scholar's, half booster's—that one academic after another, upon climbing onto the Hawkes bandwagon, has since taken as his own. Without bothering to identify himself as Hawkes's teacher, mentor, and sponsor, Guerard lets fly the accolades; he situates Hawkes on a level with Kafka, Faulkner, and Djuna Barnes (doing so "advisedly," he claims, in a wonderful imitation of scholarly circumspection, because "I think the talent, intention, present accomplishment and ultimate promise of John Hawkes are suggested by some conjunction of these three disparate names"), and with a number of other imposing figures. Yet the terms in which Guerard executes this comparison are peculiar indeed. To him, the magnificence of his protégé's talent is demonstrated by the fact that Hawkes "is now, at the outset of his career and at the age of twenty-three, a rather more 'difficult' writer than Kafka or Faulkner, and fully as difficult a writer as Djuna Barnes"; that "as a picture of the real rather than the actual Germany, and of the American occupant of that Germany, *The Cannibal* is as frankly distorted as Kafka's picture of the United States in *Amerika*"; that *The Cannibal* is characterized "by a very distinct reluctance (the reluctance of a Conrad or a Faulkner) to tell a story directly"; that, in *The Cannibal,* a degree of "difficulty and distraction is provided, as in Djuna Barnes, by the energy, tension, and brilliance of phrasing often expended on the relatively unimportant"; that *The Cannibal*'s "total reading of life and vision of desolation [are] as terrible as that of Melville's *Encantadas*"; that "as Kafka achieved a truth about his society through perhaps unintentional claustrophobic images and impressions, so Hawkes . . . has achieved some truth about his." In short: *The Cannibal* is as difficult, as distorted, and as depressing as the work of many great writers. Therefore *The Cannibal* is a great book and Hawkes is a great writer.

If such characteristics automatically made a book great, then *The Cannibal* would be a work of the utmost distinction. The novel is nominally set in an imaginary German town, Spitzen-on-the-Dein, in 1914 and 1945, but things are so surrealistically confusing that the novel cannot really be said to have anything so pedestrian as a setting.

Similarly, Hawkes gives us several names, but nothing resembling a human being ever takes form around any of them, so he's safe there, too: no real characters here. He's not out to evoke a particular place, time, or person but "to render [as he confides in *Humors of Blood and Skin*] my own vision of total destruction, total nightmare." Perhaps the best way to understand what Hawkes means by "vision" is to describe *The Cannibal,* or at least its first few pages, in some detail.

The book begins with the release of inmates from a mental institution near Hawkes's mythical town. One of the inmates, a pseudo-character named Balamir, makes his way into the town, and Hawkes provides an inventory of the things he passes along the way: the "fallen electric poles," the "piles of debris," the "same tatters of wash hung for weeks in the same cold air." By the end of the first page, we've gotten the point: this place (though we can hardly recognize it as a place) has suffered total destruction. But Hawkes is just getting started. He doesn't want merely to establish that everything in sight is broken to bits, falling apart, or rotting away, and then move on to something else. Heavens, no. He wants to create a *vision.* And since this is not Vladimir Nabokov or Nathanael West (or, for that matter, Edmund White, James Purdy, or Truman Capote), what that means is that we get more of the same—and more, and more, and more:

> Piles of fallen bricks and mortar were pushed into the gutters like mounds of snow, smashed walls disappeared into the darkness, and stretching along the empty streets were rows of empty vendors' carts. . . . Book-stores and chemist's shops were smashed and pages from open books beat back and forth in the wind, while from the split sides of decorated paper boxes a soft cheap powder was blown along the streets like fine snow. Papier-mâché candies were trampled underfoot. . . .

Evocative, yes. But it's also quite enough. Not for Hawkes. He drops Balamir for the moment, tosses a few more disembodied names at us—Madame Snow, her daughter Jutta, the Mayor, the Signalman, the Census Taker—only to return, immediately after introducing each of them, to his catalogue of the smashed, the moldy, the trampled, the fallen. Hawkes informs us that the legs and head were lopped off the town's statue of a horse, that the "rattling trains" were halted by "the curling rails," that "the empty shops and larders" were filled "with a pungent smell of mold," that the only horse left in town was "one gray beast" who "trampled, unshod, in the bare garden, growing thinner each day, and more wild," that "banners were in the mud, no scrolls of figured words flowed from the linotype, and the voice of the town at night sounded weakly only from Herr Stintz's tuba," that "there was nothing to eat . . . and tables were piled on one another, chipped with bullet-holes," that the town was full of "piles of cold rubbish and earth." *Et cetera, ad infinitum.*

This is what Hawkes means by vision. This crumbling town is supposed to rise up and haunt one, the way Stonehenge does at the end of *Tess of the D'Urbervilles.* But it doesn't work. Why? One reason, at least, is that there are people in *Tess,* people we believe in and care about, who give those weathered stones symbolic meaning, who make them matter. The same holds for James's golden bowl, for Woolf's lighthouse, for Fitzgerald's green light at the end of *Gatsby.* Reading *The Cannibal,* one wants desperately to be moved, but one isn't; in spite of Hawkes's prepossessing litany of broken buildings and smashed statues, the lack of human dimension makes the whole thing surprisingly inert.

Nonetheless, *The Cannibal* achieved what it was meant to. It was no bestseller, but, largely thanks to the attention Guerard attracted with his prefatory puffery, it was a *succès d'estime.* And Hawkes's subsequent novels—eight of them published between 1951 and 1982—solidified his position as a leading visionary novelist. Of course, none of this *succès* came about without help. As Hawkes's body of work took shape, so did an equally noteworthy body: the John Hawkes "fan club," a well-defined group of academic critics who have gathered around Hawkes and his works in the manner of a corps of disciples, and who have been instrumental in the rise of Hawkes's fortunes. Among them are Leslie A. Fiedler; Robert A. Scholes (Hawkes's colleague at Brown University), who included a chapter on Hawkes in his influential 1967 study *The Fabulators;* Donald J. Greiner, Frederick Busch, and John Kuehl, authors of critical studies of Hawkes's work published in the mid-Seventies; John Graham, editor of a collection of essays on Hawkes's novel *Second Skin;* and of course, Guerard, who has published a number of articles on Hawkes. The fan club convenes irregularly, at university symposia and MLA conventions, to discuss Hawkes's work. Its chief document is an outré volume entitled *A John Hawkes Symposium: Design and Debris* (1977), which contains the proceedings of a conference at Muhlenberg College whose speakers included not only most of the gentlemen listed above, but—just to establish beyond a doubt that the real purpose of this conclave was not criticism but celebration—

Hawkes himself. To keep things entirely in the family, *A John Hawkes Symposium* was published by (ahem) James Laughlin.

T he locust-like descent of scholars upon a contemporary novelist is, of course, hardly remarkable; many a writer has had the dubious honor of being paraphrased to death in dissertations and misinterpreted from the lecterns of hotel conference rooms. But few, if any, have seemed to pay so much attention to their academic expositors, or have owed them so much, as has John Hawkes. And few have been the subject of such unqualified veneration. For as far as the club members are concerned, Hawkes is *the* litmus test for the modern critic. "It's interesting, you know," Guerard says in his keynote address at the Muhlenberg gala, "that some of the alleged 'modernists' [during Hawkes's Harvard days] really didn't like Jack's work. . . ." The operative word is *alleged:* these self-styled modernists, simply by failing to admire the work of their colleague's undergraduate protégé, proved themselves to be Victorian fuddy-duddies. "The fact is," Guerard complains elsewhere, "that older and professional readers, with a few honorable exceptions, did not like Hawkes's work at all. They incorrigibly looked to those elements of fiction Hawkes saw as his 'enemies' at the beginning of his career." Well, you know these dishonorable, incorrigible critical types: they just go around *looking* for trouble.

Not like the members of the Hawkes fan club. The Hawkesians, at least on the subject of Hawkes, agree on just about everything. It is hard to read through their criticism without inferring that they have all subscribed to some party platform. They all, for example, enjoy complaining that Hawkes is ignored outside the academy. "There has been marked discrepancy," writes Kuehl, "between the academic and the general reception of John Hawkes's novels. Eminent literary critics such as Albert J. Guerard, Leslie A. Fiedler, Robert A. Scholes, and Tony Tanner have praised his art, yet Hawkes commands only a small following, many of whom are college teachers and students." Greiner echoes this sentiment, referring continually to Hawkes's "obscure reputation," his "lack of readers," his being "unknown and unread." He calls this obscurity "deplorable" and "a cause for concern." "I do hope that what I have to say will encourage more serious readers to pick up his novels," declares Greiner. "A writer of Hawkes's genius deserves a wider hearing."

One would hardly know that these men are carrying on about someone who, as a result of the efforts of their cabal, has long since escaped obscurity—who has been front-paged in *The New York Times Book Review* and the other major literary periodicals for over two decades; whose books clog the shelves of literary bookstores; who has been sanctified by the Ford, Rockefeller, and Guggenheim gods; and who is a member of the American Academy of Arts and Letters. To be sure, this Hawkes-is-neglected routine started decades ago, when it was somewhat less of an untruth. Fiedler, for example, wrote in his introduction to *The Lime Twig* (1961) that Hawkes was "perhaps . . . the least read novelist of substantial merit in the Unites States," and described an ad in which Laughlin denounced the editors of *Partisan Review* for not printing "the work of such writers as Edward Dahlberg, Kenneth Patchen, Henry Miller, John Hawkes, and Kenneth Rexroth." Fiedler noted: "God knows that of all that list only John Hawkes really needs the help of the *Partisan Review.*" Well, in the past two decades— thanks to the puffery of partisans like Fiedler—Hawkes has eclipsed all those writers, except Miller, in celebrity. But the Hawkes-is-neglected theme plays on. A typical complaint of a Hawkes clubman today is not that Hawkes can't get into the *Partisan* but that he does not have the readership of his fellow "black humorist" Joseph Heller—whose books are, of course, huge bestsellers. How famous, one wonders, can you become and still be considered obscure?

The clubmen also like to delude themselves (and mislead everybody else) with the notion that if Hawkes is less well known than he should be, it's because only academics have what it takes to appreciate him. Kuehl puts it this way: "Popular reviewers and their audiences [i.e., everybody off-campus], failing to comprehend how his work operates, also fail to understand what it expresses." This is merely a variation on the familiar academic conceit that everyone outside of academia is (to be kind about it) out of touch. It pleases the club to spread this sort of self-flattering fertilizer, and to feel that the novels of Hawkes are an all-in-the-family thing—of-the-academy, by-the-academy, for-the-academy. This possessiveness surfaces almost embarrassingly in Fiedler's introduction to *The Lime Twig:*

> Who . . . reads John Hawkes? Only a few of us, I fear, tempted to pride by our fewness, and ready in that pride to believe that the recalcitrant rest of the world doesn't deserve Hawkes, that we would do well to keep his

pleasures our little secret. To tout him too widely would be the equivalent of an article in *Holiday,* a note in the travel section of the *Sunday Times,* might turn a private delight into an attraction for everybody. Hordes of the idly curious might descend on him and us, gaping, pointing — and bringing with them the Coca-Cola sign, the hot-dog stand. They've got Ischia now and Mallorca and Walden Pond. Let them leave us Hawkes!

So why is this Ischia among novelists appreciated only in the academy? Because he's *difficult,* of course. Guerard's characterization of Hawkes as "a rather more 'difficult' writer than Kafka or Faulkner" is echoed by Kuehl ("his manipulation of complicated techniques and attitudes makes him one of the most difficult American novelists since Faulkner") and by Greiner ("Hawkes is as important a writer as Updike and Nabokov. As difficult as they sometimes are, he is difficult constantly").

Hawkes is great because he's difficult. And he's difficult because of that unconventional vision. Writes Kuehl: "Those who expect formal and conceptual materials associated with traditional realism are perplexed, for Hawkes mocks these as anachronistic. Substituting 'vision' for 'novel' and 'reality' for 'realism,' he would support Robbe-Grillet's contention that verisimilitude is no longer the issue. Old familiar fictional elements... seem banal to an anti-realist who rightly considers himself unique." This is the key to the fan club's defense of Hawkes. Whatever shortcomings non-club critics may fault him with, the club's answer is simple: Hawkes doesn't write by the old rules, so you can't judge him by old rules. Characters that never come to life? Instead of characters, Hawkes gives us *voices.* Greiner declares of two characters in *The Beetle Leg* that neither "is meant to be fully developed. It is their voices that count." No plot? Instead of plot he gives us *vision.* "The difference," explains Greiner, "is between the conventional novel with its structure based on meaning and the experimental fiction with its coherence based on imaginative vision." "There is no room for characters," asserts Frederick Karl about *The Beetle Leg,* "as there is no room for narrative or plot. The ten episodes ... are connected only by landscape and language. Just as the former is a state of mind more than a place, so the latter exists more in Hawkes's imagination than in the ordinary resources of language." What, one must wonder, makes voices without characters better than characters without voices? Why is an "experimental fiction" based on "vision" without "meaning" preferable to a conventional novel that has both?

The fan club divides Hawkes's oeuvre—and quite rightly, too—into two distinct visionary epochs. Some of the boys call the first one the "waste land" period. Besides *The Cannibal,* it includes three novels: *The Beetle Leg* (1951), *The Lime Twig* (1961), and *Second Skin* (1963). The books read almost like rewrites of one another: the "visions" are virtually identical; only the pseudo-characters and pseudo-settings are different. *The Beetle Leg* has, in place of a German village and asylum, a town and dam in the American West. A man named Mulge Lampson is buried in the dam; ten years after his death, we peek in on the surrealistic lives of his shadowy survivors. Hawkes tries to build the dam up into a major symbol, but, as with *The Cannibal,* the lack of human dimension defeats him. *The Lime Twig,* though pretty much a rerun, is a step in the right direction. In a gray, grim pseudo-London, a fat, pathetic, lonely pseudo-man named Hencher and his landlord Michael Banks join in a scheme to kidnap a racehorse named Rock Castle. Early in the novel, Hencher gets kicked to death by the horse, and later on Banks and his wife Margaret meet equally unpleasant ends; one cannot help but feel that Hawkes kills off Hencher so early because he perceives that Hencher is turning into (horrors!) a real human being for whom the reader might actually develop (God help us!) sympathy.

The last "waste land" novel is *Second Skin.* The narrator is Skipper, whose present is the Edenic bliss of a tropical island, and whose past is a parade of suicides—his father's, his wife's, his daughter's—and the murder of his son-in-law Fernandez. There are some genuinely affecting passages in *Second Skin,* and they are affecting because Skipper is at least the beginning of a real character, and the settings and situations through which he moves are the beginnings of real settings and situations. Indeed, the movement throughout these four "waste land" novels is quite distinctly away from the ineffectual "visionary" method of *The Cannibal* and toward a more nearly effective, and conventional, approach. Thus, though none of these four early novels works as a whole, the last two, at least, hold promise.

In the novels that follow *Second Skin,* unfortunately, Hawkes goes off in a new direction, chasing a new "vision." This might be called his pornographic period, for if these books were more disciplined in style and structure, they would make fine additions to any adult bookstore. Guerard called the first three Hawkes's "trilogy of sex," but with *The Passion Artist* (1979) the trilogy became a tetralogy, and then in 1982 a fifth came along in the form of *Virginie: Her Two Lives,* and it was suddenly embarrassingly clear that this wasn't a nice, naughtily adventurous little cluster of Updikean or Rothean sex novels but a whole new career founded on prurience. Gone is the desperate attempt to avoid characters, settings, plots; not that Hawkes suddenly develops a great talent for these things—he simply doesn't struggle against them. Since the "vision" of these later books is almost exclusively carnal—focusing, for the most part, on very clearly defined types of sexual interaction between people with very clearly defined relationships—it is all but impossible for Hawkes to stay as far from the conventional novel as he would like.

Still, he does his best. He manages to set *The Blood Oranges* (1971) in some unnamed tropical demi-paradise that never does come into focus. The book is about two men who swap wives: Cyril, the "sexually liberated" narrator (whose puerile philosophical mots—e.g., "the only enemy of mature marriage is monogamy"—Hawkes seems to take completely seriously), initiates the swap; the other man, Hugh, a pornographic photographer, eventually comes down with terminal guilt pangs and commits suicide, after which his wife Catherine is institutionalized and Cyril's wife Fiona leaves, taking with her Hugh's three children. *Death, Sleep and the Traveler* (1974) is about one Allert, a collector of pornographic albums who has been sharing his wife Ursula with his friend Peter, a psychiatrist; Allert takes a cruise, on which he has an affair with one Ariane. She disappears at sea; Allert is accused of murder; Ursula testifies in his behalf, then clears out. *Travesty* (1976) is a *récit;* the unnamed narrator is driving a car across France; in the backseat are his daughter Chantal and Henri, a poet who has been sleeping with both her and the narrator's wife Honorine. At the beginning of the book the narrator tells his passengers that he's going to smash the car into a wall a few miles up the road and kill them all; the remainder of the book consists of his recital, along the way, of anecdotes about sex with his mistress and his delight in pornography. *The Passion Artist* is about a man named Konrad Vost whose surrealistic sexual adventures involve his daughter, a prostitute, and his mother, a prison inmate. *Virginie: Her Two Lives* is about an eleven-year-old French girl who lives in two centuries. In 1945 she lives in a "Sex Arcade" with her brother, a raunchy cab driver named Bocage; in 1740 she lives with a "sensualist" named Seigneur, whose kept women burn him to death at the end of the book.

The attitude toward sex in these novels is sub-adolescent, and the eagerness (and utter inability) of the author to appear hip is pathetic. Hawkes wants desperately to come across as a roué, but he only succeeds in sounding like a middle-aged English professor who wants desperately to come across as a roué. Even a giggly twelve-year-old would soon tire of Hawkes's unrelieved preoccupation with clothing, underwear, and naked bodies—a fetishistic obsession which causes some sections of *Death, Sleep and the Traveler,* for example, to sound like fragments of letters to *Penthouse:*

> Ursula made no attempt to defend herself against the handfuls of heavy lotion which Peter, as I could now clearly see, was smearing across the tight rounded surfaces of Ursula's translucent underpants.

> I was sexually aroused in the depths of my damp swimming trunks as I had not been since long before the disappearance of the ship's home port. . . .

> "Let me hear what you can do with your flute."
> "Very well," she answered then. "But it may not be as easy as you think. You see, I play in the nude."

Parts of *Virginie,* meantime, read like excerpts from a poor translation of an X-rated French movie:

> "Do you think I could ever wear such foolishness? Sylvie," she cried, "Sylvie does not wear the frilly underpants!"

> "Look there," whispered Sylvie. "See how gently Monsieur Pidou uses the soap!'"
> "And little Déodat," whispered Yvonne, "how buttery he is, and how red!"

> "Oh, the endless buttons of sailor pants!"

This sort of nonsense, however, is innocuous compared with the sadomasochism that pervades the later novels. In *Travesty,* for instance, the narrator boasts about spanking his mistress Monique, and of her coming after him immediately thereafter with a whip: "I thought she meant only to whip me lightly to ejaculation, a process, which, at that moment, I imagined as a fulsome and brilliant novelty." But she flays him bloody, and does so "with joy" and "with superb contempt." And as a result: "In my defeat and discomfort I too felt a certain relief, a certain happiness for Monique. . . ." Cyril, the philosopher of *The Blood Oranges,* asserts that "most of us enjoy the occasional sound of pain, though it approaches agony." And the grubby gamboling of *Virginie* inspires such lines of dialogue as the following:

> "Virginie!" she called in a breath of pure amusement, "fetch the kettle. We are going to introduce Lulu to the raptures of steam!"

> "Mesdames!" Seigneur cried happily, and to me surprisingly, as he came at last among us and took his place at my table. "Mesdames, she who loves well punishes well!"

I will not dwell on Hawkes's obsession with little girls, or with bestiality; but reference must be made to the scene in *Virginie* that begins with Seigneur delivering the following speech to one of his kept women, Colère:

> "No creature is too deformed to love," he said. "No act is too unfamiliar, too indelicate to perform. Repugnance has no place in the heart of a woman such as you. By embracing an animal, or several animals, you do no more than embrace the very man, those very men, for whom you are now preparing yourself in the art of love. Adoration cannot live without debasement, which is its twin. I must ask you to disrobe."

Whereupon Colère proceeds to have a sexual encounter with two dogs and a pig—mainly with the pig, a scene to which Hawkes devotes four pages. Apparently this is what Frederick Karl refers to when he describes Hawkes's later novels as creating a "vision . . . of breaking out, of movements beyond matrimonial convention, of developments in individual sensibility," and what William Gass means when he speaks of the "glorious sensuality" of these books. There's certainly nothing very glorious going on here between people: men and women are forever abusing, abandoning, and betraying one another, the point apparently being that this is what intimate relationships are all about. They are founded not on love (there's very little of *that* in these books) but on passion, which in Hawkes's novels comes off as a form of totalitarianism.

Though Hawkes's career breaks up neatly into two periods, certain qualities run through all the novels. There's that prolix, pretentious style; that endless, amateurish pounding away at words like *agony* and *desolation;* that penchant for metaphors that sometimes don't make much sense but must sound powerful to his ear (in *The Blood Oranges,* for example, the "distant fortress . . . cupped in the shriveled palm of desolation"); those endless series of rhetorical questions:

> Why then this decided sensation of erotic power? Why the implication of some secret design? What brilliant and, so to speak, ravaging guile could possibly be concealed inside that slender and merely partial form? Why did I smile immediately and Fiona cry out in happy recognition at the black hole driven so unaccountably into that small portion of the stone which, realistically, should have revealed no more than sexual silence?

Most of the novels contain violence—murder, suicide. Hawkes remains clinically detached from his creations, but the obsessive cataloguing of chaos in the early books, and the exhaustive examination of sexual degradation in the later ones, makes it hard to overlook the possibility that this whole oeuvre is the product of a psyche desperate to dissipate its despair about mortality, entropy, and sin. This possibility, however, neither makes the early novels less tedious nor the later ones less offensive. The fan club seems to sense this, and has worked out explanations for all the gloom and grubbiness. Some suggest that Hawkes's books are profound commentaries upon the near-psychotic extremities of human despair (in the early novels) and passion (in the later novels). Others insist that his works are not meant to be taken seriously; they're supposed to be humorous, and if you don't see that, you're just obtuse. Hawkes seems to believe this himself. Witness the title of his new collection, *Humors of Blood and Skin,* and a few of his introductory remarks therein: "In *The Cannibal* I discovered an impulse toward comedy"; "*The Beetle Leg* is a mock . . . 'Western'"; *Travesty* is "a comic novel." Hawkesian humor is the subject of Greiner's book, *Comic Terror,* in which he singles out for comment the scene in *The Beetle Leg* where Mulge's mother Hattie dies and is buried above him in the dam: "Face down, eyes in dirt, she peered through the sandy side toward her son below, where he too lay, more awkward than she, feet up and head in the center of the earth." Greiner's gloss on this passage: "This kind of humor is not for everyone." *Humor?* Hawkes's comedy, you see, is "irreverent comedy at its best, designed not to amuse nor to provide a moment of quiet pleasure but to outrage," to "counter . . . complacency."

Countering complacency: that's what it comes down to. The club's favorite explanation for the gloom and grubbiness in Hawkes is, straightforwardly enough, that gloom and grubbiness are good for us. "One must confront the conceptual ugliness of human depravity," says Kuehl, and no writer helps one to do so better than Hawkes, whose visionary fiction "communicates objectively and uncompromisingly the nightmarish aspects of irrational twentieth-century existence." This notion of literature-as-emetic is common in academia, where the more nightmarish the picture a novel paints of the contemporary world the more seriously it is likely to be taken; but the Hawkesians have carried the claims for the value of negativism to unprecedented lengths. Guerard, in his introduction to *The Cannibal,* set the fan club's tone for all time when he wrote that "John Hawkes clearly belongs, perhaps this is to his credit, with the cold immoralists and pure creators who enter sympathetically into their characters, the saved and damned alike. Even the saved are absurd, when regarded with a sympathy so demonic: to understand everything is to ridicule everything." What Guerard is doing here is singing the praises of a sensibility that sees very little distinction between virtue and evil, except perhaps for a tendency to be bored by the former and charmed by the latter. Does Guerard really consider immorality creditable and virtue absurd? Does Hawkes? Of course not—not in real life, anyway. But for the "demonic" Hawkes, and for the club members who have echoed Guerard's praise through the years, moral values in life are one thing, those in literature another. It all just goes to show how little regard they have for a humanistic notion of the novel as a means of understanding life and how strongly they're chained to an academic notion of the novel as a playing field for professors. Although it is hardly intended as such, *Humors of Blood and Skin* is the perfect testament to Hawkes's lifelong indifference to the one conception, and his perpetual inability to break the ties that bind him to the other.

Guy Davenport:
Fiction à la Fourier

DECEMBER 1984

I t's hard, these days, not to be suspicious of experimental writing. So much of it seems to be produced by ego-happy no-talents whose main reasons for writing in an unorthodox manner are that (a) they are incapable of writing in the usual way, and (b) they know that it is a great deal easier to attract attention in some critical quarters by being different than by being good. So familiar is this phenomenon in the land of letters that when a genuinely gifted writer, having a very clear idea of what he is doing and why, attempts to reach us by an unfamiliar route, we are often, understandably, less than willing to pack up our gear and meet him half-way. Guy Davenport is such a writer. *Apples and Pears* is his fourth volume of stories (the first three were *Tatlin!*, *Da Vinci's Bicycle,* and *Eclogues*), and he has yet to give us anything that an average contemporary reader would recognize as a conventional short story. Not for him the isolated incident, the limited setting and time frame, that have been the earmarks of the form since Edgar Allan Poe; not for him the deadeningly spare prose, the commonplace characters, and the no-ideas-but-in-things approach of the Bobbie Ann Masons and the Raymond Carvers. To Davenport—whose wide range of tastes and talents has been amply demonstrated by his poetry (*Flowers and Leaves*), classical translations (*Archilochos, Sappho, Alkman*), scholarly editions (*The Intelligence of Louis Agassiz*), and critical essays in literature, art, history, and philosophy (*The Geography of the Imagination*)—life is a banquet and most short-story readers are starving to death.

The typical Davenport story, then, is a smorgasbord of colorful people, intriguing ideas, and rich, resonant language (plus, quite often, striking illustrations by the author, who is, on top of everything else, a very gifted artist). In "Tatlin!", Vladimir Yevgrafovich Tatlin, the Russian Constructivist artist, engineer, and theoretician, zips through the world of Nicholas II, the Revolution, Lenin, Stalin, *Kultur-bolschewismus, la vie tzigane,* Chagall, Picasso (who tells him, "Plan nothing: make"), Diaghilev, Nijinsky, Jacques Lipchitz, Moholy-Nagy, and Juan Gris, making buildings and airplanes, painting with a "wild boldness [that] was a childhood, a drunkenness of style," and philosophizing ("Art must die and be reborn in everything"; "A house is a vocabulary. A city is a language"; "Cézanne + Lenin = Konstruktivizm"). In another story from *Tatlin!*, "The Airplanes at Brescia," Kafka and Max and Otto Brod go to Brescia for an air show put on by Blériot and Curtiss, walk in the footsteps of Da Vinci, cross the paths of Puccini and a strange man who turns out to be Wittgenstein, and observe that modern ideas and inventions have made the world new again: "This new thought was naked and innocent; the world would wound it in time. . . . Did men know anything at all? Man was man's teacher. Anyone could see the circle in that." In "The Haile Selassie Funeral Train," from *Da Vinci's Bicycle,* James Joyce (d. 1941) and Guillaume Apollinaire (d. 1918) ride the funeral train of the Ethiopian emperor (d. 1975); while the train takes them "down the boulevard Montparnasse, which was in Barcelona," they talk about man, war, art, God, energy, Ibsen, and Orpheus.

It should be clear by now that Davenport has tended to pluck his protagonists from the most rarefied purlieus of twentieth-century intellectual and cultural history. He is, needless to say, a foursquare modernist; more than that, he's a devout Poundian, whose first three volumes of stories—with their profusion of philosophical tidbits, cross-cultural references, dropped names, and foreign words—inevitably recall the *Cantos.* Davenport even embodies the same paradoxes as Ezra Pound. His obsession with ideas goes hand-in-hand with a profound suspicion of them ("The mind is a washout," says a Davenport character who seems to speak for her creator. "Only the soul counts. Only feeling"). And his flat-out antipathy for the twentieth century is more than balanced by an overweening enthusiasm for the thinkers and artists who have helped to define it.

Apples and Pears is, essentially, more of the same. It's a Poundian's paradise from the word go, borrowing its epigraph from Ezraphile Louis Zukofsky and the title of the first of its four stories, "The Bowmen of Shu," from a poem by Pound ("The Song of the Bowmen of Shu" appears in *Cathay*). Perhaps no Davenport story is as purely Poundian as this one. It takes as its subject the life of the sculptor Henri Gaudier-Brzeska, Pound's friend and fellow Vorticist, who died in the First World War at the age of twenty-three and whose first biographer was *il miglior fabbro* himself. As Pound makes clear in *Gaudier-Brzeska,* he valued the young sculptor because he was an artist "as independent as the savage" who, like the Paleolithic cave painters, put instinct over reason every time. "The Bowmen of the Shu" reflects this view. Its form also owes a great deal to Pound's book, which is a grab bag of straight biography, anecdotal memoir, reprints of Gaudier-Brzeska's theoretical writings on art, the texts of his letters from the front, and photographs of his major works. "The Bowmen of Shu" is a disciple's distillation of all this—a *Canto*-like mosaic in words, illustrated by two Gaudier-Brzeska drawings and a dozen or so drawings by Davenport of Gaudier-Brzeska sculptures. It's as if Davenport has tried to put together the sort of thing Pound would have manufactured himself, had he chosen to memorialize his friend in a prose poem (which is what "The Bowmen of Shu" really is) rather than a book. Davenport aims, all at once, to convey the horror of the war in which Gaudier-Brzeska died, to persuade us of the astuteness of the man's artistic theories, and to give us a sense of the disparity between his humble origins and the glorious artistic and literary circles he ended up in. The result is a *tour de force* of compression. Davenport gives us forty-two paragraphs—none of which is connected by either time, setting, perspective, or logic to its neighbors, and many of which are only a line long—and in that confined space manages to carve a vivid word sculpture of his subject. In one paragraph, he has Gaudier-Brzeska describe the trenches ("white smoke and drizzle of sparks blowing across barbed wire in coils, the stink of cordite"); in another, he adumbrates the sculptor's relationship with Sophie Brzeska (" S O P H I E/All night by her bed, imploring her. It is revolting, unspiritual, she said"). Davenport drops every name remotely worth dropping (among them Flint, Hulme, Tancred, Mansfield, Jacob Epstein, Modigliani, and Lewis) and quotes every theoretical statement worth quoting—as, for example, these first few sentences of Gaudier-Brzeska's "Vortex" (originally published in *Blast*):

SCULPTURAL ENERGY IS THE MOUNTAIN
Sculptural feeling is the appreciation of masses in relation. Sculptural

ability is the defining of these masses by planes. The Paleolithic Vortex resulted in the decoration of the Dordogne caverns. Early stone-age man disputed the earth with animals.

The idea of the modern age as a return to the primitive—to the "Paleolithic Vortex"—is as central to Davenport's philosophy, and to "The Bowmen of Shu," as it was to the art of Gaudier-Brzeska. Davenport's story is, in fact, perhaps best understood as presenting what is to its author an archetypal and profoundly ironic modern tragedy: namely, that Gaudier-Brzeska, an artist whose imagination has been liberated from convention by a Paleolithic Renaissance, is destroyed by a civilization that has, at the same time, abandoned its Victorian self-control and reverted to the instinctive savagery of primitive man. (As anthropologist Robert De Launay says to Gaudier-Brzeska in the trenches: "we are learning the Paleolithic in a way that was closed to us as *savant* and *sculpteur*.") When the penultimate paragraph of "The Bowmen of Shu" records Gaudier-Brzeska's death ("C O R P O R A L H E N R I G A U D I E R/Mort pour la Patrie. 4 Octobre 1891 – 5 Juin 1915"), the lesson we are supposed to take away with us is, manifestly, that life in this century is as ugly as its art is beautiful. If *Apples and Pears* is, in a sense, a one-man symposium on the problems and promise of the twentieth century, "The Bowmen of the Shu" is a clever and concise keynote address.

The forty-two views of Gaudier-Brzeska are succeeded by "Fifty-seven Views of Fujiyama," whose title recalls Wallace Stevens's "Fourteen Ways of Looking at a Blackbird." Like Stevens's poem, Davenport's story—composed of fifty-seven long, unlinked paragraphs—is something of an exercise in perspective. The odd-numbered paragraphs constitute the first-person account of a journey to the north of Japan by the late-seventeenth-century poet Matsuo Bashō, and are based on Bashō's own writings. During the course of his travels, Bashō observes, communes with, and writes poems about nature—sometimes in the company of the fellow poets whom he meets along the way:

In Obanazawa I visited the merchant poet Seifu, who had often stopped on business trips to see me in Edo. He was full of sympathy for our hard way across the mountains, and made up for it with splendid hospitality. Sora was entranced by the silkworm nurseries, and wrote: *Come out, toad, and let me see you: I hear your got-a-duck got-a-duck under the silkworm house.* And: *The silkworm workers are dressed like ancient gods.* We climbed to the quiet temple of Ryushakuji, famous for being in so remote and peaceful a site. The late afternoon sun was still on it, and on the great rocks around it, when we arrived, and shone golden in the oaks and pines that have stood there for hundreds of years. The very ground seemed to be eternity, a velvet of moss. I felt the holiness of the place in my bones; my spirit partook of it with each bow that I made to the shrine in the silent rocks. *Silence as whole as time. The only sound is crickets.*

Remote, peaceful, silent, holy: this is the world of Bashō as described in the odd-numbered paragraphs of "Fifty-seven Views of Fujiyama."

The even-numbered paragraphs are a more complicated proposition. Some of them form the first-person account of a contemporary American male who goes hiking in the Vermont woods with a seventeen-year-old girl, "with no purpose but to be in the wilderness, to be in its silence, to be together deep among its trees and valleys and heights." But things don't go well. He sees a mill that turns out not to be there; they lose the trail, stray into a swamp, get cold, hurt, and upset; and when they skinny-dip in the shallows of a brackish lake, they are intruded upon by a Boy Scout leader with "a Biblical air." Some of the even-numbered paragraphs describe what appear to be the same man's encounters with various noteworthy survivors of the modernist period, notably Ezra Pound (an extremely similar account appears in "Ithaca," a story in *Da Vinci's Bicycle*); some paragraphs describe his trip (in the company of a number of bourgeois tourists) to historic sights in Greece; and a couple of paragraphs constitute cut-and-dried textbook descriptions of the provenance of various species of plants:

> *Sequoia Langsdorfii* is found in the Cretaceous of both British Columbia and Greenland, and *Gingko polymorpha* in the former of these localities. *Cinnamomum Scheuchzeri* occurs in the Dakota group of Western Kansas as well as Fort Ellis.... *Cinnamomum Sezannense,* of the Paleocene of Sezanne and Gelinden, was found by Heer, not only in the upper Cretaceous of Patoot, but in the Cenomanian of Atane, in Greenland....

The point of this inventive (though surprisingly unanimated) fugue seems to be that whereas Bashō, in his time and place, could perfectly and harmoniously integrate the roles of historian, wayfarer, poet, and naturalist, contemporary Western man suffers from a dissociated sensibility; the way our society is structured, and the way we have been taught to think and behave, make it impossible for us to bring the disparate elements of our lives into a happy conjunction, and to experience the natural world, in all its manifestations, as fully as possible. This is, as I say, what Davenport *wants* us to get out of the story. The actual effect of "Fifty-seven Views of Fujiyama" is something else again. The Bashō sections, which at first seem to possess a luminous and fragile beauty, soon begin to sound mechanical and monotonous, and eventually evoke a picture of medieval Japanese life and poetry that is, alas, so numbingly dull that, at the end of the exercise, one is almost inclined to fall to one's knees and thank God for being born in the Atomic Age. This is, one can be sure, not quite what Davenport had in mind.

"The Chair" is the shortest and slightest story in *Apples and Pears,* and the only one in which the paragraphs cohere throughout in the manner most of us are used to. It describes an encounter at Marienbad between Franz Kafka and the Rebbe from Belz, and seems to have been written so that Davenport could ask, "Who will write the history of affection?" (answer: *he* will, in the following story), and so that Kafka, at the end, could offer up a prayer to God, acknowledging that it is "absurd . . . for one insignificant creature to cry that it is alive, and does not want to be hurled into the dark along with the lost. It is the life in me that speaks, not me, though I speak with it, selfishly, in its ridiculous longing to stay alive, and partake of the presumptuous joy in being." Modern literature as a cry of life, an assertion of the joy in being: this is the perfect note for Davenport to strike at this point in *Apples and Pears.*

For the next (and last) item in the book is the novel-length "Apples and Pears," which is by far Davenport's longest work of fiction and arguably his most ambitious and adventurous exploration ever of life, art, thought, and affection in the twentieth century. To a large extent, the purpose of the three stories that precede "Apples and Pears," is simply to prepare us for it. If "The Bowmen of Shu" means to remind us what this cruel, primitive century is capable of doing to brilliant, primitive modern artists, "Apples and Pears," set in 1981, presents us with a young artist named Alexander Floris who is as primitive and modern as Gaudier-Brzeska but who, unlike that painter who died "pour la Patrie" in World War I, rejects the world and its alarms entirely and finds thereby a happy, fulfilling life. If "Fifty-seven Views of Fujiyama" implies that the contemporary Western sensibility is a shattered one, "Apples and Pears" purports to depict some contemporary Western Europeans who recover for themselves the simple, natural harmony that Bashō knew. And if "The Chair" describes the desperate desire of Franz Kafka, that prototype of the tortured modern mind, to "partake of the presumptuous joy in being," "Apples and Pears" seeks to show a group of modern types partaking, *Angst*-free, of all that life has to offer.

The subtitle of "Apples and Pears" is "Het Erewhonisch Schetsboek, Messidor-Vendémiaire 1981." According to a copyright notice in the front of *Tatlin!*, *Het Erewhonisch Schetsboek* is the title of a book by one Adriaan van Hovendaal from which parts of Davenport's story "The Dawn in Erewhon" (published in *Tatlin!*) are derived. Some of the characters of that story, set in the 1950s, reappear in "Apples and Pears," and there's no indication whether, and to what degree, the characters and situations described in "Apples and Pears" are actually taken from the works of van Hovendaal. At any rate, the story does, as the subtitle suggests, take the form of the diary-*cum*-notebook of van Hovendaal, a middle-aged Dutch philosopher, who describes therein his "complex friendship" with the aforementioned Alexander Floris, a nineteen-year-old Dutch painter whose serenity, sensitivity, sensuality, and lack of inhibition are all equally remarkable, and whom Adriaan has apparently helped, over the past couple of years, to educate and civilize. Like Gaudier-Brzeska, Sander (as the young painter is called) is a born savage who puts instinct over reason ("All I'm doing, Adriaan, is what I know how to do. I don't know what it means"). He and his sister Grietje are lovers, and Adriaan makes love to both of them, sometimes one at a time, sometimes à *trois*. After a brief ramble through Paris and an interval on an idyllic island, the three of them move into a cheerful, unpretentious little house in Amsterdam that they name Florishaus, and there they live a simple, natural life full of affection, creation, and contemplation. And that's about it. What action there is in the 240-page story consists largely of the comings and goings of the various members of the supporting cast, which includes: (a) two pubescent boys, Hans (Adriaan's nephew) and Jan, who are in love with each other and who (when they are not modeling nude for Sander) couple endlessly; (b) Joris Oudveld, a bashful eighteen-year-old German Lenin groupie (he kisses his bust of Vladimir Ilyich when he leaves his room) who thinks of his "hankering to hug gossoons" (i.e., young boys) as a form of Marxist rebellion; (c) Olaf, also eighteen, a Danish gymnast who runs a YMCA-like "wolfden" in Copenhagen where pubescent lads make love to each other (and to him); (d) Godfried Strodekker, "chairman of the Nederlands Student en Arbeiterverbond voor Pedofilie," who gives closely argued lectures on pederasty; (e) Sweetbriar, an English philosopher; and (f) Wolfgang, a little street orphan whom Adriaan takes into Florishaus as Sander's assistant and (eventually) lovemate.

Depraved? Well, yes. But Davenport doesn't mean it to come off that way. On the contrary, he wants us to be enchanted—and, to a remarkable degree, he succeeds. Though a synopsis may make "Apples and Pears" sound like a low-budget pornographic movie, the story is actually quite reminiscent of pastoral poetry. Like the shepherds in Theocritus and Virgil, Davenport's characters are impossibly good, happy, and affectionate, and they live (for the most part) in a world that is impossibly lovely, tranquil, and timeless. For them, there are no taboos—they feel affection for one another, and sex (whether with man or woman, child or sibling) is their way of expressing it. Might such indiscriminate carrying-on be wrong? The question arises only fleetingly. "Why must we try to figure out why we're hugging anybody . . . ?" asks Grietje. "Love is love." "Human affinities," says Olaf, "come from any direction. My *slubberter* here are after affection one way or another, and are also heroically generous in giving it. Their puppy longing to hug and lie close is as God intended." Simple as that.

In "Apples and Pears," nobody feels hurt or jealous or guilty; nobody's being abused or psychologically damaged, nobody's in danger of contracting a social disease; there's no real conflict, no significant threat at any point to anybody, no substantial changes from day to day, no money worries, no authorities from the child protection bureau knocking at the door (though Grietje does mention this possibility at one point). Even Hans's and Jan's parents, liberal-minded folk that they are, are amenable to the exceptional goings-on at Florishaus. None of it, of course, is believable; but we believe. Davenport, magician that he is, *makes* us believe in (and even cherish) this bucolic never-never-land where everyone is innately good, no one does anyone harm, and love conquers all.

"Apples and Pears," then, is about the human race not as we know it, but as Davenport would like it to be. His vision derives largely from the work of a man whom he has called "the only philosopher of happiness," the French philosopher François Marie Charles Fourier (1772– 1837), to whom *Apples and Pears* is dedicated and whose pres-

242 · *Bruce Bawer*

ence in it is even stronger than that of Ezra Pound. Indeed, after lurking
in the background of Davenport's previous books of fiction, Fourier,
with *Apples and Pears,* takes center stage in Davenport's fiction. This is
not to say that Davenport takes Fourier's philosophy seriously *qua* philosophy. Like his character Sander, he thinks of Fourier as "a sweet
idiot," and considers his sincere proposals for the alteration of human
society to be utterly impracticable, but "is nevertheless taken with the
vision." The vision in question (which Fourier spent most of his life
constructing) was of a utopia called Harmonium, where man's natural
virtue (as posited by Rousseau, and believed in devoutly by Fourier)
would, through the elimination of the tensions that destroy human society, be permitted to prevail, and where, as a result, everyone would
live in peace, happiness, and harmony. And how would those destructive tensions be eliminated? Sex. Fourier felt, you see, that if we took
the fetters off our various passions—sexual attraction being the primary
one—and indulged them fully, all those tensions would vanish and life
would be a dream. In short, as Davenport observes in "The Dawn in
Erewhon," Fourier felt the answer to mankind's problem was "a life
that would cooperate with the instincts rather than deplore them." To
this end, Fourier urged the establishment of "phalansteries," communities that would constitute a sort of proving ground for Harmonium.
And this, more or less, is the idea in "Apples and Pears." Though nobody in the story ever quite says so, Florishaus (whose residents aim for
"society as poetry rather that the newspaper prose of history") is to all
intents and purposes a Fourieristic phalanstery.

But Fourier is not the only utopian in the picture. The names of
Samuel Butler and his novel *Erewhon* crop up frequently in "Apples and
Pears," and with good reason; for like the Erewhonians, Davenport's
people detest machines, which more than anything else have made the
twentieth century what it is. "Butler's insight," notes Adriaan, "was
that the machine enslaved us, changing all work to drudgery. All work
became pandering to the reproduction of the machines." He reflects

> that no phalanstery anything like Fourier's is possible without an
> Erewhonian revolution, canceling machines. To return movement to
> walking, horseback riding, and the true dance. To return music to the in-
> strument and occasion. To return love to passion as it arises. To return
> work to communal duty, to the sense of usefulness. To have the begin-
> ning and end of everything kept in sight and in the discourse of the whole

phalanstery. To take happiness from money and restore it to the harmony of work and its reward, ambition and its achievement. To put mind and hand in concert. To reorganize society after its disastrous dispersal by train, automobile, airplane. . . .

There's another thing the characters in "Apples and Pears" share with the Erewhonians: they're extremely attractive and wellbred, and have a nearly Nazistic regard for youth, strength, and beauty. This regard, as it happens, is as much Fourieristic as it is Erewhonian. "Physique is character," which might well have been a Hitler Youth slogan, is a Fourieristic principle quoted in "Apples and Pears."

As should be clear by now, "Apples and Pears" is only partly narrative. Though constructed chronologically, it is formally similar to "The Bowmen of Shu," with its mosaic of disconnected paragraphs that jump from narration to reflection to recondite quotation. Within a single diary entry, Adriaan is likely not only to tell us what he and Sander did, discussed, and ate today, but to quote passages (from a variety of poets, biologists, philosophers, and the like) that apparently strike him as affirming some tenet or other of Fourierist doctrine, and to recite chunks of grand-sounding gibberish (for example, about a parade of *chérubins et chérubines* and *séraphins et séraphines*) that don't even begin to make sense unless one is familiar with Fourier's complicated and bizarre blueprints for Harmonium. There is the usual Davenport-manteau of dropped names (e.g., Poussin, Picasso, Proust, Stravinsky, Satie, Schiele), but there are some unfamiliar names too. As if to emphasize that his story does not take place in the real world (as well as to acknowledge the story's indebtedness to a philosopher who lived during the Napoleonic new order), Davenport has Adriaan give dates according to the Napoleonic calendar; thus "Apples and Pears," set in summer and autumn, takes us through the months of Messidor, Thermidor, Fructidor, and Vendémiaire. Davenport's elegant, accomplished illustrations—which capture the story's exuberant and innocent sensuality in styles based variously on the Greek *kouroi*, Athenian vase paintings, and the works of Mondrian, Picasso, Braque, and other modern artists—similarly underscore the otherworldliness of the story's "elemental, clear joy." And Davenport's offbeat diction serves much the same purpose; when he is not using strange English words (such as *snurf, snurp, nicker, fritz, thrip, quiddit,* and *tallywhacker*), he is using Dutch words—most of them, fortunately, cognates (*erotisch, kameraad, puberteit*)—or dipping into French, German, Danish, Latin, or Greek. Often these deviations in diction occur when the subject is sex. Hence, Davenport describes Jan and Hans as "wucking and snuffling," and has one boy entice the other to disrobe by saying, "Come on, *vriendje . . . poedelnaakt* like me."

Which brings us to the major problem with "Apples and Pears": namely, that every so often it stops being a lyrical portrait of an otherworldly world ruled by affection and becomes—well, something else.

Sometimes, for instance, affection steals away into the background, leaving behind nothing but sex, sex, sex. At such moments, Davenport—as in some of his earlier stories—is likely to break into detailed descriptions of the male sex organ (for which he has more names, in English *and* Dutch, than the Eskimos have for snow) or of the extremely skimpy briefs and swim trunks that are the subjects of many of his illustrations (boxer shorts, like machines, seem to be *défendu* in Davenportland). At other times, more disturbingly, Davenport injects politics into his pastoral, apparently taking seriously his characters' beliefs that a universal "faith in good will" can be substituted "for the Capitalist assumption that all exchanges are of something for money"; that it is possible "to breed meanness out of human nature" simply by taking the world economy "from the greed of merchants and the vicious manipulation of the stock market and put[ting it] into the care of children on ponies"; and that Western society's refusal to allow children "erotic affection and a fully sensual life is an injustice too long imposed by puritanical prejudices, ignorance, and the narrowness of bourgeois propriety." Such silly rhetoric is hardly new to Davenport's fiction; like Pound, he has always tended to blame certain failings of human nature on Western democracy.

And that's a shame. But, as with Pound, the perverseness of Davenport's politics in no way negates the value of his work or the significance of his contribution to American literature. And make no mistake about it, that contribution is considerable. At a time in history when the prime criterion of excellence in American short fiction seems to be a sort of mindless, impersonal monotonousness, Guy Davenport's inimitable adventures in the realms of philosophy, language, and literary form are to be treasured. Davenport at his best reminds us how exciting and valuable literary innovation can be. And he does something else that is even more important: he reminds us of our humanity, and (however bizarrely) of the importance of affection. Dostoevsky, it is said, found Fourier's social program ridiculous, but praised him nonetheless for his obvious "love of humanity." He might well, one thinks, have done the same for Davenport.

The Human Dimension: E. L. Doctorow

December 1984

In the introduction to his only play, *Drinks Before Dinner,* E.L. Doctorow says he's tired of what he calls "the theatre of pathos." By that, he means plays in which

> a story is told about this man or that woman to reveal how sad his or her life is, or how triumphant, or how he or she does not realize fulfillment as a human being, or does realize it, or is trapped in his or her own illusions, or is liberated from them, or fails to learn to communicate love, or learns, or is morally defeated by ethnic or economic circumstances, or is not defeated.

If you think that list covers just about everything from *Oedipus Rex* to *Hurlyburly,* you're right. Doctorow doesn't care much for any play that takes the emotional life of human beings too seriously. He's proud to say that *his* characters "have no domestic biographies to offer, no childhoods to remember, no religion, no regional identification." As little human dimension, in short, as possible.

What they do have is ideas. Doctorow loves ideas. He favors plays "in which the holding of ideas or the arguing of ideas is a matter of life and death, and characters take the ideas they hold as seriously as survival." The main idea in *Drinks Before Dinner,* as postulated by one Edgar (the author's mouthpiece), is that thanks to TV and the Bomb, we've all "dispose[d] of our humanity." "I am no longer distinguishable from anyone else," complains Edgar, "nor is anyone distinguishable from me.... We could all be each other." This, Doctorow means us to understand, is why he's not all that excited about writing plays that center on emotional conflicts: we nuclear-age Americans are automatons and cannot be expected to have any emotions, let alone emotional conflicts, worth writing about.

Doctorow's novels sell a similar bill of goods. The pre-World War I Americans in the pellucid, often powerfully written *Ragtime,* with their plain-wrap names ("Father," "Mother," "Younger Brother," etc.), and the Depression-era Americans in the often confusing and pseudo-surrealistic 1980 novel *Loon Lake* (in which the histories of the major characters are presented as cut and dried *Who's Who* listings) are as free of human dimension as the contemporary dramatis personae in *Drinks Before Dinner.* Doctorow doesn't blame the truncation of these lives on TV and the Bomb, of course. On what, then? Partly on Freud, whose ideas, he says, "destroy[ed] sex in America," but even more, predictably enough, on a native son: Henry Ford, whose assembly line turned workmen into "nameless faceless" cogs (*Loon Lake*) and "interchangeable parts" (*Ragtime*). The characters in *The Book of Daniel* are somewhat rounder, but even they are defined almost exclusively in terms of their relationship to the American system; as the book is supposed to be Daniel's doctoral dissertation, its form allows Doctorow to interpolate mini-think-pieces on, among other things, Disneyland as the ultimate symbol of depersonalization in modern America.

What about Doctorow's first novel, *Welcome to Hard Times*? It's a Western, and therefore takes place pre-assembly line, but its characters—the settlers who help Blue, the mayor of a Dakota Territory town named Hard Times, rebuild it after its destruction by the marauding Man from Bodie—are perhaps the dreariest and most dimensionless of all Doctorow's creations. Why are *they* like this? Doctorow apparently wants us to feel that it has something to do with their common dream: the American dream of taming a frontier, of working hard and reaping rewards. Near the end of the novel, when the local mine turns out to contain nothing but fool's gold, Blue observes that the worthless stone is "like the West, like my life: The color dazzles us, but when it's too late we see what a fraud it is, what a poor pinched-out claim." Soon afterward, when unemployment results in the final destruction of the town and the death of many of its residents, Blue comments, "If I hadn't believed, they'd be alive today." Believed, in other words, in the American dream.

That the American dream is a pretty bad deal for all concerned is, of course, a controlling idea in Doctorow's fiction. The dream is responsible for all of it: the mass-produced cars, the TV sets, the Bomb and even, in the end, the full-scale destruction of humanity. The dream, as Emma Goldman explains in *Ragtime,* causes the masses to "permit themselves to be exploited by the few" by "being persuaded to identify with them." As for the few, all the dream does for them is bury them alive in a depersonalized consumer Disneyland. (Not coincidentally, Doctorow has filled his novels with images of live burial: Houdini buries himself alive and J. P. Morgan sleeps in a pyramid in *Ragtime;* a mine disaster in *Loon Lake* buries workers under tons of rock; the Man from Bodie locks a man in a horse-drawn hearse.)

The dark side of the American dream is, needless to say, a familiar literary theme, and by no means an unworkable one. It served Fitzgerald well in *The Great Gatsby* and Dreiser in *An American Tragedy.* But it has yet to work for Doctorow. His approach is closer to Upton Sinclair's than to Fitzgerald's: rather than recognize that the novel's path to truth leads, of necessity, through the human soul, he peoples his novels with characters that are little more than hunks of plywood, each with its own sharply defined didactic function. There are victims of the system, such as Coalhouse Walker (the pianist whose car is trashed by firemen and, whose fiancée, Sarah, is killed by a militiaman in *Ragtime*) and Susan Isaacson (whose parents are executed for treason in *The Book of Daniel*). America betrays these victims, takes the lives of their loved ones, drives them to madness, anarchy and violence. Walker commits murder; Susan, suicide.

Then there are the bourgeois apologists, people like Robert Lewin (who adopts Daniel and Susan in *The Book of Daniel*) and Father in *Ragtime.* They're aware of the system's injustices—against the Isaacsons and Walker, respectively—and even try to do something about them. Lewin "belongs to committees, and practices law for poor people . . . is big in the ACLU" and is "a demonstrator against Dow Chemical recruiters," and Father puts up bail for Walker. But it isn't enough for Doctorow, as he makes clear in the last sentence of the paragraph about Lewin: " When he has the time, he likes to read *The New Yorker.*" To Doctorow, it's all clear-cut: Lewin and Father, for all their humanitarianism, are part of the system. They've bought the dream, and unlike Isaacson and Walker, they are not about to chuck it for a one-way trip to the barricades. Doctorow goes out of his way to make them look silly on this account: when Susan argues with Daniel about her involvement in a revolutionary movement, Lewin complains, "If you can't conduct a civil discussion I'd prefer no discussion at all"; when Father bails Walker out of jail, he's "put off because Coalhouse Walker was barely civil in his gratitude."

That there's so little room amid all the betrayal and injustice, the madness and violence, the noble anarchy and detestable civility, for a little individual human psychology makes following the fortunes of Doctorow's characters a frustrating experience. What is it, one cannot help but wonder, that makes Coalhouse Walker so intractable? What makes him, of all the black Americans ever harassed by racists, refuse to walk away from trouble? Why does the death of Sarah transform him into a twentieth-century Nat Turner? Doctorow throws a line in somewhere about "the violence underlying all principle," and we understand we are to recognize that Walker is a man of principle, who takes the ideas he holds—ideas about justice, dignity and vengeance—as seriously as survival. Fine. But how did he get that way? Doctorow gives us no clue. To him, Walker is merely a victim of the system.

The way Doctorow sees it, we're all victims. Sometimes it seems he reserves his pity for those who make it: Mindish, the Isaacsons' supposed Communist collaborator in *The Book of Daniel*, who spends his declining years in bourgeois Santa Barbara bliss; Tateh, the destitute socialist in *Ragtime* who strikes it rich in Hollywood and gives himself a title; Joe, the working-class drifter in *Loon Lake* who is adopted by a millionaire and rises through the ranks of the Central Intelligence Agency, eventually becoming an ambassador. Happy endings? Not at all. The way Doctorow sees it, America has played its dirtiest trick on such rags-to-riches figures. By making them well-to-do, it's robbed them of the integrity and independence of mind they derived from being down and out. Success has buried them alive.

And that, believe it or not, is the general idea at work in "Lives of the Poets," the "novella" in Doctorow's new book, *Lives of the Poets: Six Stories and a Novella.* Actually, it's not a novella at all; it's a sixty-page spiel by a speaker who, like Doctorow, is a successful fiftyish liberal New York Jewish novelist. This novelist goes on about his mistress, his children, his broken marriage, his friends' marriages, his health and age, the erosion of America's moral values, the rise of ridiculous religions, the number of minorities in New York, and his memories of Kenyon College (where Doctorow also went to school).

Above all, the novelist goes on about his "commitment." He's always been deeply committed, but it's not as easy as it used to be. His problem is this: he's a rich, famous writer, a friend of "Norman," a regular on the fashionable dinner-party circuit in Manhattan. He's *buried alive,* don't you see? He's oppressed by success. He's being killed with comfort. At a party at the Dakota apartment house, he watches his writer friend Leo do some serious drinking because "He's quite brilliant and has never made a dime"; but our hero knows who's *really* suffering here: "Oh Leo, I think, when you make a little money from your work you'll see what trouble is." And he's serious.

But he hasn't given up. He has abandoned his wife, kids, and suburban home to live in a Greenwich Village high-rise with his young mistress. Clearly, this is meant to be taken, at least in part, as a heroic act: the man's trying to climb out of that middle-class grave, to renew his "commitment." He's like Younger Brother in *Ragtime,* who leaves his white-bread family to put on blackface and join the Coalhouse Walker gang. And—what do you know?—the man pulls it off. At the end of the story, he overcomes his stasis, his love of bourgeois comfort, and takes a family of Central American refugees into his high-rise flat. But you don't believe it for a minute. For one thing, it's out of character. For another, our novelist's act of mercy is a tired conceit that Doctorow has overused. His Ins are always harboring Outs, thereby exposing themselves to a therapeutic measure of adversity and anarchy otherwise unavailable to them. In *Welcome to Hard Times,* Blue takes in Molly and Jimmy after the devastations wreaked by the Man from Bodie leave them homeless; in *The Book of Daniel,* the Lewins take in the Isaacson children; in *Ragtime,* Mother takes in Sarah and her baby; in *Loon Lake,* the millionaire F. W. Bennett takes in Joe. Thanks to its ending, "Lives of the Poets" manages to seem both aimless and contrived, a neat trick.

The same is true of other stories in *Lives of the Poets.* Most of them are about lonely, estranged, or disturbed people who are the victims of nature (symbolized variously by snow, shadows, water), history, and/ or America. "The Writer in the Family," for instance, begins promisingly as a story about a New York City boy in 1955 whose salesman father has died and who writes letters in his father's name to convince his grandmother that the family is alive and well in Arizona. "To the immigrant generation of my grandmother, Arizona was the American equivalent of the Alps, it was. . . . success." The premise is intriguing, and we expect the boy to grow in some way as a result of his letter writing;

but what we get instead is yet another diatribe about dehumanization. The boy notices his father's collection of sea novels as if for the first time and realizes with a start that his father never aspired to spend his life buried alive in a deadly-dry place like Arizona—what he wanted was to escape, to go to sea. End of story.

"Willi" also has a boy hero. His mother and tutor have an affair; the boy tells his father; the father attacks the mother; the boy protects her: "I was enraged, I pushed her back and jumped at him, pummeling him, shouting that I would kill him." Doctorow sets this story in Galicia in 1910 so that his narrator can close by saying, "All of it was to be destroyed anyway, even without me." The story, you see, is really about betrayal, violence, World War I and, above all, the advent of the American century.

And so it goes. In *Lives of the Poets,* there are no lives and no poets, only a handful of familiar ideas. The styles are familiar too. In some of these fictions ("Lives of the Poets," "The Writer in the Family," "The Hunter") Doctorow spells things out in that scrupulously simple *Ragtime* prose; in others ("Willi," "The Water Works," "The Foreign Legation," "The Leather Man") he tries to be artsy and mysterious in the manner of *Loon Lake.* Play it one way or the other, the song is always the same.

Don DeLillo's America

APRIL 1985

Try as one might, it is difficult to avoid Don DeLillo forever. He may not be a bestseller, but his books seem—at times anyway—to be ubiquitous. His new novel, *White Noise,* is his eighth, and it has all but one of its predecessors to keep it company on bookstore shelves. For DeLillo has, somehow, managed to become a member of that elite circle of writers whose books are kept in print. It's strange: there are titles by Fitzgerald, Hemingway, and Faulkner that are not easy to locate even at reputable literary bookstores; but at many such establishments one can, without any trouble, find the novels of DeLillo in attractive, attention-getting Vintage paperback editions, their uniform front covers decorated with striking, surrealistic, black-and-white photographs, their back covers (and front matter) crammed with critical testimony that this fellow is, no question about it, *the* novelist of our times. "He has a chillingly persuasive view," writes Bruce Allen, "of who we are in the Twentieth Century and where we might be going." He is a master of "modern alienation and violence" (*The Washington Post*); he, "more than any other novelist to emerge in this decade [the Seventies], . . . knows the spoiled goods of America" (Thomas LeClair in *The New Republic*); he is in touch with "the sinister ambiguities, the floating ugliness of America's recent history" (John Updike); he meditates "on the excesses of contemporary thought" (Christopher Lehmann-Haupt); he reflects "our era's nightmares and hallucinations" (Abe C. Ravitz, *The Cleveland Plain Dealer*).

Our era is, indeed, much on DeLillo's mind. Another author might write a novel because he has found himself possessed by a character, a setting, a single line of dialogue that resonates in his mind and demands that he listen. Not Don DeLillo. Most of his novels were born out of a preoccupation with a single theme: namely, that contemporary American society is the worst enemy that the cause of human individuality and self-realization has ever had. In one semi-surrealist opus after another, DeLillo has told the story of a conspicuously successful American who jumps off the assembly line and, in one way or another, tries to—well—"find himself." *End Zone* (1972), for instance, is the story of Gary Harkness, a college football player who is revolted by the doctrine of "team spirit"; America, he says, is "becoming a nation devoted to human xerography," and he wants to be more than a photocopy. So he leaves a promising gridiron career at Penn State and ends up playing ball at an obscure college in west Texas. *Great Jones Street* (1973) is about a rock star, Bucky Wunderlick, who, convinced his fans are not responding to him as individuals anymore but simply as a mob, drops out of his band in the middle of a successful tour and moves into a seedy East Village flat, where he becomes the focus of a bizarre drug plot straight out of Thomas Pynchon's *The Crying of Lot 49*. In *Players* (1977), a young stockbroker named Lyle Wynant leaves Yuppiedom behind when his fascination with a murder at the Stock Exchange leads him to become involved with terrorists. In *The Names* (1982), James Axton, an international businessman disenchanted with the life of a corporate jet-setter, is intrigued by an unusual series of cult murders in Greece and the Mideast; like Wynant, he becomes increasingly obsessed—and, ultimately, involved—with the killers.

One thing that these novels all share, aside from the goodbye-American-dream motif, is a stunning implausibility. Representation of reality is not DeLillo's strong suit. It's hard to accept most of his characters as living, breathing human beings, or to conjure up a clear picture of Logos College in *End Zone* or the huge, futuristic scientific institute called Field Experiment Number One in *Ratner's Star* (1976), or to believe in the existence of all these cliques, clans, and cabals—the conspiracy in *Players,* the Transparanoia Corporation and Happy Valley Farm Commune in *Great Jones Street,* the cult in *The Names,* or the secret intelligence network, Radial Matrix, in *Running Dog* (1978). "There are no stockbrokers, terrorists, or wives—dehumanized or not—in *Players,*" writes Stephen Koch. "There are only words, inky squiggles on a page, telling us things that we do not believe." Robert Towers makes a similar observation about *The Names:* "[T]he very existence of the cult, which is crucial to the central action of the novel, is never made plausible—at least to me." Me neither.

But then, these novels are not meant to be true-to-life tales. They are tracts, designed to batter us, again and again, with a single idea: that life in America today is boring, benumbing, dehumanized. Not only has the American system robbed us of our individuality; the era's despicable technological innovations have afflicted us all with a dreadful condition known as "sensory overload"—a term introduced by a character in *Great Jones Street:*

> "A man in Missouri spent a hundred and sixty-one days in a deep cavern. . . . He ate canned food, he drank water, he burned over nine hundred candles. He said it's the first time in his life he wasn't bored. Sensory overload. People are withdrawing from sensory overload. Technology. Whenever there's too much technology, people return to primitive feats. . . . "

Return to primitivism: this, in different ways and to varying degrees, is what the protagonists do in most of DeLillo's novels. Harkness's tiny Texas college, Wunderlick's East Village flat, Wynant's terrorists, and Axton's cult are all versions of the Missourian's cave—they are places to escape to, refuges from a technologically overdeveloped society whose major achievement, DeLillo would have us believe, is to have dragged us further and further away from our true selves.

And what *are* our true selves? DeLillo's answer to that question is clear. To DeLillo, to be human means to be, at heart, a primitive beast; those of us who live in high-tech America are, therefore, more out of touch with our humanness than any humans who have ever lived. To "find oneself" one must, like the Missouri caveman, return to primitivism; and in the world according to DeLillo, returning to primitivism means, in essence, entering into a community, conspiracy, or subculture governed largely by primitive violence. In DeLillo's overly diagrammatic world, savagery is the only alternative to depersonalization by means of sensory overload; only through a pure, brute physicality can one reclaim one's selfhood. Of course, the violence has to be the right sort of violence; in America, you see, we don't even *murder* properly. "We do the wrong kind of killing in America," says James Axton in *The Names.* "It's a form of consumerism. It's the logical extension of consumer fantasy. People shooting from overpasses, barricaded houses. Pure image." The American brand of violence is, in other words, too impersonal, too deliberate, too media-oriented. The right kind, of course, is the intimate, unconsidered kind. "Mindless violence," says Azarian, Wunderlick's manager in *Great Jones Street,* "is the only true philosophical violence." "One way of betraying the revolution," says a terrorist in *Players,* "is to advance theories about it. . . . Theory is an effete diversion. . . . The only worthwhile doctrine is calculated madness." At the heart of each of DeLillo's novels is the assumption that, deep down, all human beings long to wreak havoc, to run wild, to kill. The narrator of *Players* alludes to "the glamour of revolutionary violence . . . the secret longing it evokes in the most docile soul," and Axton, in *The Names,* suggests that "There must be times when a society feels the purest virtue lies in killing."

It is not only the conspiracy-happy protagonists of *Players* and *The Names* that are drawn to barbarism. Harkness, in *End Zone,* who enjoys reading about atrocities, manifestly considers football to be a wonderful savage ritual of sorts, and the inflicting of pain upon other players a primal sacrament; he speaks longingly of "kill[ing] with impunity," of "d[ying] in the celebration of ancient ways." Wunderlick, in *Great Jones Street,* feels much the same way about his music, which he wishes could be as destructive ("destruction is such fun"!) as football: "What I'd really like to do," he says, "is injure people with my sound. Maybe actually kill some of them. They'd come there knowing full well. Then we'd play and sing and people in the audience would be frozen with pain or writhing with pain and some of them would actually die from the effects of our words and music. . . . That's art, sweetheart." DeLillo is not being facetious here, not making fun of Wunderlick, hard as it may be to believe; each of his novels provides ample evidence that, to DeLillo, art—in present-day America, anyway—has got to confront the primitive yearning, deep inside every human soul, to kill, maim, and destroy.

Why? Because if you don't, you're denying your humanness. It's better, DeLillo seems to say in one novel after another, to be a marauding, murderous maniac—and therefore a *human*—than to sit still for America as it is, with its air-conditioners, assembly lines, television sets, supermarkets, synthetic fabrics, and credit cards. At least when you're living a life of primitive violence, you're closer to the mystery at the heart of it all. That's what life is to DeLillo: a mystery, an enigma. His books are full of codes, ciphers, secret names and places and organizations. Most of the books take the form of suspense stories (why is the cult murdering these people in *The Names?* what do the conspirators want with Wunderlick in *Great Jones Street?* what's the meaning of the interplanetary radio signal in *Ratner's Star?*) but—significantly—the clues never add up to much of anything. By the end of the typical DeLillo novel, in fact, things are hovering pretty near the point of utter incomprehensibility. What is always clear, however, is that one is supposed to come away from these novels convinced that life is a teleological puzzle that no novelist (or scientist, for that matter) is ever going to piece together—a mystery that technological advances can only serve to distance us from.

DeLillo's newest novel, *White Noise,* represents yet another go at these rapidly aging nihilistic clichés. This time around, the passenger on the Primitivism Express is Jack Gladney, professor of (like it or not) Hitler Studies at a large Eastern college. Though, like all DeLillo heroes, Jack is a connoisseur of destruction, and though he starts making gibes about our stifling assembly-line culture on the first page of the book, it takes an "airborne toxic event" in his hometown to make him truly frantic about his mortality and the unrelieved emptiness of his life. It doesn't help any, either, when he discovers that his wife Babette, a teacher of posture, has slept with another man, a quack doctor who claims to have developed a drug that eradicates the fear of death. Though it is less surrealistic than any of his previous novels, *White Noise* —as is par for the course with DeLillo—grows steadily darker, more fantastic, its direction less and less clear. Jack, like Axton in *The Names,* grows obsessive, loses touch with his family, breaks out of his structured existence. He learns from his colleague Murray that "there are two kinds of people in the world. Killers and diers. Most of us are diers" (mainly, it seems, because we don't have the guts to be killers). "Violence," Murray explains, "is a form of rebirth," murder a means of self-liberation. Jack decides he is a killer. He starts carrying a gun with him to school; eventually he steals the neighbors' car and, rod in tow, seeks out the quack doctor.

There should be profound emotions at work here, but *White Noise* is, like its predecessors, so masterfully contrived a piece of argumentation that believable human feelings and actions are few and far between. There is hardly a natural moment in the whole book. Characters do not

think, they cogitate; they do not talk, they engage in dialectic and deliver endless monologues about the novel's major themes. It is often
difficult to tell them apart when reading a stretch of dialogue, because
they all sound exactly alike. Indeed, with rare exceptions, they all *think*
exactly alike. When they are not pondering the significance of one contemporary American phenomenon or another (e.g., supermarkets, TV
commercials, the *National Enquirer*), they are contemplating life, death,
and the cosmos. And when their mouths open, they produce clipped,
ironic, self-consciously clever sentences full of offbeat metaphors and
quaint descriptive details.

The first conversation in *White Noise* is typical. Jack has returned
home from campus, where he has watched the new students and their
parents arriving for the beginning of the fall term; he tells Babette,
"You should have been there," and describes for her the long line of station wagons: "Blue, green, burgundy. They gleamed in the sun like a
desert caravan." Babette replies:

> "It's not the station wagons I wanted to see. What are the people like?
> Do the women wear plaid skirts, cable-knit sweaters? Are the men in
> hacking jackets? What's a hacking jacket?"
> "They've grown comfortable with their money," I said. "They genu-
> inely believe they're entitled to it. This conviction gives them a kind of
> rude health. They glow a little."
> "I have trouble imagining death at that income level," she said.
> "Maybe there is no death as we know it. Just documents changing
> hands."

They're off. And for the remainder of the book, that's how Jack and
Babette talk, to each other and everyone else. It's consistently fast
paced and facile, and occasionally witty, and absolutely *never* sounds
like two married people talking to each other. Most of the time it
sounds just like what it is: an author's collection of stale cultural barbs,
broken up, essentially at random, into lines of dialogue. It's bad enough
that the above passage, with its interchangeable quips about the station-
wagon set, should occur on the fourth page of the book, when we
should be getting to know the characters; what's even more silly is that,
later in the novel, when Babette tells Jack about her motel-room liaison
with the quack doctor, their conversation is equally superficial. "You
entered a motel room," says Jack, "excited by its impersonality, the
functionalism and bad taste of the furnishings. You walked barefoot on

the fire-retardant carpet. . . . You lay on the bed, embracing. Then he entered you." Babette's response, naturally, is: "Don't use that term. You know how I feel about that usage." *Functionalism, fire-retardant, usage* — is this the language of a bitter husband and a contrite wife? Of course not. It's the language of a novelist who's more intrigued by words than by the feelings they are supposed to represent, more concerned with slipping in a brief, banal set piece on the bland impersonality of American motel rooms than with trying to understand, and render as faithfully as possible, the feelings his characters would be likely to have in the situation he has put them in.

Life—life itself, that queer entity that Flaubert and Tolstoy and Thomas Mann somehow never grew tired of describing—does not interest DeLillo at all; for him, life seems to exist so that we can theorize about it. He never leaves anything alone and just lets it *be*. His narrator and characters, in *White Noise* as elsewhere, are always knee-jerk generalizers. The introductory description of Babette, for instance ("Babette is tall and fairly ample. . . . Her hair is a fanatical blond mop"), turns within a couple of sentences into a broad, seemingly frivolous general statement, the only apparent purpose of which could be to reduce Babette to a stereotype: "If she were a petite woman, the hair would be too cute, too mischievous and contrived. Ample women do not plan such things. They lack the guile for conspiracies of the body." Later in the novel, Jack observes that his teenage son's hairline is receding, wonders guiltily whether he might be at fault ("Have I raised him, unwittingly, in the vicinity of a chemical dump site . . . ?"), and before you know it has happily found himself a suitable generality: "Man's guilt in history and in the tides of his own blood has been complicated by technology, the daily seeping falsehearted death." DeLillo's, quite clearly, is a mind that lets itself be violated by any old idea that happens along.

If you like your novels studded with these kinds of Philosophy McNuggets, you'll love *White Noise*. Lead a character in this novel into a supermarket, bank, or kitchen, and—presto!—he launches, unbidden, into an impromptu interpretive essay, the thrust of which is that deep beneath the surface of our plastic culture lurk the manifold mysteries of human existence. When Jack runs into Murray at the supermarket, for example, Murray explains to him that the market—a key setting in the novel—"recharges us spiritually, it prepares us, it's a gateway or pathway. Look how bright. It's full of psychic data." To be sure,

"Everything is concealed in symbolism, hidden by veils of mystery and layers of cultural material. But it is psychic data, absolutely. The large doors slide open, they close unbidden. Energy waves, incident radiation. All the letters and numbers are here, all the colors of the spectrum, all the voices and sounds, all the code words and ceremonial phrases. It is just a question of deciphering, rearranging, peeling off the layers of unspeakability. . . . "

Jack goes to the bank, checks out his account balance on the computer, and launches into an ironic rhapsody when the computer's figures match his: "[t]he system had blessed my life. I felt its support and approval. The system hardware, the mainframe sitting in a locked room in some distant city. What a pleasing interaction. . . . The system was invisible, which made it all the more impressive, all the more disquieting to deal with. But we were in accord, at least for now. The networks, the circuits, the streams, the harmonies." (Cf. *The Names:* "It's the inner consistencies we have to search for. The symmetries, the harmonies, the mysteries, the whisperies.") Even Bee, Jack's twelve-year-old daughter by a previous marriage, finds it necessary to set the symbolism out on the table. Speaking of her mother's kitchen, she says: "It's not a kitchen at all. It's her life, her middle age. Baba [Babette] could enjoy a kitchen like that. It would be a kitchen to her. To Mother it's like a weird symbol of getting through a crisis, except she hasn't gotten through it." (Does any twelve-year-old actually talk this way?)

Of course, supermarkets and banks and kitchens can hold symbolic meanings for people. But why, pray tell, must those meanings be talked about endlessly, with such awesome banality and at such tiresome, unrevealing length? DeLillo's purpose in having his characters carry on about supermarkets and banks, of course, is chiefly ironic: to him, such phenomena are paramount signs of the dehumanization of America. He is, as might be expected, especially devoted to the tiredest of all contemporary clichés, the one about the tyranny of television. In *White Noise,* as in *Players* (at the beginning of which Lyle Wynant is a cathode-ray addict of psychotic proportions), DeLillo portrays the American mind, high and low, as being haunted constantly by sounds and images from the tube. At times, to be sure, he comes close to a perceptive characterization of the role that commercial slogans, jingles, and brand names play in some TV-centered American households, interpolating, for instance, stray sentences from the Gladney family's television set into the stream of dialogue. But DeLillo defeats any hope of verisimilitude by going way overboard. During the "airborne toxic event," he has Jack describe the huge black cloud of poisonous Nyodene gas (the novel's major symbol) as "resembl[ing] a national promotion for death, a multimillion-dollar campaign backed by radio spots, heavy print and billboard, TV saturation." This description does not help the reader to see the cloud, or serve to consolidate its symbolic pre-eminence in the book; it tends, rather, to diminish it. It is inconceivable that a man whose family was threatened by a cloud of toxic gas would describe it in such a way. The simile is an utterly contrived one, dictated not by the author's intuitive gift for imagery but by his polemical motives, his obsession with commercialism. The only image it fixes in the mind is one of DeLillo himself, sitting at his typewriter, mechanically tapping out his book.

This sort of heavyhanded theme-mongering goes on throughout *White Noise*. When the Nyodene cloud forces the Gladneys to evacuate their house and spend the night at an emergency relocation center, Jack hears his daughter Steffie mutter something in her sleep. "It seemed important," Jack tells us, "that I know what it was. In my current state, bearing the death impression of the Nyodene cloud, I was ready to search anywhere for signs and hints, intimations of odd comfort." As he listens to Steffie mumble in "a language not quite of this world," he struggles to understand:

> I was convinced she was saying something, fitting together units of stable meaning. I watched her face, waited. Ten minutes passed. She uttered two clearly audible words, familiar and elusive at the same time, words that seemed to have a ritual meaning, part of a verbal spell or ecstatic chant.
> *Toyota Celica.*

How does DeLillo get away with such stale gags?

DeLillo's people don't talk about things, if they can help it; they talk about the *nature* of things. Jack's smug, brainy fourteen-year-old son Heinrich (the successor of obnoxiously brilliant adolescents in *The Names* and *Ratner's Star*) likes to expatiate upon the nature of modern knowledge: "What good is knowledge if it just floats through the air? It goes from computer to computer. It changes and grows every second of every day. But nobody actually knows anything." Murray, for his part, discourses pretentiously about "the nature of modern death": "It has a life independent of us. It is growing in prestige and dimension. . . . We can take cross-section pictures of it, tape its tremors and waves. . . . But it continues to grow, to acquire breadth and scope, new outlets, new passages and means. The more we learn, the more it grows." The less DeLillo's characters have to say, the more they talk.

And when they do, quite often they talk in questions. Not single questions, but long series of questions. Heinrich, who unfortunately never seems to tire of epistemology, responds to a query about what he would like to do by saying, "Who knows what I want to do? Who knows what anyone wants to do? How can you be sure about something like that? Isn't it all a question of brain chemistry, signals going back and forth, electrical energy in the cortex? How do you know whether something is really what you want to do or just some kind of nerve impulse in the brain?" And so on, for a longish paragraph, to no apparent authorial purpose. Jack, for his part, is always wondering. When he learns that a doctor has "tapped into [his] history," he wonders about that "history": "Where was it located exactly? Some state or federal agency, some insurance company or credit firm or medical clearinghouse? What history was he referring to? I'd told him some basic things. Height, weight, childhood diseases. What else did he know? Did he know about my wives, my involvement with Hitler, my dreams and fears?" When Jack learns that his ex-wife, who lives in an ashram with a swami, wants Heinrich to visit her, he wonders: "Did swami have twinkling eyes? Would he be able to answer the boy's questions where I had failed, provide assurances where I had incited bickering and debate? How final is the Age of Darkness? Does it mean supreme destruction, a night that swallows existence so completely that I am cured of my own lonely dying?" And when Jack catches up with Babette's quack doctor, he wonders some more: "His nose was flat, his skin the color of a Planter's peanut. What is the geography of a spoon-shaped face? Was he Melanesian, Polynesian, Indonesian, Nepalese, Surinamese, Dutch-Chinese? Was he a composite? How many people came here for Dylar [the fear-of-death drug]? Where was Surinam? How was my plan progressing?"

Perhaps the most disturbing aspect of *White Noise* is Jack's fascination with Hitler. The dictator is the subject not only of his professional research but of his private obsessions. He has hitched his wagon to Hitler because, as Murray tells him, "You thought [Hitler] would protect you." Jack admits as much when he explains why he named his son Heinrich: "I thought it had an authority that might cling to him. I thought it was forceful and impressive and I still do. I wanted to shield him, make him unafraid." He tells his daughter Denise:

> "There's something about German names, the German language, German *things*. I don't know what it is exactly. It's just there. In the middle of it all is Hitler, of course."
> "He was on again last night."
> "He's always on. We couldn't have television without him."
> "They lost the war," she said. "How great could they be?"
> "A valid point. But it's not exactly a question of greatness. It's not a question of good and evil. I don't know what it is. Look at it this way. Some people always wear a favorite color. Some people carry a gun. Some people put on a uniform and feel bigger, stronger, safer. It's in this area that my obsessions dwell."

Keep in mind that this is DeLillo's idea of a sympathetic character. Indeed, we are clearly meant to see Jack as the archetypal twentieth-century victim—a victim whose sense of helplessness is so profound that he cannot help but succumb to the temptation, shocking but psychologically understandable, to identify with the aggressor; and since Jack is the archetypal twentieth-century victim, whom else could DeLillo have him identify with but the century's premier aggressor, Adolf Hitler?

White Noise is not, as it happens, the first DeLillo novel in which Hitler has made an appearance. Quite the contrary. Germany, Nazism, Hitler haunt DeLillo's novels the way Maud Gonne haunts the poetry of Yeats. The reason is obvious: Hitler is the ultimate example of twentieth-century man reverting to primitivism. If the nature of humanity is essentially a dark mystery, Hitler is the murderous monster at the heart of that darkness. He is (so DeLillo seems to feel) all of us writ large. This, presumably, is why there is a rock group in *Great Jones Street* named Schicklgruber and, in *End Zone,* a character named Hauptfuhrer; it is why, in the latter novel, there is a student who wants to "get my hair dyed blond so everybody will think I'm one of those small blondie boys with that faraway look in their eyes who used to be so big on the Himmelplatz three or four decades ago." It's why the putative pornographic film at the thematic center of *Running Dog* turns out to be not pornography at all but a film of Hitler, in derby, wing collar, baggy pants, and boutonniere, doing an imitation of Charlie Chaplin. It's why, in *White Noise,* Jack and Murray compare notes on their respective scholarly subjects, Hitler and Elvis, and discover that the two men were really very much alike. DeLillo's point, throughout, is unmistakable: Hitler was just like us. We are all Hitler.

Am I alone in finding this whole business extremely offensive? DeLillo's offense, to my mind, is that he refuses to make distinctions. To him, as to Jack Gladney, the question of Hitler is simply "not a question of good and evil." Nor, it is clear, do moral considerations enter into his appraisal of any human act. A craving for primitive destructiveness dwells deep in all our hearts, DeLillo's books insist; it is what makes us human. But is DeLillo honestly interested in what makes us human? I submit that he is not. His characters are little more than authorial mouthpieces, all but interchangeable with one another. And what makes human beings fascinating, and worth writing novels about, is their differences. Real people talk differently and think differently and have different interests and tastes and fears. None of this is reflected in DeLillo's novels. It is impossible, in the end, to accept his characters as human beings, or to take his novels seriously as representations of reality. All they amount to, really, is documents in the history of nihilistic chic.

But it is probably *déclassé* of me to try to discuss DeLillo's novels as representations of reality. "Surely," I can hear DeLillo's devotees saying, "you realize his true subject is not 'real life' at all, or even *ideas* about life, but words, words, words—language, codes of every kind, the whole question of signification?" Very well, it's true: DeLillo's narrators and characters *are* constantly talking about language. Football, Harkness tells us in *End Zone,* "is the one sport guided by language, by the word signal, the snap number, the color code, the play name." The murders in *The Names* are likewise guided by language: Axton's cult chooses its victims by their initials. DeLillo's characters are, as a rule, unusually sensitive to words, often worrying, in casual conversation with friends and family, about whether they've used *le mot juste.* (Pammy, in *Players*: "Is that right—'precipitate'?" Lyle: "I think so. . . . Maybe not quite.")

Words—the very sound or look of them, utterly divorced from their meanings—alternately hurt and comfort these people. A man named Wally Pippich, in *End Zone,* tells Harkness that "[s]ome names produce a negative gut reaction in my mind. Cyd Charisse. Mohandas K. Gandhi. Xerxes." Billy Twillig, the fourteen-year-old mathematical genius who is the protagonist of *Ratner's Star,* similarly finds that "[s]ome words frightened him slightly in their intimation of compressed menace. 'Gout.' 'Ohm.' 'Ergot.' 'Pulp.' These seemed organic sounds having little to do with language, meaning or the ordered contours of simple letters of the alphabet. Other words had a soothing effect. . . . " Lyle Wynant in *Players* is soothed by words, too. He finds the names of certain suburbs "wonderfully restful. They're a liturgical prayer, a set of moral considerations." In *End Zone,* Harkness recalls a sign ("WHEN THE GOING GETS TOUGH THE TOUGH GET GOING") that his father put in his room: "The sentiment of course had small appeal but it seemed that beauty flew from the words themselves, the letters, consonants swallowing vowels, aggression and tenderness, a semi-self-recreation from line to line, word to word, letter to letter. All meaning faded. The words became pictures. It was a sinister thing to discover at such an age, that words can escape their meanings. A strange beauty that sign began to express." Owen Brademas, an archaeologist in *The Names,* also finds beauty in words without meanings. Speaking of the stone tablets he has uncovered, he says, "I've begun to see a mysterious importance in the letters as such, the blocks of characters." He finds "those beautiful shapes . . . so strange and reawakening. It goes deeper than conversations, riddles. It's an unreasoning passion."

"Liturgical prayer," "strange beauty," "unreasoning passion." There is a distinct parallelism in these novels: as characters escape high-tech civilization, so words escape their meanings. The latter escape, like the former, appears to represent to DeLillo some triumphant, ritualistic shedding of false trappings. And indeed, in many a DeLillo novel, when the protagonist bids adieu to his xerographic former life, his language becomes reduced to meaningless sounds or disconnected words. Harkness, in *End Zone,* refers to his year at Logos College as a time of "words broken into brute sound." Pammy Wynant, in *Players,* after watching a movie in which a boy suffers "reduced sensibility" (meaning that he is "either unable to speak or refusing to") passes under a sign that reads "TRANSIENTS" and is confused by it: "It took on an abstract tone, as words had done before in her experience (although rarely), subsisting in her mind as language units that had mysteriously evaded the responsibilities of content." And Bucky Wunderlick, who in *Great Jones Street* goes into hiding knowing that his closest followers are waiting for him to "return with a new language for them to speak," is in the end injected with a drug that will make it impossible for him to put words together to create meaning. As a result he spends "[s]everal weeks of immense serenity" on "that unimprinted level where all sound is silken and nothing erodes in the mad weather of language."

There is more, much more, to be said about language in the novels of Don DeLillo—especially in *The Names* and *Ratner's Star,* which are absolutely chock-full of references to the "secret power" of names, to "[t]he mystery of alphabets, the contact with death and oneself," to the notion that "a secret name is a way of escaping the world . . . an opening into the self," that "[t]he universe is the name of G-dash-d," that "[m]eaningless sounds, abstract symbols . . . have the power of creation," and so forth. Though DeLillo's philosophy of language is not perfectly coherent or consistent, it is clear that his preoccupation is not with language as a means of communicating sophisticated ideas and complicated feelings, but with language as ritual. The ultimate purpose of language, DeLillo seems to feel, is not to convey meaning but simply to affirm one's existence. Language—especially language freed of the rhetorical trappings of "civilization" and the illusion that scientific progress leads to greater understanding—is, simply, the cry of human identity. This idea dominates the end of *The Names,* when James Axton, at the Parthenon, is surrounded by people speaking a variety of tongues and realizes that "[t]his is what we bring to the temple, not prayer or chant or slaughtered rams. Our offering is language." The fundamental importance of language as a ritual of identity is likewise suggested toward the end of *White Noise,* when Jack wonders: "Is there something so innocent in the recitation of names that God is pleased?"

One cannot deny that all this is at least theoretically interesting. And it is certainly conceivable that a compelling novel of ideas might be built on an intellectual foundation much like the one I have outlined. DeLillo, however, has yet to write it. Though his preoccupation with the philosophy of language occasionally yields thought-provoking, or at least memorably expressed, observations (e.g., "Mathematics is what the world is when we subtract our own perceptions"), it generally results in little more than one discouraging battery after another of pointless, pretentious rhetoric. He does not develop ideas so much as juggle jargon.

What makes the case of Don DeLillo especially unfortunate is that he does have real talent. He has always had a flair for humor—dark humor, naturally, of the Vonnegut-Heller sort—and that gift, in particular, is demonstrated in *White Noise* more abundantly than in any of DeLillo's previous books. But his continuing lack of interest in developing his characters and ideas, and his stubborn adherence to a stylish, schematic view of modern America as a great big xerox machine, continue to cripple DeLillo as an imaginative writer. It's ironic. While those of us who live in the real America carry on with our richly varied, emotionally tumultuous lives, DeLillo (as *White Noise* amply demonstrates) continues, in effect, to write the same lifeless novel over and over again—a novel constructed upon a simpleminded political cliché, populated by epigram-slinging, epistemology-happy robots, and packed with words that have very little to say to us about our world, our century, or ourselves. If anyone is guilty of turning modern Americans into xerox copies, it is Don DeLillo.

Flesh and Faith:
John Updike

SEPTEMBER 1986

John Updike once wrote that Vladimir Nabokov was possibly the finest author in America "whose books, considered as a whole, give the happy impression of an *oeuvre*, of a continuous task carried forward variously, of a solid personality, of a plenitude of gifts explored knowingly." It is a revealing comment. The typical late-twentieth-century American novelist, I think it is safe to say, doesn't tend to think in terms of compiling a coherent, respectable *oeuvre* but aims rather to produce one or more distinctive masterpieces, Great American Novels, each of them standing gloriously and impudently on its own. Not Updike. Even more than Nabokov, perhaps, he has consciously striven, throughout the more than quarter century of his literary career, to assemble a body of work worthy of standing alongside the productions of Balzac, Thackeray, Trollope; remove the dustjackets of his hardcover books—from his first volume of poems, *The Carpentered Hen and Other Tame Creatures* (1958), to his newly published twelfth novel, *Roger's Version*—and you will see that they form a matched set, identical down to the design and typeface on the spine. From the very beginning, evidently, Updike has sought to create an *oeuvre* worth collecting.

In the judgment of many, needless to say, he has been extraordinarily successful in this endeavor. He has won the National Book Award, the Pulitzer Prize, the American Book Award, the National Book Critics Circle Award; when *Esquire* recently asked several famous American writers which famous American writer should next win the Nobel Prize, no name was mentioned more than his. Critics celebrate Updike as a witty, acutely realistic observer of contemporary middle-class American life, and though several of his novels have been characterized by non-American settings and non-realistic approaches—*The Centaur* (1963) blended contemporary reality with Greek myth, *The Coup* (1978) chronicled the adventures of an anti-American sub-Saharan dictator, and *The Witches of Eastwick* (1984) explored a fantastic coven of Vietnam-era New England witches—Updike is, in the popular mind, thought of almost exclusively as the bard of the American bourgeois, the creator of *Rabbit, Run* (1960), *Couples* (1968), and other studies in middle-American *Angst* and *ennui*. And indeed, it could be convincingly argued that in their own ways even such novels as *The Centaur* and *The Coup* are fundamentally commentaries on the American way of life.

Updike is also recognized, quite justly, for his magnificent style, his unerring sense of sentence rhythm, his exquisitely precise choice of words; indeed, to read almost any passage of Updike—whether it be fiction or poetry or critical prose—is to recognize how much he loves words, is charmed and dazzled and bemused by them. (To be sure, his poetry, like that of most major American novelists—why is this so?—is quite undistinguished; his criticism, on the other hand, is consistently serious and thoughtful, and often truly splendid.) He is, in short, a master of the English language in an age when, to many, it seems amusingly old-fashioned to speak of a contemporary writer in such terms.

But not all critics revere Updike. Many academics, in particular, are unhappy with him because he writes so gracefully; they feel (incorrectly) that there can be little room, between the lines of his elegant prose, for the sort of ambiguities that they make it their business to deconstruct; their characteristic cry, accordingly, is that Updike is "more style than substance." This is, of course, a foolish cry. But there are justifiable complaints to be made about Updike, complaints that apply not only to one or two lesser works but to the bulk of his fictional *oeuvre*. These complaints might be briefly summarized as follows: first, that his vision of middle-class America is consistently facile and predictable, a vision founded upon the fashionable conceit that the average American lives a life of failure, compromise, misery, frustration, and unabating sexual urges. Second, that Updike's view of sexuality is little short of puerile, that when his male heroes think and talk about sex (and they rarely think or talk about anything else) they sound frighteningly like teenaged boys. And third, that Updike is frequently too distracted by public events and trends to focus properly upon the handful of imagined private lives that he has taken it upon himself to examine.

These things are certainly true, to a considerable extent, of *Roger's Version*. The novel's protagonist and narrator is Roger Lambert, a former Methodist minister, Ohio-born, who is now (the novel takes place in 1984–85) a fifty-two-year-old professor of divinity at a major metropolitan New England university. (Both university and city go unnamed, though in most respects Harvard and Boston seem to fit the bill.) After being defrocked in 1970 for committing adultery, Roger tells us, he divorced his first wife, Lillian, married his young mistress, Esther, and brought her East, where the two of them have for several years lived a quiet, affluent academic-couple-type life with their son, Richie, who is now twelve years old. Though Esther is increasingly moody and distant these days, and though Richie seems more at home with the folks on *Gilligan's Island* than with his family, Roger, who spends most of his time immersed in the recondite history of the early Church Fathers, claims to be happy; what he really seems to be, however, is bored and lonely and relatively serene in the knowledge that, the world being what it is, he could probably not improve appreciably upon his present state of affairs.

It is on an October afternoon in 1984 that Dale Kohler, a friend of Roger's teenaged niece Verna, disrupts this settled (if less than perfect) existence. Dale, a graduate student in computer research and a devout Christian, visits Roger to propose using the university's powerful computer system to prove the existence of God—"i.e., of a purposive and determining intelligence behind all phenomena"—and to request a grant from the School of Divinity to support his research. The most recent scientific findings, he says, support a belief in God; they demonstrate that the earliest cosmic events could *not* have occurred randomly and still have resulted in the formation of galaxies, of life, and (ultimately) of human intelligence, and that every supposedly arbitrary mathematical constant—the value of the weak force, the mass of the neutron, and so forth—had to be exactly what it was in order for mankind to develop. Therefore, Dale insists, there must have been a God present at the beginning to get things going in precisely the right way.

Roger's reaction to this young man is mixed. He is repelled by the "luminescence in his eyes," attracted by his enthusiasm, grateful to him for bringing something new into his life; he envies the young man's burning faith, but is at the same time appalled by Dale's urgent need to uncover a scientific foundation for his beliefs, his desire to (as it were) trap God in a computer. For Roger is a "Barthian," an adherent of the theology of Karl Barth (1886–1968), to whom *Roger's Version* is, one surmises, something of a centenary tribute. The theology of Barth is unalterably opposed to the way of thinking that Dale Kohler represents. Barth posits a God whose majesty is forever beyond the sordid reach of man. "The real God," he has written, "the God men do not invent, is *totaliter aliter* — Wholly Other. We cannot reach Him; only He can reach us." (Which he does, Barth declares, by way of revelation — in the form of Christ.) "There is no way from us to God," he has elsewhere observed, "not even a *via negativa* — not even a *via dialectica* nor *paradoxa*. The god who stood at the end of some human way . . . would not be God."

Both of these quotations patently mean a great deal to Updike: he cites them in a review of a Barth book in *Assorted Prose* (1965) and, in *Roger's Version,* has Roger Lambert recite them approvingly. And appropriately, too — for the novel's essential thematic concern, as it soon becomes clear, is an unmistakably Barthian one: the inability of man to make contact with the Infinite, and his obligation to face, day after day, the uncertainty, corporeality, and finitude of real life.

This theme is consistent with the philosophy not only of Barth but of Kierkegaard; and, though *Roger's Version* is unquestionably more of a "novel of ideas" than anything Updike has ever written, it should be noted that both of these thinkers have exerted an important influence throughout Updike's *oeuvre.* For, appearances to the contrary, Updike has always been as fascinated by God as by sex, as obsessed with the eternally inaccessible Great Abstractions as with the ubiquitous wonder of physicality. (If most of the time this obsession has not been readily apparent, it is doubtless because he has tended to communicate his theological interests with a good deal more subtlety and finesse than he has his sexual preoccupations.) Indeed, Updike has written that "Barth's theology, at one point in my life, seemed alone to be supporting it (my life)."

Barth, with his stubborn denial of the power of science either to prove or to disprove God's existence, is a major support of Roger Lambert's life as well. In his tense scientific disputations with Dale (which occupy an extraordinary amount of space in this novel), their roles seem ironically reversed: the young computer whiz argues that there's a God out there waiting to be discovered; the older ex-minister maintains that the computer will find nothing. Despite his strong theoretical opposition, however, Roger is so intrigued by Dale's ideas, and so impressed by his faith and fervency, that he helps the young man secure a grant. He also looks up his troubled, childish niece Verna (who, rejected by her conservative Ohio parents, is living on welfare in a housing project in Roger's city with her half-black infant daughter, Paula). Both Dale and Verna dine at the Lambert house for Thanksgiving, and before long Roger and Esther are involved with the two of them in ways that need not be described to anyone who has ever read an Updike novel.

For, novel of ideas or not, *Roger's Version* is set in familiar Updikean territory. Indeed, in many respects Roger is something of an intellectual variation upon that archetypal Updike hero, Harry Angstrom of *Rabbit, Run* and *Rabbit Redux*. Like Harry in his most recent incarnation (*Rabbit is Rich,* 1981), Roger is preoccupied with blacks (finding them frightfully dangerous but enviably full of life), homosexuals (threatening but fascinating), and a certain variety of sexual intercourse that shall go nameless here; like Harry, Roger worries whether his house is nicer than his neighbors', worries about miscegenation, and worries that he will never again have sex with anyone except his wife (and, like Harry, proves to be wrong). Esther, like Harry's wife, Janice, is cool and snooty, but sexy; his son, Richie, is as much of a television-centered deadhead as Harry's son, Nelson; his niece Verna, though irresponsible and self-indulgent like Nelson, lights Roger's fire the same way Nelson's wife, Melanie, lights Harry's.

As in *Rabbit is Rich,* moreover, the action of *Roger's Version* takes place against a neatly contrived background of current events, which Updike would apparently have us take as apocalyptic signs. In the earlier book, set in 1979, Harry despairs about double-digit inflation and the long filling-station lines, and laments that "the . . . world is running out of gas"; in the latter book, Roger (uncheered, apparently, by the stable dollar and the availability of gasoline) muses miserably about Reagan's re-election and the advent of AIDS—which, Verna suggests, is going to get us all.

Roger also contains elements of Tom Marshfield, the protagonist of *A Month of Sundays* (1975). Like Roger, Tom is a minister, a Barthian, and the center of a parish sex scandal; is married to a woman considerably younger than himself whom he met in church (Tom's wife, Jane, was an organist; Esther was a member of the choir); and is angry and unhappy about God and his marriage. What's more, Roger entertains certain fantasies about Esther and Dale that are remarkably similar to Tom's fantasies about Jane and a younger man named Ned Bork. (Both younger men, incidentally, are pale, slim, acned, and thirtyish, both are suspected by our protagonists of being homosexual or asexual, and both live dormitory-style.) And while Tom discovers, to his distress, that not his wife but his young lover Alicia has been sleeping with Bork, so Roger seems more worried by the possibility that Verna may be sleeping with Dale than by the fact that Esther is.

In *Roger's Version,* then, the *via Updikea* leads as always to Carnality, with few (if any) stops along the way for struggles of conscience or thoughts of morality. As Esther once stole Roger away from the ministry, so, with hardly any trouble at all, she steals Dale from Christ. To the eternally phallocentric Updike (whose once-scandalous descriptions, always more clinical than sensuous, of his characters' private parts and sexual gyrations now seem merely tiresome and embarrassing), this is the way the world works: faith, for all its attractions, can't compete with the flesh. (In the end, interestingly, there is a feeble echo of that great American novel of flesh and faith, *The Great Gatsby,* when Dale, having seen enough of the corruption of the East, returns home, like Nick Carraway, to the Middle West.)

If loyal Updike readers are put off by *Roger's Version,* it will probably not be because of the customary coital sequences or the overt theology but because of the aforementioned scientific discussions, mostly between Roger and Dale, about the origins of man and his universe. (So much space do these conversations take up, indeed, that it sometimes seems as if the story exists only to carry us from one conversation to the next, in the same way that the book of a musical comedy carries the audience from song to song.) Those who are not quite certain what a neutron is, or what the weak force is, will be hopelessly lost in these passages; those who know, but could not care less, will be utterly bored. Readers who are interested in science, however, may well join this reader in finding these passages, dramatically static though they be, to be absorbing in and of themselves. (Indeed, such readers may even end up judging *Roger's Version* to be a good deal more congenial, page for page, than the average Updike opus.)

And yet, taken as a whole, *Roger's Version* compares unsatisfactorily with most of Updike's novels. For, when one reaches the end, one cannot help but realize how far short Updike has fallen of doing justice to a tremendously ambitious theme. To be sure, Updike deserves only respect for confronting the question of religious faith in the late twentieth century, for attempting to probe the relations between God and technology, man and Infinity, human and artificial intelligence. But, though he devotes many an intriguing page to all of these topics, it must be said that he simply doesn't succeed in making a well-rounded novel out of them. He establishes dramatic conflicts, but they seem, in large part, trivial and vulgar in their conception, thematically irrelevant in their development, and uninspired, even half-hearted, in their resolution; by the end of the novel he appears to be uncertain of what he has been trying to say, of where to direct emphasis. In the last analysis, what Updike has done in *Roger's Version* is to essay a few esoteric variations upon—and detours from—his usual formula. The result is yet another beautifully written, intermittently thoughtful, and seriously flawed contribution to the five-foot Updike shelf.

Tom Wolfe's

The Bonfire of the Vanities

OCTOBER 1987

When it was announced, a couple of years ago, that Tom Wolfe planned to write a novel, and that the rock-'n'-roll magazine *Rolling Stone* would run it chapter-by-chapter as it issued from his typewriter — just the way the nineteenth-century English quarterlies once published Dickens and Trollope — I was more than usually intrigued. Not only by the plans for serial publication — which, in the 1980s, seemed as daringly old-fashioned as Woody Allen's use of black-and-white film — nor even by the association between Wolfe, the reactionary (though hip) social critic, and *Rolling Stone,* the not-very-conservative bible of Bon Jovi and Springsteen fans. No, mostly I was intrigued by the very idea of Tom Wolfe, one of the foremost practitioners of the New Journalism, composing a work of fiction. What sort of novel, I wondered, could Tom Wolfe write? Granted, such books as *Radical Chic, The Painted Word,* and *From Bauhaus to Our House* had demonstrated his ability to present an argument in the form of a fluid narrative; and *The Right Stuff* had boasted a storyline as strong as that of many a novel.

But there is a difference between writing such books and composing a novel. Besides, the hallmark of Wolfe's work is his eccentric, attention-getting style — a style which is often effective in his non-fiction but which one can imagine being inappropriate to a novel. It is a style thick with sarcasm, with cutesy catch phrases (*"tout le monde"* is a special favorite), with interjections (*"Mmmmmmmmmmmmmmmmm,"* he writes in *Radical Chic,* describing his reaction to some cheese balls) that make it look as if one of his typewriter keys has gotten stuck, with deliberate repetitions (a piece in *The Kandy-Kolored Tangerine-Flake*

Streamline Baby begins with the word "hernia" repeated thirty times) and redundancies (the third sentence of *The Painted Word* refers to "that great public bath, that vat, that spa, that regional physiotherapy tank, that White Sulphur Springs, that Marienbad, that Ganges, that River Jordan for a million souls which is the Sunday *New York Times*"). It's a style, in short, that is calculated to draw attention to Wolfe himself. Upon hearing of Wolfe's venture into novel-writing, therefore, one wondered: Would Wolfe abandon his famous prose style for this occasion? Or would he find some way of making it work in a novel, the main purpose of which should not be to convey Wolfe's personality but to depict objectively conceived characters?

The answer is that Wolfe has retained his style, and that—in large part—it works. Yes, there are some problems with characterization and stylistic overload, but to an impressive degree Wolfe's novel succeeds, style and all; at its best, it's witty, absorbing, a marvelous page-turner. One reason for this is that Wolfe has played to his strengths: *The Bonfire of the Vanities,* like most of Wolfe's non-fiction, is an audacious work of social criticism.

The novel chronicles the decline and fall of Sherman McCoy, the number-one bond salesman for the prestigious Manhattan investment firm of Pierce and Pierce. At the beginning of the novel, McCoy—a tall, handsome, thirty-eight-year-old Yale graduate with a million-dollar-a-year income and a luxurious Park Avenue apartment—is an ambitious, self-confident sort who likes to think of himself as a "Master of the Universe." The event which precipitates McCoy's downfall is a seemingly minor one. One night, he makes a wrong turn on the Triborough Bridge. He and his glamorous Southern mistress, Maria—whom he's just picked up at LaGuardia Airport—are thereby plunged into the South Bronx, where, after a harrowing ride through the unfamiliar streets, they end up at an expressway on-ramp that is blocked by a tire. The subsequent events occur very rapidly: Sherman leaves his Mercedes to move the tire; two black teenage boys approach, offering help; Sherman, assuming they're muggers, fights them off and gets back into the car; Maria, who has meanwhile taken the wheel, drives off quickly. In doing so, she inadvertently runs over one of the boys, whose name (we are to learn) is Henry. Neither McCoy nor Maria reports the incident. Through a series of unlikely but credible events, however, Henry's injury becomes a public symbol of racial injustice, and by the time a police investigation does connect McCoy with the injury, half of New York is screaming for his blood.

Wolfe does a splendid job, in these early chapters, of describing McCoy's world—a world in which "mere boys, with smooth jawlines and clean arteries, boys still able to blush, were buying three-million-dollar apartments on Park and Fifth. (Why wait?) They were buying thirty-room, four-acre summer places in Southampton, places built in the 1920s and written off in the 1950s as white elephants, places with decaying servants' wings, and they were doing over the servants' wings, too, and even adding on." The novel is full of this sort of thing—elaborate, energetic descriptions of the material circumstances and systems of value under which wealthy New Yorkers live and work in the 1980s, and of the values that guide them. It is common nowadays, of course, for novelists to fill their work with irrelevant detail, but Wolfe's details are wonderfully appropriate throughout; he is a novelist of manners who, like many a nineteenth-century English novelist, is fascinated by the manners and morals of his well-heeled contemporaries.

He is not concerned only with millionaires, however. Several not-so-rich characters figure prominently. One is Lawrence Kramer, a young Bronx prosecutor who sees in the McCoy case—with its rich white defendant—a chance to garner some publicity and to give his career a needed boost. Another is Peter Fallow, a decadent young British reporter for the sensationalist New York tabloid, *The City Light,* for whom the McCoy story comes along just in time to keep him from getting fired. Lawrence lives on the West Side, and takes the subway every day to the Bronx courthouse, a gloomy oasis of safety in a neighborhood where no one dares even to walk down the streets; Fallow lives the life of a member of New York's "Eurotrash" community, cadging meals from affluent, vulgar Americans even as he looks down his nose at them. Wolfe brings the worlds of these men to life as vividly as he does Sherman McCoy's.

Along the way, Wolfe also draws a dozen or so arresting lesser portraits. One thinks particularly of a tough old judge named Kovitsky; of "Reverend Bacon," a slick leader of the black community; of New York's unnamed (but very Koch-like) mayor; of Kate diDucci, a rich hostess whom McCoy's decorator wife, Judy, wants to cultivate; and of Arthur Ruskin, Maria's aged husband, who made his millions transporting Arabs to Mecca by air. Some of these minor characters are suspiciously reminiscent of real-life celebrities. One cannot read Wolfe's description of Nunnally Voyd, a pompous middle-aged novelist who hobnobs with high-society folk, without thinking of Gore Vidal. (Incidentally, Nunnally Voyd's is not the only name that Wolfe has fun with. McCoy's law firm, for instance, is called Dunning, Sponget & Leach.)

Every so often, Wolfe sets the plot aside for a while to offer a somewhat fuller view of the lifestyles of the rich and famous. In one chapter, for example, McCoy attends a Fifth Avenue dinner party given by "this year's host and hostess of the century"; in another, Fallow accompanies Ruskin to a chic restaurant, where Ruskin is fawned over nauseatingly by the maitre d' (who immediately turns callous when Ruskin dies at the table). Some of the details in these episodes are brilliantly—and hilariously—on target. Wolfe focuses in upon all sorts of things that many of us have noticed but probably never thought much about: for example, the emaciated look that rich middle-aged New York women seem to cultivate, and the way high-society hostesses have of greeting every newly arrived guest as if he were the dearest of friends.

These are people capable of subordinating even the gravest philosophical issues to matters of status and fashion. Take bigotry, for example. When the English baby nurse that Kramer has hired complains about "colored" people, Kramer is pleased: "Thank God in Heaven! What a relief! They could let their breaths out now. Miss Efficiency was a bigot. These days the thing about bigotry was, it was undignified. It was a sign of Low Rent origins, of inferior social status, of poor taste. So they were the superiors of their English baby nurse, after all. What a fucking relief." And take religion. Though McCoy doesn't believe in God, he tells his small daughter otherwise when she asks him. But he'd prefer not to have the question raised at all. "He had hoped he would never have to discuss religion with her. They had begun sending her to Sunday school at St. James' Episcopal Church, at Madison and Seventy-first. That was the way you took care of religion. You enrolled them at St. James', and you avoided talking or thinking about religion again."

"Low Rent" New Yorkers (to borrow his terminology) aren't safe from Wolfe's sarcasm either. He takes note of the snotty swagger practiced by certain teenage urban males, for instance—he describes it, in his inimitable way, as the "Pimp Roll"—and of the grammatical barbarisms and linguistic vulgarities ("Whaddaya, whaddaya") characteristic of certain Bronx lawyers and New York's Finest.

The novel, then, gives a colorful picture of several levels of New York life. It might even be said that New York—the city Wolfe loves to hate—is itself the book's main character. Wolfe is not, of course, the first fiction writer of the Eighties in whose work New York has figured prominently. In recent years, many writers—particularly young ones—have sought to bring the city to life in their pages; one thinks of *Bright Lights, Big City,* of *Slaves of New York,* of the novels and stories of David Leavitt, Deborah Eisenberg, Emily Listfield, and many others. But the city that appears in most of these fictions is only a pale, distorted shadow of the real thing. These young writers almost never range beyond certain areas of Manhattan, and their understanding of the city's history, culture, and social dynamics is almost invariably crippled by the outsider's illusions that they brought with them. In their fictions, New York often seems to be little more than a playground for relatively affluent young white people who grew up somewhere else and rarely have reason to venture beyond the Village or the Upper West Side. The New York of Tom Wolfe's novel is grimmer, more complex, more real. Wolfe *knows* New York, in all its boroughs, on all its class levels, and he is interested in it not as a one-dimensional backdrop but as a social organism. His book's greatest virtue resides in its portrait of the city; nowhere in contemporary fiction has the New York of our era been so richly and perceptively brought to life.

And honestly, too. Other contemporary writers who treat New York in their fiction delicately avoid the subjects of race and crime; Wolfe is not afraid to make it clear that these are matters, along with money and real estate, that New Yorkers are compelled to think about very often. Wolfe envisions New York, in fact, as the setting of an escalating, almost apocalyptic conflict between poor blacks and rich whites. In the novel's prologue, the mayor is mercilessly harassed by a Harlem audience full of blacks who are, alas, willing to follow the lead of their rudest, most radical members; in his mind the put-upon mayor castigates the city's rich white *goyim* in their "swell co-ops": "You don't even know, do you? Do you really think this is *your* city any longer? Open your eyes! The greatest city of the twentieth century! Do you think *money* will keep it yours?" The city's white neighborhoods, he muses, are temporary enclaves of safety—"little Hong Kongs, that's all!"—in a mostly dangerous, and predominantly minority-populated, metropolis; it's only a matter of time, to his way of thinking, before such communities as Riverdale, Forest Hills, and Brooklyn Heights are inundated by the blacks and Third Worlders that occupy the rest of the city. The encounter between Sherman McCoy and the black teenagers is intended to dramatize this vision of a city in the process of changing hands. What happens to McCoy, in essence, is that he comes to realize that he is far from being a Master of the Universe; for all his wealth and power, the ultimate mastery of New York rests in other hands than his.

Wolfe is concerned, then, with many uncomfortable truths and controversial themes. If at times, when he is writing about the *beau monde,* Wolfe seems a bit too smart-alecky, his sarcasm excessive and his ironies too easy, when he is writing about the city's less hoity-toity precincts his prose is often quite straightforward and forceful. His descriptions of such things as Kramer's perilous daily subway rides, of McCoy's desperate moments in his Mercedes on the dark Bronx streets, and of the dismal Bronx courthouse and its even more dismal environs (particularly of the holding pen where McCoy spends a few painful hours) are strikingly evocative. At times, to be sure, one does feel as if Wolfe is loading the dice against blacks. Though his novel has several white point-of-view characters, not a single black character is presented from the inside, as it were; thus, while Wolfe gives us an opportunity to empathize even with such an unappetizing chap as Peter Fallow, he makes certain that the deepest motivations of Reverend Bacon, Henry, and Henry's mother—to name three of the novel's most prominent black characters—remain a mystery to us. To read Wolfe's novel, furthermore, is to get the impression that all young blacks in New York are indifferent students and a potential danger to society.

There are other problems with the novel. Unsurprisingly, Wolfe's style often strikes one as too jazzy and self-conscious for the occasion. A style, of course, can be as contrived as one wants it to be, but it has to *sound,* at least, like the natural form of expression of some conceivable variety of human animal. Sometimes Wolfe's prose is so far out there that it just doesn't qualify. When Judge Kovitsky spits at some noisy prisoners in a police van, for instance, Wolfe describes the sputum as follows: "It hit the wire mesh and hung there. . . . For one strange feverish moment there was nothing in the world, in the solar system, in the universe, in all of astronomy, but the cage and this one gleaming, oozing, pendulous sunlit gob of spit." There are too many such overly feverish moments in Wolfe's prose. Most of the time, though, Wolfe's style works fine. There *are* awkward patches—but his energy, like that of a Dostoevski or a Dreiser, carries one along so rapidly that one usually doesn't have time to notice the bumps and ruts along the way.

One of the novel's weakest aspects is the characterization of McCoy. When a satirist sits down to write a novel, he automatically has a problem: how to ridicule his hero and, well, make him a *hero* at the same time? A satirist, after all, need sympathize with no one; but a novelist, under most circumstances, has to sympathize at least with his protagonist—and sympathy is not, let us say, a quality for which Wolfe's work has heretofore been noted. Wolfe's solution to this dilemma is an uneasy one. At the outset of the novel, Sherman McCoy is presented unsympathetically. He's a vain adulterer, obsessed with power, money, status, and material possessions, and Wolfe spends a lot of time making fun of him. The only admirable thing about him is that he does have *something* of a conscience; after lying to his wife about his extramarital activities, he reflects upon his sins: "The Master of the Universe was cheap, and he was rotten, and he was a liar." Bingo.

It is impossible to feel much sympathy for the Sherman McCoy whom we meet in Chapter One. By the end of the novel, however, this fatuous tower of conceit has somehow been transformed into a model of probity. In the closing chapters we are obviously supposed to regard McCoy as a decent, sensitive man destroyed by circumstance. He's so good, in fact, that when he must lie, under oath, to save his skin, he is devastated: "I'm doing something illegal!" This dishonesty, Wolfe suggests, is at odds with every fiber of McCoy's being. "In well-reared girls and boys," Wolfe writes, "guilt and the instinct to obey the rules are reflexes, ineradicable ghosts in the machine." To read this passage is to wonder whatever happened to the cheap, rotten, lying McCoy of Chapter One. (Besides, are we really supposed to believe that the top bond trader at Pierce and Pierce, in this age of insider trading scandals, has never lied or broken the law before?) Doubtless the reason for the inconsistency is that Wolfe realized, halfway through the novel, that his hero had to be sympathetic for us to care about his fate; since the serial method of publication made it impossible for him to go back and make McCoy more likable from the start, he had no choice but to change McCoy gradually and hope it wouldn't be *too* noticeable.

Another problem with Wolfe's characterization is that some of his creations are dangerously close to caricatures: the ridiculously unctuous society lady, the impossibly vulgar Low-Rent lawyer. There are times, also, when Wolfe's preoccupation with the vanity and snobbery of high-society folk seems itself a form of vanity and snobbery; as with the Truman Capote of *Answered Prayers,* one finds oneself wondering why an author so acutely aware of the mediocrity and tediousness of rich people continues to pay so much attention to them, to take them so seriously. Yes, Wolfe's moneyed characters are fascinating, but they're not as fascinating as he thinks they are.

For the fact is, after the first few engaging chapters, the novel begins to pall. By the middle of the book Wolfe has already played his best cards; much of the material in the second half is redundant, tiresome. The exhilarating inventiveness of the opening chapters gives way to an uninspired playing out of what proves to be a more conventional plot than one expected. The ending itself is particularly disappointing: rather than find a serious and meaningful way to conclude McCoy's story, Wolfe opts for a more Wolfean (and less novelistic) wrap-up, offering a last, frantic round of facile jokes about the media, superficial burlesques of New York types, and easy ironies about American civilization and culture in the Eighties. Despite this last-minute retreat into familiar territory, however, *The Bonfire of the Vanities* is on the whole a very provocative work—a study, as funny as it is penetrating, of a man who is blinded to the real values in life by his own vanity and self-aggrandizement, and of a metropolis many of whose denizens have raised the cultivation of those attributes to a high art. Wolfe is one contemporary novelist who's not out to hide his love of ideas, his zest for language, and his intellectual energy. In an era of arid, inert little novels, this big book resounds with life.

IV

True Confessions

These days, when sampling newly published works of American fiction, one often feels less like a reader than like a psychoanalyst. One feels, in other words, as if one is witnessing a confession of the writer's own personal history—or, at least, some semi-imaginative variation upon it—and is expected to respond with commentary, advice, or words of sympathy. That many of these new works are written in the first person does little to dispel this impression. This is not to suggest that there is anything wrong, per se, with autobiographical fiction. After all, such distinguished works as *Remembrance of Things Past* and *The Sun Also Rises* are heavily autobiographical (and written in the first person, to boot). But these novels represent highly accomplished acts of artistic distancing, of self-objectification; at the end of each of them one feels not merely that one has rummaged around inside a single confused soul, but that one has been vouchsafed an artist's vision of the world.

Many a novel and short-story collection nowadays, by contrast, seems confessional in the worst—the most desperate and claustrophobic—sense of the word. In such a work, the writer's main purpose typically appears to be less artistic than personal: he may seek, variously, to delineate his deepest emotions, to expiate his guilt, to prove his innocence, to account for his failures or weaknesses or neuroses. The real subject of the "fiction," accordingly, consists less often in the events of the narrative themselves than in the protagonist's *feelings* about those events. The most lamentable consequence of this state of affairs is that a comprehensive moral vision often seems wanting; one gathers that, as far as the writer is concerned, the way the protagonist sees things is pretty much the way they are.

It is especially dismaying to find this to be true of literary works that are, in various other respects, extremely impressive. *The Good Mother,* a first novel by Sue Miller (a fortyish writer who has published stories in the *Atlantic, Ploughshares,* and *Mademoiselle*), is a case in point. The novel tells the story of Anna Dunlap, who begins free-associating in the very first sentence: "The post office in East Shelton reminded me of the one in the little town near my grandparents' summer home in Maine." During the first half of the novel, Miller cuts back and forth between the events of Anna's childhood at that summer home and elsewhere, and the aftermath of her relatively recent divorce from her husband Brian, a Boston attorney. The intended connection between these two narrative threads is obvious after the first couple of chapters, even though the whole picture is not. We gather that Anna feels a great deal of remorse over her divorce and, especially, over certain still-undescribed events, involving her four-year-old daughter Molly, that proceeded from it; and we recognize that Miller is out to convince us that none of these events is, at bottom, entirely Anna's fault—that they are, instead, the consequence of her misguided upbringing.

Miller has, as a matter of fact, got her heroine's entire psychic dilemma figured out. When she was a child, her parents wanted her to be a piano prodigy, but she proved not to be good enough, so they withheld their love and approval from her. The "sense of limitless possibility" that had infused her life at the age of eleven thus quickly evaporated as soon as it became clear that Anna was no Van Cliburn in the making. And her grandparents, unfortunately, were just as cold and distant as her folks. (One would have to hunt far and wide in the annals of world literature to find so extraordinarily unaffectionate a family as the one with which Miller has saddled her heroine.) Because she didn't feel loved, Anna, taking her wanton cousin Babe as a model, became the class Jezebel in junior high school. ("I felt finally that something was being asked of me socially for which I had a gift.") She married Brian, the son of a minister, because he was the first of her several college lovers to take her erotic largesse seriously enough to make the offer. None of those lovers, however, gave her real pleasure—and that included Brian. Being married to him was a very bland proposition; he was "in every way peripheral to my life." The essential difference between Anna and Brian, in Miller's eyes, is captured in a brief exchange that takes place on the night they decide to break up. Anna remarks that "sex between us was always so . . . nothing. So terrible." Brian is surprised, stung; "I never thought so," he replies. See the difference? Anna has never had satisfying sex, but *knows* it's out there somewhere, will recognize it when she sees it, and will make the most of it; Brian, on the other hand, doesn't know about it and doesn't care. Even though he's been having an affair with a co-worker named Brenda (whom he marries directly after the divorce), we are meant to understand that this affair is a pallid, predictable little piece of business, that Brenda is a creature of "tidy asexuality," that Brian is not really interested in, or open to, the glorious sensual possibilities of human life.

After parting from this wimpy Establishment husband, Anna meets a soulful, tempestuous painter named Leo Cutter, and becomes his lover. Leo is the diametrical opposite of Brian—he's a free spirit who sleeps on the floor, talks dirty, bathes in a tin washtub, doesn't own a jacket or tie, and collects pornographic pictures. ("Leo was fascinated with the inability of painting, print, to convey a sense of the pornographic in the way photography did, and with what that suggested about the visual imagination.") He's in touch with his body, with the earth—he's *dans la vie:* "Life seemed to reach in and touch Leo in a way it never did me." Leo helps Anna discover eroticism as a means of communication between two souls, thus restoring to her that "sense of limitless possibility" that she had in childhood. When she becomes pregnant, he leads her to an abortionist and explains to her that the nice social worker who tries to comfort her is "a fascist of the soul"; to Anna, this behavior is indicative not of a deficient sense of responsibility on Leo's part but of an admirable integrity of character. (If any of this sounds familiar, perhaps that's because in many ways it's a replay of *An Unmarried Woman,* with Leo as Alan Bates to Anna's Jill Clayburgh —and with Brian, of course, in the Michael Murphy role.) Alas, Anna and Leo's palace of pleasure comes tumbling down when—well, not to ruin it for anyone—*something happens* and Brian decides it is unsafe for their daughter Molly to remain with Anna. Having had the child with him for a visit, he keeps her and sues for custody; the second half of the novel is concerned with the ensuing legal proceedings.

Let it be said that Miller handles all this marvelously. She is a highly gifted storyteller with a good sense of suspense and structure and pace; her prose, though not particularly distinctive, is smooth and elegant. Indeed, on the technical level this is the most accomplished novel I've read in some time—engaging and consistently believable.

Yet the confessional quality of *The Good Mother* weakens it considerably. In the latter part of the book, Anna discusses her situation with a psychiatrist (who reassures her that she is a good mother), and then, with the other principals, testifies in court. The "feel" of these episodes is disconcerting; Miller gives the impression that she is pleading her own case, delivering an *apologia pro vita sua*. Her main purpose seems to be to make us believe that Brian is overreacting prudishly, that Anna is the better parent—more loving, more giving—and that Anna and Leo's freewheeling, unsettled life is better for Molly than the wimpish stability of Brenda and Brian's home. And there's the rub. Because this reader, anyway, came away from the book with quite a different view of things—namely, that Anna is simply too confused, too wrapped up in herself and her feelings about Leo, to reasonably assert a greater right to custody of the child. Though she adores Molly, Anna seems less worried about what happened to Molly while in her care, and about how it may have affected the child emotionally, than with the question of how the whole sordid incident reflects on *her*. (Thus the book's title.) And Miller seems to endorse—indeed, to *share*—this view of things. Anna's implicit attitude toward life is that there are only two ways you can go: you can be aloof, like her parents and grandparents and ex-husband, or you can be dissolute, like Aunt Babe and Leo. This is the perspective of a very troubled, mixed-up person, and Miller does little to suggest that her own perspective is significantly broader.

With Linda Collins, too, one receives the impression that one is being asked to play psychoanalyst. Like Miller, Collins is a woman of middle age who is only now bringing out her first book, *Going to See the Leaves*. The stories in this book (which originally appeared in *Commentary, The St. John's Review, The Hudson Review, Mademoiselle*, and *The Kenyon Review*) are preoccupied with the passage of time, the ebbing of life, the fading of love. In every story, her method of treating these themes is to lead one or more members of a sophisticated upper-middle-class Manhattan family through a swarm of natural symbols—water and falling leaves, color and colorlessness, heat and cold, light and dark—that suggest the opposition between life and death. Several of these stories (though the word *meditations* would be equally appropriate for most of them) are delivered in the first person, with a middle-aged woman as narrator; most of the others, though written in the third person, center upon the consciousness of such a woman.

In "When the Pipes Froze," for instance, the narrator recalls the winter day (the second of January, to be specific) when she journeyed with her husband, Richard, to their house in the country, and found it to be ice cold—the heat and electricity had gone off and the pipes had frozen in the walls. They ended up spending the night at the local Howard Johnson's, where they dined on whiskey sours, cherry tomatoes, corn relish, three-bean salad, pickled beets, pimentos, carrot salad, scrod with Newburg sauce, and pumpkin pie; not till the meal was over did Richard realize that "Everything we ate was orange." Get it? Unconsciously, they were reaching out for life after seeing their house transformed into a tomblike symbol of death. This realization prompts our narrator to soliloquize at length upon the days when she and her husband were younger and, like Anna Dunlap, had delusions of limitless possibility, believing foolishly that writing, philosophy, sex, and psychoanalysis would save them from the common end.

A similar woman narrates "Driving Back from the Funeral," in which she and her husband return home across the snow-covered coal country from his brother-in-law's funeral in Harrisburg. At the funeral, she felt that "in the presence of death the little rages of the heart must scatter. Looking at [the body] I thought, We are in death's presence, and so I resolved to be tender forever. But of its own accord the chatter started again, and I was as before." A near-accident on the highway again reminds her of her mortality and she thinks: "Having given ourselves up for lost, having folded my hands and said, 'Lord, take me,' why not consider the rest of our lives a serendipity, a gift?" She remembers that, at the funeral, she "couldn't look at [the body] enough. . . . As if there were something to stare down, as if there were something to achieve by this looking, something to win."

In "Meditation on Play, Thoughts on Death," a woman dwells on the fact that her twelve-year-old son, Jacob, doesn't play imaginative childhood games anymore; instead he studies Latin, practices the violin, and plays hockey. She mourns the loss of his childhood—but what concerns her most of all is aging itself, particularly her own. At times, these meditations can be very affecting:

> We all move together in one inexorable swerve toward the end of our lives. We bear to one another different relations. To one, I am mother; to another, child or wife or friend. Some are of my age, we are agemates, and so look the same distance back and see the distance ahead shortening

by the same degree; we are bound to one another by virtue of the fact that we stand on parallel rungs of our particular ladders; we understand that what is true for one of us is likely to be true for another, whether or not we dare to touch upon these facts aloud. Then there are those younger than ourselves, our friends whose youth we may envy, pity, despise, depending upon what we think they know about these matters. And then there are our children, whose upward curve warms and chills us, whom we would like to exhort to pleasure and to whom we would call out at the same time, *Memento mori*. No, not that. Surely not that. We would never have them think on death, nor would we have them see how we are ourselves aging, how we are the moribund at the wedding feast. But still we would warn them unbeknownst, so that in the midst of their shouts and games, with cheeks feverish with joy and lips parted to sing, suck, lick, or bite at the apple of life, they should still remember, and prepare, and bear forever the name of their lord and master, death, before their eyes, upon their sleeve.

There are many such moving passages in Collins's stories, and to read any one of them is to be moved to admiration by its style and sensitivity. But to read two or three in succession is to be exasperated by an insistent monomania, often morbid in its tone. The *memento mori* motif is ubiquitous, and after a while the pointed references to darkness, cold, and such are almost comical. In "Driving Back from the Funeral": "Quick winter evening was rushing toward us." In "A Summer's Day": "The thought of time passing confused her. Everything slid away. . . . She felt she had been wheeled swiftly past the events of her life." In "Meditation on Play, Thoughts on Death": "I am growing old, and I cannot forget for a minute." In "Intimacy": "Soon it will be cold in the kitchen. So the garden will disappear and the window will show only black. Soon, in fact, they will be depressed, night-sad." In "Going to See the Leaves": "The room was cold. She heard the wind and saw that the leaves were still falling in the dark. It was a grave matter that all the leaves were falling, but she was very glad she had come to see them." Certainly death haunts us all, but eventually one wants to know why Collins and her characters seem unable to think of anything else.

The one exception to all this is the first and longest story in the book, "The Doctor's House." There is no upper-middle-class Manhattan family here, no middle-aged woman worrying over her mortality. Rather, this story is a Kafkaesque account of the pregnancy of a high-powered young Manhattan lawyer named Charles Hamilton. Hamilton is not so much astounded by this odd occurrence as he is embarrassed and inconvenienced by it (he has to abandon his practice and his impersonal sex life), and eventually changed: the pregnancy sets his moral priorities in order. But one is not sure, in the end, what Collins is getting at in the story. Is it supposed to be funny—the idea being that it would take pregnancy to make a heartless male yuppie change his stripes? Or is it meant to be a celebration of the essential things in life, of the miracle of reproduction and of life itself? If it is meant as celebration, I don't think it succeeds; a woman's pregnancy is one kind of miracle, after all, and a man's quite another. This story is odd in a way that Collins did not intend it to be—odd in the sense of perplexing, strangely incomplete. Indeed, this is an odd book—a collection of truly poignant *pensées* that eventually collapses under the weight of its own obsession.

The funniest sentence of the year may be one that appeared in *The New York Times Book Review*'s "Noted with Pleasure" column on April 20. "Laurie Colwin," it read, "swims against the tide of fashion." Now, there are many things that one can imagine people calling Laurie Colwin, but unfashionable? Never. The author of three novels and two previous collections of short fiction, Colwin has developed in recent years into a touchstone of post-Sixties literary minimalism, becoming, in the process, the idol of a whole generation of writing-workshop students, and (arguably) the reigning monarch of fiction at *The New Yorker,* where four of the eight stories in her new collection, *Another Marvelous Thing,* first appeared. (Others were first published in *Cosmopolitan, New Woman,* and *Playboy.*)

The stories recount the history of a love affair between two married Manhattanites. The middle-aged Francis (Frank) Clemens is an investment consultant; the youngish Josephine (Billy) Delielle is an economic historian. A friend of mine read three of these stories in their original magazine appearances and thought, until she was able to compare the texts word-for-word, that she had actually read the same story three times. I had my doubts about the absolute veracity of this anecdote until I read this book. The first two stories, "My Mistress" and "Frank and Billy," depict the affair in its early stages, relating many of the same episodes and details; the former is told in the first person, from Frank's point of view, the latter in the third person (over Frank's shoulder, as it were). In both stories, Colwin takes us through the tedious business of introducing the principals, filling in their backgrounds, explaining (elaborately) how they got together. There's not much character exploration. The point of the stories, apparently, is to tell us that Frank and Billy met at a party given by the *Journal of American Economic Thought,* to which they are both contributors; that Billy has "lank brown hair" and gray-blue eyes; that she teaches two classes a week at a business school; that Frank calls on Billy wearing a tweed coat; that around the house she wears "a pair of worn corduroy trousers, once green and now no color at all, a gray sweater, an old shirt of her younger brother's which has a frayed collar, and a pair of very old, broken shoes, with tassels, the backs of which are held together with electrical tape"; that she uses baby powder and Ivory soap; that she's working on a dissertation about "the effect of the medieval wool trade on a Cotswold village"; that her husband Grey, three years her elder, is "the resident economics genius at a think tank"; that Frank's wife Vera is an interior designer; that one of his sons is a security analyst and the other a journalist; that Frank's apartment is very tastefully decorated; that Billy's apartment on the second floor of a brownstone has "no style whatever"; that Billy sleeps in an old T-shirt of Grey's and buys her white cotton underwear at a five-and-ten; that on a weekend trip to their Vermont love nest they stopped and bought coffee, milk, sugar, cornflakes, bread, butter, cheese, salami, eggs, and tomato soup.

The approach is much the same throughout the book. In "French Movie" Frank and Billy see a movie called *Ghost Dogs from Outer Space.* In "A Little Something" they spend two days together while Vera is away on business. In "Swan Song" they keep talking about breaking up but never do. Any one of these stories might easily be confused with any other. The last three stories in the book are more easily distinguished from one another. In "A Country Wedding," Billy and Frank finally break up and at last we meet Grey, who accompanies Billy to her friend Penny's wedding. In "Another Marvelous Thing" Billy spends a couple of days in the hospital and eventually has a baby by Caesarian section. And in "A Couple of Old Flames" Billy, with her nine-month-old son William in a hip sling, runs into Frank at a party given by the *American Economic Review* and they go out for a bite together.

But the book doesn't add up to much. Frank and Billy never take on dimension; nor does their romance. To be sure, part of the purpose of

Colwin's flat tone is to suggest that real extramarital love affairs are not romantic and exotic, as in French movies, but trite. ("Isn't it banal?" remarks Billy, apropos their affair, in "Swan Song.") Yet Frank and Billy's affair rings just as false as any French movie romance. Neither of them ever gets excited, cries, loses control; Billy's sardonic tone never falters. Love is a transaction, and a pretty uninteresting one at that: as Billy puts it, "We're in a very unusual situation. It has to do with limited doting, restricted thrall, and situational adoration."

We learn more, in fact, about Grey's résumé, Billy's wardrobe, and the decoration of Frank's apartment than we ever do about our protagonists' motivations. What is the attraction between them? Why is Billy cheating on her charming, handsome, brilliant young husband? How does she feel about being unfaithful to him? We haven't a clue. And the few things that Colwin does tell us about Frank and Billy's feelings don't really *tell* us anything, don't resonate, don't make them grow into flesh-and-blood people in our minds; on the contrary, those cut-and-dried details seem arbitrary, little more than furnishings. Whether the subject is love or the lunch menu, it is discussed in the same terse, precise, emotionless, and matter-of-fact manner: "With the exception of her family, Billy was close only to Grey and Penny Stern. She had never been the subject of anyone's romantic passion. She and Grey, after all, had been fated to marry. She had loved him all her life." So terse, precise, emotionless, and matter-of-fact, indeed, are the stories in this book that they often read less like pieces of fiction than like tidy little business reports or case studies—full of short sentences and objective details and virtually free of metaphor, ambiguity, or anything resembling human emotion.

*T**he Wild Birds: Six Stories of the Port William Membership,* a collection of recent short fiction by the novelist, poet, and essayist Wendell Berry, is one of those books that remind one of the real purpose and possibilities of the literary art. "Yes," one says to oneself while reading it, "this is what fiction is all about." The good and simple truth to which each of Berry's stories testifies is that its author observes people carefully, understands them precisely, and cares about them deeply; bombast, pretension, and narcissism are alien to him. He writes about the inhabitants of rural Kentucky, where he has spent most of his life, but his stories bear no resemblance whatsoever to the stylized, anomic rural fiction—

the "hick chic," as Diane Johnson dubbed it recently in *The New York Review of Books*—of Bobbie Ann Mason, Anne Tyler, and company. One has the refreshing impression that Berry doesn't give a damn what's in and what's out: he writes what he wants to write. Given the present literary climate, this sort of independence of mind is a considerable achievement in itself.

The stories in this book take place in and around the imaginary village of Port William, Kentucky, over a period of thirty-eight years. The first story, "Thicker than Liquor," is set in 1930; the last, "The Wild Birds," in 1967. (Port William also served as the setting of three previous novels by Berry, *Nathan Coulter, A Place on Earth,* and *The Memory of Old Jack.*) The central character in three of these stories is Wheeler Catlett, a lawyer whose conception of the community of Port William as a "membership" is a running theme throughout. "The way we are," a farmer named Burley Coulter explains in the title story, "we are members of each other. All of us. Everything. The difference ain't in who is a member and who is not, but in who knows it and who don't." This is Berry's view of things as well. To his mind, moreover, people have unspoken obligations not only to one another but to the land they share. "The land expects something from us," Wheeler says in "It Wasn't Me." "The line of succession, the true line, is the membership of people who know it does." There's something very American, very nineteenth-century Transcendental, about this formulation; and indeed Berry describes Wheeler in "It Wasn't Me" as "a seer of visions—not the heavenly visions of saints and mystics, but the earthly ones of a mainly practical man who sees the good that has been possible in this world, and, beyond that, the good that is desirable in it." Because they are founded upon the conviction that such things as friendship, honesty, decency, loyalty, and community are important, Berry's stories may strike some readers as "old-fashioned," and it is true that the world of Wendell Berry is, as far as such matters are concerned, utterly antithetical to that imagined by writers like Laurie Colwin, to whose self-centered and superficial urban characters words like *honesty* and *loyalty* are little more than quaint anachronisms.

What distinguishes Berry from the Colwins and Masons, however, is not that his stories are old-fashioned; it's that they're timeless, reflecting an abiding awareness of and respect for the things that endure—or, at least, deserve to. The plots are simple enough. In "Thicker than Liquor," Wheeler (who has been out of law school for four years, and is practicing in Hargrave, the large town nearest Port William) goes up to Louisville to pay the hotel bill of his uncle Peach, an alcoholic, and bring him back home. Uncle Peach is nothing but a nuisance to Catlett, who has had to do this sort of thing many times. When Uncle Peach begins vomiting on the train, Wheeler is disgusted, and cannot figure out why he goes to so much trouble on the man's behalf. "He did not need Uncle Peach, so far as he was aware, for anything—not him nor the likes of him. So far as he was aware, nobody did." But during the buggy ride from the train station to Uncle Peach's place, he realizes otherwise:

> It was a long six miles. Uncle Peach's stomach objected as strenuously to the motion of the buggy as it had to that of the train. He had long ago emptied himself, but the spasms came anyhow, prolonged clenches that left him fighting for balance and breath. And each time, Wheeler had to stop the mare and hold Uncle Peach to keep him falling out of the buggy.
>
> Finally, after this had happened perhaps half a dozen times, Wheeler, who had remained angry, said, "I hope you puke your damned guts out."
>
> And Uncle Peach, who lay, quaking and white, against the seatback, said "Oh Lord, honey, you can't mean that."
>
> As if his anger had finally stripped all else away, suddenly Wheeler saw Uncle Peach as perhaps Dorie had always seen him—a poor, hurt, weak mortal, twice hurt because he *knew* himself to be hurt and weak and mortal. And then Wheeler knew what he needed from Uncle Peach. He did need to be comforted. That was all. He put his arm around Uncle Peach, then, and patted him as if he were a child. "No," he said. "I don't mean it."

In "It Wasn't Me," the local farmer Old Jack Beechum has died, and his daughter Clara, who is now living in Louisville, comes to claim her inheritance. Wheeler, who was privy to Old Jack's final but unwritten wish—to let his tenants, Elton and Mary Penn, purchase the farm for two hundred dollars an acre—"assume[s]s that Clara ... [will] be bound by it as a matter of course." But Wheeler proves to be mistaken; the world, he is reminded, is *not* "ruled by instinctive decency." Clara, no longer part of the delicate, intricate web of obligations that is Port William, and no longer able to recognize, as her father could, "the irreconcilable division ... between the things of this world and their value in money," determines to put the farm up at auction. Wheeler does all he can to secure the farm for the Penns, whatever the expense.

"The place," he says to Elton, "is not its price. Its price stands for it for just a minute or two while it's bought and sold, and may hang over it a while after that and have an influence on it, but the place has been here since the evening and the morning were the third day. The figures are like us—here and gone."

So important is the land to Berry that at times it seems to surpass people on his list of concerns. People, after all, grow old quickly (Wheeler changes in the blink of an eye, in this slim book, from a young man into an old one) while the land remains. In "The Wild Birds," wherein Wheeler (now in his sixties) is apprised of Burley Coulter's wish to pass his farm on to his needy, illegitimate, and theretofore unacknowledged son, Danny Branch, Wheeler's first instinct is to think of the good of the farm rather than the good of Danny. Wheeler would prefer that the farm go to Burley's nephew Nathan, who doesn't want or need it. "It has been a comfort to Wheeler to think that the Coulter place, past Burley's death, would live on under that name. . . . That is what he longs for, the passing on of the land, in the clear, from love to love, and it is in grief for that loss that he is opposing Burley."

If there is a failing in these stories it is that on occasion they threaten to degenerate into tracts on farm policy. Both "Thicker than Liquor" and "The Wild Birds" were previously published in *Mother Jones,* of all places, and not until the fourth page of "The Wild Birds" can one understand what the editors of that magazine could possibly have seen in these gentle stories about rural life. On that page we find Wheeler writing a speech—for no apparent reason or occasion—in which he wants to clarify "the process by which unbridled economic forces draw life, wealth, and intelligence off the farms and out of the country towns and set them into conflict with their sources. Farm produce leaves the farm to nourish an economy that has thrived by the ruin of land. In this way . . . *price* wars against *value.*" This brief detour is one of the weakest parts of the book.

But *The Wild Birds* is far more memorable for its strong than its weak moments. Among these strong moments are the evocation of old Mat Feltner's last walk through the woods in "The Boundary"; Wheeler's reflections, at the beginning of "The Wild Birds," about the changes that time has wrought in Hargrave; and Andy Catlett's description, in "That Distant Land," of Elton and Nathan and Danny's tobacco cutting: "They drove into the work, maintaining the same pressing rhythm from one end of the row to the other, and yet they worked well, as smoothly and precisely as dancers. To see them moving side by side against the standing crop, leaving it fallen, the field changed, behind them, was maybe like watching Homeric soldiers going into battle. It was momentous and beautiful, and touchingly, touchingly mortal. They were spending themselves as they worked, giving up their time; they would not return by the way they went." *The Wild Birds* makes one feel good about the fate of fiction. It is a lovely book.

All in the Family

NOVEMBER 1986

A decade or so ago it would have been all but inconceivable for a young American writer to make his name with a collection of short stories. Yet when David Leavitt published *Family Dancing* two years ago, shortly after his graduation from Yale, the book's success was phenomenal: it received enthusiastic reviews, it sold briskly for several months at all the best bookstores, it was nominated for both the National Book Critics Circle Award and the PEN/Faulkner Award. Leavitt, who had previously published two stories in the *New Yorker,* one in *Harper's,* and one in *Prism,* was suddenly—to judge by the way everybody was talking about him—a Major American Literary Figure.

Yet the stories themselves were, by and large, exasperatingly commonplace. Throughout most of them Leavitt (who had written his first serious fiction scarcely three or four years earlier, as a member of Knopf editor Gordon Lish's workshop at Yale) adhered religiously to the rules of current literary fashion: the characters were flat, the prose dry and passionless, the plots jejune; the stories were preoccupied with surfaces, crowded with banal domestic details. What made this familiarity more disturbing than usual, however, was that Leavitt—as he demonstrated in his best stories, "Dedicated" and "Territory"—was capable of finer things. Above all, these two fresh and poignant stories revealed a remarkable sensitivity toward his characters that one wanted to see more of. Oddly, it was in these same two stories that Leavitt dealt most overtly with the theme of homosexuality (which hovered in the background of the other stories); it was as if this subject, and none other, inspired Leavitt to write with feeling and originality.

Like most of the stories in *Family Dancing,* Leavitt's first novel, *The Lost Language of Cranes,* is out to remind us how rare and difficult it is for people, whether friends or lovers or even members of the same family, to know and understand each other, and how wonderful it is when, if only for a brief moment, they make meaningful contact. The novel, like the stories, is about an educated upper-middle-class family under stress, its members out of touch with each other; as in "Territory," the stress is caused primarily by the intrusion of homosexuality into the family circle. Like *Family Dancing,* then, the novel brings together two seemingly incompatible milieus—the family and the homosexual sub-culture—presenting us thereby with a world in which the paramount human ritual is not a young person's marriage but his "coming out" to his family, a world in which two very different kinds of love are continually striving for peaceful coexistence.

The book, alas, is founded upon a gimmick that might be more appropriate to a soap opera than to a serious novel. The gimmick is this: unbeknownst to one another, both Owen Benjamin, the mild-mannered, middle-aged admissions director and English teacher at an exclusive Manhattan boys' school, and his bright, sensitive, twenty-five-year-old son Philip, an editor of romance novels, are homosexual. The son, who lives on the Upper West Side, is "out" to his friends and, after years of lonely awkwardness, has finally (he thinks) found true love with a wealthy young freelance copywriter named Eliot Abrams, and is ready to come out to his folks; the father—who, with his anomic wife, Rose, a copy editor for a small publishing house, is under the threat of losing his rent-stabilized East Side apartment in the co-op boom—has spent the last couple of decades secretly haunting homosexual porno theaters on Sunday afternoons. Though all three Benjamins (as well as many of the supporting characters) are professional communicators, all of them are to some degree alone, isolated, spiritually incommunicado. The novel, which follows this unusual family through a single winter, bids us wonder: What will happen when Philip comes out to his folks? Will Owen come out too? And *then* what? How will Rose (the sole heterosexual member of the clan) handle all this? Will the family grow closer or shatter completely?

Given this contrived premise, it is surprising how effective parts of the novel are. Leavitt is particularly good at evoking the desperation of loneliness, the joy of achieving a human connection, the small private agony of failing to. Certain episodes along these lines—for instance,

Philip's two nocturnal visits with a friend from college and Owen's pathetic phone call to a stranger—are unusually affecting. (The latter episode causes one to feel genuine sorrow, pity, and embarrassment—emotions in which, along with fear and panic, Leavitt seems at times to specialize.) The pictures of Manhattan life are realistic, what with the constant talk of rents and sublets and apartment availability; and the title—whose meaning is explained in a brief chapter near the middle of the book—proves to be nicely allusive. As for Leavitt's prose, it is lucid, graceful, and free of affectation; though sometimes he appears to be on the verge of descending into the detail-heavy insipidness of *Family Dancing,* he rarely in fact does so.

Philip, the book's central figure, is Leavitt's most convincing creation by far. Like the protagonists of "Territory" and "Dedicated," he is a likable and touching figure, openly romantic, even childlike, in his affections; he is also (like one or two earlier Leavitt characters) outrageously insecure and self-analytical, inclined to speechify about how he feels, to ask his friends and parents how they feel about how he feels, and to explain thereupon how he feels about how they feel about how he feels. (Leavitt, fortunately, does not fail to see the humor in this.) In particular, he is burdened by an overwhelming compulsion to broadcast his sexual orientation to the world and longs for the world to smile upon his acceptance of it. He is also nostalgic, and some of his memories of childhood (as well as his musings about them) feel so real that one cannot believe them to be otherwise; the delicate and honest perceptiveness of these passages is very special. That it is impossible not to identify Philip with his creator does not mitigate the skill with which Leavitt brings him to life.

This is, then, a novel of considerable virtues. Despite them, however, it has significant—and, alas, all but crippling—weaknesses. Its presiding consciousness, for instance, is characterized by a callowness which—though rather appealing when viewed in the light of the jaded grubbiness of many a gay novel—cannot but be viewed as a substantial failing. There are numerous structural problems as well. Leavitt includes no fewer than four full-dress coming-out episodes (plus several other episodes in which characters simply talk about how they came out). He devotes a good deal of attention to the development of a subplot involving Eliot's adoptive father—a children's writer whose gentle fantasy stories Philip adored in his childhood—and then drops it without warning; he does the same with the Benjamins' apartment crisis.

Nor does he find much for Rose to do besides roam the streets of Manhattan and the rooms of her apartment thinking dark thoughts. Indeed, both Rose and Owen are less convincing than Philip, and their relationships with each other and with their son feel synthetic.

But the book's most significant failing is that the gimmick at its center never stops feeling like a gimmick. The fact that these two homosexuals are father and son doesn't help us to understand either of them better, and doesn't serve to tie their stories together in any significant way. (Nor does it pay off in an explosive reversal or an illuminating climax.) For the most part, Philip and Owen might as well be total strangers inhabiting different novels. Of course, this is Leavitt's whole point — Philip and Owen *are* worlds apart, and he wants us to recognize how tragic (but true to life) it is that a father and son can go a quarter of a century without seeing an essential part of each other, without recognizing a common bond. Yet the novel doesn't dramatize this tragedy effectively: aside from the fact that Leavitt fails to draw a clear picture of Philip and Owen's relationship, one is simply too aware of the gimmick *qua* gimmick to be moved by it. (And one is uncomfortably aware, as well, that the whole thing reads like a homosexual wish-fulfillment fantasy — for what could make a homosexual young man, eager for unreserved parental acceptance and approval, happier than the notion that his father too is a homosexual, and an even more mixed-up one than himself?)

What *Family Dancing* suggested, and what *The Lost Language of Cranes* unfortunately affirms, is that David Leavitt is a fine young writer who labors under a severe and singular set of limitations. He is at his best when writing about homosexuals (especially young ones), at his worst when trying to create convincing heterosexuals; but he's not willing to be just a writer of "gay lit," a supplier of fiction to the homosexual community. He wants to show homosexuals and heterosexuals in contact, wants in fact, it sometimes seems, to justify the ways of one to the other; Leavitt leaves the impression that some part of him truly believes that if homosexual children can persuade their parents to accept them without reservation then somehow the natural drawbacks and frustrations of homosexual life — and perhaps even the essential isolation of human existence itself — can be vanquished. One hopes that such matters will eventually cease to weigh so heavily upon his mind, and that he will in time prove capable of broader interests and sympathies.

Louise Erdrich too is a choreographer of family life, acutely aware of the impediments to mutual understanding and acceptance that families face. Erdrich, a half-German-American, half-Chippewa writer whose first novel, *Love Medicine,* won the 1985 National Book Critics Circle Award for fiction, has now written a second novel, *The Beet Queen,* which resembles its predecessor not only in its preoccupation with family but also in a number of other ways. Like *Love Medicine, The Beet Queen* consists of a series of alternating first- and third-person chapters; it has several protagonists of equal prominence, all of them friends, neighbors, or relatives of one another, most of them bearing exotic names like Sita Kozka and Wallace Pfef; and it is steeped in the grotesqueries of rural Roman Catholicism and twentieth-century Chippewa mysticism, and, above all, in the stark atmosphere of the North Dakota prairie (an atmosphere reminiscent, in some ways, of *Winesburg, Ohio*). Some of the characters in *The Beet Queen* even appeared previously in *Love Medicine.* But there are some welcome differences between the two books. In *Love Medicine,* the chapters jumped around chronologically, from 1981 to 1934 to 1948, and so forth, and never seemed to find a center. The characters, furthermore, were dull and unvaried, their voices indistinguishable from one another, their outrageous antics ultimately monotonous and predictable. In *The Beet Queen* these flaws have been remedied to some extent: aside from the welcome fact that its chapters are in chronological order, the book has focus, it has warmth, its characters are engaging and distinctive; although it is in its own way as outrageous as *Love Medicine,* the outrageousness seems to be brought into play with greater discrimination.

The story begins in 1932. Abandoned by their widowed mother, Mary and Karl Adare, aged eleven and fourteen respectively, journey by boxcar from Minneapolis to their aunt's hometown of Argus, North Dakota. Upon their arrival in Argus, a dog chases them, and the children run in different directions—Mary heading toward her aunt's house, and Karl hopping back on the moving freight train. As a result of this chance canine encounter, Mary and Karl do not see each other again for twenty years. They spend most of their lives apart—she growing up in Argus, a sexless homebody, and he becoming a promiscuous, rootless traveling salesman. Yet their seemingly antithetical lives are alike in their emptiness and loneliness; profoundly wounded by their mother's abandonment, both Mary and Karl find it impossible to trust, to love. They are not, to be sure, the only abandoned or solitary souls in *The*

Beet Queen. Mary's vain, pretentious cousin Sita Kozka, her good-hearted bachelor neighbor Wallace Pfef, and her friend Celestine James —all of whose lives are as central to this novel as Karl's and Mary's—are likewise, in their different ways, the victims of rejection or isolation or unrequited love, and, as their lives proceed, the abandonments and frustrations multiply apace.

Erdrich brings these individuals to life with extraordinary facility. Yet the book's structure, though more effective than that of *Love Medicine,* is troublesome. Erdrich thinks less like a novelist, in terms of gradual character development over a relatively long period of time, than like a short-story writer. *The Beet Queen,* accordingly, consists mostly of self-contained, tightly organized chapters—each focused upon a single character, each charting a single course of action, and each building to its own climax. (Indeed, many of them have been published as short stories in periodicals, including *Ms., The American Voice, Formations, The Atlantic Monthly,* and the *Kenyon, New England, Georgia,* and *Paris* reviews.) Most of them center upon epiphanies in the lives of their principal characters; the recognitions and reversals follow one another at a breathtaking clip, with the ten or twenty years between each character's successive appearances omitted as mere chaff. Erdrich patently operates upon the assumption that people do not change gradually but abruptly, and that every human life can thus be handily summarized in four or five intensely dramatic key episodes.

In accordance with this vision of the human condition, Erdrich's characters are the sort who make sudden resolutions following traumatic incidents and stick to them forever. After climbing back into that boxcar in Argus, for instance, Karl (in one of the book's most moving episodes) seeks affection and comfort in the arms of a young vagrant, only to be rejected, and silently vows "not to cry on the lap of anyone again"; a few years later, Mary, having been similarly spurned by one Russell Kashpaw, makes a fateful vow of her own: "I would never go out of my way for romance again. Romance would have to go out of its way for me." They are, moreover, the sort of characters who know with absolute certainty things that in real life no one could possibly know for certain. For instance, after an intimate liaison with Wallace Pfef at a Minneapolis farm-equipment convention, thirty-four-year-old Karl knows from Pfef's "stricken" stare that "if I wanted I could have him for life." The world according to Louise Erdrich is, in short, a decidedly melodramatic one; Mary and Karl's mother does not just run off—she flies away at a Minneapolis carnival with a barnstorming pilot she has never met before.

The positive side of this approach to the novel is that it produces a crisp and lively book, a book as dense with plot twists as *Raiders of the Lost Ark;* the negative side is that we end up feeling that we don't know the characters nearly as well as we'd like to. The chapters concerning Karl, for instance, present us in turn with several different incarnations—a shy and sweet adolescent, a slick and cynical thirty-year-old salesman, and so forth—without showing him developing from one stage to the next. Clearly we are meant to understand that it is his mother's abandonment of him that makes him cynical; but not to *show* this sweet boy losing his sweetness, month by month and year by year, is to refuse to use the form of the novel to its best advantage. It is, indeed, to refuse to write a novel, per se.

Yet there is a unifying idea here. Much as Leavitt keeps us wondering whether the barriers will come down between the embattled Benjamins, so Erdrich teases us with the question of whether any members of the Adare family will ever be permanently reunited, whether in fact any of the novel's principals will leave behind the sad and traumatic past, put an end to the relentless cycle of abandonment, and take up the burden of loving and being loved. Over the years, one opportunity after another for reunion presents itself. But it is not until the closing chapters of the book, set in 1972, that the suspense is relieved. Erdrich's deft weaving together of the novel's plot strands in these brief closing chapters proves to be audacious, coincidence-heavy, and ultimately quite affecting—a *sui generis* mixture of the tender and the absurd, the realistic and the magical.

For magic is the major theme in *The Beet Queen.* In her first novel, Erdrich's characters, unable to "get love right," sought to secure it by means of an Indian potion, a "love medicine." In *The Beet Queen,* Mary—a devotee of fortune tellers, palm readers, psychics, yarrow sticks, Tarot cards, and Ouija boards—is touched by magic. On a memorable night in her early twenties, she awakens to find her hands glowing; on a winter day in her childhood, when she smashes face first into the ice on the Argus school grounds, the nuns see the resulting pattern on the ice as the face of Jesus and announce a "miracle"; Mary, for her part, sees it as the face of Karl, whom she loves and misses. Later in the novel Wallace identifies Karl (who has abandoned him as well as Mary) not with Jesus but with Satan. Meaning what? Perhaps, simply enough, that we are all part Jesus and part Satan, able to embrace or spurn our fellow man, and that our challenge in life is to act in accordance with the best that is in us. Certainly a reverence for the everlasting possibility of redemption, of human communion, is at the heart of Erdrich's novel. Like David Leavitt, she places great value upon both romantic and familial bonds, recognizes how delicate they are and how easily damaged, and celebrates the enduring love and the qualities of character that make their renewal possible.

*E*nchantment, a first outing by Daphne Merkin, is not a novel so much as it is—in the diplomatic words of Walker Percy's jacket blurb —a "remarkable memoir, fictional or not." And actually it's not even a memoir so much as it is 288 pages of whining about what torture it is to be a spoiled rich brat who grew up in a huge, well-appointed Manhattan apartment and a Long Island summer house (complete with swimming pool), with a laundress, a cook, a nurse, and a chauffeur at her beck and call, and a charge account at Bloomingdale's from the age of fifteen. There's no story here, just a jumbled collection of memories that reads like a transcript of several marathon sessions on the psychiatrist's couch; and there aren't any real characters, either, for our narrator's parents, siblings, servants, and classmates—not to mention the clerks who wait on her in Bloomingdale's and the women she chats with at fund-raising dinners at the Waldorf—exist in this book only insofar as their lives touch upon hers. Hannah Lehmann—for such is the name that Merkin gives her heroine—has no interest in other people as separate individuals, with lives and thoughts and feelings unrelated to her own, and neither apparently does Merkin.

About Hannah: she's twenty-six years old, one of the six children of two German Orthodox Jews; her father, Walter, is a kind, indulgent, rather distant Wall Street stockbroker and her mother, Margot, is (Hannah keeps telling us) cruel and neglectful. Indeed, Margot's purported cruelty and neglect—and Hannah's inability, at the same time, to stop loving her, to break free from her—are the principal themes of *Enchantment:* "The enchantment I am under is stifling, a witch's cloak. My mother is the Wicked Witch, but she is also the object of desire. She is the first I have known of love—of the deception of love. I don't believe the world is any different away from her." The evidence of Margot's witchery is formidable: when Hannah was a little girl Margot made her skate at the Wollman Rink in Central Park (with all the Puerto Ricans!) rather than at Rockefeller Center. And then (shades of Kuznetsov's *Babi Yar*) there was the time that Margot took Hannah to Lord & Taylor and bought her a plain gray wool coat that made her look like a doorman. No wonder that, "[a]fter I learned about the Nazis in detail . . . I decided that my mother had been Ilse Koch, chief female S.S. officer at Auschwitz, before she married my father."

In reality, Hannah's mother appears to be a more or less typical mother of the German-Jewish variety—possessive but emotionally undemonstrative, generous but given to occasional (and extremely mild) acts of thrift. She loves and cares about Hannah but has five other children and other things in her life—and it is for this that Hannah is unable to forgive her. Hannah wants a perfect love—which, to this spoiled rich girl, means complete, undivided attention; she wants a mother, in other words, who is a mother and nothing else. In her psychiatrist's office she imagines *his* mother, "sweet but negligible, standing over a hot stove and stirring soup—the mother I always wanted. With a mother like that, who couldn't take on the future?" Later she tells Margot: "Maybe you're not simple enough to be a good mother." Hannah likes putting Margot down like that.

"The world doesn't revolve around you," Margot tells Hannah at one point. But this whole novel testifies to Hannah's inability to accept this proposition. Nothing interests her—not geography, not books, not the people she passes on the street—unless she can relate it, in some way, to herself, to her own feelings. Merkin, to be sure, is aware that her heroine's view of things is less than perfectly objective. She knows Hannah has a problem; Hannah knows Hannah has a problem. (Why else has she been going to a psychiatrist since the age of eleven?) And yes, there *is* some intentional irony here and there in this good-sized book. But there's not anywhere near as much of it as there should be. Merkin seems really to believe that Hannah is suffering—indeed, that she has experienced a variety of pain that those of us who *aren't* rich Jewish girls will never know. As she puts it, "To people without money, all other griefs run a distant second, and even craziness can seem a luxury." In other words, only rich people really know what it feels like to *feel*. And Merkin means it! Oh, those lucky poor people—since her teens, Hannah has been consumed by envy (a patronizing envy, to be sure) for them:

> If I were poor, my mother would stand on the fire escape in summer, and everyone for miles around would see what she was doing to me, that she had absorbed me like a sponge, made it so there was no "away" away

from her. But my mother never wore rollers in her hair or walked around in bedroom slippers outside as though the world were her home. No pock-faced, leather-jacketed boy ever lounged against the neighborhood stoop and said, "Your old lady's crazy, isn't she?" Outside her own home you couldn't tell much about her.

And again:

Money, I felt, even before I knew it, wasn't the issue [in the Lehmann home], the way it was in *Little Women* or *Five Little Peppers*. What was missing was less clear-cut but no less impoverishing: some allowance for the spill of our personalities, the clamor of distinctive selves—a turf for each of us to stake out, mess up, tack drawings to the wall of, declare *Mine*. When I saw the rooms of friends, I became conscious of a difference, the voice they had been given in the choice of a ruffled bedspread, a white and gold desk. But it is not until I am grown up, when I will have friends with children of their own, that I am struck by the thought that what was absent from the rooms my siblings and I slept in was, simply, us.

Hannah envies not only poor urbanites but middle-American *shiksas*, though she takes it for granted that their lives are dull and mindless: "The opposite of terror [i.e., Hannah's life] is blandness—a snub-nosed girl from Dayton, Ohio, who regards her family with the same lack of guile with which she regards the sky when it is blue." The models whose photographs she examines while getting her hair done on Madison Avenue are "women with names like Kelly and Dawn, who come from tiny towns in Texas and Washington, who are tall and thin, and who don't appear to be burdened by any pasts to speak of." Sure, nobody has a past except Hannah; no one *feels* except her; everybody's a stereotype. What's ironic is that she herself, though her author doesn't seem to realize it for a minute, is the stereotype to end all stereotypes. For what Merkin has written here is one long Jewish-princess joke:

Bloomingdale's always makes me lonely: all the choices, so many possible ways to look, everything requiring an output of energy, a core of solid conviction—*This gray sweatshirt is me*. Nothing I buy can't be bought or worn by thousands of other people....

It is almost embarrassing to have arrived in my mid-twenties from a background of no visible hardship and not to have seen Italy. "Italy!"

people say: "How can you skip Italy? How is it possible *you* haven't been to Italy?"

Enchantment is, of course, like *The Lost Language of Cranes* and *The Beet Queen,* concerned above all else with families, with the things that drive them apart and the things that, after all is said and done, bring them back together again. "Families are all there is," Hannah overhears one woman say to another on the Central Park West bus. "Families are monstrous," she muses while crossing Central Park in a taxi, "but without them there is no one to tell you not to go into Central Park at night." Like Leavitt and Erdrich, Merkin is preoccupied with the theme of alienation—"Why is it that we get our first taste of isolation within families?"—and with the realization that "families are a secret." Yet *Enchantment,* unlike Leavitt's and Erdrich's novels, is not only informed by personal experience; it seems to consist of nothing *but* personal experience. One keeps waiting for a sign that Merkin is aware of the impression she's making, for a switch, perhaps, to another narrator (Margot or Walter or even one of the other children), for some escape from the claustrophobic solipsism of Hannah Lehmann. But there is no escape. Certainly no "novel" has ever appeared to be more blatantly confessional. Yet one hesitates to commit oneself to the statement that *Enchantment* is an autobiography in disguise, for the simple reason that it seems incredible that anyone could really write and publish so shamelessly narcissistic a document; surely, one thinks, this book must be a pure piece of invention, an ingenious attempt on Daphne Merkin's part to capture the workings of a self-obsessed Jewish princess's mind. But to what conceivable purpose?

And yet, for all this, *Enchantment* is far from unreadable. For one thing, even in the present era of "happy-talk" news programs, tell-all movie-star autobiographies, and late-night talk shows, you don't get to see such pure, unabashed egocentrism very often; in this regard, Merkin's book is gruesomely fascinating—a tour de force of a decidedly unliterary sort. For one thing, the book is so sumptuously written that, ridiculous as it is, many a reader is likely to stick with it to the end simply to enjoy the music of Merkin's prose. It is dismaying to see such promising gifts squandered on what may well be the most inane book of the year.

Peter Taylor was writing about families long before Merkin and her contemporaries were gleams in their fathers' eyes. Indeed, though many a celebrated writer of his generation (he was born in 1917) has tended to take the family for granted and to confront flashier subjects, Taylor's wonderful short stories—many of which were collected in *The Old Forest and Other Stories,* last year's PEN/Faulkner Award winner—have consistently demonstrated a preoccupation with the relations of parents and children, and have examined those relations with insight and sympathy. Taylor has, moreover, provided in his prose a model of tautness, purity, and elegance; so restrained and rigorous, as a matter of fact, is his writing that a reader unfamiliar with his work—especially one who has recently been exposed, say, to the free-wheeling confessional manner of a Daphne Merkin or to David Leavitt's grab bag of subplots and minor characters—may well feel constricted, suffocated. This is, as it happens, an utterly appropriate response to Taylor's fiction, for the fine, well-to-do Southern families of his stories are often confining families, subtle dictatorships whose younger members, though they may travel far from home to make their lives, can never completely break the bonds of enchantment. Quite frequently, then, in the world of Peter Taylor, you can't help but go home again—and again, and again—in one sense or another.

Yet Taylor's perspective upon this state of affairs is as different as it could be from Daphne Merkin's. He is a supremely objective writer, whose stories, though they are doubtless grounded in profoundly felt and comprehended personal experience, are at the same time exquisitely shaped aesthetic objects—pure fictions; even when he writes in the first person, there is little temptation to identify him with his narrator. This is the case with his first novel in thirty-six years, *A Summons to Memphis,* which tells the story of a middle-aged Manhattan editor named Phillip Carver, whose two sisters call him back home to Tennessee to help thwart their widowed father's plans to remarry. After informing the reader of the summons, Phillip attempts to fill in the background on his "old-fashioned family," with an eye to explaining how they managed to stay so old-fashioned, why he and his sisters are all unmarried, why his sisters are so eager to destroy the old man's chance at happiness. It all goes back, Phillip explains, to the single event, way back in his early teens, which changed not only his life but the lives of all the Carvers: the betrayal—and, almost, the financial ruin—of his father, a prominent Nashville attorney, by his father's best friend and principal client, a Mr. Lewis Shackleford.

Betrayal, it should be noted, is a favorite theme of Taylor's. In his story "First Heat," a naïve young politician suffers his "baptism of betrayal," and learns how to forsake his own principles; in "Miss Leonora When Last Seen," a retired spinster schoolteacher is betrayed by her former students, now members of the town school board, who sue to condemn her house and build a new school on her property. If the theme of betrayal is often present in Taylor's work, it is indubitably because betrayal represents, to him, a forsaking of "old-fashioned" virtues—honor, loyalty, moral rectitude—for the modern values of expediency, self-interest, "progress" at any price; to him, betrayal manifestly symbolizes the moral price that twentieth-century humanity pays for its life of convenience and comfort.

Mr. Carver being a man of old-fashioned virtue, his reaction to Lewis Shackleford's betrayal was dignified and decisive: he quietly removed his entire family from Nashville to Memphis, breaking off all relations with Shackleford and all connections with his Nashville career. Though his career recovered splendidly, his family, alas, did not; on the contrary, the move had a devastating lifelong effect upon all the Carvers. The reason for this, according to Phillip, resides in the differences between the two cities. Nashville, he explains, is a more genteel city than Memphis; its "best" families participate in horse shows, fox hunting, serious literary evenings, and formal dinner parties, whereas Memphis is a place of golf games, card parties, and "hotel society." Memphians are offended by "Nashville pretension"; Nashvilleans look down upon Memphians' lack of ambition. (For example, the typical Memphis parents of Alex Mercer, Phillip's friend since childhood, "were convinced that any deviation from what they considered the Memphis norm, any eccentricity or any excellence of any kind amounted only to exhibitionism.") In short, "Memphis was today. Nashville was yesterday. Mother was willing to forget Nashville. Father wished to live Nashville in Memphis." What had once been a cohesive family, then, and an integral part of Nashville society, became in Memphis a house that was both divided against itself and set apart from the city around it. Phillip's mother, for instance, having gained "a kind of personal liberation for which she was not prepared and of which she did not know how to make an advantage," was no longer able to play "her role in the family unit":

[F]rom the day we arrived in Memphis it seemed she never under any circumstances had any sense of what was fitting or any feeling of responsibility with regard to the role of a mother in an old-fashioned family like ours. She continued to be affectionate with each of us individually but any idea of the family or of herself as mother seemed as meaningless to her as all the silly debutantism that her daughters had to go through and the life in the business world that Father was caught up in.

Soon after the move to Memphis, indeed, Phillip's mother stopped wearing her daytime clothing and became a virtual hermit. Similarly, Phillip's sisters, Josephine and Betsy, were frozen by the move "in the roles of eternal young ladies." As for Phillip himself, who as a boy wanted to be a poet, the move meant a death of the soul.

This is, at least, the way Phillip sees things—or claims to. Yet there are significant, and disquieting, inconsistencies in his testimony. On page five he says that his family is not "a genuine Memphis family," having lived there (as of his mother's death two years before) "only thirty years." Rather, they are a "Nashville family." But he later mentions (on page 176, to be exact) that the Carvers had in reality resided in Nashville for only six years, having moved there from the small (and fictitious) Tennessee town of Thornton. Even the statement that they'd lived in Memphis for thirty years is contradicted on page seventeen, where Phillip states that the family moved to Memphis "[m]ore than forty years ago." (It should be added that Phillip dates the move in 1931—which leaves some question as to when the "present" of this novel is supposed to be.) Phillip's liberal use throughout the novel of the words "of course"—sometimes four or five times per page—becomes an irritating tic, but it seems to be, on Taylor's part, an intentional one, designed to point up the fact that we cannot take anything that Phillip tells us for granted. He is self-deceptive and therefore unreliable; behind his seemingly clear-eyed view of things lies a more comprehensive truth of which we can get only occasional glimpses. But some facts do become plain. We come to realize, most importantly, that the sad fates of Phillip, his mother, and his sisters have less to do with the move to Memphis, per se, than with the fact that Lewis Shackleford's betrayal turned Phillip's father into a heartless tyrant whose family was incapable of challenging his power in any constructive way. Over the course of the novel Phillip comes to accept some—if not all—of these truths.

Like Ford Madox Ford's *The Good Soldier,* then, *A Summons to Memphis* is a domestic tale of jealousy and betrayal, a tale many of whose most important details the book's seemingly sensible and civilized narrator manages to ignore or to misconstrue, and whose ultimate lessons he largely fails to perceive. But the book is more reminiscent of Taylor's own work than it is of any other writer's. For instance, the story "Dean of Men," which is told in the first person, concerns a middle-aged academic (who has much in common with Phillip Carver's English-professor friend Alex Mercer) whose well-born, prosperous, and highly principled father (a businessman) and grandfather (a politician active in Tennessee state government) were both betrayed by friends and consequently became embittered tyrants. A passage in which the father's disloyal crony fails three times in succession to come to town by train to explain his shady dealings reappears, in essentially the same form, in *A Summons to Memphis*. In the novel, as in the story, the narrator compromises with his ambitions but not with his principles, and the father and his treacherous friend are reconciled in their very old age—the point being that, though people are indeed capable of corruption, "[a] man must go on living among men."

Likewise, earlier versions of Alex Mercer and Phillip Carver may be found in the story "Daphne's Lover"; Phillip's trip home—and his father's cruel domination—are foreshadowed in "At the Drugstore"; and the novel's use of Memphis and Nashville as the backdrop for a quarrel between two public men is prefigured in "The Captain's Son." *A Summons to Memphis* echoes a host of Taylor's best stories, furthermore, in its depiction of life as a patchwork of unexamined memories, unarticulated feelings, and repressed desires, of moral compromises that people are incapable of acknowledging even to themselves, and of thoughts and statements and actions that are emotionally authentic if logically inexplicable. The novel suggests, as do many of Taylor's stories, that to live in a family is to be forever a child, to some extent, tortured repeatedly by a child's conflicts and guilts, regrets and resentments, and that maturity means being willing to let go, as fully as possible, of these preoccupations, and to attempt to live with one's family as amicably as one is capable of doing. And finally, *A Summons to Memphis* is consistent with Taylor's earlier work in its quiet but forceful affirmation that, in a world obsessed with fashion, with newness, with revolution for its own sake, there are certain timeless values that are worth preserving—indeed, that without a sincere and fervent faith in the vital importance of those values, there can be no such thing as a civilized life. To Peter Taylor, in other words, the writing of fiction is a moral act—and he brings to it a reverence for language, for the art of narrative, and for the human spirit that many of his younger colleagues would do very well to emulate.

The Literary Brat Pack

Spring 1987

Meg Wolitzer. David Leavitt. Peter Cameron. Susan Minot. Elizabeth Tallent.

In the past couple of years these names, and one or two others, have become extremely familiar to readers of book sections, high-toned magazines, and articles about The Future Of American Literature. These are the writers, we are told time and again, who are revolutionizing American fiction, who have initiated a short-story renaissance. They publish their stories primarily in *The New Yorker,* are invited to participate in symposia with their distinguished literary elders, and are reviewed prominently and respectfully; despite their youth—most of them are in their twenties and early thirties—universities clamor to have their services as teachers of creative writing. Honors abound. It was Leavitt, for instance, whose first book, the 1984 short story collection *Family Dancing,* was nominated for the National Book Critics Circle Award in fiction; it was Leavitt, again, who was asked by the editors of *Esquire* to follow in the footsteps of F. Scott Fitzgerald and William Styron by writing, for the magazine's May 1985 issue, the decennial essay on his generation of Americans. It was Susan Minot whose first book, *Monkeys* (1986), was the subject of one of the most unequivocally positive reviews to appear on the front page of the *New York Times Book Review* in recent memory.

And yet, when one turns from the breathless critical encomia to the works of these young writers, they strike one—to be kind about it—as decidedly modest accomplishments. So great, in fact, is the disparity between the public image and the performance that one is tempted to refer to this overly hyped circle of writers as the Literary Brat Pack. Like the Hollywood Brat Pack, they have an excessive sense of their own importance in the scheme of things, and—by means of the enthusiastic blurbs and reviews that many of them have given to each other—have helped to distract the attention of their audience from many of their more deserving contemporaries. Like the Hollywood Brat Pack, finally, the members of the Literary Brat Pack have one outstanding skill: they promote themselves extremely well.

Where, one might ask, did all these young writers come from? Many are graduates of that most peculiar of contemporary American cultural institutions, the university writing workshop—a place where literary trends are assiduously followed and where the history of American short fiction tends to be thought of as extending back no further than 1961 or so (the year J. D. Salinger published *Franny and Zooey*). David Leavitt, for instance, wrote his first serious fiction for a Yale writing workshop taught by Gordon Lish.

Lish—who is a senior editor at Alfred A. Knopf, Inc., the publishing house which issued Leavitt's *Family Dancing* —figures in the histories of many of the Brat Packers. Amy Hempel studied under Lish in the Columbia University writing program and dedicated her first book, the Knopf short story collection *Reasons to Live* (1985), to him: "For the teacher, Gordon Lish." Other Brat Packers' connections to Lish go back even further. Meg Wolitzer, whose book *Sleepwalking* (1982) was also published by Knopf, is the daughter of novelist Hilma Wolitzer, who used to write for Lish when he was an editor at *Esquire* and whose 1977 book *In the Flesh* carried the dedication: "Special thanks to Gordon Lish."

In a recent profile for *Spy* magazine, Mimi Kramer referred to Lish as "the Joseph Papp of American fiction." He's an editor who "claims not to believe there's any such thing as genius or talent," a teacher who tells his students that any of them can become the writer of their time. For "greatness," to Lish—and to the countless students who have made his sensibility their own—is less a matter of literary excellence than it is of cheap Hollywood-like celebrity. Lish tells his students that "he wants . . . to be the teacher who produces the greatest number of important writers." And, since Knopf is (as Kramer notes) "the most prestigious publisher of new American fiction," Lish is in a splendid position to create "important writers"—that is, writers who will be reviewed widely and discussed seriously by literary critics.

And make no mistake, Lish is far from shy about publishing the work of his own students and protégés; in fact, perhaps the majority of the modish young fiction writers of our day—many of them ex-students of Lish—had their first books published by Knopf. It is fair to say, then, that the Literary Brat Pack is in large part the product of the Gordon Lish fiction factory, and consequently of the Gordon Lish sensibility—a sensibility that equates greatness with notoriety, that seems to consider talent somewhat less important than P.R.

Speaking of P.R., the principal document in the study of the Literary Brat Pack is an article—"New Voices and Old Values"—which is one of the neatest pieces of literary public relations that I've ever seen. The article appeared on the first page of the May 12, 1985, issue of the *New York Times Book Review,* and its author was David Leavitt, who is presently the most celebrated—and, it must be said, is probably the most talented—of the Brat Pack writers. Leavitt's article trumpeted the arrival on the literary scene of "a new generation of writers who are re-cording through their fiction the changes in the way young people think about family, marriage, love and loyalty." Leavitt listed the names of these writers, modestly omitting himself from the lineup: Marian Thurm, Elizabeth Tallent, Peter Cameron, Meg Wolitzer, Amy Hempel. These writers, he observed, "have in general limited themselves to the short story, a form they seem to find appropriate to the age of shortened attention spans, fractured marriages and splinter-ing families in which they grew up."

And perhaps, one wonders, appropriate to their own limitations as well? Leavitt's assumptions about the short story form are disturbing, to say the least. I, for one, have always thought of the short story as a form which, far from being designed for readers whose minds wander, is more tightly compressed than a novel and therefore often demands greater powers of concentration on the part of the reader; as a form which, far from being appropriate to an era of fragmenting families, at its best tolerates far less disorder than does the novel. Leavitt's apparent failure to recognize these things—to respect, in short, the exquisite pos-sibilities of the short story form—seems endemic among the Literary Brat Pack; reading their work, one continually gets the impression that they are writing short stories not because they find the form challenging but because they find it easy.

But enough. To return to Leavitt: "What they [Thurm, Tallent, *et al.*] share is not only their youth—there are many other notable young writers whose work differs vastly from theirs—but their predilections and obsessions, both in style and content. Stylistically, their work owes a strong debt to older writers such as Raymond Carver, Ann Beattie and Mary Robison, but the concerns of their fiction are as specific to their generation—especially the precariousness of families and the ways young people react to the shattering of the familial or parental edifice."

There's a shorter, blunter way of putting all this, of course. Namely: "All of us Literary Brat Packers write exactly alike." Well, *almost* exactly. Almost everything they do derives directly from Carver, Robison, and—perhaps most of all—Beattie, whose aggressively flat, affectless, detail-happy manner is faithfully represented by this passage from her 1976 novel *Chilly Scenes of Winter:*

> He drives to a store and buys a big package of pork chops and a bag of potatoes and a bunch of broccoli and a six-pack of Coke. He remembers cigarettes for Sam when he is checking out, in case he's well enough to smoke. He buys a National Enquirer that features a story about Jackie Onassis's face-lift. James Dean is supposed to be alive and in hiding somewhere, too. Another vegetable. Not dead at all. *East of Eden* is one of his favorite films. He saw it, strangely enough, on television after he and Laura went to a carnival and rode on a Ferris wheel. . . .

And so on. Beattie's prose is plain and unsurprising, often written in the present tense and the first person; her characters, in the main, are dull and passive ciphers. Her fiction is chock-full of the names of TV shows, movies, celebrities, popular songs, and consumer items; it's as thick with irrelevant (or, at best, only tangentially relevant) concrete particulars as it is thin on character development.

If anything, the typical Brat Pack fiction outdoes Beattie in these regards. David Leavitt's hero in "Territory" runs across his mother's daily list of things to do (which Leavitt reproduces *in toto*) and "observes the accretion of names, *the arbitrary specifics that give a sense of his mother's life.*" (My emphasis.) Too often, the writers of the Literary Brat Pack seem truly to believe that it is precisely out of such "arbitrary specifics" that convincing, flesh-and-blood fictional characters are made.

Thus, if a character in a Literary Brat Pack story is taking a course, the writer will almost certainly tell us the full name under which it is listed in the college catalog; if there's a song playing down the hall or a book lying on a bedside table, we'll know the title of it; if somebody goes out for groceries, we don't have to wonder for a moment whether it's an A & P or a Safeway. (Actually, it's usually 7-Eleven.) The Brat Pack writers are more likely to give a detailed run-down on the contents of a given character's cupboard or clothes closet or television viewing schedule than to provide a coherent and convincing set of clues to the contents of that character's soul. After reading a story by one of the Brat Packers, in fact, it's often difficult to describe any of the characters in such a way as to distinguish them from numerous similar—and equally superficial—characters in other Brat Pack works. Sometimes the only noticeable differences are the external ones—the names they go by, the TV shows they watch. Read enough Brat Pack stories in a row and the young characters begin to run together in your mind—and the same goes for their mothers and their fathers, their apartments and their jobs, their parents' divorces and cancer cases, and (above all) their failed and failing "relationships."

Back in college, I remember, an English professor of mine joked about the hyperrealism of early French realists like Champfleury and the brothers Goncourt, who, he told us, actually reproduced balance sheets in their novels! Had we ever heard of such a thing? The class laughed—but that was ten years ago. Now professors in university creative writing programs tell their students that this is the way to write: load up on concrete details, relevant or not. The more particulars, the better. Who could've imagined?

The Brat Packers are especially big on the details surrounding "relationships": his brand of cologne, her favorite song. They seem to believe that one of the principal purposes of literature is to provide readers with a sort of pop sociology of young romance. Leavitt's "New Voices" piece, accordingly, is full of sentences like this: "No matter how seriously Miss Tallent's people commit themselves to each other, they can never really make the connections that form the foundation of lasting relationships." Commitments, connections, relationships: perhaps these words, better than any others, suggest the attitudes and assumptions that shape the typical Brat Pack novel or story.

What's frustrating about these fictions, of course, is that the set decorations—the bags of groceries, the copies of *GQ* and *People* and *Vogue,* the BMWs and MTV and *Sound of Music* cast albums—tend, time and again, to overwhelm the frail narratives. In one pale, passionless Brat Pack narrative after another, we are presented with young people—or young people and their families—who are in extreme emotional crisis, victims of divorce or cancer or a death in the family or an "inability to communicate," but who as a rule speak to each other only about the most banal domestic matters—about, in other words, the stories' furnishings.

These families are almost always broken (or breaking), almost always upper-middle-class. They have summer places and boathouses and swimming pools; the mothers have time to do volunteer work (usually for liberal causes). The young heroes and heroines—if they're not teenagers or pre-teens who are still living at home—tend to reside in small, seedy sublets in Manhattan, where they either (a) take courses at Columbia, NYU, or the New School or (b) hold down marginal, funky jobs in second-hand clothing stores or travel agencies or publishing firms. Often they own a cat. Judging from their cultural references, they grew up on lots of television and on the scores of *My Fair Lady* and most of Rodgers and Hammerstein.

There are about four basic Brat Pack story themes: the folks' divorce (Thurm's "Starlight," Leavitt's "The Lost Cottage"), the troubled relationship with Mom (Cameron's "Memorial Day," Leavitt's "Territory"), the frustrations of romance (Cameron's "The Last Possible Moment," Thurm's "California," etc.), and dead or dying mothers (Cameron's "Fast Forward," Thurm's "Aftermath," Leavitt's "Counting Months"). Many of these mothers die of cancer, and in fact cancer is a particularly popular topic in Brat Pack fiction: in one story after another, characters talk about their chemotherapy, undergo tests, or mention friends with leukemia.

Some Brat Pack stories are unusually similar to one another. Cameron's "Jump or Dive," about a boy whose uncle lives with his male lover in Arizona, is reminiscent of Leavitt's "Danny in Transit," about a boy whose father lives with his male lover in Greenwich Village. And Cameron's "Excerpts from Swan Lake," in which a nice, sensitive young gay man spends a week at his grandmother's house with his grandmother and his boyfriend, reminds one immediately of Leavitt's "Territory," in which a nice, sensitive young man spends a week at his mother's house with his mother and his boyfriend. Cameron's "Memorial Day," with its strained mother-son relationship, also seems to echo "Territory": the intelligent but tragically distant mother in the former story, who tells her son "You are breaking my heart," is barely distinguishable from the intelligent but tragically distant mother in the latter, who tells her son, "I wanted you to grow up happy. And I'm very tolerant, very understanding. But I can only take so much."

There are numerous other—and more recondite—recurrent motifs. For instance, there are several Brat Pack stories in which children (escaping, presumably, from the lovelessness and anonymity of real life) pretend to be putting on TV shows. In Leavitt's "Danny in Transit," Danny invents "an episode of 'The Perfect Brothers Show,' the variety show on his personal network." In Susan Minot's *Monkeys,* the children imitate acts that they see on the Ted Mack and Ed Sullivan shows. And in Cameron's "Odd Jobs," a man named Keith and his daughter, Violet, play "a game they called Christmas Special.... Violet was pretending she was Marie Osmond; Keith was Perry Como—the choice was him or Andy Williams. They had linked arms and were strolling through the snow, in a small circle, singing."

And there are T-shirts galore. One of the principal tenets of the Literary Brat Pack's creative philosophy, it sometimes seems, is that all you need to do to define a character is to put him in a T-shirt that has something printed on it:

> He was wearing an old T-shirt that showed an anatomical drawing of a heart, the separate chambers carefully labeled.
> > —Elizabeth Tallent, "Comings and Goings"
> > from *In Constant Flight* (1983)

> Lynn is wearing maternity jeans that she cut down into shorts at the beginning of the summer, and a red T-shirt, size Extra Large, which says "Coke Adds Life" in white letters that have turned pink from the chlorine.
> > —Marian Thurm, "Floating"
> > from *Floating* (1984)

> Lonnie gets up and walks over to me, trowel in hand. He has on plaid Bermuda shorts and a Disney World T-shirt.
> > —Peter Cameron, "Memorial Day"
> > from *One Way or Another* (1986)

> The husband wears a fraying T-shirt that says "The Only Safe Fast Breeder Is a Rabbit."
> > —Elizabeth Tallent, "Natural Law"

> Sam drops down on the carpet in the living room. He is large-boned and slightly overweight and is wearing a T-shirt with a subway map of New

York City on it. In his lap he holds a dispenser of Windex, a sponge, a rag, and a plastic bottle of ammonia.
—Marian Thurm, "Winter"

Both of the boys are wearing T-shirts which say *Coca-Cola* in Arabic.
—David Leavitt, "Danny in Transit"
from *Family Dancing* (1984)

Petrovsky makes his way toward us through the crowd. He is thin, wearing a Star Wars T-shirt and tattered Adidas.
—Elizabeth Tallent, "In Constant Flight"

Ray was Alex's much-younger brother, a commercial artist in his late thirties who dressed in jeans and T-shirts with pictures of rock bands on them, and who, in Grace's mind, was about as grown-up as a college student.
—Marian Thurm, "Grace"

In his "New Voices" piece, amazingly enough, Leavitt looks upon the sameness of Brat Pack fiction as a virtue. Summarizing one short story after another, he continually points up the parallels between them, as if numbing monotony itself were some sort of virtue. He observes, for instance, that the parents in these stories are all alike in that "The one thing [they] seem to feel they can count on is disappointment, inevitably and repeatedly, and they hammer their fatalism relentlessly into the heads and hearts of their children." These parents, moreover, are "usually leaving each other and taking up with unsuitable partners." As for the young people in these stories, they're "dreamy, supersensitive youths" who "do not believe their vulnerability, bewilderment and sadness set them apart in any way from the rest of humanity."

But they've got one thing over on their sad, selfish, screwed-up folks. "Where the younger characters differ from their parents," Leavitt writes,

is in their energetic insistence on rallying in the face of potential disaster. Born in an era of flux and instability, they are blessed with remarkable flexibility. They can weather changes that would floor their elders, while at the same time they cling to the values of family and marriage with a tenacity unknown to their alternately wayward and crippled parents. By necessity and disposition, they are willing to compromise—with their families, with one another and the history into which they were born.

In short, Brat Pack families are all unhappy, and they are all unhappy in precisely the same way. And the young protagonists of Brat Pack stories are all heroic in the same way, too. (The capacity of some of these writers for jejune self-celebration is often breathtaking.) That this sameness—not only of content, as Leavitt cheerfully reminds us, but of style—might be considered by a discriminating reader to be artificial, modish, and representative of a woeful lack of imagination doesn't seem to have occurred to Leavitt.

It's not just Leavitt, though, who's convinced of the Brat Pack's supreme importance: it's the whole lot of them. In an article published last August 31 in the *New York Times,* reporter Colin Campbell retailed some literary anecdotes that he'd picked up in Long Island's exclusive Hamptons district. One of them concerned Leavitt and Wolitzer and a few of their friends (including Gary Glickman, a close friend of Leavitt's whose first novel, *Years from Now,* is to be published this spring by Knopf). The whole gang, according to Campbell, was driving around the Hamptons in a car when Meg Wolitzer asked "what it might mean to the future of American fiction if they crashed." Strong though the temptation may be, I'll refrain from answering that. But I will say that the remark sums up, better than anything else I've read, these kids' single most irritating collective characteristic: namely, their insularity, their smugness, their fatuous certainty that—in a country populated by a quarter of a billion people—they and their tepid, adolescent little fictions represent the future of the national literature.

Time, of course, rolls on. Since the publication of "New Voices," one or two of the Brat Pack writers have published their second books, and the reviews have been mixed, many of them surprisingly cool—cool, at least, compared to the warm praise that greeted their previous books. More and more critics, it would seem, are beginning to look more critically at Brat Pack fiction. Why? Part of the reason almost certainly is that the once-worshipful critics are tiring of the narrowness of the Brat Pack writers' interests, the flatness of their styles, and the monotony of their characters and settings. The similarities that unite the Literary Brat Pack, in short, have perhaps become—or, at least, may well be on their way to becoming—a definite liability.

This may explain why Leavitt, in his introduction to a recent issue of the *Mississippi Review* for which he served as guest editor, made a slick 180-degree turn. The issue, entitled "These Young People Today," consisted mostly of stories by Thurm, Hempel, Cameron, Glickman, and two or three skilled Brat-Pack imitators. "While it's true," Leavitt said in the introduction, "that these stories provide a generational perspective on the world which is unique, and true as well that common concerns and themes link many of them, I'm struck more by the diversity of voices, concerns and locales, as I read them over, than I am by the parallels." Though, he assured us, he's generally "given to looking for commonality," it was "the rich difference—not the narrowing sameness—which made me want to read these stories over and over again." And just in case we hadn't already gotten the point, he repeated it once more in his penultimate sentence: "All together," he insisted, these stories "comprise a gathering of stunningly unconnectable voices."

Amazing, isn't it, how a group of strikingly similar voices can, in only a year or so, become "stunningly unconnectable"? But whether this amusing switch marks the beginning of the end of the Literary Brat Pack's heyday, or merely indicates the beginning of another chapter in a saga that has yet to reach its climax, only time can tell.

Notes

The Novel in the Academy

1. Flannery O'Connor is also on his list, but merely (one suspects) as a token female; his discussion of her work makes it clear that he doesn't regard her as highly as he does the others. The reason for this should be obvious.

2. No doubt Mailer's huge, daunting *Ancient Evenings*, published too late to be considered in *American Fictions*, would have raised Mailer's position in Karl's eyes.

Reading Denis Donoghue

1. It is perhaps worth noting that Donoghue's admiration of Burke is far from a one-sided affair. Burke has written about Donoghue—and very favorably, needless to say—more than once. In 1977, for example, Burke reviewed Donoghue's book *The Sovereign Ghost: Studies in Imagination* in *The New Republic*. The tenor of the review is expressed in its first sentence, which reads as follows: "Any text that deserves some measure of appreciation can consider itself lucky if Denis Donoghue chooses to write about it."

The *Pushcart Prize* Story

1. Henderson's essays "The Great American Novel" (published under the name Luke Walton) and "At Pushcart" both appeared in *The Publish-It-Yourself Handbook*, ed. Bill Henderson, revised edition (Pushcart/Harper & Row, 1980). "On Pushcart Press" appeared in *The Little Magazine in America: A Modern Documentary History*, ed. Elliott Anderson and Mary Kinzie (Pushcart, 1978).

2. It must be mentioned that the editors of *The Little Magazine in America* let a Trojan horse into the gates in the form of Gene Lyons, whose "Report on the Fiction Collective" dares to question the "fearless innovator" pose of Baumbach and his fellow Collectivists. A number of Lyons's observations would apply as well to other enterprises whose histories are chronicled in the book. For example: "A large part of the Fiction Collective's case against commercial publishers in fact rests upon (the publishers') alleged hostility to, or incomprehension of, what is 'new,' or 'innovative,' or 'experimental.' In the organization's lexicon all of those words are good ones, as 'traditional' and 'commercial' are bad." Lyons's wit, intelligence, and critical standards put most of the editor-chroniclers in the book to shame.

A NAKED WOLFE

1. Field is not the only critic to have mined Wolfe's minor writings recently. Richard S. Kennedy, the author or editor of several previous volumes on Wolfe, is the editor of *Beyond Love and Loyalty: The Letters of Thomas Wolfe and Elizabeth Nowell* (University of North Carolina Press, 164 pages, $18.95); Kennedy contributes a foreword to Suzanne Stutman's *My Other Loneliness: Letters of Thomas Wolfe and Aline Bernstein* (University of North Carolina Press, 390 pages, $30). The former book, composed mostly of routine exchanges between author and agent, does include three or four interesting letters in which Nowell offers suggestions for changes in Wolfe's stories; the book also includes the text of a rather Kafkaesque Wolfe story, "No More Rivers" (published for the first time), which profited greatly from Nowell's blue pencil. The latter book, originally a dissertation directed by Kennedy, presents us with the most unattractive Wolfe: Tom the lover, whose hostile, abusive letters to the woman he ostensibly loved betray a self-centered, insensitive young man full of guilt, resentment, and suspicion. Some of the letters are fascinating and revealing, and they make one appreciate Wolfe's ability, in his third novel, *The Web and the Rock* (which was, essentially, about his relationship with Bernstein in the late Twenties), to describe his own neuroses objectively. The book is far too long, however; a selection, rather than a complete correspondence, would have been desirable. The apparatus in both books is poor; the letters are not placed in context, as in Nowell's excellent *The Letters of Thomas Wolfe,* published in 1956 (before many of the letters in these two volumes were available for publication). Instead, the editors find it necessary to footnote the correspondents' passing references to Esperanto and the "Internationale." Stutman is particularly obtuse; her title for a chapter full of tense, argumentative letters between Wolfe and Bernstein is "Idyllic Years." She means it.

SALINGER'S ARRESTED DEVELOPMENT

1. A total of twenty-one Salinger stories, published in the "slicks" between 1940 and 1948, have never been allowed by Salinger to appear in book form. Almost all of these stories are contrived productions of little or no literary interest.

CAPOTE'S CHILDREN

1. In *Conversations with Capote,* published last year, Lawrence Grobel asks: "Have you ever wondered why you are able to relate so well to murderers?" Capote replies: "Because right away they realized that I wasn't passing any judgment on them. I had no opinion about them as a person regarding the fact that they'd killed. . . . " The book—which consists mostly of insulting remarks about nearly everyone Capote ever knew—was published by New American Library (244 pages, $14.95). Also recently issued is *Three by Truman Capote,* which includes *Other Voices, Other Rooms, Breakfast at Tiffany's,* and *Music for Chameleons* (Random House, 358 pages, $12.95).

2. Interestingly, as far back as 1964, Norman Mailer had foreseen both *Answered Prayers* and its consequences. In his famous *Esquire* piece, "Quick and Expensive Comments on the Talent in the Room," Mailer wrote of Capote: "I would surely suspect he hesitates between the attractions of Society which enjoys and so repays him for his unique gifts, and the novel he could write of the gossip column's real life, a major work, but it would banish him forever from his favorite world."

Works Cited

The Novel in the Academy

Karl, Frederick R. *American Fictions 1940–1980:*
A Comprehensive History and Critical Evaluation. New York: Harper & Row.

Criticism in Extremis

Newman, Charles. *The Post-Modern Aura: The Act of Fiction in an Age of Inflation.*
Evanston: Northwestern University Press.

Reading Denis Donoghue

Donoghue, Denis. *Reading America: Essays on American Literature.*
New York: Alfred A. Knopf.

"The Story of English" on PBS

McCrum, Robert; Cran, William; MacNeil, Robert. *The Story of English.*
New York: Elisabeth Sifton Books/Viking.

Behind the Images: Fitzgerald and Cheever

Cheever, Susan. *Home Before Dark: A Personal Memoir of John Cheever.*
Boston: Houghton Mifflin.

Mellow, James. *Invented Lives: F. Scott and Zelda Fitzgerald.* Boston: Houghton Mifflin.

On Ernest Hemingway

Griffin, Peter. *Along with Youth: Hemingway, the Early Years.*
New York: Oxford University Press.

Hemingway, Ernest. *The Garden of Eden.* New York: Scribners

Lynn, Kenneth S. *Hemingway.* New York: Simon & Schuster.

Meyers, Jeffrey. *Hemingway: A Biography.* New York: Harper & Row.

No Angel

Donald, David Herbert. *Look Homeward: A Life of Thomas Wolfe.* Boston: Little, Brown.

A Naked Wolfe

Field, Leslie, ed. *Thomas Wolfe: The Autobiography of an American Novelist.*
Cambridge: Harvard University Press.

All About Norman

Manso, Peter. *Mailer: His Life and Times.* New York: Simon & Schuster.

Talking Heads: The Novels of Saul Bellow

Bellow, Saul. *More Die of Heartbreak.* New York: William Morrow.

John Hawkes's Fan Club

Hawkes, John. *Humors of Blood and Skin: A John Hawkes Reader.*
New York: New Directions.

Guy Davenport: Fiction à la Fourier

Davenport, Guy. *Apples and Pears and Other Stories.* Berkeley: North Point Press.

The Human Dimension: E.L. Doctorow

Doctorow, E.L. *Lives of the Poets: Six Stories and a Novella.* New York: Random House.

Don De Lillo's America

De Lillo, Don. *White Noise.* New York: Viking.

FLESH AND FAITH: JOHN UPDIKE

Updike, John. *Roger's Version*. New York: Alfred A. Knopf.

TOM WOLFE'S *The Bonfire of the Vanities*

Wolfe, Tom. *The Bonfire of the Vanities*. New York: Farrar, Straus & Giroux.

TRUE CONFESSIONS

Berry, Wendell. *The Wild Birds: Six Stories of the Port William Membership*. Berkeley: North Point Press.

Collins, Linda. *Going to See the Leaves*. New York: Viking.

Colwin, Laurie. *Another Marvelous Thing*. New York: Alfred A. Knopf.

Miller, Sue. *The Good Mother*. New York: Harper & Row.

ALL IN THE FAMILY

Erdrich, Louise. *The Beet Queen*. New York: Henry Holt.

Leavitt, David. *The Lost Language of Cranes*. New York: Alfred A. Knopf.

Merkin, Daphne. *Enchantment*. San Diego: Harcourt Brace Jovanovich.

Taylor, Peter. *A Summons to Memphis*. New York: Alfred A. Knopf.

COLOPHON

This book was designed by Tree Swenson.

The type is Bembo, composed by The Typeworks.

Manufactured by Edwards Brothers.

Library of Congress Cataloging-in-Publication Data

Bawer, Bruce, 1956–
    Diminishing fictions.
    Bibliography: p.
    1. American fiction—20th century—History and
criticism.   2. Criticism—United States—History—20th
century.   I. Title.
PS379.B36   1988   813'.5'09   87-83084
ISBN 1-55597-109-1